PAUL FOOT

PAUL FOOT

A LIFE IN POLITICS

MARGARET RENN

VERSO

London • New York

First published by Verso 2024

1 3 5 7 9 10 8 6 4 2

Verso
UK: 6 Meard Street, London W1F 0EG
US: 388 Atlantic Avenue, Brooklyn, NY 11217
versobooks.com

Verso is the imprint of New Left Books

ISBN-13: 978-1-80429-190-0
ISBN-13: 978-1-80429-193-1 (US EBK)
ISBN-13: 978-1-80429-192-4 (UK EBK)

British Library Cataloguing in Publication Data
A catalogue record for this book is available from the British Library

Library of Congress Cataloging-in-Publication Data

Names: Renn, Margaret, author.
Title: Paul Foot : a life in politics / Margaret Renn.
Description: London ; New York : Verso, 2024. | Includes bibliographical
　references and index.
Identifiers: LCCN 2024012674 (print) | LCCN 2024012675 (ebook) | ISBN
　9781804291900 (hardback) | ISBN 9781804291931 (ebook)
Subjects: LCSH: Foot, Paul, 1937-2004. | Foot, Paul, 1937-2004--Political
　activity. | Journalists--Great Britain--Biography. | Socialists--Great
　Britain--Biography. | Socialist Workers' Party (Great Britain)--History.
Classification: LCC PN5123.F45 R46 2024 (print) | LCC PN5123.F45 (ebook)
　| DDC 070.4/44092 [B]--dc23/eng/20240524
LC record available at https://lccn.loc.gov/2024012674
LC ebook record available at https://lccn.loc.gov/2024012675

Typeset in Minion by Hewer Text UK Ltd, Edinburgh
Printed and bound by CPI Group (UK) Ltd, Croydon CR0 4YY

Contents

Introduction: Our Left Foot

Red flags filled the air as a great crowd of mourners brought Golders Green to a standstill on a sunny summer's day. Paul Foot's family, and a lifetime of friends, comrades and colleagues, made their way through the streets of North London in a long procession, to be greeted by a steel band as they filed into Golders Green crematorium.

Paul Foot's death on 18 July 2004, at the age of sixty-six, made the evening news, the next day's papers, and a joke in *Private Eye*: 'RIP Paul Foot 1937–2004. A Great Journalist. Died in time for press day.'

Obituaries appeared in newspapers across the country – the nationals, weekly and monthly journals and magazines, dozens of local newspapers and international papers alike. The BBC website asked for tributes, which poured in. There were special supplements in *Socialist Review* and *Socialist Lawyer*, as well as in *Private Eye*, which would become a book, *My Friend Footy*, written by Richard Ingrams, Paul's friend for almost his entire life.

Tam Dalyell MP described Paul as 'the staunch friend of lost causes', while Richard Stott, his editor for many years at the *Daily Mirror*, reflected that Paul 'had a rare ability to make our trade feel noble'. The *Economist* described his politics as 'potty' but his journalism 'revelatory'. On the journalists' Fleetstreet Forum website, one posted: 'So, farewell then Footie. I'm sure that crooks and swindlers the length and breadth of the country are breathing a sigh of relief.'

Paul's coffin, a wicker basket draped in a red flag, a Plymouth Argyle scarf and a West Indian cricket rosette, was carried into a venue so small that his family had to issue tickets for those who needed to be inside. Meanwhile, a huge crowd listened to the speeches relayed on loudspeakers in the summer sunshine in the crematorium gardens.

'For god's sake, cheer up', his friend Jim Nichol began. 'That's what Paul would have wanted.' And then, at the request of Paul's young daughter Kate, *I'm a Gnu* by Flanders and Swann rang out to a sea of smiles, balanced later by a lively rendition of the socialist 'Internationale', sung with great gusto. Many knew the words already, but for safety's sake they were printed on the funeral card. His son Matt caught the mood with his reference to another song. On the night before he died, Paul, walking with the help of two sticks, had left home with his son Tom, also on crutches, singing, 'Anything you can do, I can do better'.

His three sons, John, Matt and Tom, remembered the father who was always losing his keys and spectacles, but never forgot telephone numbers. Who never lost his passion for life. Who was loving and friendly, until his partner Clare beat him at tennis or golf, when he turned into a furious, sulky child. They finished by reciting one verse each from the ending to Shelley's poem 'The Mask of Anarchy'.

There was the odd glitch. No one had thought about who was going to press the button, and the coffin snagged before disappearing from sight. Then, as many as could made their way back to Stoke Newington for a curry in the Abney Hall.

Three months later the Hackney Empire was sold out for a celebration of Paul's life. Clips of old television footage and photos ran between his children's stories about trips to have his hair cut and his delight in eating meringues and Liquorice Allsorts. The comedians he worked with were there to tell old jokes and new, and Dave Spart, the eponymous lefty of *Private Eye* fame, made an appearance, as told by Richard Ingrams. Some of the people he had campaigned for were also present: the sisters of Samar Alami and Jawad Botmeh, two Palestinians locked up for the 1994 bombing of the Israeli embassy in London, which Paul was sure was a miscarriage of justice; Pam Dix, whose brother died in the Lockerbie bombing; Gurpal Virdi, a black police-man drummed out of the force by his racist colleagues; Colin Wallace, who suffered a similar fate from the British army in Northern Ireland. And the widow of Harry Stanley, shot dead in the street by a Hackney policeman.

Of course there was politics, courtesy of Tony Benn and Eamonn McCann, among others. 'I've never known a man', said McCann, 'who could laugh so much at the absurdity of the system we live under.'

The evening, however, belonged to Michael Foot. Ailing and infirm, he was helped on to the stage, and in a halting voice delivered a love letter to his devoted nephew. 'It's terrible to think of waking up in a world where there's no Paul Foot. It is a very sad thing indeed', he began. With his shaking hands and poor eyesight, Paul's uncle's sadness at the death of his nephew caught at everyone's throat. But Michael, politician and journalist, was a typical Foot, and had no time for a great show of sentiment. 'I owed so much to Paul. We had a few arguments which were still going on right up to the end. And I won't go into who was winning them.'

His chosen theme was a book, a revolutionary leader, and a poem. The first was *The Black Jacobins*, C. L. R. James's history of the slave revolt in Haiti, the best book about the history of slavery, Michael explained, and 'one of the greatest books on socialism ever written'. It was a book that Paul had read and reread, and he coveted Michael's first edition: 'He had an eye on my books, you know.'

The leader was Toussaint L'Ouverture, the black Jacobin and leader of the Haitian slaves. And the poem was Wordsworth's homage to Toussaint, written to his fallen hero, and read by Michael in memory of his fallen nephew:

Yet die not; do thou
Wear rather in thy bonds a cheerful brow:
Though fallen thyself, never to rise again,
Live and take comfort! Thou hast left behind
Powers that will work for thee; air, earth and skies.
There's not a breathing of the common wind
That will forget thee;

'That's what we think about Paul', Michael interjected.

> There's not a breathing of the common wind
> That will forget thee; Thou hast great allies:
> Thy friends are exhultations, agonies,
> And love, and man's unconquerable mind.

1

Mangoes in the Bath

Paul Foot was born in 1937 in Palestine, although he did not live there for long. From his birth until the age of seven he moved around the world with bewildering speed – from Palestine to England, back again to the Middle East, then on to South Africa, Cyprus, and finally Jamaica.

Paul's father, Hugh Foot, was the reason for all the moving. After attending a Quaker school, followed by four years at Cambridge University, Hugh had decided that his father's career as a lawyer, Liberal politician and Methodist preacher was not for him. Instead, he joined, on a whim rather than for any high-minded reason, the Colonial Service, entering what he called a life of voluntary exile.

Hugh's was, he acknowledged, a privileged upbringing in a large family of five brothers and two sisters, all of them devoted to their parents. But 'the greatest privilege of all', he wrote in his memoir, 'was to have been brought up in a good liberal, Methodist home', and he adopted from an early age his father's hatred of cruelty and injustice. As a child, when his family was living at St Cleer on the edge of Bodmin Moor, he liked to escape to the gypsy encampments, where he sat with the children round their campfire. Their contempt for the settled life of people who lived in the comfort of their own homes appealed to him, and he was put out when his mother objected to him bringing his young gypsy friends home to tea: 'This struck me as gross discrimination, an intolerable social injustice.'[1]

Hugh began as an administrator in the Colonial Service and rose through the ranks to become governor of Jamaica, and then of Cyprus.

But his first posting was to Jerusalem, where he arrived in August 1929 at the age of twenty-one. He took quickly to life in the Middle East, becoming an Arab enthusiast, learning Arabic and giving up drinking and smoking. His enthusiasm for the region even stretched to driving out into the desert, carrying his own rations, guns and a tent, to sleep under the stars. He learned to work with both Arabs and Jews, and to respect rebels: 'I often idly wished to be on their side of the barricades instead of on the side of authority.'[2]

The British administration in Palestine was small, just twenty people, and Hugh was soon promoted to assistant district commissioner for Samaria, which extended from north of Jerusalem to south of Nazareth, and from the Jordan River to the Mediterranean Sea, a vast area that covered around 300 Arab villages and a group of Jewish settlements that were soon to increase and multiply. He was based in Nablus, but each weekend he would travel to Jerusalem to prepare for his examinations in Arabic. Whenever he could, he would drive north in his enormous open Buick to Haifa, where he was courting Sylvia Tod. The daughter of a Scottish father who worked in the oil industry and an Italian mother, her family had left Italy to escape the fascists. Sylvia was good company. She was elegant, played tennis, loved music, had a sense of humour and could herself be witty – an important asset for anyone marrying a Foot. After their wedding in 1936, they set up home together in Nablus, just as life there was becoming increasingly unsafe.

Hitler's attacks on Germany's Jews escalated in the mid 1930s, and the number of Jewish refugees moving to Palestine grew, as did Arab alarm and resistance. It began with occasional skirmishes between Palestinian Arab forces and Jewish police and paramilitaries, but, by 1937, a full-scale rebellion was under way. Each morning, Hugh would look through the long list of disorder and destruction: telephones cut, bridges damaged, trains derailed, convoys ambushed, the outbreaks of fighting in the hills. Almost every day brought news of casualties on both sides, including men Hugh knew. 'For two years I never moved without a gun in my hand', he was later to write. 'We soon learnt that it was useless to have a gun in the holster.'[3]

As Nablus became less safe, the heavily pregnant Sylvia was evacuated back to Haifa, where Paul was born on 8 November 1937. But by the following year, Hugh had reached the top of the assassination list issued by the Arab rebel command in Damascus, and the British high commissioner, Sir Arthur Wauchope, decided the family would have to leave. Under guard, Hugh, Sylvia and baby Paul made their way to their ship in Port Said. They were on their way back to London.

At first they moved into a tiny flat near Battersea Park, which they shared with Hugh's younger brother Michael, then just starting out as a leader writer on the *Evening Standard*. The arrangement did not last long. As war threatened, children were the first to be evacuated out of the city, and Paul was sent to stay with his grandparents Isaac and Eva in Cornwall. His parents soon followed, when pregnant women were ordered out of London. They got no further than Bath, where Paul's sister Sarah was born in September 1939. The chance for father to dote on daughter was short lived. On the day she was born, Hugh received a telegram telling him to report back to London. He was on his way back to the Middle East, on the Orient Express to Istanbul, his first stop en route to Amman in Transjordan. Once she could travel, Sylvia packed her bags, gathered up her two small children and set off by ship to join him, accompanied by a nanny and Hugh's younger sister Jennifer.

Sylvia had barely arrived when they were evacuated for a third time. As the war in Europe spread to North Africa and the Middle East, all European families were ordered to leave, and the extended family – Sylvia with her two children, her father and mother, her sister Dorothy, and Dorothy's two daughters Christina and Elizabeth – joined a ship sailing for South Africa. It was a journey fraught with danger. The Atlantic convoys frequently came under attack from German naval vessels, and the ship alongside theirs was sunk with all lives lost. But Paul and Christina were too young to grasp how dangerous it was and whiled away the hours playing games with the young sailors, as their nanny, overcome with seasickness, was confined to her cabin below.

In South Africa, the family lived in a house near the city of Durban which, Christina remembers, featured smooth black tiles on the front steps to keep out the snakes. Their English nanny, whom they called Nurse, turned out to be extremely bossy, and Paul didn't like her. He often found it difficult to eat his meals with Nurse telling him off all the time – something that Sarah thought very odd, as she could never stop eating.

When it was considered safe to travel again, the family returned to the Middle East, and in 1943 they joined Hugh on his first tour of Cyprus. They had been away for three years; Paul was six and Sarah four. It was a peripatetic life being married to a colonial officer, and each of Sylvia's four children was born in a different country – Paul in Palestine, Sarah in England and, later, Oliver in Jamaica and Benjamin in Nigeria. The nearest thing to home the family had was Hugh's father Isaac's rambling house in Cornwall, which Paul and Sarah both loved. It was there that the family found themselves as the war ended, a stay that coincided with the 1945 general election. A total of four Foots were standing. Grandfather Isaac, who had already served two terms as the Liberal MP for Bodmin during the 1920s and '30s, was standing in Tavistock for the Liberals. His eldest son Dingle, a lawyer like his father, hoped to retain his seat as the Liberal MP for Dundee. John, who had not yet successfully run an election campaign, was now the Liberal candidate in Bodmin, Isaac's old seat. And Michael, the renegade as far as the family were concerned, had abandoned the Liberals and was standing as a Labour candidate in Plymouth, Devonport. All this had been explained to the small boy.[4]

The outcome was dramatic. The war hero and Conservative Winston Churchill was out, Labour were in. The Liberals were decimated, and it was Michael, the certain loser, who was the only member of the family to win his seat. Although only seven at the time, Paul was aware that something extraordinary had happened, but he wasn't yet sure what. And no one cared to explain, least of all his grandfather, who shut himself up in his bedroom for five days and refused to speak to anyone.

Then the family were off again. Hugh Foot's next appointment was as colonial secretary of Jamaica. Life in the Caribbean, Paul's sister Sarah remembers, was so much better. 'We had a wonderful Jamaican nanny', she later wrote, 'very different to the English one we had in South Africa. She spoilt us both and she sang songs to us and gave us mangoes in the bath. We thought she was wonderful.'

Paul was seven when he arrived in Jamaica, and his parents enrolled him in a school on the Old Hope Road, Kingston. Housed in a large, white-painted colonial building with deep, cool verandas, and surrounded by tall palm trees, Priory House educated a mix of boys and girls. The girls wore white summer dresses, the boys knee-length shorts. Only the headmaster sported anything so formal as a tie. Paul was in the youngest class. He was a clever boy who loved books like his grandfather, and loved quoting from them. He came top of his class at Christmas, and was given a beautiful edition of *The Pied Piper of Hamelin*.

Those days in Jamaica stayed with Paul for one reason above all others: cricket. 'Ever since, at the age of eight, I bowled four balls in a net off the Old Hope Road, Kingston, Jamaica, to George Headley (the greatest batsmen in the history of the world)', he would write over thirty years later, 'I have experienced only one completely uncomplicated pleasure: watching West Indian batsmen in full flood.'[5] Paul played as often as he could, and photos survive of him with his own team, all of them Jamaicans, except for Paul, the skinny little white boy at the end of the row.

It was idyllic, but it couldn't last. After just two years in Jamaica, the family, including Paul's new baby brother Oliver, were on the move again. They set sail for England, just as the Empire Windrush would do a few months later, and there they separated. Paul's parents, his brother and sister were off to his father's new posting in Nigeria, while Paul stayed behind. He was nine, and it was time for him to go to boarding school: Ludgrove was waiting.

It was not going to be easy in post-war Britain. Food was rationed, and Paul's cotton shorts were replaced by scratchy grey worsted, the Jamaican sun by English rain; he was now in a boys-only school in Berkshire. But Paul claimed he loved it, and at Ludgrove he flourished. During one class, the headmaster, Alan Barber, read out an essay that Paul had written on Jonah and the whale. At first he couldn't understand why, but Barber had liked some of the phrases Paul had used, and suggested to the other boys that they too should try writing like that. 'I've never understood why I can write better than others', he later said. 'But Alan Barber was the first person who really suggested to me that I could.'[6]

There were other reasons for Paul to love school, and one of them was his classics tutor, Ken Morrison. Very early in the morning, over a pot of tea and biscuits, Morrison took the bright boys for extra lessons in Greek and Latin. 'He taught us almost to think in elegiac couplets', Paul remembered.[7] While the school might not have devoted a great deal of attention to music or drama, there was an emphasis on hitting and kicking a ball. There are photos of Paul with the school second XI cricket team, with their stripy caps, and another more informal snap in which he is sporting the blue cap with the bold capital L of the Ludgrove first team.

Paul's sister and his cousins remember his time there rather differently. One problem was Morning Parade. Every day after breakfast, the boys lined up outside the toilets and a master issued them with toilet paper. As the boys came out, each had to report on the success of their mission: Correct (successful) or Not Correct. It was an archaic system, which was abolished in the 1970s. Richard Barber, nephew of the headmaster and the school's biographer, says it did nothing but encourage small boys to lie. 'As a sensitive boy, Paul would have felt it was pretty insulting.'

Looking back, Paul thought Ludgrove a ludicrously snobbish school. The fabulously wealthy Duke of Devonshire had already passed through by the time Paul arrived, as had the eccentric Marquess of Bath. Long after Paul, the princes William and Harry would also study there. As he told Richard Barber, 'the fact that it's accessible to only a very tiny section of the population' means it becomes 'a central prop of the whole divided nature of our society'.[8]

The long school holidays were mostly spent with one group or another of his aunts and uncles. The Tods, on his mother's side, took up residence at Beeleigh Falls in Essex every other summer. Or they went to Italy, to Paul's maternal grandparents', where they swam, and played tennis and ping pong. Paul even managed to impress the family with his command of Italian. *Un gelato si prega?*, he would ask at the village ice cream parlour, until the others realised it was almost the only Italian he knew.

If he was not with the Tods, he was with the Foots. His uncle, John Foot, with his American wife Anne and their children Kate and Winslow, lived in Crapstone, a village in Devon on the edge of Dartmoor, a few miles north of Plymouth. Kate was Paul's age, Win two years younger, the same age as Sarah. They lived in an elegant town house with a large garden, Yew Tree Cottage, in the middle of the village. For the young Paul, Crapstone became a home from home, and his uncle and aunt became like second parents to him.

The Foots' was a lively household. In the garden, with its high old walls, there were endless games of football and French cricket, which would last until sheer exhaustion would bring the game to an end. There was tennis, and Monopoly, and at the dinner table there were jokes and word games, and a much-prized quiz book. 'At meals my father would read out questions and we would try to answer them', remembers Paul's cousin Kate. 'We loved it. We went through that book several times.' They were free to wander where they wanted, and roamed about on Dartmoor. 'No one ever worried about us, where we were or that we were going to come back. It was a lot of fun.'[9]

A disused airfield on the moors, built for fighter planes during the war but never used, was a fantastic playground for Paul and Win. 'It was full of bits of military stuff that had been left behind', Win remembers. 'There was a fake farmhouse where we would go and make these boats that we raced.' They were carved out of bits of wood, and Paul could never make his go properly.

There were dances too, run by local families, at the Women's Institute and the village hall, or, if it was a real Hunt Ball, at some grand house. Win and Paul would dance Scottish reels. 'Paul and I were fanatic about that! Our holidays revolved around the dances and the romances.'

At Christmas, the extended Foot family would gather at Isaac Foot's house across the valley in Cornwall. Michael believed that Isaac had bought the great rambling Victorian house called Pencreber, in the village of Callington, because Isaac's previous home in Plymouth was so full of books he'd run out of space for more.[10] Books were Isaac's great passion; they were 'the light of his life', according to Michael, who described his father as a 'bibliophilial drunkard'. At Pencreber the volumes were piled high in every room, and stacked up the stairs. To get to the lavatory required some delicate manoeuvring around the stacks, and in the old laundry, no longer used for its original purpose, books were everywhere. There were 2,000 volumes on the French Revolution alone; one room was stacked with modern poetry, another with detective novels; and one of the front bedrooms was called the Greek Testament room after its 450 volumes in Greek.

'Often you would find people sitting down in the passage or on the stairs', Sarah remembered, 'having found a book they had always wanted to read, starting to browse through it and soon forgetting where they were.'[11] When, in 1959, Isaac paid three of his grandsons two shillings and sixpence each to count the books, they reached the magnificent total of 59,900.

While reading, Isaac would make notes in small hardback note-books, so that nothing would be forgotten or lost, filling several hundred of them in the course of his long and well-read life. He would often read aloud to his own children, and he encouraged all the children to read and to learn texts by heart. While he was teaching himself French, he read them *Les Miserables*, translating as he went, and when he decided to learn Greek, so that he could read the New Testament in its original language, he paid Paul's father – then at school – a shilling an hour to tutor him. Paul and his cousin Kate each received half a crown for learning Macauley's *Horatius*, and two shillings for Tennyson's poem *Revenge*. Shakespeare was a shilling a go for shorter speeches. 'Paul was so much better at it than I was', says Win. 'Isaac got Paul to read Gibbon's *Decline and Fall* and I think he got £5, which was a huge amount of money in those days.'

Occasionally, Paul would join his own family for the holidays, wherever they might be. Janet Cunliffe-Jones, the daughter of the lieu-tenant-governor of West Nigeria while Paul's father was chief secretary, remembers playing tennis with Paul in Nigeria in the late 1940s, and in the summer of 1951 there was one memorable holiday in Jamaica when a hurricane hit the island. Paul was fourteen, and his father had returned to Jamaica as governor. The family home was in the grandly named King's House, set in beautiful gardens with a magnificent collec-tion of tall royal palms. The hurricane struck earlier than expected, while Sylvia was busy helping the Red Cross prepare and Hugh was broadcasting to the nation. He barely made it back home, having to abandon his car and driver at the gate and crawl to his front door. In the house he found his four frightened children and two of their friends. He dragged mattresses onto the floor of an inner room and huddled the children together. Benjie, the youngest and not yet two years old, was in tears. Water was coming in on all sides. A river was cascading down the main staircase. Out of the window, in a flash of lightning, Hugh could see 'the great royal palms sixty feet tall banging their heads on the lawn and then whipping back like fishing rods'.

Nature had gone wild. 'Strange forces were let loose and sweeping the every-day world away. Half horrified and half fascinated, I wanted to shout with a mad sense of elation', he wrote in his memoir.[12]

In the summer of the hurricane Paul finally left Ludgrove. He had won the school classics prize, commemorated with a copy of *The Tragic Drama of the Greeks* by Arthur Elam Haigh. He was on his way to Shrewsbury.

2

An Inky Little Boy

In the summer of 1951, two boys arrived at Shrewsbury School on the same day. One was Christopher Booker, the other Paul Foot, and they were there to sit for the school's scholarship exam. Shrewsbury was a traditional, conservative sort of place, stuck in a late-Victorian time-warp, with traditional games, chapel every day and twice on Sundays, and, according to Laurence Le Quesne, a young master of history who arrived at the same time, committed to the idea that the classics were the benchmark of a good education.

When Paul and Christopher returned to Shrewsbury in the autumn of that year, they found themselves in different houses, where boys studied, took their meals and slept. Scholarship boys like them were automatically in the classics department, for those pupils were considered to be the school's brightest and most distinguished, although those who excelled at sport ran them a close second. The classical scholars studied Greek and Latin, and little else. They were expected to pass an O-level in maths (Paul had to sit the exam several times before he did) as well as English and a modern language, but otherwise it was all Greek and Latin – hours and hours of it, day in and day out, week after week. History was ancient Greek history; poetry was translating English verse into Greek; they even read the Bible in Greek. Such a preoccupation with classics even permeated the common language of the school. While most public schools had a system of 'fagging', in which new boys ran around making tea and cleaning the boots of older boys and prefects, at Shrewsbury, fagging was known as 'douling', after the Greek *doulus*, a slave. To become a prefect and have power over the douls was, for some, the height of privilege.

'There were special privileges for prefects', Christopher remembers, 'a special room of their own, their own desks. They could have radios, they had command over the douls and scum [scum were first and second years], and there were little details like being able to keep your coat open and wear a special tie. And those who were very grand in the school hierarchy – those with scholarships to Oxford, or in the first eleven – could even walk on the grass.'

Christopher's house was, he says, more liberal than the others, 'to the point of using Christian names'. Perhaps more importantly, 'We simply stopped the beating.' The beating: that was the issue for Paul.

In School House, Paul's house throughout his years at Shrewsbury, the cry would go up: 'The Housemaster wants to see [surname, first name, initials would follow] and there would be a great roar of laughter along the corridors. We all knew what was going on.' The memory of that shout belongs to Piers Brendon, a couple of years younger than Paul but also in School House. The victim was his contemporary, a beautiful young boy who Piers believes would prefer – even now, more than sixty years later – to remain nameless. Both Paul and the nameless boy were victims of the same housemaster, Anthony Chevenix-Trench.

Chevenix-Trench ran School House as a sado-masochistic dictatorship, according to Brendon. He was a serious classical scholar, and his pattern of behaviour was to offer to help the boys with their Greek studies. There was chocolate for success and a beating for failure, starting at three mistakes. 'Three mistakes could usually be found', wrote Paul some years later. 'Trench explained that I had a "choice", the cane with trousers on; or the strap, with trousers off', Paul wrote. 'When the relatively painless strap was nominated, he became extremely cheerful and excited. Clapping his hands in joyful anticipation, he would lead me out of the study to his upstairs sitting room on the "private side" of the house, where he locked the door, pulled down my trousers and pants, lowered me onto his sofa and laid into me with his belt. The blows hardly hurt at all, though the humiliation was excruciating.'[1] Paul was fifteen.

The occasion of Paul's long piece recounting these memories in the *London Review of Books* was the publication in 1996 of Chevenix-Trench's biography. Its author, Mark Peel, opened his book with the news about Chevenix-Trench's rise within the hierarchy of public schools: 'As Britain awoke from the long, hard winter of 1962–63', Peel wrote, 'the news that Anthony Chevenix-Trench had been appointed Head Master of Eton brought a spring to the step of all those who bemoaned the growing sense of drift and complacency in the country.'[2]

Whether or not the appointment put a spring in the step of the country, it certainly put a spring in the step of two Eton schoolboys – both in the direction of *Private Eye*. Hume Shawcross, son of the famous lawyer Sir Hartley Shawcross, and his friend Caspar Fleming, son of Ian Fleming, the creator of James Bond, had been expelled from Eton by Chevenix-Trench. They arrived at the *Eye* offices in 1969 and poured out a tale that Paul already knew by heart. A short piece duly appeared under the headline 'Jolly Beating Weather': 'Rumours that Mr Trench will be retiring were being strenuously denied in official circles this Easter', wrote Paul. Within months, Chevenix-Trench and Eton had parted company, under the public pretext of his ill health. The problem with Eton was that Chevenix-Trench had made the mistake of whipping the heirs of earls as though they were run-of-the-mill manufacturers' sons, as at Shrewsbury.[3]

What riled Paul was Trench's remorseless rise through the public school system: from housemaster at Shrewsbury, to headmaster at Bradfield, and then to the pinnacle of the English public school system at Eton. And all along the way, those who should have known better looked the other way or pretended not to know. Or they simply made excuses – pointing to Trench's terrible experience in the war, building the Burma railway while a prisoner of the Japanese. After Eton he was appointed to yet another headmastership, at Fettes in Edinburgh, from which he was also sacked.

'While he was at Shrewsbury, I remember Paul following my mother around saying, "It cannot be right that boys get beaten"', his cousin Elizabeth (Lily), recalls. 'He hated Chevenix-Trench. He thought he was a monster. But I don't know if he ever told my mother what was happening with him. I think this was the beginning of his sense of injustice.'

He didn't tell Lily's mother, and he certainly didn't tell his own: 'The key to Trench's rise in the public schools was his mastery of public relations', wrote Paul. 'He spent hours gushing to parents about the brilliance, wit and sporting prowess of their sons. The parents, kept in the dark by that instinctive solidarity with which adolescents protect each other against the adult world, adored him. Not one of us would have dreamt of "sneaking" on Trench to our parents or to any other adult.'[4]

Life in School House could be grim. All house prefects kept a record of their time in office. Writing in the *Fasti* (*fasti* – Latin for book or record) at Easter 1953, a young prefect by the name of G. J. Peel described Paul, then just fifteen, in less than flattering terms. 'The Weed lost no time at all at the beginning of the term', he remarked,

> in telling the study (as if they hadn't heard already) that his father was Governor of Jamaica, and that he had two distinguished uncles . . . before the end of term the study got sick and tired of hearing about the Weed's relations. Despite the High rank of his parents and relations No. 3 was forever short of money and food and he had to content himself with Aniseed balls . . . He was scruffy beyond words; one would think that no one had ever cared for him.[5]

Paul's father was indeed the governor of Jamaica – a position that elevated him to the title Lord Caradon. And his two famous uncles were Dingle Foot, who had by then lost three successive elections as a Liberal candidate and was about to switch parties and become the Labour MP for Ipswich, and Michael Foot, the Labour MP for Plymouth, Devonport – a seat he lost in 1955, before taking Aneurin Bevan's seat in Ebbw Vale, after Bevan died. Paul's lesser-known uncle – not least because his attempts to get a parliamentary seat had eluded him – was John Foot, Paul's surrogate father, who would eventually go to the House of Lords as a Liberal peer.

If there was one saving grace from G. J. Peel's account, it was that Paul 'was extremely amusing and good natured'. So good natured, in fact, that when Paul came to write his own study *Fasti* two years later, he seemed determined to find the positive in everyone. Of his second-in-command he wrote:

> I could not have believed it possible that one and the same person could be cheerful and amused through a Lent Term in which the weather and everything else has done its best to make us miserable. But seeing is believing. Every moment of the day a broad grin seemed to be stretched across his face, and his laugh . . . was constantly ringing throughout the room.

At number three was another boy with a fine sense of humour, and 'he, too, is always ready to laugh and be laughed at'.[6]

That easy-going attitude won Paul a reputation. When he became a prefect – or 'praepostor', as the school preferred to call them – he refused to take part in one of the nastiest practices at Shrewsbury: the collective beating of boys. At the school, punishment was in the hands of the boys, not the masters. A praepostor had the power to punish a younger boy for any misdemeanour, but if the offence was considered especially serious, the punishment escalated. The praepostors would gather with their victim, and the cane would pass from hand to hand, each taking a turn to thrash the boy. There could be as many as twelve prefects present. Paul would have none of it, and such a challenge to the school's authoritarian regime shocked most of the masters. But it cheered the younger boys enormously, as well as the young master Laurence Le Quesne.

After the departure of Chevenix-Trench, the new master of School House promptly promoted Paul to praepostor, and head of house. 'Paul was so civilized that he was regarded as a wimp', says Piers Brendon. 'He didn't subscribe to the values of the house. We were allowed to talk in the bedrooms and, while other monitors would read James Bond, Paul read P. G. Wodehouse. I remember his delight in the language.'

Now that Paul was in the sixth form, things were looking up. He was still studying the Greco-Roman classics, but he had time to go to Le Quesne's history lectures and join in the lively discussions. Paul was a great debater, even at school, and in Le Quesne he found a teacher willing to encourage his students to read the weekly leader in Kingsley Martin's radical and anti-establishment *New Statesman*.

There was also Kek. Frank McEachran, Kek to everyone who knew him, had a method of teaching boys that would later inspire Alan Bennett's play *The History Boys*. A teacher of modern languages, his passion was literature, and in particular poetry. He was a friend of the poets W. H. Auden and T. S. Eliot, and he encouraged the boys to read D. H. Lawrence, Dylan Thomas, W. B. Yeats, James Joyce, Stephen Spender and Louis MacNeice, along with Shakespeare and the Bible, Milton's *Paradise Lost* and Dante's *Inferno*. Spinoza and Kierkegaard stood alongside Rilke and Heine, and lines were read in both Latin and Greek. In class, the boys in Kek's charge would be called out to stand on a chair and recite from memory. Paul must have been in his element. Literature coursed through his veins, and from the earliest age he had learned passages of it by heart.

Kek collected his quotes into a book, *Spells*, published while Paul was still at school. On each left-hand page are the quotes, the spells, and on the facing page the explanatory note, the source of the quote and its meaning. As you read, you can imagine a boy standing on a chair and quoting Spell 9, from Coleridge's poem *The Rime of the Ancient Mariner*:

> The fair breeze blew, the white foam flew,
> The furrow followed free;
> We were the first that ever burst
> Into that silent sea.

In his note, the reader can hear Kek talking to the boys about what they have just heard: 'Coleridge. *The Ancient Mariner*. The magic ship has sailed to the South Atlantic, rounded Cape Horn, and entered the Pacific. Note the effect of movement in the verbs "blew", "flew", "followed", rising to a climax in "burst". The crescendo is reinforced by the three b's – breeze, blew, and burst, and so on.[7]

Kek understood the power of reciting poetry, and credits the boys at Shrewsbury for inventing the term 'Spells' for these short bursts of recited verse. 'Tomorrow for the young the poets exploding like bombs' – a line taken from W. H. Auden's poem 'Spain', written during the Spanish civil war – evoked what Kek thought poems could do for young minds.[8]

Kek was an eccentric, and his classes thrilled and mesmerised his students. They certainly made a lasting impression on Paul and another boy sharing those moments, Richard Ingrams. He was in the year above Paul, so there was little opportunity for friendship. But he had stayed on for an extra year to sit his Oxford scholarship exam (which he failed), and in that final year the two sat next to each other.

'Any of those who sat in Kek's classes, as Paul and I did', Ingrams later wrote, 'had a lasting bond in that we had in our heads these little spells and could recite them to one another for the rest of our lives.'[9] They adored Kek.

Richard's great friend in school was Willie Rushton. They were the same age, and though they were in different houses in school, they lived near each other in South London and spent their holidays going to the cinema together, where they watched the films of Jacques Tati and the Marx Brothers over and over again. They also shared a sense of humour, which found its outlet in the school magazine, *The Salopian* – a typical school publication crammed with cricket results and news of old fellows. But in it they carved out a space for something different. Richard contributed the words and jokes, Willie Rushton, an all-round buffoon according to one master, the drawings and cartoons. As the school solemnly commemorated its 400-year history, they produced a 400-year-old edition of the *Salopian*, printed by Caxton, with no old boys' news, because there weren't any. They were joined by Christopher Booker, who penned editorials and added a further subversive element: 'We attacked speech day, which inspired a fine Willie Rushton cartoon, we attacked the cadet force', recalls Christopher. And then along came Paul.

Laurence Le Quesne had overall responsibility for the magazine, though the boys did all the writing and editing, and in 1955 he proposed Foot join the *Salopian* editorial team. Richard, who as editor kept the minute book, was disparaging about the development: 'Le Quesne proposed P M Foot (SH) who had done *nothing ever* for the Salopian and was proposed merely in that he would serve as a good "contrast" to the other editors (Rushton and myself) and represent a more serious line of thought.'[10] Paul joined the team, and in his last year in school found himself somewhat in awe of Richard. 'I worshipped him and wanted to be near him', he told Richard's biographer, 'In our last year we sat next to each other in the Classical Upper Sixth. I was in a position of total hero-worship to him.'[11]

Le Quesne was impressed by these four bright boys – Richard Ingrams, Willie Rushton, Christopher Booker and Paul Foot – all of whom would go on to become so important in the life of the future *Private Eye*. For now, though, there were other things to think about, not least the meetings of the Literary Society and the Forum Society, the purpose of which was to promote 'the study of current social, political or economic problems'. Richard, Paul and Christopher were members, and the Forum Society's invited speakers ranged from Austen Brooks of the League of Empire Loyalists, on the extreme right of British politics, to Paul's Uncle Dingle.

On one occasion the school invited two Shrewsbury old boys, Michael Heseltine and Julian Critchley, to debate the proposition: 'This House disapproves of the Public School System'. Heseltine, Paul would remember, raved against the snobbery and sports culture of public schools, denouncing their regime of corporal punishment. 'There were "oohs" and "ahs" throughout the hall when he mentioned homosexuality', Paul wrote.[12] Opposing him was Chevenix-Trench and a rather boring master called Michael Hoban, who would go on to become headmaster of Harrow. 'The debate was tense. The vote was close. The result, announced to prolonged cheers from cheeky youngsters like me, was victory for the Reds. The motion was carried by 115 to 105.'[13]

News of the debate duly appeared in the gossip column of the *Daily Express*. Heseltine was accused of selling the result of his debating triumph, and the school meted out the most severe punishment it could: Heseltine was struck off the old boys' register. Of course, as Paul pointed out some years later in the *New Statesman*, once he became a Tory minister and amassed a great fortune, he was allowed back in.

There was music, too. John Stainer, grandson of the Victorian composer of the same name, taught singing to Paul and Richard, and, in the tradition of such public schools, a great deal of sport, which came in every shape and form: cricket, football, rowing on the River

Severn, athletics, cross-country running, and fives – a game something like squash, but played with a hard ball, a leather glove, and no racket.

Paul also played a lot of cricket. There is a photograph of him lined up with the rest of his team, smiling at the camera from under their school caps. In a gossip column piece written for Paul's fortieth birthday, Christopher Booker jokingly remembered Paul's skill with the cricket bat: 'Since the retirement of Graveney and Cowdrey, there is no classical stroke-player I would prefer to watch.'[14] Paul also rose to be captain of the School House boxing squad. Willie Rushton hated boxing, and his memory may also be tongue-in-cheek when he describes in the same article withdrawing his house from the school boxing competition: 'Foot got very angry and punched me on the nose. I slotted him straight back, knocked him out cold. I decided I was such a good boxer I should give it up on the spot.'

In the summer of 1956, it all came to an end. National Service beckoned, and then university. Richard Ingrams, Willie Rushton and Paul went their separate ways for the next two years, serving in different regiments on different continents, but would meet again at Oxford. Christopher Booker, who managed to avoid National Service, was off to Cambridge.

Paul enjoyed his time at Shrewsbury, despite the beatings – especially in his last year, when Chevenix-Trench was replaced at School House by the kind and courteous Michael Charlesworth. 'In that last summer of 1956 there was no cruelty or sadism endured or inflicted', he later wrote in the *London Review of Books*. 'I was sad to leave, and naturally grateful to the public school system for its many advantages.'[15] Although Paul would change his view on public schools, in his autobiography Charlesworth quoted one of Paul's letters written not long after he left the school: 'I remember far more good than evil. Journalist, yes. Socialist, yes. But always an upholder of the Public Schools. We may find each other in that last ditch!'[16]

Paul's memory is forgiving. There was one last outburst of mindless brutality, and this time Paul decided he would tell everyone about it. He sat down, dipped his pen in the ink, and wrote a story about power and the abuse of power for the *Fasti*. It is a story he continued to write for the rest of his life.

'It was a large mountain, treacherous and steep. The plain below was a pleasant one, full of people who could become your friends. The mountain towered grimly over the happiness below.' This was the mountain of Authority, with its twin peaks Discipline and Leadership. The boys who tried to make it up the mountain in pursuit of power become bitter and cruel. And, Paul wrote, 'I hate them all.' He preferred the plain, where things were different and the boys were cheerful, helping each other and being helped.[17]

The piece was provoked by an incident in School House in which an older boy had resorted to his fists. Paul couldn't stand it. We might never have known about Paul's plea for justice and tolerance but for a curious turn of events. Shrewsbury School, then as now a major public school, keeps an extensive archive which includes the School House *Fasti*. But the volume covering the year 1956 had a chequered history. It disappeared in the 1970s, and only reappeared in 2016, when two ladies arrived at the school to return it. The reason for the theft is not known, but it is presumed that it had something to do with a visit to the school by the Queen to celebrate the school's 400th centenary in 1952. She lunched in School House, the largest of the dining rooms, decked out in regal oak panelling, and signed the *Fasti*. On the lined pages of this rather ordinary notebook is the flowing 'Elizabeth R', followed by the flourish of 'Philip'.

Paul's allegory runs over several pages, and then he too finishes with a flourish: 'I am heartbroken to leave, more sorry than I ever imagined, or I am sure than anyone else I know here.' He loved the place, and he loved the boys. 'I have made so many friends and have now suddenly to break off and start all over again.' He will miss their cheerfulness, their good humour and their intelligence. He will miss 'the wonderful feeling that whoever I meet – whether it be in the base-ments, the studies, or the long stone passages – I will know him, be on level terms with him enough to laugh and joke, to be serious or sarcas-tic, as the mood demands.'

After signing his name, Paul adds a quote from Shakespeare's *Richard II*:

Throw away respect
Tradition, form and ceremonious duty . . .
I live with bread like you. Feel Grief,
Taste Want, need friends – Subjected thus
How can you say to me – I am a King.

Michael Charlesworth must have known about the essay when he wrote Paul's final school reports, where he described Paul as an inky and grubby little boy when he arrived, young for his years and rather shy. He had failed to develop during his first three years, although he had made up for this in his last term. His regime as head of house was very liberal, 'for he hated being firm and liked to be on friendly terms with all. He disapproved of many things about "the public school system" for he was an idealist. Yet he loved his life more than most.'[18]

3

Paradise on Earth

Paul and Richard had been out of school for two years by the time they arrived at Oxford, having completed their compulsory national service. The scheme, intended to keep the British armed forces up to strength after the war, was on its way out; but in 1956 there was no option except to delay and go to university first, or to be excused on health grounds. Both decided to get it over with.

Richard had a grim time. Public school should have been the only qualification necessary to be offered a commission, but he had messed up his interview board. When asked what he played, he replied 'the cello', when the answer should have been rugby or cricket. Without a commission, he was appointed to the army Education Corps and sent off to Korea (the more peaceful part), and then to Malaya. At least one good thing came out of it: it was there that he met an officer in the Gurkhas named Andrew Osmond.

Paul, on the other hand, did get a commission, eventually. His army career began at Copthorne, just down the road from his old school, from where he moved to the barracks in Strensall, near York. He described it as a reign of terror. The company sergeant major would shout and call for volunteers for fire picket – a long watch for the imagined enemy – and Paul remembered how it was 'You, You and You (always Me, somehow)'.[1] He hated the bullying, the hierarchy, and the general atmosphere of unpleasantness that a military structure depends on. Shouted at constantly, he sought solace in church, as the only place he could find some peace. His failure to show the necessary leadership qualities for an officer resulted in more of the same at the end of his officer training: three more months of mindless potato peeling. He was, he later told a BBC television programme, the worst officer ever to get a commission, so he was very low down on the list for a job once his training was complete. Then came some respite and some luck; the people who decide these things found him a regiment in Jamaica.

But there was, said his interviewing officer, a downside. The Jamaica Regiment was a native regiment. That would be all right, Paul told him. 'Now I don't think you fully understand, Foot, there are also natives in the mess, officers, do you realise?' Paul did understand, and said that would be fine, too. For having to put up with such a state of affairs, he would get an additional eight shillings a day. 'We call it wog money', said the officer.[2]

Paul was absolutely delighted. Not about the money, or the language used, but because he loved Jamaica. He had spent two happy years there as a small boy, playing cricket with his young Jamaican friends. And his family were also there.

These were the days when the comings and goings of important people warranted a photograph in the local newspaper, and his arrival made the pages of the *Gleaner*. A photographer was on hand at the airport to record the moment when he hugged his mother, now Lady Foot, with a great grin on his face and a tennis racket tucked under his arm. There would be tennis and swimming when he was not on duty, and endless hours in huts in the heat counting out gaiters and other pointless tasks when he was. It was, he said, a complete waste of his time.

He did occasionally have to stand to attention. There are photos of Second Lieutenant Foot of the Duke of Cornwall's Light Infantry on parade, standing upright and stiff in his long khaki shorts, sword pointing skyward, opposite his father the governor, and on another occasion while Princess Margaret inspected the troops. The sword was a problem. Chris Hall, who worked with Paul in the mid '60s, remembers that Paul had to draw the sword from his scabbard and then return it with a great sweeping motion. 'I had it from Paul that he was very worried about swiping off the head of the guy next to him.'

The other advantage of being stationed in Jamaica was the very congenial company he could keep on his days off. Sabina Park,

Kingston's Test cricket ground, was not far from his barracks, and for two whole days in 1958 Paul sat on a tin roof watching the great West Indian cricketer Gary Sobers play. 'I watched him knock off the highest ever score in a Test Match as if he was playing French cricket in a back garden', he later wrote. 'He wasn't remotely worried if he failed to get the runs, because he would then take the new ball, and try another record. If that failed, he could turn on his slow Chinaman, which he bowled better than anyone else in the world.'[3]

Paul lived at his barracks while his family was living in the grandeur of King's House, with its colonnades and verandas, dinners outdoors in the cool night air and glamorous visitors. There were so many that his father once described it as a hotel, where the bookings were 'brisk – particularly in the tourist season'. There were presidents and heads of state from across the world: Winston Churchill stayed for three weeks in 1953, and Princess Margaret for five days, which included a trip down the Rio Grande on a wooden raft with Paul's mother. Noël Coward, who Paul's mother adored, was a regular. One compensation for Paul's father was riding out in the early mornings and watching the sun come up over the Blue Mountains, 'a daily view of paradise'.

Sylvia did not mind the endless stream of guests. She was in her element as a hostess, with thirty servants on hand to help – fifteen in the house and another fifteen out of doors. Each day for her was a round of visits, to the local Girl Guides or the Red Cross, and lunches, teas and dinners to be organised at King's House. Not all of these were for interesting guests – some were sugar barons and other businessmen passing through, and many were uninvited. But the upside for Sylvia was the glamourous formal occasions, as when the Queen and Prince Philip came for a banquet at the start of their round-the-world tour of the Commonwealth in 1953, and she could dress in a ballgown and tiara.

Paul arrived in October 1957, but by mid November his family was gone. His father was needed in Cyprus. There was a farewell banquet at the house, Paul dressed smartly in a starched white uniform and seated next to Norman Manley, a future premier of an independent Jamaica. At the farewell service held in Coke Methodist Church in downtown Kingston, two-and-a-half thousand people heard Hugh

Foot say how proud he was to hear his son Paul read the lesson. Paul's brother Benjamin and sister Sarah were also present, but Oliver, who was born in Jamaica, was away at school in England. His father described how proud Oliver was to be a Jamaican, and said 'he will fight any English boy who is rash enough to speak a disparaging word about a West Indian'.[4]

Paul and Richard Ingrams arrived at University College, Oxford, on the same day in the autumn of 1958. Neither knew the other would be there, and Paul was surprised to hear someone call his name. They were delighted to see each other and very quickly became close friends – much closer than they had been at school.

Richard had chosen the college because his father went there, Paul for the opposite reason. 'He has refused to enter for colleges with which his family has had connections for he has wanted to stand on his own feet', Michael Charlesworth wrote in his Shrewsbury School reference to the College. 'He has got his short-comings, but I am convinced that he is a very good long-term bet.'[5] His father hoped so, too: 'Get a First, be President of the Union', he telegrammed.

Paul did eventually become president of the Union, although he did not get a first. He studied law, something of a family tradition, and not a subject to inspire him to hard work: 'Your pass was rather a close shave', he was warned at the end of his second term by his new masters.[6] He knew that choosing to study law had been a mistake, but did not have the guts to change. Richard, meanwhile, continued with classics. It was, he says, the only subject he knew anything about.

For Richard, Oxford meant freedom: 'Freedom to come and go as you pleased, meet in pubs, to choose what lectures to go to, to talk late into the night over endless cups of Nescafé.' For Paul, it was his 'idea of Paradise on Earth', as he wrote in a letter to Michael Charlesworth. 'I seem to spend most of my time in amazement at the joy of the place.'[7] Here there were no rules about how to wear your tie, and no barking sergeant majors.

Oxford also had a lot more to offer than simply a chance to study classics and law. There were plays to be acted in and music to be made, and the never-ending question of girls, now that they were no longer in an all-male environment. 'He gave me politics, I gave him music.

We came together in journalism', wrote Richard.[8] Within a very short time, Richard's irrepressible desire to find the ridiculous side of life found its outlet in *Parson's Pleasure*, a pocket-sized magazine about college life, whose editor, Adrien Berry, needed to study for his finals and was looking for someone to take it over. Richard and Paul happily obliged.

Richard said he had expected Oxford to be full of funny people, and was rather disappointed to find that it wasn't. 'People like me, Foot and Osmond [the Gurkha officer from Malaya who had also arrived at Oxford] just wanted to fart around' – and *Parson's Pleasure* was the ideal space for that.[9] Richard did the jokes and Paul wrote reviews of the Oxford Union debates. Paul's rooms, looking out over the quadrangle at the front of University College, became the registered address for the magazine, and here young women would gather to help them put it together over endless cups of tea and the occasional glass of sherry. They kept it afloat financially with ads for *Tribune*, where Paul's uncle, Michael, was then the editor, and for which Michael apparently paid out of his own pocket. Berry hadn't faced this problem – his father owned the *Daily Telegraph*.

There were other, more serious and conventional Oxford publications – *Isis* and *Cherwell*, both named after the local rivers – against which, for the moment anyway, they set their faces: 'Between the turgid waters of Isis and Cherwell we will steer our jolly little barque', wrote Richard.[10] They attacked the grey men who hung out in the libraries, attacked the left, and attacked the rich. But it did not last. The *Tribune* ads soon disappeared, and the magazine temporarily collapsed at the end of their first year. Fortunately, another was just starting up: *Mesopotamia*, a magazine 'of dedicated lunacy', the brainchild of Peter Usborne, who would also be the brains behind *Private Eye* in the years to come. In an early edition, Usborne is listed as editor, Richard Ingrams as caterer, Willie Rushton for special effects, Andrew Osmond as pencil sharpener, while Paul Foot was at the Typewriter. Issues of the magazine contain spoof film reviews and spoof obituaries, and Paul contributes the secretary's minutes: 'The third meeting of the Committee was held on Thursday, 5th February, at 2 p.m.'. This is followed by a long item about the cost of teacups. The magazine was funny, original and often experimental: one edition had a hessian cover embedded with seeds, another a prayer wheel clipped to the back; one even came with an advent calendar on the cover, its little windows popping open to the familiar faces of world leaders. They mocked people for taking themselves too seriously, for pretension, for any kind of humbug.

They met for what some called breakfast and others called lunch every day in the Town and Gown, a greasy spoon café off the High Street in the city: Richard and Paul, along with Andrew Osmond, Peter Jay – the heavyweight intellectual of their group – Noel Picarda and John Wells, who had met Richard during his National Service stint in Korea. At weekends they were joined by Willie Rushton who travelled up from London, where he was then working in a solicitor's office, having completed his two years of National Service in a tank regiment on the Rhine. Around the gang gathered a group of young women, some of whom also came to the café – Margaret Callaghan, daughter of Labour MP and future prime minister, Jim Callaghan, who would marry Peter Jay, and Candida Betjeman, daughter of the future Poet Laureate. Women were in short supply, as most Oxford colleges were all-male institutions, the female numbers only slightly boosted by the local typing and technical colleges.

The rather backward attitude to women at Oxford at the time was amply demonstrated in November 1958, when the Oxford Union debated the proposal that 'the emancipation of women has exposed their political incapacity'. Peter Jay – a staunch supporter of the Labour Party and a future British ambassador to the United States – remembers with some shame that he proposed the motion, in spite of the visible proof to the contrary in the form of Barbara Castle, speaking in opposition. The fiery Labour MP gave as good as she got, describing what she saw as 'a closed vestry of self-perpetuating masculine exclusiveness'.[11] It was to be another two years before women were allowed into the debates. And when Paul became president in his final term, he tried, and failed, to let them be allowed to speak.

During his first year at Oxford, Paul spent Christmas with his family in Cyprus. It was the first time that Paul, his two brothers and his sister had been together for Christmas, and by then Benjie, the youngest, was already nine years old. Paul's godfather Stewart Perowne was there, as well as Paul's cousin Christina.

As governor, Hugh Foot was overseeing the complicated negotiations for independence, but in Cyprus the situation was even more fraught than it had been in Jamaica. EOKA, the Cypriot nationalists, were in armed rebellion, and that December there was to be a hanging of two young EOKA supporters for murder. It was one of the onerous responsibilities of the governor to sign the death warrants, and the evening before the hanging, the Foots gathered for supper on the upper veranda. Although it was family, it was also formal: the women wore evening dresses, the men dinner jackets. Paul's father, too stressed by events to eat – knowing that in signing the death warrants he was 'signing my own political death' – was lying down in his room. 'Hugh was in a terrible state', remembers Christina. 'I'd sent the telegram to London saying he didn't want to do it. The government had replied: you have to.'

Fearing unrest, the director of prisons had brought forward the execution from dawn to fifteen minutes past midnight. As the clocks ticked towards the dreaded hour, the phone rang. It was London. A meeting in Paris between the foreign ministers of Greece and Turkey had agreed that the execution would be a disaster, and all hopes of a peaceful settlement would be destroyed. It was now ten minutes to midnight. Hugh grabbed Paul and they rushed to the prison, still dressed in their dinner jackets. By the time they arrived, a huge crowd had gathered, praying and shouting slogans. Opposite them, the British garrison was at the ready.

Inside the gloomy prison the political prisoners 'howled to an unheeding heaven'. The hangman, flown out from England, was standing by. Hugh had arrived just in time to retrieve the death warrants. Paul later described how the recently condemned men, 'cool and handsome in their simple clothes', calmly thanked his father for their stay of execution, as a great roar of applause rose within the prison walls: good news travels fast.[12]

On his return to Oxford after the holidays, Paul wrote about his experience in *Oxford Opinion*, and in February 1960 was invited to America to debate the death penalty. CBS wanted to film a live debate between two students from the Oxford Union and two from

Northwestern University, for and against the abolition of capital punishment. At the time, the case of Caryl Chessman, who had been sentenced to death over a decade earlier for rape and kidnap, was dividing public opinion in America.

Paul's fellow student at the debate was Robert Rowland, who had just completed his term as president of the Oxford Union. The two young men were driven by car to Heathrow where, in those early days of air travel, things were a little basic. Check-in took place in a huge tent, and there were no security checks. Once on board their Comet, they dined on caviar and wrote their speeches, before touching down in New York in the late afternoon. 'Fry him for breakfast', was the considered opinion of their cab driver on the fate of Chessman.

'The death penalty is an absolute punishment based on a relative judgment', argued Rowland as he opened the debate. 'It admits of no mistake. Unless a court of law can claim infallibility, with all that that involves, the death penalty should never be considered.' Lee Huebner, opening for Northwestern in favour of retention of the death penalty, was supported by John Roberts. Each side had the opportunity to question the other, Paul taking a rather hectoring tone. And then he had the last word: 'The case of Caryl Chessman has shown all the anomalies and illogicalities that go with the death penalty. That it does not deter, it does not reform, that on no moral criteria can it be regarded fair retribution.'[13]

'The debate was lively', remembered Rowland many years later, 'with Paul Foot being passionately patrician, sweeping the American arguments away like autumn leaves.'[14] They were told that Chessman watched the debate. Having lost his final appeal, he was executed three months later.

Back in Oxford, Paul spoke in a Union debate on the grim subject, after which Hugh Stephenson, another Oxford contemporary, wrote in *Isis* that 'Foot made the best undergraduate speech so far this term. He has got that authority which allows him to use the emotions of the House to his purpose and which you get so seldom apart from the guests.'[15] The proposition that 'capital punishment must be abolished immediately' was carried. Paul's opposition to capital punishment would not waver until it was finally abolished in Britain by a change in the law in 1965. Too late for a young man called James Hanratty – but more of him later.

Paul returned briefly to Cyprus in August 1960 for the final departure of his father as British governor. Hugh Foot had negotiated with the two sides, determined that the island should not be divided, and left an independent country with a federal structure which lasted for several years. The family sailed away in a Royal Navy ship supplied for the occasion.[16]

The Oxford Union debates were serious, formal affairs. A photo of the line-up for a debate in 1960 shows Paul in waistcoat and tails with a white bowtie. To be a named speaker, whether for or against the motion, was the top accolade. In his second year at Oxford, Paul shared the platform with his uncle Michael. Two months later he was speaking again with fellow undergraduate and future television dramatist and playwright, Dennis Potter. Later, in November 1960, Paul spoke again on the increasingly prescient issue of nuclear weapons.

The Campaign for Nuclear Disarmament had been launched two years earlier, in February 1958, at a public meeting in London that attracted 5,000 people. It was to become a focus of attention for scientists, religious leaders, writers, actors, musicians, and of course students. Michael Foot, then temporarily out of parliament, sat on the campaign's organising committee; during this period the issue of nuclear disarmament was tearing the Labour Party apart. Unilateralists, who wanted immediate disarmament by Britain, were pitted against the multilateralists, who wanted disarmament when it was agreed by the other nuclear powers. Michael Foot led the unilateralists, while Hugh Gaitskell, leader of the Labour Party, led for the other side.

Two months after the launch, over Easter weekend, the first CND march set out from London to Aldermaston, where Britain's nuclear weapons were being developed. It was a long way – fifty miles – requiring overnight stops in local schools and community halls, yet thousands of people joined. The marches continued each Easter, though taking the opposite route, from Aldermaston to London, so they could finish in Trafalgar Square. Paul's first attempt to join the march was a bit of a fiasco. He was with his cousin Kate on the long drive up from Devon when his car broke down with a blown gasket. Paul, never known for his facility with anything mechanical, was overcome with confusion when he was given the spare part and told to get on with it. The journey took them twelve hours. From that rather difficult start, Paul made a point of going on the march each year, complaining bitterly to his cousin Christina about the blisters he had acquired from having walked all the way, and showing off to his uncle Michael, who had only managed part of the route.

During his Oxford years, Paul would make regular trips to London to see his aunt Dorothy and his cousins Christina and Lily, or he would drive down to Devon to stay with uncle John and his cousins Win and Kate. A car, any car, was a rare thing among Oxford students, and Paul's was the mark of a certain level of privilege. He drove an old Jowett, a sturdy vehicle made in Bradford (later replaced by a nippy white Sunbeam Alpine, a very chic sports car, that belonged to his father). In the summer of 1959, at the end of their first year at college, Richard joined Paul for the long drive south. It took hours in those pre-motorway days. They planned to spend a few days with Paul's grandfather Isaac in Cornwall, and then with uncle John's family in Devon. Years later, Paul would recall the trip. 'The summer of '59 was absolutely wonderful', he said. 'We would sit for hours on Cornish cliffs, or the hills of Bodmin Moor; and I was always amazed by the fact that [Richard] could just sit for hours without doing anything. He could cope with his own resources. I could never do that – I always had to be doing something or talking to somebody.'[17] Paul put this down to Richard's melancholic streak and his deep religious commitment, although Richard says that 'indolence was probably a more plausible explanation'. It is hard to imagine the opportunity to be indolent when staying with grandfather Isaac. 'In the evening after supper he asked Paul to read out some of his old speeches in Parliament', remembers Richard. ' "Louder! Louder!" he insisted.'[18] Although he was in his seventies, Isaac was learning to play the piano so that he could play Bach, and as soon as he discovered that Richard could also play, he insisted he have a go at some of the Preludes and Fugues.

There was a lot of fun to be had in both Oxford and London. Christina and Lily remember Paul arriving at their mother's flat at Albert Hall Mansions in Kensington, with varying combinations of the crowd that would go on to work at *Private Eye* – Richard, of course, as well as Willie Rushton, John Wells, the actor Noel Picarda and Andrew Osmond. They planned shows and plays, and Paul and Richard would write headlines and jokes for their Oxford magazines, firing them at each other, Lily remembers, as they walked along Kensington Gore. At the back of a small notebook, between a long essay on the Emperor Hadrian and notes on translations of Virgil's *Georgics*, there are the workings of a series of these jokes, with snaps taken in a photo booth of Paul and his cousin Lily. The Sellotape is brown with age, but the photos are as clear as if they were taken yesterday: Lily looking whimsical, 'I'll say yes if you ask'; Paul frowning, 'You make me feel so young.' And, in a portent of what was to come, an eager-faced Paul wore a mackintosh and hat: 'Could I have a few words, Miss Munroe, on your feelings for your husband.'

There was serious entertainment, too. Richard and Paul both appeared in the Oxford Union's Dramatic Society production of Shakespeare's *Coriolanus*: 'Ninety hours rehearsing for one line in my case, and five lines in Richard's case. We weren't any good, either of us', Paul told Richard's biographer.[19] He recognised soon enough that acting was not a career option, although he became fascinated by the politics of the play. He had seen Laurence Olivier in the 1959 production at Stratford, and from then on went to see every production he could.

The group around Richard and Paul were a mixed bag. Another young man with a car was Grey Gowrie, younger by a couple of years as he had not done National Service, who would sit at Paul's feet hoping for words of wisdom. 'He was very, very attractive and interesting and not like people I knew', remembered Gowrie, who developed something of a crush on Paul. There was one subject, he noticed, that troubled Paul, and that was women. 'He would talk about it a lot. It wasn't an easy subject for him.' Gowrie had no such trouble himself. He went to Oxford mainly to meet girls, and the best place to meet them was on the left – something he had learned from Paul.

Women may have buzzed around Paul and Gowrie, but it was Richard who was the real attraction. 'He was shy', says Gowrie, 'but he was formidable. He was intense and sceptical, but he could be very funny. That was very attractive.' He was also a powerful figure in all their lives. 'When we got a new girlfriend we went and showed her to Richard, like showing her to your grandmother the Dowager Duchess.'

Paul had a similar experience with Richard. Monica Beckinsale was a student at St Hugh's College who went along to one of the parties in Paul's college rooms. At the time she was engaged to the exotically named Prince Nicolas Ouroussoff, much to the delight of the gossip in *Parson's Pleasure*. The engagement did not last, and soon after Monica and Paul became a couple. She was very attractive to men, according to her friends – quick-witted, intellectually exciting and worldly-wise, having spent a year at Princeton High School in the United States. Although it is now unclear what exactly motivated Richard, he wrote Paul a letter, asked others of their friends also to sign it, suggesting to Paul that he drop Monica. Paul took no notice.

Paul's first taste of office was as president of the Liberal Club. He was a Liberal because those were the politics of his grandfather, and as president he invited the speakers he knew – on one occasion, his uncle Dingle; on another, Jeremy Thorpe, then the Liberal MP for North Devon, a future leader of the Liberal Party, and a great friend of Paul's uncle John. But liberalism did not have the answers Paul was looking for. During the term when he was president, he also attended meetings of the Labour Club, and heard some of the arguments for socialism. 'To my horror and embarrassment', he later remembered,

> they seemed unassailable. I managed to cover up my confusion by committing myself to the Campaign for Nuclear Disarmament, which included Liberals as well as socialists. But by the time I left Oxford I was a keen supporter of the left-wing weekly *Tribune* (proprietor my Uncle Michael) and the *New Left Review*.[20]

The New Left had emerged in Oxford in the years just before Paul arrived. It was a loose collection of socialists and Marxists disillusioned with the communist politics of the Soviet Union after the invasion of Hungary in 1956, and equally disillusioned with British and French imperialism after the ill-fated invasion of Suez in the same year. While at one of the Labour Club meetings, Paul met Stuart Hall, the first editor of *New Left Review*, which started publication in January 1960. Hall, a Rhodes scholar from Jamaica who was deeply involved in the Oxford left, soon became one of Paul's heroes; for now,

Hall was offering something that explained the world better than liberalism.

Paul also began to write regularly for the university publications from 1960. He started with a 'Foot Loose' column in *Cherwell*, followed by another column in *Isis*, a magazine he was to edit in his final year. It was to be a very short editorship, however. Soon after he took on the role, Paul hit on the idea of publishing reviews of lectures, penned by a fellow student and published under the pseudonym 'Spartacus'. A lecture on Dante was described as using 'cosy, prosy' evasions, the net result being 'dull and void'. Attendance at another lecture was minimal. The lecturers were not happy with such public scrutiny, and Paul was hauled before the proctors (the University police) and ordered to stop.

The effect of the ban was weeks of undiluted publicity. Paul was interviewed by the BBC, and there was outrage in the national press. In the next edition he ran a blank page with 'Censored by the Proctors' stamped across it in large black letters. There were to be no more reviews.

Paul again made the headlines when Oswald Mosley, former leader of the British Union of Fascists, was invited to speak at the University. A piece in *Isis* spelled out exactly who the visiting speaker was: 'Sir Oswald Mosley has done his best for 30 years to stir up racial violence in East London, Notting Hill and elsewhere.' On reading the comments, Mosley's solicitors demanded an apology. Holywell Press, the publishers of *Isis*, agreed. Paul had nothing to do with the apology, was opposed to it, and promptly resigned as editor after just six weeks.

Max Mosley, Oswald Mosley's youngest son, was a contemporary of Paul's at Oxford – as was Robert Skidelsky. When Skidelsky published his biography of Oswald Mosley in 1975, Paul wrote a damning review for the anti-fascist magazine *Searchlight*. Paul's main bone of contention was the way in which Skidelsky shifted responsibility for the growing anti-Semitism of the British Union of Fascists in the mid 1930s onto the Jews themselves. The Jews, Skidelsky wrote, 'must take a large share of the blame for what subsequently happened'. This was an echo, Paul thought, of a speech Mosley had made to a packed Albert Hall in March 1936, where he had said that 'the Jew himself has created anti-Semitism . . . Even Hitler himself was not anti-Semitic before he saw a

Jew.' Skidelsky was, he wrote, always ingratiating when they worked together on *Isis*, but had been seduced by the glitter of the Mosley family. His book was 'meticulous in the extreme. The textual notes are all in the right order, the proofs superbly read. It is a masterpiece of modern scholarship – and utterly disgusting.'[21]

Alongside Paul at *Isis* was Grey Gowrie as poetry editor. Although their paths would diverge radically – Gowrie would become a minister in Margaret Thatcher's Conservative government – he saw in Paul something that would become the hallmark of his future journalism: 'He was clever, he knew about things, in a questioning and sceptical way, which was against the grain. He was a *tester* of ideas.' As Paul began his term as president of the Union, Gowrie wrote a piece for *Isis* which described Paul's socialism as 'armchair', suggesting that he would never make a 'practical politician' and that, like many others whose most passionate concern is the well-being of the working class, he was 'little at ease with its members'.[22]

A concern for the working class was definitely a new sort of politics for Paul in his last months at Oxford. Besides the meetings of the Labour Club and the New Left, Paul had been arguing with a politics don called Colwyn Williamson. Colwyn ran a Marxist study group, to which he invited anyone he thought might be attracted to socialist ideas, and they kept their discussions going through the days and nights of the Aldermaston March at Easter. 'On the Sunday night we were sleeping on the floor of a schoolroom, Colwyn, Paul, myself and three or four others', remembers Ian Birchall, another Oxford student. 'We talked until 4 a.m., arguing whether you could detach the issues of nuclear weapons from questions about capitalism. Colwyn was arguing that you couldn't. It had a huge impact on me, and probably on Paul too.' Colwyn and Paul continued to argue and discuss political ideas for the rest of Paul's life.

In a long essay for *Isis*, written as he was preparing to leave Oxford, Paul set out some of his new political thinking, rejecting liberalism as totally inadequate. Liberalism was about the individual, and Paul now thought the collective mattered more. 'In a society split into classes', he wrote, 'separated into elites, canonised by the emotions of contempt, disrespect and, most often, plain fear, the concept of individual liberty is little more than a shabby fraud.' Within the working class, by contrast, the idea of collectivism ran deep: 'I passionately believe that where the spirit of collectivism exists, there is the hope for the creation of a just and humane society.'[23]

In his last term Paul was finally elected, upon his third try, as president of the Union. His father was inordinately proud. Hugh Foot had been president of the Cambridge Union, and he would later write about the special treat of sitting in the gallery of the Oxford Union, hearing his son speak and seeing him occupying the president's chair: 'He had something in his accent of my brothers and my father too. A wonderful thing to hear one's father speaking in the voice of one's son.'[24]

As their time at Oxford ran out, Richard Ingrams retreated to his rooms to revise for his exams, although it did him little good. Paul also retreated to study for his exams – but only in the last three weeks, and then to Monica's parents' house in Oxford with its sunny garden.

Then he and Monica went to stay with his sister, and Paul went to bed. He had glandular fever, had in fact had it for some time, and wouldn't recover until long after he had moved to Glasgow. Stuck in bed, he wrote to Monica's mother asking if she could send on his books: 'the Orwell *Essays*, *Spanish Civil War*, R. Willliams' *Culture & Society* etc. which are all in the shelf in the top room. I am getting very short of reading and will badly need some shortly.'[25]

4

No Mean City

When Paul left Oxford, the future looked rosy. 'I'd been a great star at Oxford', he told one interviewer, 'and I thought that when you left that it was the same in life – you tried to become a star. And if you could become president of the Union and editor of *Isis* it was not a very big step to become editor of some paper or a Labour MP or a Labour minister.'[1] His first step along this glittering path was to write to Hugh Cudlipp, the managing director of Mirror Newspapers, who knew Paul's father. Cudlipp immediately offered Paul a job on the *Daily Record* in Glasgow, where, he told Paul, he would learn a thing or two.

Glasgow in those days was grim: an industrial city of tenements and families living in single-ends – flats so small they should have been illegal. It was a city that had built an empire, and along the Clyde the clang of steel on steel could still be heard in the shipyards and engineering works, which employed thousands of workers. And it rained, a lot.

The *Record* provided a daily diet of tragedy and triumph. There were stories of murder and divorce, abandoned children and found ones, collapsed buildings and crashed lorries, and workers on strike. The royal family featured prominently when taking its holidays in Scotland, while the Duchess of Argyll's divorce fed the gossip columns. There was nothing too long, and nothing too arduous.

Writing for the *Record* would be very different from writing for *Isis*. It had a huge circulation – half a million copies a day – to a predominantly working-class readership. Paul learned fast, and he could write. 'I work so fast that every now and then I outstrip the bosses, and I am left with nothing to do', he began a letter to Monica's mother.

> I am enjoying the job even more now that I have come on to the 'Features' staff. This means that I can write about things I want to write about (within reason), and about twice a week a nice big article appears by Paul Foot, which is very encouraging, and does a lot for my vanity.

His by-line first appeared on a story about the plight of blind people and the abysmal failure of the Scottish authorities. Through the local Labour Party, Paul met a blind telephonist. The resulting piece is a rather sentimental one about the difficulties he faced, but one with, as Paul would later remember, 'a bit of a bite and some point'. It provoked a huge response, and the story ran and ran, with examples of blind workers being sacked from their jobs and school children raising money for guide dogs. It also changed the attitude of the Glasgow newsroom to Paul. 'The fact that I'd had something printed that most of them rather reluctantly admitted was quite a good thing did me the power of good.'[2]

The story appeared in November 1961. Paul had just celebrated his twenty-fourth birthday. His career as a journalist was under way.

Articles soon followed on children locked up in remand homes and children beaten in school. He wrote about over-the-top profits at the Post Office and the fate of local shipyard workers, and later the trial of Nelson Mandela, the racist history of South Africa, and the call for a boycott.

After a year at the *Record*, 'Paul Foot investigates' appeared for the first time, on a piece about the failings of the driving test system. His articles were not always highbrow: 'Paul Foot probes the world of women's hairdressing', read a strap in early 1962.

There was one lesson Paul did learn at the *Record* which he never forgot. Not long after he arrived, he was sent to the High Court to collect a man acquitted of murdering his wife and escort him back to the paper for an exclusive interview. But exclusives had been promised by the man's lawyers to all the main Glasgow papers, and an appalling battle followed as the competing journalists tried to secure their prey. Complaints were made, and the National Union of Journalists in Glasgow brought the subject up for discussion at its monthly meeting. Instead of the usual six people, there were a couple of hundred who hammered out a response against the proprietors and their cheque-book journalism. The meeting began, Paul remembered, with, 'You bastard, you seized our man', but soon changed as the alternative view was put forward by the trade unionists, who said, 'This is rubbish, we're all doing this job together and we're being created into hood-lums by our newspapers.' The union was absolutely opposed to chequebook journalism, and it was going to make sure that it never happened again.[3]

Paul was planning to spend Easter 1962 on the Aldermaston march. The world was 'balancing on the rim of hell', he wrote in the *Record* – a prescient view just months before the Cuban Missile Crisis. Scotland's own particular hell was about to arrive in the shape of American Polaris nuclear warheads. Based in Holy Loch, in the Firth of Clyde, Polaris sparked protests across Scotland and the north of England, where thousands of young people came out to demonstrate.

Paul had arrived in Glasgow with some useful names of CND supporters in his pocket. The Buchans were friends of uncle Michael, ex-communists, members of the Labour Party and supporters of *Tribune*. Norman Buchan would become a Labour MP, and Janey a member of the European Parliament. For now, she took one look at Paul and put him to bed; he was still suffering from the illness that had laid him low after his exams. He stayed with them and their young son Alasdair until he was well enough to move into his own digs, on Cecil Street.

Another name in his pocket was that of Jean McCrindle. Paul stuffed a note through her letterbox: 'I'm working in Glasgow. I've been given your name by Mike Rustin. Can we meet? Long live CND.' Jean, another ex-communist, had been born and brought up in Glasgow and, after university, had returned to work as a lecturer for the Workers' Educational Association. She suggested Paul join her and the other Labour Party Young Socialists as they entertained the folk taking the Sunday evening air up and down Sauchiehall Street, one of the city's main thoroughfares. The pubs were closed in Scotland on a Sunday, and television was still a minority entertainment, so people would walk up and down and listen to – as well as barrack and heckle – the socialists and the god-botherers standing on their soapboxes.

'Paul watched us for a while that evening', recalls Jean. 'He offered to speak the next Sunday, but he did have a weird haircut as well as a voice from his public school days', and he looked a bit scruffy. Young Glaswegians were very particular about their appearance on their days off work. A local barber transformed his severe army side-parting into the Beatles pudding-basin style that was to be his for the rest of his life, and a suit was bought. As for the voice, it was as though he were a foreigner – not just southern, but posh too. He could do little about it, and would have to make up for it with the skill of his argument. Even if it was tough speaking on the street and being heckled, it was better than speaking to 'ten nice old ladies from the Co-Op, who are all opposed to the Common Market for reasons which they find difficult to formulate. They regard me as rather strange', he wrote in another of his letters. The old ladies came with the day job.

The person who helped Jean sort Paul out was Gus Macdonald, who invited Paul to a meeting of the Govan and Gorbals Young Socialists, in the heart of industrial Glasgow. The audience was mostly young apprentices and workers from the shipyards and engineering factories. Paul's chosen topic was the risk of a nuclear war starting accidentally. By his own account, he delivered a very good Oxford Union speech. But he did speak at length, and Gus, chairing the meeting, knew they had a problem: 'The pubs shut at 9.30 p.m. and the night shift started at 10 p.m., so people were getting agitated.' Finally, someone in the audience shouted out: 'Wars don't start by accident, capitalism starts war.' It brought the meeting to an abrupt end, and the entire audience rushed for the door. Paul had been in Glasgow for just three weeks.

The Young Socialists meetings were held in an old fruit shop on Weir Street. Gus lived along the street, as did Bob Gillespie and a host of other people Paul would get to know. For Paul, they were the real working class, not some theoretical version in the pages of *New Left Review*. Gus was an apprentice engineer in the shipyards, where the apprenticeship was long and wages low, with no guarantee of a job at the end. He was also a union man and an agitator, as well as a great reader – not just of political periodicals like *Tribune*, but Marx and the philosophers, too. The tradition of working-class self-education was very much alive in the Glasgow of the 1960s, and in his lunchtimes Gus would meet with some of his fellow workers to discuss what they had read: 'There were hundreds and hundreds of men working in that yard, so there were a lot of very smart guys there.'

A year earlier there had been a great strike of apprentices along the Clyde and across the country. They were on strike for weeks and, when it was over, these young men needed somewhere to flex their newly developed political muscle. 'I had a bit of a political background', explains Gus, 'because my father read *Tribune*, which I'd been reading and selling in the shipyard, and my parents were in the Labour Party, so we joined the Young Socialists.' Out of that strike, the Govan and Gorbals Young Socialists became something unique: a Young Socialists branch made up entirely of young industrial workers, male and female.

Politics in Glasgow was then still dominated by the Communist Party, particularly in the trade unions, and anyone on the left who wanted to challenge the CP would have to be sharp about it. So, as a form of political education, Gus invited two speakers up from London for a weekend school. Paul had gone with him to the British European Airways Terminal in St Enoch Square to collect them. It was late in the evening when the two men arrived, and Paul was struck by the differences between them: 'Michael Kidron was impeccably dressed, urbane and charming. His companion, Tony Cliff, short and scruffy, was plainly terrified of being bored.' Brothers-in-law, they were the earliest members of what became the International Socialists.[4]

The weekend was something of a revelation, not just because Tony Cliff turned out to be a great speaker, but also because of 'his ability to explain an issue with such clarity and force that I could not help laughing at my own inability previously to understand it', as Paul would later write of that meeting. The issue they argued over was one that preoccupied the whole of the left at the time: Was Russia socialist? – a rather arcane issue when Paul reflected on the meeting in the 1990s, and even more so three decades later.

The Communist Party of Great Britain was formed in 1920, in the wake of the Russian Revolution. Like its fellow parties around the world, it attracted workers and intellectuals to its radical view, particularly during the turbulent 1930s, when capitalism was still reeling from the effects of the Great Depression and fascists were on the march across Europe. But these high ideals were soon soured by Stalin's purges and trials, and his signing of a pact with Hitler. In the 1950s, the Soviet invasion of Hungary further dented the CP's reputation. But loyalty is a powerful force in politics. The militant trade unionists, who had grown up under the influence of the CP, found it hard to let go. The '60s generation was different – too young to remember or, like Paul, from another political tradition entirely. They may have retained some residual notion that Soviet planning offered a better way of organising society, but there was not the same commitment. Among them, alternative ideas found a willing audience.

When he arrived in Glasgow, Paul had no firm view on this issue. On one of his early attempts on Sauchiehall Street, a drunken heckler soon sorted him out. 'What about Russia?' he shouted. As Paul tried to explain, he followed up with, 'What about the Berlin Wall?' Paul tried again. The wall was there, he explained, to keep out 'bourgeois elements' who wanted to sabotage the socialist experiment. 'It's there, you bampot', his heckler bawled, 'to keep the workers in!'[5] Paul had no idea what a bampot was, but accepted that such crude common sense had something to it. If the workers disliked the state they were living in, it was probably not a socialist state at all. He took up the argument that, although there had been a revolution, and there had been planning, a Stalinist bureaucracy had taken over.

Tony Cliff, having wrestled with the various descriptions of what Russia might be, eventually concluded that it was not socialist at all, but capitalist. Not capitalist in the Western European and American sense, but 'state capitalist'. The transfer of power and wealth had not been to the workers, but to the class that ran the state. Russian workers were just as much cut off from economic and political power as they were anywhere else in the world.

The effect of Cliff's argument on Paul was dramatic. Like many of his fellow Young Socialists, he wanted to believe Russia was somehow better, that it provided some hope against America, its nuclear arsenal and its aggressive foreign policy. 'It was devastating', he remembered.

It threatened not only a residual sympathy for what seemed at least like state planning in Russia, but also a whole view of politics, including, crucially, the notion that socialist change could come from the top of society, planned and executed by enlightened people, educated ministers and bureaucrats.[6]

Change would have to come from below.

Gus was impressed, too. He had first seen copies of the *International Socialism* journal in London, and had liked the intellectual style of its writing. Michael Kidron edited the journal alongside the Scottish philosopher Alasdair MacIntyre. Gus also saw something in Tony Cliff that could carry even a Glasgow audience: he was funny. He soon joined Cliff's tiny political organisation, the International Socialists, and Paul joined the following year, along with Bob Gillespie and eventually Jimmy McCallum. They remained in the Young Socialists, belonging to both simultaneously.

This was a fluid time for politics. Young people were joining one organisation or another, testing ideas, trying out different groups. In its early days, the New Left, including as it did several former members of the Communist Party, was generally hostile to the followers of Trotsky. Stuart Hall had suggested to Paul that he should 'sort out the Trots' when he got to Glasgow. Paul had agreed, although he had no idea who or what a Trot was. As it turned out, the International Socialists who Paul now joined were the very Trotskyists that he had been warned about.

Jimmy McCallum, an apprentice in one of the big engineering factories, was younger than the others – just a teenager. Paul made a distinct impression on him: 'He was attractive because he was not middle class but from the haute bourgeoisie', he recalls. 'He was the first person I ever heard speaking in that voice. He was terribly, terribly posh.' Jimmy wanted to know why Paul had come to Glasgow, a city in which he seemed so out of place. Paul explained that it was partly because of his reading of *No Mean City*, Alexander McArthur's book from the 1930s, based on his experience as an unemployed Glaswegian.

No Mean City follows gang leader Jonnie Stark, beginning with his home life in the Gorbals, where he lives in a single-end, a one-room apartment with a cavity bed: a small, windowless closet. He is short of work and short of rent, the drains are blocked, and the place is infested with bugs. The story is unremittingly grim, and life for Stark and those around him ends badly. But it is Govan and the Gorbals that are at the heart of the story: Govan, where the shipyards dominated the skyline, and the Gorbals, a byword for bad housing. 'Paul came looking to see if that experience was real', says Jimmy. 'He found out it was very real, and I think it changed him in a way perhaps he had never thought about.'

Little had changed in Glasgow since McArthur's book was first published – certainly not for those like Bob Gillespie, who also lived in a single-end. 'It was the first worker's house Paul was in', he recalls. 'My single-end was a single room, with a bed in a recess, a fireplace, a window and a sink. That was it. The baby's cot was next to the bed.' The toilet was communal. Paul was rather taken aback when he visited, and would eventually lend Bob the money to move out.

Bob was the same age as Paul, and had also been in the army, having signed on at sixteen. He still had 'Hong Kong' tattooed across his knuckles from his years in service. 'I came from a broken home. My mother was sick. In the army I got some discipline, three square meals a day, and a level playing field with the other fellows.' Out of the army and back in Glasgow, he became a printer, a trade unionist and a socialist. One evening, he invited Paul around for supper: Chips in the pan, a tin of spam, and tinned pears to follow. Paul was enthusiastic. 'This is amazing', he said as he tucked in. It was a Paul thing: he found every meal that someone prepared for him amazing, even those out of a tin at Bob's, or served in a greasy spoon down the Hackney Road in London.

There were two other influential Glaswegians Paul got to know during his time there, both called Harry. The first was Harry Selby, a small, voluble man in his late forties who worked out of his own barber's shop. He toured the Young Socialist meetings with a bag full of political tracts: Marx and Engels, Lenin and Trotsky. Paul borrowed a pamphlet by Engels on Germany for three pence, and when he returned it Selby explained the text and added a haircut. Selby had, thought Paul, some electrifying ideas about how the ugly and cruel capitalist society could swiftly be changed by a revolution. Although he was a revolutionary, Selby was also obsessed with the Labour Party, in which he buried himself, eventually becoming a rather ineffectual MP for Govan in the 1970s.

The second Harry was Harry McShane – another resident of Weir Street, but one of a different generation. Nearly seventy when he and Paul first met, with a political pedigree that went back decades, McShane had become a revolutionary in 1908, and agitated against the First World War. He was an organiser of the Unemployed Workers' Movement in the 1920s, and joined the Communist Party in 1923. During the post-war years, while a journalist for the Party's newspaper, the *Daily Worker*, he began to have doubts about the direction the CP was heading in, particularly after the treatment of ordinary party members and workers in Czechoslovakia in 1948 and in East Berlin in 1953. That year, after being disciplined for not taking part in a standing ovation for a party official, he left. Unable to continue at the *Daily Worker*, he went back to the shipyards as a labourer when he was already in his sixties. He was a man of enormous principle.

Paul and Harry would sit and talk for hours in the Gondola Café in the Gorbals, where Harry would blend his knowledge of history with the politics of the day. Harry urged Paul to go with him to the meetings of the Glasgow Trades Council, where the representatives of all the trade union branches in the city met – perhaps a couple of hundred people on some occasions, almost all of whom were in the CP. The two often spoke together at meetings large and small, and even, on one memorable occasion, outside John Brown's shipyard in Clydebank, to no one at all. No matter the audience, Harry was always patient. 'Things will come up again, Paul', he said as they trooped home from a very small meeting on nuclear disarmament in Edinburgh. 'When they are not listening, then it's even more important that we keep the ideas alive.'[7]

Although they agreed about much, Harry did not join Paul in the International Socialists. In his politics, Harry was closer to Raya Dunayevskaya, a Russian-American Marxist and former secretary of Trotsky, who was then based in Chicago. The British section of her group called itself the Marxist Humanist group, and had just three members. They had all left the CP at the same time, and were all delegates to the Glasgow Trades Council. They produced a type-written bulletin, and met in a café in Renfield Street, where Paul would sometimes join them. There Harry had given Paul a copy of Dunayevskaya's book, *Marxism and Freedom*, in which she argued that Marxism had been reduced to a rump of dry economics that had nothing to say about the lived experience of working men and women. 'Marxism is a theory of liberation, or it is nothing', she wrote.

Paul held her in some regard. In a review for *Tribune*, he argued that in the modern Labour movement there had been a 'headlong stampede from theory', for fear of reviving that old and terrible ghost, Karl Marx. 'For someone brought up to believe (by liberals scoffing; and by Stalinists rejoicing) that the Russian Revolution and Lenin led inevitably to the horrors of Stalinism, Raya Dunayevskaya's book came as a tremendous liberation and relief.'[8] The downside, however, was her sectarianism. When Paul wrote to thank her for her book, she wrote back furiously denouncing him for joining the International Socialists, rather than turning those three men in Renfield Street into four.

Paul read everything he could lay his hands on: books about the German revolutionary Rosa Luxemburg; the writings of Lenin and Trotsky; and the vast biography of Trotsky by Isaac Deutscher, the third volume of which was published in 1963. Monica gave Paul a copy – 'in gay Glasgow on his birthday', she wrote inside. There were several books that Paul claimed, at different times, had changed his life. One was Ralph Miliband's *Parliamentary Socialism*, which he also read in Glasgow. 'It put me off my plan to be a Labour MP for life.'[9] Another was a slim volume written by Karl Marx.

On Friday afternoons, on his way home from the *Daily Record* offices, Paul would often stop off at Clyde Books, a bookseller that stocked communist and socialist literature, to see what was new. It was there that he found a copy of Marx's *The Civil War in France*, written in 1871 in the aftermath of the Paris Commune. Many years later Paul talked about his find at a meeting. 'I took it home, reading as I went', he said, 'bumping into people on my way, then on the bus, and finally finished it that night.'[10] Paul's talk doesn't offer the usual portrait of Marx, the ageing philosopher, beard and boils, writing *Das Kapital* in the British

Library. It shows Marx as a young man, just twenty-nine, with a young family, émigrés recently arrived in London. There were jokes, of course: Paul doing funny voices as Marx, too busy to go to meetings: 'No I will not come to your piddling meeting', and, making it more topical for his audience: 'No bloody branch meetings or committee meetings or meetings of any kind.'

But, of course, Marx did go to meetings. He couldn't resist knowing what was going on, being where the action was. And this was why, when the Paris Commune was crushed in 1871, Marx wrote this short pamphlet. Thousands died as the French military retook Paris, amid scenes of the most revolting barbarism, and thousands more were imprisoned. Marx was indignant at the scale of the atrocity, but, said Paul, he understood why this democratic experiment had been put down with such brutality. When the workers of Paris took over the running of the city, they challenged the old order, which 'writhed in convulsions of rage at the sight of the Red Flag, the symbol of the Republic of Labour, floating over the Hôtel de Ville'.[11] 'In one blow', Paul told his audience, 'this book smashed all my exciting parliamentary ambitions. It was quite obvious to me that there was no point whatsoever in engaging in such activity.'

Paul, Gus and the others were then young men. They drank and smoked, went to dances, made up jokes, wrote and sang songs. The singing took Paul and fifty others from the folk-singing section of the Young Socialists all the way to a miners' club in Lanarkshire, where they worked their way through the traditional folk numbers, *The Blackleg Miner*, *Bold Robert Emmet* and *Dark as a Dungeon*, to little interest and little applause from the Lanarkshire miners and their wives. Then one of the miners came to the mic and sang Cole Porter's *All the Way* in the style of Frank Sinatra, to great acclaim.

They also played football. Alongside Gus on the apprentices' strike committee was a young man called Alex Ferguson, who then played football in the Scottish League. Gus played for the Scottish youth team, and at various times Jimmy McCallum also played with Gus. But you really had to choose. Gus and Jimmy chose politics. Alex chose football.

The longer Paul stayed in Glasgow, the more his involvement in the International Socialists grew. The three of them, Paul, Gus and Bob, travelled around speaking at meetings: Aberdeen, Edinburgh and Dumfries, Liverpool, Newcastle and, on one occasion, Skegness, for the Labour Party Young Socialists gathering. Photos show Paul and Gus, young and eager in their long woolly jumpers and CND badges, and Paul looking a bit awkward surrounded by young women and men holding pints of beer.

There was considerable tension between the Young Socialists, generally on the left, and the leadership of the Labour Party. It came to a head in 1962, when Hugh Gaitskell, the Labour leader, arrived in Queen's Park in Glasgow to deliver his May Day speech. Banners were held aloft protesting the party's position on nuclear arms, and Gaitskell was heckled as he took to the stage. That tensions should focus on this issue was not surprising. Just two years earlier, the Labour Party conference had voted in favour of unilateral disarmament and, in response, Gaitskell had vowed to 'fight, fight and fight again' to get the decision overturned – something he eventually succeeded in doing. The problem for Paul that day, as Gaitskell addressed the crowd, was that whoever was holding up the Woodside Young Socialist banner was too slow in hauling it down. Plain for all to see, the constituency was accused of organising the rough reception for Gaitskell, and suspensions and threats of expulsion followed.[12]

Glasgow Woodside was Paul's constituency, and it was already in dispute with the leadership over the selection of the left-winger Neil Carmichael as its candidate for the 1962 parliamentary by-election. Paul had been at the selection conference, as had a law student from Glasgow called John Smith. Naturally, Paul was supporting the left-wing candidate Neil Carmichael, Smith his right-wing opponent.

'Some of us were rather surprised to see John as a delegate to the conference', Paul wrote many years later. He was not known in the local Labour Party, and there were so many people at the meeting that an inquiry was set up into their credentials.[13] It was eventually revealed that John Smith had come along from a union branch which no longer existed and which, when it had, represented women cleaners at a municipal bus depot. This did not impede his advance to the very top of the Labour Party.

As the election loomed in November 1962, Paul was in difficulty again. The previous year he had written an article for *Young Guard*, the paper of the radical left inside the Young Socialists, which stood for unilateralism and a Labour government committed to workers' control. The Glasgow City Labour Party deemed writing for *Young Guard* a breach of their rules. They called Paul in and threatened to withdraw his party card.

'It was a very civil meeting, and I haven't heard anything since', he was quoted as saying in the London *Evening Standard*.[14] But none of this stopped a Labour agent from trying to persuade him to stand as a candidate himself – a proposal he politely declined. As for Neil Carmichael, he won the selection against the odds, and then won the by-election, turning a Conservative seat Labour.

The political infighting in the Labour Party mattered less as Paul devoted more of his time to the International Socialists and their monthly paper *Labour Worker* – just four pages, for the price of three old pennies. Paul took over as editor in 1963. Harry McShane and Bob Gillespie joined him on the editorial board and, from his flat in Glasgow, Paul persuaded people to write articles, wrote their head-lines and did whatever editing was required, before sending the copy to London to be typeset and printed. Editing the paper involved a lot of badgering. One of those he canvassed for pieces was Colin Barker, a student IS member from Oxford. Paul asked for snippets of trade union news, and encouraged Colin and the other IS members to do whatever they could to contact workers inside the local Cowley car plant by 'generally hanging around seeing if anyone is interested or would like to come to some meetings'.[15]

The *Labour Worker* print run was tiny, at just 1,500 copies. Every sale was precious, and so, while the bookkeeper was on his summer holidays, Paul took on that task, too. He sent round a duplicated letter asking how many copies each small branch or individual wanted, anxious not to waste copies because of the costs involved. Colin Barker's letter contained Paul's further anxious handwritten line: 'Also desperate for money for the last issue.'[16]

Despite *Labour Worker*'s meagre resources, its pages teemed with articles by workers about their own industries and unions, as well as local and national strikes and campaigns. Even the occasional global event was addressed, like the Washington March for Jobs in August 1963. In his article, Harry McShane focused on the political debates and divisions that arose on the march, between the radicals and those who would have been content with legislative improvements.[17]

As editor, Paul didn't always get it right. But he was always happy to acknowledge mistakes and gaps in his knowledge. He had heard that a piece about the miners had gone down badly with Lawrence Daly, an NUM official and socialist from Fife. Paul wrote to Daly begging him to write a letter, short or long, for the paper. Paul's explanation for what had happened was frank. The reason the piece was no good, he explained, was that it was 'written by someone whose only knowledge of miners comes from statistical surveys and accounts – i.e. myself. Criticism from someone who does understand would, I think, be much more valuable than the original article.'

Besides editing *Labour Worker*, Paul also wrote a short pamphlet for it on the growing numbers of unemployed in Scotland. Government reports and plans had been appearing since the 1930s, he argued, but none made any difference. They looked good on paper, but changed nothing. The workers would have to fight for themselves: for five days' work or five days' pay, for sharing work in place of sackings, and for workers' control.[18]

'Sir Hugh's Son Weds' ran the headline in the *Sunday Express* over a photo of Paul and Monica on their wedding day. Monica looked stunning in a very '60s hat, while Paul sported a red carnation and his CND badge, and rather pompously told the paper there was no engagement ring because rings were 'too bourgeois'.[19]

The wedding plans were fraught. Monica's mother was a deeply religious Catholic and wanted a church wedding. Monica would have gone along with it just to humour her, but Paul – 'thank god', she said, looking back – would not. All through the autumn of 1961 they argued with each other about the wedding and all through the Christmas holiday they argued with her parents, Monica taking Paul's side. Paul felt very low about it. Back in Glasgow after Christmas, he wrote a long and rather tortured letter to Monica's mother to try and explain the situation, and to make amends for the conflict. Although he had been brought up in a religious family, he wrote, he now found himself on the other side, against the church.

In the last three months, when for the first time in my life I have come into contact with poor people and destitute people, I have been horrified at the effect the Church can have upon them – horrified at the acceptance of dogmas, orders, etc. passed down by the Church (all the churches).

His problem was not religion *per se*, he said. He believed in the Christian ethic. He also believed in marriage – just not in a church. Monica's mother had clearly put up something of a fight, comparing a register office wedding to a visit to the Dog Licence Office. Her argument did not bother Paul one bit. But he was bothered by the hurt to her. 'Breaking this to you has been one of the most difficult and horrible things I've ever had to do', he wrote.[20]

Finally, on Saturday, 23 June 1962, the young couple married in the Oxford Register Office, followed by a great party in the grounds of University College. Paul's mother was there, but his father could not be. Paul's godfather Stewart Perowne took his place and, in the tradition of the Foot family, gave him a collection of Samuel Richardson's novels as a wedding present.

From Oxford, Paul and Monica travelled to London and stayed with his aunt Dorothy and his cousin Christina in his aunt's flat in Albert Hall Mansions. Christina was fascinated: 'Paul doted on Monica,' she remembers. 'He would feed her morsels and call her "my little bird"'. Monica made quite an impression on Christina's sister, Lily, who thought her very avant-garde. At the end of their stay, they were off to Glasgow to start a new life together.

Their first home was a rented flat that Paul found. But paying £350 a year in rent seemed rather a poor use of their funds if they were going to stay in Glasgow for some time, as they planned. So, with the help of his father and a loan from the Glasgow Corporation, they bought a flat on Kersland Street, a wide street with grand-looking houses near the Botanical Gardens. It was spacious; but, though it might have looked grand, Monica's sister Mary remembers it being incredibly cold, and the mats lifting off the floor in the drafts.

Monica might not have been Richard Ingrams's choice for Paul, but when she moved to Glasgow she had plenty of admirers. 'She was quite flirty', remembers Jimmy McCallum, barely out of his teens when he first met her. 'She was a good-looking, skinny lady. She had a bit of spirit.' She had even, it was rumoured, danced with JFK – a story that added a sprinkle of stardust to her image. In truth, the story had become exaggerated in the telling. Monica had been invited to the United States in 1960 by an old friend, and had been taken to Kennedy's inaugural ball, where his entourage made absolutely sure Kennedy was seen dancing with his own wife and no one else.

There was no interruption in the flow of letters to Monica's mother, whatever the arguments over the wedding. 'We are very happy. I seem to fall more in love every day', Paul wrote to his mother-in-law once they were settled. But there was a downside. What Monica desperately needed was more confidence. 'She turns to me for more, unhappily, than I, in my disgusting self-confidence and brashness, can ever give her.' Her job helped, now that she was working for Scottish Television, but 'like the economy, she is prone to slumps and booms'.[21]

Besides her day job as a television researcher, Monica also got involved in Glasgow's political life. She too joined the Young Socialists; she worked on the design of *Young Guard*, producing some innovative and clever front pages, as well as writing book reviews. A love of literature was one of the things she shared with Paul. But her sister was alert to the contradictions of their life in Glasgow: Paul was trying to understand the working class, while Monica was buying wine and sherry and an orange-coloured coat.

Paul's Oxford friends were not standing idly by while Paul was busy in Scotland. They wanted to continue with something akin to *Parson's Pleasure* and *Mesopotamia*, the satirical magazines they had produced in Oxford. Once Peter Usborne, the publishing brains behind *Mesopotamia*, decided to put some effort into the project, *Private Eye* was born.

The first issue was published in October 1961. Peter was the publisher, Christopher Booker the editor, and Richard Ingrams and Willie Rushton made up the editorial team. The one person missing was Paul. 'I'm part of a movement now', he wrote to Richard, politely declining an offer to join the old gang.[22] And that was that. Until the question of the Kinross by-election arose.

In October 1963, the increasingly unpopular Harold Macmillan resigned as prime minister due to poor health, and Sir Alec Douglas-Home, a Conservative peer, was chosen as his successor. Douglas-Home was not a particularly attractive figure. An old Etonian, he was pilloried by the Labour leader Harold Wilson as out of touch. As Richard put it, 'It seemed like Macmillan's final gesture of contempt for democracy to elect this half-witted Earl who looked and behaved like something out of P. G. Wodehouse.'[23] Being an earl, he sat in the House of Lords. To sit in the Commons as prime minister, he had to give up his peerage and stand for election.

There happened to be a vacancy in the seat of Kinross and Western Perthshire, the third-safest Conservative seat in the country, that stretched across vast acres of Scottish moorland mainly occupied by sheep and pheasants. Douglas-Home was in his element. Dressed in an old tweed knickerbocker suit, thick wool socks and stout shoes, he set off to drum up support among the country set of the constituency.

The anointing of Douglas-Home as the future prime minister did not go down well at the *Eye*. During a lunchtime session in the Coach and Horses pub in Soho, Willie Rushton was persuaded to stand against him. Thus Willie, the resident cartoonist for *Private Eye*, and by now a star on BBC television's satirical *That Was the Week That Was*, became Willie the parliamentary candidate. To support Rushton, the entire staff of *Private Eye* decamped for Scotland, staying in the publisher John Calder's house, where Paul was reunited with them to cover the election for the *Record*.

'The people of this constituency are being fobbed off', Paul quoted Rushton. 'They are being used as pawns in the Whitehall game.' Rushton called on the voters to register their protest and vote against this mediocrity of a man.[24] When the results came in on Friday 8 November, Rushton received forty-five votes, and never stood for parliament again. Douglas-Home, on the other hand, received over 14,000 votes – a huge majority over the Liberal runner-up – and duly took his seat in the Commons. His was to be one of the shortest stints as prime minister. The Conservative government was engulfed by the fallout from the scandalous Profumo affair. Within a year, they had been voted out.

◆

Paul was increasingly in demand as a speaker. Jim Nichol, a recruit to the International Socialists in Newcastle, remembers meeting him over the Whitsun holiday in 1964. The two of them went to a friend's house after a meeting – Paul to stay the night, Jim just for the company. In the end they both stayed, sharing a bed-settee with a mouse that scurried around inside the mattress. There was little sleep to be had under the circumstances so, instead, they talked until the early hours, mostly about politics, but also about Jim's pending engagement, about which he was uneasy. Paul made him promise not to go ahead, and Jim agreed. Until the following day when he went to a jeweller's and bought a ring.

Jim, a clerk in the coal mines, was just one of dozens of young men and women in and around the International Socialists who made their way to London in the 1960s, crashing at Tony Cliff's until they made other arrangements. 'I was moving from colliery to colliery, eastwards towards the sea', he remembers. 'In the end, I did a twenty-mile bus journey to work each day. The writing was on the wall.' Blyth, on the coast, was one of the last pits he worked at.

The same was happening in Glasgow. As he neared the end of his apprenticeship, Gus was put on the night shift – a sure sign, he says, that there would be no permanent job for him. In 1963 he moved south, where he also stayed in Tony Cliff's spare room. Gus proved popular in the capital. 'Macdonald could sell the New Testament to rabbis', Cliff joked, and they worked alongside each other, Gus eventually taking over as editor of *Young Guard*. But in the end he was too interested in a wider range of political ideas than the IS could offer, and he, Cliff and Michael Kidron parted company. With help from Paul's uncle Michael, Gus took a job as circulation manager for *Tribune*, eventually becoming the journalist he had always wanted to be.

Not much later, Paul also returned to London.

In the end, those Glasgow Trots had sorted out Paul, rather than the other way around, and Glasgow had changed his life:

What I read there (and heard in the debates among the Young Socialists) seemed to fit the reality of the city of Glasgow far more closely than anything I had read before. It seemed suddenly clear that society was cut into classes, and the classes were forever at war with one another.[25]

5

The Leper

An overnight telegram raced south in April 1964: 'Expect Grandchild in November – Paul and Monica'.

The young couple followed the telegram. Paul and Monica were returning to London to pursue their careers and bring up their family. At first, they moved into a basement flat, courtesy of a friend's mother, while they looked for a more permanent address. And then, with the financial help of Paul's father, they found something better, a flat on Haverstock Hill, with Hampstead Heath to the north and Primrose Hill to the south. It was a nice part of London, even then.

Monica was happy. She had friends in London, and one of them organised a cocktail party on their return. She now found herself in a more congenial setting, surrounded by a radical social circuit that included many of the rising stars among writers and actors. Jack Duncan, an old friend from their Oxford days and aspiring theatre director, lived just up the road. And while waiting for her baby to arrive, she was writing a prolific number of book reviews for the *Scotsman*.

Paul, having served his three-year apprenticeship on a local paper, had had another useful conversation with Hugh Cudlipp, the friend of his father who had sent him to Glasgow. This time, he offered Paul a job on a national newspaper in London, at the *Daily Herald*, which was about to be relaunched as the *Sun*.

In the 1930s, when it was jointly owned by the Trades Union Congress, the *Herald* had been the country's biggest-selling daily newspaper. But by the 1960s its sales were in decline, advertising revenue was falling, and its latest owners, the International Publishing Corporation, decided something had to be done. Paul arrived just before the relaunch, joining the team on a new column, 'Probe', which promoted itself as a 'new technique in daily journalism, taking you right behind the news'.

The first edition of the *Sun* appeared on 15 September 1964. The Conservative government had just called a general election, which gave the Labour-supporting paper and its Probe team plenty of scope. The next day, Paul had his by-line on the column with a piece on the competing candidates. Most of them, he wrote, were aged between forty and fifty-five. Only one in twenty were women. And, in a very characteristic comment, he noted that 'not a single one of the half million car and cycle workers in Britain is standing as a candidate for one of the three major parties'. There were a good number of teachers and college lecturers, and a vast array of lawyers, and three-quarters of the Conservative candidates went to public school – one in seven of them to Eton. Only one Tory candidate worked a manual job.[1] This was a flying start for Probe.

In fact, the Probe column wandered all over the place. It appeared twice a week, sometimes by Paul, sometimes by others in a team that also included Chris Hall, another young journalist. Occasionally it was written by the science editor, or the motoring correspondent – or, if they were lucky, by one of the foreign correspondents. At the end of September, Paul wrote a Probe piece on the pressing issue of the price of dog food. Monica says Paul hated working on the column – not least having to say 'Probe here' every time he answered the phone.

That year's general election was to be held on Thursday, 15 October. Harold Wilson was now leader of the Labour Party, following Hugh Gaitskell's sudden death the year before, and Alec Douglas-Home was the sitting Conservative prime minister. All the papers in what would later become the Mirror Group had a mainly working-class readership, and were straightforward about where their allegiances lay: for a Labour victory and an end to Tory rule. But this election turned out to be unique for a reason most editors had not anticipated. Besides the usual damning of each side by the other, word was that something nasty was going on in the Midlands constituency of Smethwick.

In the run-up to the election, the Probe team spread out into the towns with a high concentration of new black voters. They visited Southall in West London, Bradford in Yorkshire, and Smethwick in the West Midlands, where the Conservative candidate was a teacher and local councillor called Peter Griffiths. Griffiths ran a racist campaign. If Labour lost the seat and Griffiths won, the Probe column argued, 'it will look to the world as if the people of Smethwick really are afraid of getting "a n****r for a neighbour".[2]

That slogan was not of Griffith's making; but he defended those who used it, in a that's-what-people-are-saying sort of way. His election address called for restrictions on immigration. He talked up dirty and overcrowded living conditions, and focused on a decline in moral standards and the need to make the streets safe at night. If Griffiths believed racist scaremongering would win him votes, then he was absolutely right: when the result was announced, he had overturned a Labour majority that had been maintained since 1945. Yet Smethwick, as the Probe article pointed out, was not a depressed part of the Midlands. People had jobs, mostly in manufacturing, local employers were looking to recruit, and wages were good. The number of immigrants was not large. But, by fanning the flames of racism, Griffiths showed that you could win votes against the national tide that had brought Labour to power nationally.

The election result was announced on the front pages on Friday, 16 October 1964. The fallout from the Profumo affair contributed to the Conservative government's defeat, giving Labour the narrowest of majorities – just four seats. In the end, 'those famous Foot brothers', as the Sun described them on its front page, did well: Dingle would be solicitor-general; Hugh, Paul's father, was to be minister of state at the foreign office, in which capacity he would head the UK's delegation at the UN and sit in the House of Lords as Lord Caradon; and Michael Foot was back in parliament as MP for Ebbw Vale – a seat he won with a whopping 83 per cent of votes cast.

After hauling down the British flag in Cyprus in 1960, Paul's father had briefly returned to Cornwall before he was asked by the prime minister, Harold Macmillan, to join Britain's mission at the UN in New York. He was now an ambassador with a particular responsibility for newly emerging nations, which he knew something about after his years in Jamaica and Cyprus. But less than a year later he resigned, after it became clear that the British government was going to kowtow to the white minority in Rhodesia, led by Ian Smith. In their internal memos, the government circulated the idea that Hugh Foot had only resigned because he had another job lined up. But this was not true; his departure was a matter of principle. He had promised Joshua Nkomo, the founder of the National Democratic Party – and when that was banned, the Zimbabwe African Peoples Union, or ZAPU – that he would do just that if there was no concession to the black majority.[3]

While Hugh travelled between the Foreign Office in London and the UN in New York, he needed somewhere permanent that his family could call home. Trematon Castle was advertised in the early 1960s by the Duchy of Cornwall, on a long lease and at a peppercorn rent, and it was where Hugh moved the family in 1961. With its ancient keep, built at the time of the Norman conquest, it had a tower and a gatehouse that provided the backdrop for an elegant Georgian house with a stunning view across Plymouth Sound, and lawns ideal for endless games of French cricket. The house had gardeners and a housekeeper, and all was well until the roof needed repair. To pay for it, the ever-practical Sylvia went on a speaking tour in the United States to raise the necessary funds.

At Trematon Sylvia could be a real mother to her younger boys, and a grandmother to Paul's first son, John. Although Cornwall was quiet compared to the busy life Sylvia had led in Jamaica and Cyprus, and she was often lonely there, she was able to maintain her duties as a hostess, as the guests kept coming. They included the Queen, who stopped by in July the following year on her way to board the Royal Yacht *Britannia*.

On the Monday following the general election of 1964, Paul was writing in the *Sun* about the tin mining industry in Cornwall – no doubt he had found a good reason to spend some time during the election campaign with his family. But the election also provided Paul with an idea for a book. Within days of Harold Wilson's victory, Paul wrote a long letter to Tony Godwin, chief editor at Penguin, with 'a very rough sketch' for a book on the politics of immigration. 'It has been done hastily', he wrote.

Tony Godwin was enthusiastic, and Paul got the go-ahead. By January 1965 a contract had been signed, and within four months the manuscript was almost finished. This was thanks in part to the people running the Institute of Race Relations in London, who kept a newspaper cuttings library that Paul devoured. Nicholas Deakin, an old Oxford friend, was working on his own book for the Institute, and was impressed both by Paul's phenomenal energy and by his endless barrage of questions.[4]

In the early summer of 1965, Paul wrote again to Godwin about the urgency of getting the book published. The chances of an election that October were running very high, the pundits in Fleet Street were telling him. He and Monica were off to France, and he would complete it there. They would be staying with Ronald Segal, an exile from apartheid South Africa who had a house on the French Riviera. Segal helpfully edited the manuscript for Paul and telegrammed Penguin: 'Paul pleased reaction stop. Edited manuscript will arrive with Paul end month.'[5]

When it arrived, Godwin was delighted. It was, he claimed, 'the most explosive political book I have published since I have been at Penguin'.[6] There were still some long discussions to be had about the title, the cover design and the date of publication, but in the end *Immigration and Race in British Politics* was published, after a lengthy libel read, in August 1965.

The problem with post-war Britain, Paul wrote, was its massive labour shortage. A voucher scheme existed for East Europeans and war refugees stuck in Italy who could apply for jobs, but the numbers it provided were insufficient, and the terms harsh. To let in larger numbers, the government needed to repeal existing legislation, established during the First World War, which kept out those it referred to as aliens – in short, anyone the government disliked – under the flag of 'undesirables'. But just as the labour supply was drying up, on 8 June 1948 the *Empire Windrush* set sail from Kingston, Jamaica, with hundreds of people on board, many of them Jamaicans. They had come to the 'Mother Country' to find work.

The British Empire, which at its peak in the nineteenth century encompassed vast swathes of the world, including India and large parts of Africa, and stretched from Canada in the north to Australia in the south, had offered citizenship to its new subjects in return for the exploitation of those countries' natural resources. 'No one, apparently, foresaw the one crucial privilege which citizenship entailed – the obvious right of a British citizen was to come freely and live in Britain', wrote Paul.[7] Thousands of others would soon follow the *Windrush*, at first from the West Indies, then from India and Pakistan.

For the Tory government after 1951, and the country's labour-hungry employers, 'this must have seemed a heaven-sent gift. The Commonwealth citizens came in freely – unhindered by the legislation applying to aliens. They cost the Government nothing.'[8] Neither government nor employers had to provide housing or language courses, or even additional school places for children. The migrants were left to shift for themselves. And while the numbers were relatively small at first – just 2,000 in 1953, according to Paul, rising steadily throughout the 1950s, until 125,000 people arrived in 1961 – a degree of pressure on services provided the right conditions for Griffiths's campaign in Smethwick. While the Tory Party had been reluctant to support him during the election, once it was over two factors immediately commended him to them: he had won, and he had got away with it.

Harold Wilson, the new Labour prime minister, was appalled by the election of Griffiths. He called on the Conservatives to disown him, and remarked that, if they would not, the 'Smethwick Conservatives can have the satisfaction of having sent a member who, until another election returns him to oblivion, will serve his time here as a parliamentary leper'.[9]

Uproar followed in the House. But with the exception of Wilson's withering speech, Griffiths was welcomed, and became a model of respectability. He was courted by the press – invited to speak at universities and to Young Conservative rallies – while the party distributed his speeches. 'The story of the Conservative Party's reaction to Commonwealth immigration is a story of undiluted cynicism, chauvinism and human neglect', wrote Paul.[10] And although he had campaigned for years on immigration, when Griffiths got to parliament he barely raised the subject. 'His mastery of the *volte face* has, indeed, charmed thousands of liberal conservatives', wrote Paul. 'He has succeeded in fooling almost all of the people all of the time.'[11]

The Labour Party seemed incapable of countering Griffiths. Their candidate in Smethwick had been Patrick Gordon Walker, the sitting

MP. Although he had started on the left of the party, and talked of socialism and the working class, by the 1950s Walker had moved across to the extreme right – a position from which, Paul wrote, no traveller has ever returned.

From 1950 until 1951, during Clement Attlee's second term, Walker had been the Commonwealth secretary, and while in the role had prevented Seretse Khama from returning to Bechuanaland (later Botswana) as his country's leader because he had married a white woman. He was also a long-time advocate of immigration controls, and even resorted to that damning phrase, 'the British must come first'.[12] Clearly, he was no match for Griffiths. His only hope, it seemed, was that the issue would go away, or that voters would get bored with it. Yet so vicious and long-standing was the anti-immigrant campaign in Smethwick that Paul concluded even the most brilliant candidate would have lost. Labour could of course have taken a different course, Paul argued – one of welcoming immigrants, providing help with housing and schools, urging trade unionists to accept immigrants gladly, recruiting them and fighting for better wages for all. 'If he faces the subject without fear or evasion,' Paul wrote, 'appealing constantly to the decency and solidarity of the working class – if he does all this, he may not win many votes. He may even lose some. But he plants the seed of principle which will grow.'[13]

There were Labour MPs who had taken just such a principled position. Paul quoted Josiah Wedgwood, a Liberal MP during the First World War who had joined the Independent Labour Party in 1919. Wedgwood spoke out against the renewal of the aliens' legislation: 'Generally speaking', he said in the parliamentary debate on the bill, 'aliens are always hated by the people of this country. Usually speaking, there has been a mob which has been opposed to them, but that mob has always had leaders in higher places.' He believed in the greater good:

> The interests of the working classes everywhere are the same . . . the brotherhood of man and the international spirit of the workers is not merely a phrase but a reality. We know that the whole of this Bill is devised in order to satisfy the meanest political spirit of this age.[14]

In 1964 there was little that was principled or honourable at Transport House, Labour Party headquarters. It wanted party workers and spokesmen to keep quiet on the topic. They were hobbled throughout the election, wrote Paul. All they could argue was that Conservative controls were ineffective. As the election campaign went on, the drift towards demands for increased control became more marked. The shadow home secretary eventually turned to that well-worn phrase, 'if it must be done', to justify a Labour government tightening controls, and capitulating in the face of what it believed to be public opinion. Its greatest fear was the fear of losing votes.

Griffiths had laid the fuse. On the last page of his book, Paul reproduced Griffiths's final election address in its entirety: 'The only Smethwick Candidate who has ALWAYS called for the strictest control of immigration is Peter Griffiths. Remember this when you cast your vote.' Twenty-four words; one issue.

If Penguin feared a libel action, then it needn't have. There was one solicitor's letter on behalf of John Bean, of the British National Party, complaining that Paul had described his party as a fascist organisation. It was not, he wrote, even if

> it is perfectly true that the British National Party believe that further immigration by people of non-European stock should be prohibited and that those non-Europeans already in this country should be encouraged to return to their countries of origin as soon as possible.[15]

Penguin's lawyers noted that they would resist this one, and suggested Paul might like to leak it to *Private Eye*. The Birmingham Immigration Control Association also complained they had been misquoted. But it all went nowhere.

Paul appeared on television to promote his book, and did the rounds of the studios, not just the BBC Home Service, but also local radio and the African and Caribbean services. He returned to the Oxford Union to debate the issue and, speaking brilliantly according to one student present, at the London School of Economics. He was very much in the public eye. Yet not everyone was so enthusiastic. No national newspaper would take the serialisation rights, while the editor of the *Sunday Times* found the book 'emotional', and was more interested in an extract from one of Penguin's gardening books. The *Observer* and *Sunday Telegraph*, where Paul worked from 1965 to 1967, also gave it the thumbs-down.

'Mr Paul Foot is clearly a very angry young man', wrote Norman St John-Stevas in his review for the *Sunday Times*. 'He lashes out at virtually every political figure who has been involved in the immigration controversy.'[16] St John-Stevas was a new MP, and would share the Conservative benches with Peter Griffiths. Meanwhile, the review for the *Observer* was written by another of the new intake of MPs, Roy Hattersley, Labour MP for Birmingham Sparkbrook. He did not like the book one bit, describing Paul as a zealot:

> Since he believes only a tiny proportion of the politicians of either major party will do anything better than compromise with prejudice, he castigates them collectively and individually in a way which is often gratuitously offensive and occasionally ludicrously biased.

Hattersley's view was that the excesses of someone like Griffiths were disgraceful, but exceptional.[17]

An American edition was briefly mooted. 'I've just learned from your proud papa that you are engaged in doing a book and I'd like very much to know something about it', wrote Michael Bessie, the publisher of the first volume of Michael Foot's biography of Aneurin Bevan in the US, who had met Paul at Michael's house. But, having read it, Bessie rejected it: it was admirable, he said, but not likely to sell widely in the US.[18]

By chance, in the week of the book's publication in Britain, rioting erupted in Watts, Los Angeles, setting off alarm bells in the British media. Could riots happen here? Those predicting similar events in Britain had got it wrong, Paul wrote in the *Sunday Telegraph*. There was a vast difference between the historic roots of colonialism and 'the grim heritage of anti-Negro savagery rooted deep in American history'.[19]

Paul made clear throughout the book that immigration could be used successfully by Conservative candidates to surmount the party's most awkward obstacle, 'the loyalty to Labour of the industrial working class'. But was it loyal? Would the industrial working class keep voting for a party that took a principled stand on immigration? Paul tackled this question head-on in an extended article for the *International Socialism* journal in the autumn of 1965. He argued, as Keir Hardie had done in 1904, that immigration control was a deceit, doing nothing to solve the problems that workers' faced. What they needed was better wages and better housing. But that argument had given way among Labour MPs to lofty appeals to the ideal of the 'Mother Country' and the sanctity of the Commonwealth. Against such hollow phrases, Paul put the internationalist case, just as Josiah Wedgwood had done years before, in favour of a world in which workers were not forced to move to provide their labour to greedy capitalists, where they could come together to carve out a better life for all.

With the book to keep him busy, Paul quit the *Sun* in early 1965 and moved to the Mandrake column on the *Sunday Telegraph*. This was an unlikely home, but it was just three days a week, which gave him the time he wanted to write. The Probe team at the *Sun* had not been a happy ship. Chris Hall blames it on the column's editor. Soon after the election, the Labour government had introduced a bill to end capital punishment, and the team suggested a background feature. Their editor's response was enthusiastic. How much does an execution cost? How much money would a ban save? He had previously been a City editor at the *Express*, and thought of everything in terms of profit and loss. The journalists' enthusiasm turned to dismay, and within six months the entire team resigned.

Alongside the writing of the immigration book and his work at the *Sun* and the *Sunday Telegraph*, Paul continued both to edit and write for *Labour Worker*. In February 1965 he penned an obituary of the man who had been hailed the greatest living Englishman: Winston Churchill. Half the nation watched the former prime minister's funeral on television, and the obituaries sometimes tipped into drivel. 'Sir Winston Churchill will spend his time from now on, in heaven, painting', Paul quoted from the *London Evening News*. 'Children who look up and see a rainbow in the sky will know that Winston is at work.' This was the same man who thrived on war, both patriotic war and class war. It was the miners who were his particular foe – first in Wales in 1910, and then during the general strike of 1926.[20]

Churchill's habit, wrote Paul, was of seeing the good in bad people, being particularly charmed by 'Signor Mussolini's gentle and simple bearing' during a visit to Italy in 1927. As for Hitler, Churchill had written in 1937, 'One may dislike Hitler's system and yet admire his patriotic achievement.' Yet, Paul wrote, 'This monstrous, battle-hungry thug is hailed as the greatest Englishman who ever lived.'

Paul's first son, John, was born on Paul's birthday in November 1964, just as he was starting the immigration book. Two years later, in early September 1966, his second child was due. Paul and Monica planned to move out of their flat and into a house in Gondar Gardens, West Hampstead, before the baby arrived. Monica's mother helped with the finances, for which they were particularly grateful. She also agreed to come and stay for a few days when Monica came out of hospital following the birth. Paul had asked her to come, because, he thought, Monica would be 'both tired and depressed'.

He wrote her a thank-you note once the dust had settled on baby Matt's arrival. He was still working at full throttle. 'I am finding it more and more difficult to do everything I want to', the note said. 'It is as though the entire journalistic field was spread before [me], with the possibility of writing almost anything for anyone. It is all very exciting.' Monica was also busier than ever, and he hoped she would be able to give up some of her reviewing work: 'She really does have far too much on her plate now, and she finds it very difficult to wind down', wrote Paul. With the letter, Paul enclosed a copy of his latest article for *Queen* magazine about the case of James Hanratty, convicted of murder and rape, and later hanged. He wanted to write a book about it, he said – but he had agreed with Penguin to write a book on Harold Wilson, and Penguin wanted that first.

Sir Allen Lane, the founder of Penguin Books, had written personally to Paul promising he would publish both:

I feel deeply the Wilson book is needed otherwise I wouldn't bugger you around on the Hanratty when you're so obviously primed to go. But once the Wilson's done, then I'd LOVE to publish the Hanratty. I'll sign a contract now if that's what you want. You have only to ask.[21]

With a small boy, a baby, his job at the *Sunday Telegraph*, the articles, the radio appearances and one or other of the books, Paul was very busy. Finally, following Matt's birth, he decided he had to stop editing *Labour Worker*, although he stayed on the editorial board. After his resignation, Roger Protz took over; he and his wife Christine also moved into Gondar Gardens, in the small flat at the top of the house. Paul knew them both well: Christine had typed up the manuscript of his immigration book, and he and Roger had worked together on *Labour Worker*. It was a good place to live, with a large garden where their nanny Dibby ran an informal children's playgroup, and there were interesting neighbours: Doris Lessing lived a few doors down.

Paul and Monica continued to make the newspaper gossip columns. In May 1968, Monica had been spotted on a demonstration outside the French embassy with Tariq Ali, then the most famous of all the revolutionaries in Britain, who was carrying her three-year-old son John on his shoulders. The *Sunday Express* thought it so sensational that they phoned Monica's mother, as well as Paul's father in New York, and even Monica herself. 'Tariq is a very old friend', Monica told the paper, and her children loved him. 'He often carries John on demonstrations. I trust my children with him – he's fantastically nice and very gentle.' In response to her mother's fears that the children would be frightened by the experience, she had her own answer: 'I can't see the difference between pushing the pushchair down Oxford Street with a crowd of shoppers and pushing it down Oxford Street with a crowd of non-violent marchers.' Paul's father simply laughed it off: 'We start politics early in my family.'²²

Working at the *Sunday Telegraph* had its advantages. The Mandrake column was a space for news about the arts and politics, and not an onerous slot. It was edited by Lionel Birch, one of the great names in journalism at the time, and it left plenty of time for Paul to work on his books. But the *Sunday Telegraph* was not his natural home, and after nearly two years of working there he started discussing with Richard Ingrams the possibility of joining the staff at *Private Eye*, which was published every other week. One week for journalism and one week for book-writing seemed a very attractive proposition.

6

A Bee to the Honeypot

There had been changes at *Private Eye* since its founding in 1961. Richard Ingrams was now editor, having ousted Christopher Booker some years before. Booker's inability to keep to a deadline was one aggravating factor, and Richard's desire to be editor perhaps another. There were other changes as well. Andrew Osmond, who had put up the money to get the *Eye* going, had returned to his career in the Foreign Office and sold his interest to Peter Cook – a decision that delighted everyone. Cook was a star of the satire scene and, rather than come into the office and behave like a traditional publisher, he came in to help write the jokes.

He and Paul had a lot in common. They were born in the same week, to fathers in the colonial service, and they were both shipped home from foreign parts to public schools, spending the holidays with popular aunts and uncles in the West Country. As a consequence, they both supported hopeless football teams: Torquay United in Cook's case, Plymouth Argyle in Paul's. The only difference was that Cook avoided National Service, and instead went to university before establishing himself as a comic star after *Beyond the Fringe* took London and Broadway by storm in the early 1960s. And while Cook's comedy may have signalled his obsession with the absurd, there was also a deep seriousness to him. In an interview in 1962 he told the *Sunday Pictorial*:

People at the top make out that they know everything. What pompous rubbish . . . the government and the Establishment dismiss the population with a combination of arrogance and disdain. My main aim is to try to get the people treated like rational human beings.[1]

There had been other changes at the *Eye*, too. Peter Usborne had departed for greater things in publishing, and Willie Rushton had more or less gone, to stardom on the stage and television. He still drew cartoons, but his layout skills had been passed down to his younger cousin, Tony Rushton, who maintained the *Eye*'s trademark amateurish design. This was partly a technological issue: hot metal had given way to typesetting, and anyone with an old Remington and a tin of Cow Gum could cut and paste their pages ready for the printers.

Claud Cockburn had also joined the magazine. An old hand, he had published his own very successful magazine, the *Week*, in the 1930s, dedicated to information about the political establishment that other papers would not touch. He had an instinct for gossip, believing that it usually contained some grain of truth. In the summer of 1963, Cockburn edited an edition of the *Eye* while Richard was on holiday. That issue, number forty-three, announced on its cover that the prime minister's wife was having an affair with another MP; called Lord Astor a liar; and, to cap it all, named the head of MI6, the UK's spy service. It was the last of these that caused the most panic; in those days it was a closely kept secret. Sales of the magazine rocketed; and then, as is the way with rockets, they fell back to earth. But, in less than two years, *Private Eye* had established itself.

Paul provided copy for what had become Cockburn's regular section of the magazine, the 'Illustrated London News'. According to Claud's son, Patrick, Paul and his father got on extremely well. Paul was good at ferreting things out, and permanently sceptical. What bound them together was 'a passion for discovering and exposing awkward facts about British society in which no one seemed interested.'[2]

The *Eye* attracted all kinds of nutters with an axe to grind, and what impressed Paul about Claud was the time he would spend with such people and how, more often than not, they had stories. 'Listen to the loons' was his first lesson. Both were also on the extreme left, albeit in very different quarters. Claud had been in the Communist Party, and had a general distaste for anything Trotskyist – just as Paul did for

Stalinists. But they both liked people who were politically serious, and so they got on handsomely.

It was while Paul was providing stories for Claud's column that the *Sunday Telegraph*'s news editor sent him to cover an unusual burial.

In 1966 the body of James Hanratty was moved from Bedford prison to a cemetery in Watford. Hanratty had been convicted in February 1962 of the A6 murder, the case taking its name from the road where the bodies of Michael Gregsten and Valerie Storie had been found. Valerie had been raped and shot, but survived; Gregsten did not. The death sentence was then mandatory. After the hanging, Hanratty's body was buried in the prison yard, as prescribed by law. Now, because the law had changed and capital punishment suspended for five years pending its abolition, his body could be exhumed and reburied in consecrated ground. 'There may be trouble', the news editor antici- pated, as capital punishment was still a contentious issue.

There was no trouble. Nothing remarkable happened at the burial, and Paul had nothing much to report. But his interest in the case was piqued. All James Hanratty's family were there, and they invited Paul to join them for the wake at their home, where he met the people who knew everything about the story – Hanratty's father, also called James; his mother Mary; his brothers, in particular his younger brother Michael; and Jean Justice, an early campaigner for an enquiry into the case.

'Hanratty: The Case for an Enquiry' – 6,000 words long, running across six pages – appeared in the glossy *Queen* magazine in September 1966. Paul named the possible murderer as Peter Alphon. Alphon had been the police's first suspect, and had made – but later withdrawn – a confession. Paul had warned Jocelyn Stevens, the editor and proprie- tor of *Queen*, that calling a man a murderer was not merely civil libel but criminal libel, which could result in a jail sentence. 'I'd love to go to jail for this!' came Stevens's reply.[3] Paul's article summoned a wealth of facts, almost all of them authenticated in writing, on tape or aired during two parliamentary debates, and all supporting the demand for an enquiry. 'There is no need for an emotional appeal to make the case for an enquiry', wrote Paul. 'It is possible that an innocent man has been wrongly executed. Is this not argument enough?'[4] Two months later, the *Eye* also devoted two whole pages to the Hanratty story – in particular to one important aspect of it: Hanratty's alibi.

Had Hanratty spent the night of the murder in Rhyl, North Wales, in a boarding house with a green bath in the attic, as he claimed? If he had, he could not have committed the murder. Mrs Grace Jones, the landlady from Rhyl, who did indeed have a green bath in her attic, had given rather shaky evidence at the trial, and the jury had dismissed the alibi. Hanratty's story was that he took the train from London to Liverpool to look for a man who might buy some stolen jewellery he wanted to sell. Unable to find him, he instead took the bus on to Rhyl, in North Wales – 200 miles from the scene of the crime on Deadman's Hill, on the A6 near Bedford. There were other witnesses, eight in total, who remembered some detail or other of Hanratty's movements in Rhyl. One had been known to the police but not to the defence, and was therefore not called at trial. A BBC *Panorama* team found the other seven. Paul had travelled to North Wales with the *Panorama* team, and in his long article for the *Eye* he named each of the eight witnesses. He also denounced the *Sunday Telegraph*, where he still worked, for devoting so much time and energy to rubbishing the claims of the BBC programme and its alibi witnesses. It was hardly surprising, then, that within weeks Paul had upped sticks and, in February 1967, made the move from Fleet Street to Greek Street.

Many might have considered this move a poor one. The *Eye*'s offices at 22 Greek Street were above a strip club and next to a betting shop. Its finances were shaky and its circulation modest and variable. But for Paul there was something much more important at stake: 'I still recall the almost overwhelming sense of liberation. Off my back were the cloying hierarchies, the silly office intrigues and petty censorships which stifled so much writing in the official press.'[5]

Paul had two whole pages all to himself – that was the attraction. He was drawn to it, he said, like a bee to a honeypot. 'Writing for *Private Eye* is the only journalism I have ever been engaged in which is pure enjoyment. It is free publishing of the most exhilarating kind.'[6] In March 1967 the promised two pages made their first appearance, under the heading 'Footnotes'.

The format was simple: several stories, or the occasional longer piece stretching sometimes to a whole two-page spread. Paul wrote about any story that grabbed his attention: at home, the police, comprehensive schools, the costly development of that great white elephant in the sky called Concorde, gun-running to Northern Ireland; abroad, the beleaguered Palestinians, the war in Vietnam, the political sell-out in Rhodesia and BP's sanctions-busting (Paul's father was a great source of information on Rhodesia). There was politics, too, including stories on the prime minister, Harold Wilson, and after him Ted Heath, as well as on the trade unions, strikes and incomes policy. The pages provided a fortnightly snapshot of things you might not know about stories in the news – including stories that should have been in the news but were not.

One story that Paul would return to for years to come was about a young Conservative politician called Jeffrey Archer, who had been elected as the MP for Louth in Lincolnshire in a December 1969 by-election. It just so happened that Paul had some information about the young politician's rather excessive expenses while working for the United Nations Association, a charity that supported the work of the UN within Britain. Archer had claimed for a number of expensive lunches at high-end restaurants, like the Savoy and the Carlton Towers – lunches which, as it turned out, had been paid for by someone else.[7]

Along with stories that would run in only one issue, others ran across several editions, including that of 'The Man with the Golden Hands'. These were the hands of Dr Christiaan Barnard, a South African surgeon and the pioneer of heart transplants. The breakthrough was not the surgery itself, wrote Paul, as any experienced cardiac surgeon should be able to transplant a heart. Tissue matching was also improving, and the odds of a match between the transplanted heart and the recipient were narrowing each year. The sensational advance was in the most intractable problem of all: how to get the new heart into the body before the heart was irretrievably damaged. For a kidney transplant, the surgeon has half an hour or so. A heart must be transplanted in as little as three or four minutes.

'Professor Barnard and his team have discovered a "solution" to this tricky problem: namely to remove the heart *before it has stopped beating*', wrote Paul. The first patient, Mr Louis Washkansky, received the heart of a woman killed in a car accident. He lived for just eighteen days. The second patient received the heart of Clive Haupt, a young black man who collapsed with a brain haemorrhage. He was transferred in an unseemly rush from the hospital in False Bay to the transplant unit several miles away at Groote Schuur, Cape Town. If the hospital had really wanted to save his life, argued Paul, they would not have moved him. But transferred he was, and when he finally died some hours later, the transplant patient was ready and waiting.[8]

By late 1968, Paul's articles had caught up with events when the third transplant took place. This time Dr Barnard would not name the donor, and the reasons soon became clear: there was the heartless body of a dead African woman in the morgue. When her husband and her brother arrived to collect it for burial, they were shocked to discover what had happened, and wanted to know why no one from the hospital had asked their permission. We didn't know who she was, came the hospital's feeble reply. Not true, wrote Paul. The South African newspapers had uncovered a rather different story. Evelyn Jacobs, a black domestic worker from Gugulethu, collapsed as she left work. Her employers called a doctor, and he pinned a label to her clothes with her name on it before she was taken to Groote Schuur. Deceit and disrespect followed, as Miss Jacobs was whisked directly into the transplant unit, avoiding the usual admissions procedures and any effort to save her life.

In each case, Paul detailed the sequence of events: the failure to try to save the dying donors, the failure to consult the donor's relatives, and the desire for success at any cost. But while he might tour the world, in love with the attendant publicity, Barnard also preferred to avoid the difficult questions. Paul asked them anyway – in particular about Barnard's lack of transplant experience, having carried out just one kidney transplant before his first heart. More crucially, were his donors actually dead?

In December 1968, all the articles were gathered together in the *Eye*'s first special, a twelve-page pamphlet, *Hearts and Grafts*.[9] Paul's source for much of the detail in his later articles about transplants was Dr Geoffrey Spencer, a specialist in intensive care at St Thomas's Hospital in London. He had predicted that a lot of people would be hanging around in intensive care 'like a group of vultures', just waiting for people to die. Dr Spencer lived next door to Peter and Margaret Jay, and he had sent a short piece to the *Eye*, which Paul picked up. They talked repeatedly on the phone over the whole of that year. Dr Spencer understood the critical issue: for transplants, you needed beating-heart donors, and it can be quite hard to decide whether someone is dying or dead.

After the initial craze had abated, the transplants more or less stopped. Why? 'Because it didn't work', Dr Spencer explained.

Paul invited Dr Spencer to the monthly *Private Eye* lunch. It was hoped that, for the price of a steak and a plate of chips in the local pub, the people in the know who they invited along would share their knowledge and their gossip. Politicians were always on the list, as well as disgruntled journalists and lawyers; they all had something to say. It was the politicians that Paul liked, particularly the Tory mavericks like Alan Clark and Richard Shepherd. Surprisingly, according to Richard Ingrams, he rather liked Margaret Thatcher. 'They met on the radio programme *Any Questions*' he remembers, 'and he invited her to a lunch, and she came, twice. They got on very well. She must have been in opposition. Like his dad, he always saw the good in people.'

The lunches were in the upstairs room of the Coach and Horses, just around the corner from the *Eye* office. It was where its journalists would gather on a working day, around a table at the back. One of those who joined them was Patrick Cockburn, Claud's youngest son, who spent time as a teenager doing work experience at the *Eye*. 'It was pretty intimidating', he remembers. 'I had scarcely been in a city, as I lived in Ireland and went to school in Scotland. I thought the adults at the *Eye* were typical of all adults.' Rather than treating him as a teenager en route from school to university, they treated him as if he were a seasoned journalist. Patrick was expected to make calls, ask questions, and do the work of journalism with the rest of them. But there was one small problem: 'Paul and Richard knew everything about the establishment and had nicknames for well-known figures.' To the uninitiated Patrick, it was not always clear which name was real and which was just a nickname, and he was sometimes in danger of using the wrong one. 'It was good for me. I tried to get up to the mark. You don't know how good Paul was until you met other journalists.'

❦

In the early morning of 16 May 1968, Ivy Hodge, a fifty-six-year-old woman who had just moved into a corner flat on the eighteenth floor of Ronan Point, Newham, got up early to make herself a cup of tea. As she struck a match to light the gas, her stove exploded, and an entire corner of the twenty-two-storey block collapsed, killing four people and injuring seventeen others.

System-built tower blocks like Ronan Point were springing up across the country in the 1960s. Built of pre-cast concrete slabs for the walls and floors, they were brought to the site ready-made and lifted into position by cranes, the walls slotting together on steel pins, the floors sitting on a narrow lip in the wall. In the *Eye*, Paul devoted an entire column to the disaster. The Danish design, he wrote, was never intended for such large construction projects. Instead, it was intended to be used for low-rise, five- or six-storey buildings. The article was illustrated with a drawing that showed how just one-and-a-quarter inches of each four-ton floor slab rested on the wall on each side. If anything moved the wall by a quarter of an inch or more, he wrote, the floor slab would fall in a 'progressive collapse'. This was exactly what had happened that day at Ronan Point.[10]

At the Committee of Inquiry into the disaster, Taylor Woodrow Anglian, the builders, and the London Borough of Newham, which had commissioned the building, argued in their evidence that, in this case, the explosion was so violent that no building could have withstood it: a fantastic 600 pounds per square inch. But was that true? The Building Research Station carried out an experiment for the inquiry, using the same Larsen Nielsen design system on a two-storey building. There was some astonishment when it collapsed at 1.6 pounds per square inch. The chairman of the inquiry contacted the minister of housing the same evening to suggest that the gas be turned off in all similar high-rise blocks.

Just as Geoffrey Spencer had helped with the story of Christiaan Barnard, Paul found someone who could help him with his investigation into Ronan Point. Sam Webb, an architect who had been collecting information about system building since the early sixties, knew all about what might have gone wrong. In the end, Paul's sources were so good that he was able to predict the outcome of the inquiry before it had published its report. 'To deafening sighs of relief from the building industry, the Government and the local authorities', he wrote, it would go easy on all three.[11] Its recommendations would include, Paul predicted, improvements to existing buildings and drastic modifications for those not yet started or completed. But as the builders and the government would be found not culpable, the taxpayer would have to cough up. Once it was published, much as Paul had predicted, the inquiry's report was so soft on the construction companies that, as *Construction News* reported, of the ten top companies involved in building this type of tower block, not one suffered a fall in its share value.

Paul's contact on *Construction News* was Laurie Flynn, a young journalist who had the job partly thanks to Paul, who had written him a reference. It was while Paul was rallying the students at the London School of Economics, during the great student protests of 1967, that he first met Laurie and another student, Martin Tomkinson. The two of them would help Paul piece together the most sensational story of all.

In April 1970, Laurie spotted an article in the Bradford *Telegraph and Argus* titled 'The Master Builder', about a particularly powerful man in Yorkshire whose stamp was on town centres throughout the North of England. This was an architect who had the ear of politicians, a man so successful that he had made himself enormously rich. Who, the article asked, was the real John Poulson?[12] *Construction News* sent Laurie off to Wakefield to meet Ray Fitzwalter, the author of the piece. When he got back to London, he went round to Paul's flat where they spent the weekend working on a long article for the *Eye*. What might have piqued Paul's interest was the name of one of Poulson's business associates: Reginald Maudling MP, deputy leader of the Conservative Party, whose name was already familiar to *Eye* readers because of his involvement in the Real Estate Fund of America (REFA), run by a crook called Jerome D. Hoffman. Maudling had bought shares in the company because, he said, he wanted to 'build up a little pot of money for my old age'.[13]

In truth, Poulson was not much of an architect, wrote Paul. But he was a brilliant entrepreneur who had designed or advised on city shopping centres, hospitals and public swimming pools. This he did by diligently making contacts within local authorities, buttering up the people who could agree contracts. While many of his contacts were on the right of politics, he also had strong links with T. Dan Smith, leader of the Labour group on Tyneside Council, and the man who helped him establish contacts in Labour-held authorities. But none of this could last. Poulson's business interests began to slide. 'People are praying that whatever happens to the Poulson empire', wrote Paul, 'its affairs will be conducted with the minimum of publicity, and that, if Mr Poulson goes down, he goes down alone.'[14]

The story was met with a stony silence from the rest of the media. That is, until two years later, when Paul sent Martin off to what Martin anticipated would be a boring bankruptcy hearing in Wakefield. In normal circumstances it would have been. But Poulson had kept detailed notes of his largesse to people who could benefit him, and the detail began to pour out in the hearings. In court, Martin heard of the many mayors and councillors who were in Poulson's pocket, from Newcastle in the north to Wandsworth in the south.[15]

Poulson would eventually go to prison – as would T. Dan Smith. Another of the characters in these stories was already in prison. REFA had collapsed, and Jerome D. Hoffman had left the country and returned to the US in a hurry, where the law caught up with him. The skids were now under the UK directors of REFA and its associated companies, including Reginald Maudling. In July 1972 it caught up with him too, and he was forced to resign as home secretary. He did not get so much as a slap on the wrist from his parliamentary colleagues, and the newspapers described him as a man of honour for resigning. Paul's view was that this was humbug. 'Mr Maudling has been found with his pants down and he has resigned for that reason', he told the BBC radio programme *Any Questions?* He had joined the fund for no other reason than to make money, that little pot of money for his old age. 'There is widespread corruption in this country', Paul said, 'because MPs and local government officials have business interests. You cannot represent two sets of people.' It was a conflict, he argued, and it should be brought to an end.[16]

Paul had hoped to write a book, *The Fall and Fall of Reginald Maudling*, and dispatched a single page to Penguin outlining his plans, covering Maudling's entry into politics, his associations with Poulson,

Jerome Hoffman and REFA, and his career as home secretary, as well as an issue pertinent to the *Eye*'s coverage of the story: the corruption of the press. Why was the *Eye* able to probe these stories and come up with the facts while the mainstream media was not?[17] But with the arrest of John Poulson, the story became sub judice, and it was left to Michael Gillard, who also worked at the *Eye*, to keep up the pressure on the Hoffman story. In the end it was Gillard who wrote a book on the affair, eventually published in 1974, with an introduction by Paul.[18]

But they were not the only people pursuing the story. Ray Fitzwalter, who had set the Poulson ball rolling, had moved on from the *Telegraph and Argus* to Granada Television, and its new investigative programme *World in Action*. There he teamed up with Gus Macdonald, who had rapidly moved up from the business side of *Tribune* to become a journalist, and then into television. But their programme on the Poulson and Maudling story was banned by the Independent Broadcasting Authority, and has never been broadcast.

Maudling felt wounded by the media attacks. He was quoted in *The Times* claiming that Paul had been 'conducting a personal vendetta' against him for years. 'I have never written anything personal about Mr Maudling', was Paul's response.

> I have confined myself to writing about his public activities and his activities as far as they affect others. I think Mr Maudling would be better advised to try to explain why he associated with Mr Poulson and Mr Hoffman rather than try to deflect attention from these matters, which are of public interest.[19]

There was a sequel for the *Eye*. Nora Beloff, a senior political writer on the *Observer*, had written an attack on the *Eye* for questioning the honour and integrity of Maudling, intended to scupper a critical piece planned by her own colleagues on the *Business Observer*. By chance or design, Paul got hold of the internal *Observer* memo that Beloff had sent to her editor, describing a meeting with Maudling. Paul printed it, and she sued for breach of copyright. The case was thrown out on the technicality that she did not own the copyright. Meanwhile, another short piece had also appeared in the *Eye*, written by Auberon Waugh, satirising Nora Beloff. It included the line that she was 'frequently to be seen in bed with Mr Harold Wilson'. It was a joke; his columns were one long joke, and he was not expecting anyone to take it seriously. But it suited her to take offence, and she won her libel action. The *Eye* immediately launched one of its great money-raisers, the Ballsoff Fund, to pay the fine and Beloff's enormous legal costs.

Auberon Waugh had been at Oxford with Paul and Richard, but was not in their gang. 'He was very suspect at Oxford', says Richard. 'He behaved like his father [the writer Evelyn Waugh], provocatively right wing and snobbish. The only time we met him he wanted to take over *Parson's Pleasure*. He came round and we made fun of him.' Nonetheless, they liked him. He joined *Private Eye*, where he contributed a diary column from 1972, and shared a tiny office with Paul, which he decorated ostentatiously with William Morris wallpaper. Whatever the difference in their political views of the world, Paul and Auberon got on extremely well – perhaps assisted by a shared connection to Cyprus.

While Paul had been counting gaiters in the sun in Jamaica, Waugh had served as an Escort Troop Commander in the British military in Cyprus. His barracks were at the bottom of the hill, and Government House was at the top, protected by trenches, sandbags, machine-guns, tin-hatted troops, searchlights, patrols and an Alsatian. During the years of the insurgency, the island saw a great deal of shooting. Armed with a different gun to the one he had been trained on, Waugh somehow managed to shoot himself, resulting in serious injury that required a surgeon remove one lung, his spleen and a couple of ribs. While he was recovering in hospital, Paul's sister Sarah and his cousin Christina visited him in the army hospital, and when his mother arrived she was put up at Government House. 'After my mother returned to England and her cows, Lady Foot took to visiting me', Waugh wrote in his autobiography. She would read to him from Lawrence Durrell's book about the island, *Bitter Lemons*.[20]

By the early 1970s, Paul was turning out headline stories for the *Eye* every two weeks. His two pages had grown to three. But his work at the *Eye* was only a small part of his output. He was also producing books at a prodigious rate.

7

Tightnits

In May 1966, a strike hit the national headlines. Members of the National Union of Seamen, who worked on the ships coming in and out of Britain's ports, stopped work, determined to improve their working conditions. The ship owners had made a derisory offer to the seamen, and as ships returned to port, often after months at sea, crews joined the strike in ever greater numbers. The longer the strike went on, the more difficult it was for the economy and the government. In response, Harold Wilson declared a state of emergency, which had little or no effect.

The government also set up an inquiry into the causes of the strike. In response, the Hull seamen criticised the inquiry's claim that the seamen enjoyed certain advantages over other workers: the interesting nature of their sea voyages, their free board and lodging, the lack of expense involved in travelling to work. 'There is a wealth of evidence we could produce', they concluded,

> to show that behind the Government, in its resistance to our just demands, stand the international banks, the financial powers which really direct the Government's anti-wage policy. The goodwill of the bankers, the ill-will of the working class. How familiar a story that is of Labour Governments.[1]

On 20 June, Harold Wilson got to his feet in the House of Commons and spoke out against the strike. He denounced the 'tightly-knit group of politically motivated men' who were keeping the strike going, endangering the economic welfare of the nation.

Everyone knew who and what he was talking about: Communists. In response Paul's uncle, Michael Foot, criticised the actions of his party leader, and the London Labour Party supported the strikers, too. Harold Wilson, it seemed, was becoming deeply divisive and unpopular. But his position remained secure. Just three months earlier he had called a general election, and had increased his majority from four to ninety-eight. By this point, he could do pretty much as he wanted.

These 'Tightnits', Paul wrote in *Private Eye*, were nothing more than the usual suspects: the Communist Party's national organiser, its general secretary, and a handful of well-known names. 'To Wilson', Paul wrote, 'any strike is the work of a "tightly-knit" body of men. Only someone utterly wedded to the conspiracy theory of politics could make such a vacuous and ill-informed speech about reds under the bed.'[2]

As disillusionment with the Labour government grew, Paul began discussing a short political biography of Harold Wilson with Penguin. *Immigration and Race* had done well, and Penguin liked their radical young author. A contract was signed in August, and Paul expected to finish by the end of 1966.

It was a busy and complicated year for Paul, with a toddler at home and a baby on the way. He was buying a house and planning a change of job. He continued to write for *Labour Worker*, which hammered home a critical message about the government, as well as the hopeless position of MPs on the Labour left. They could try to influence government policy, but it was futile – they had no power, no battalions. They were reduced, wrote Paul, 'to frenetic tactic-juggling. Opposing here; abstaining there; putting down a motion here, not bothering there.'[3] Parliamentary socialism was looking very threadbare.

Amid the turmoil, the agreed deadline for the Wilson book quickly came and went, and Paul had to admit in a letter to Tony Godwin in early 1967 that he hadn't even started writing it.

He had been diverted from his own book to write a chapter on the seaman's strike for another Penguin book, *The Incompatibles*.[4] The aim of the collection of essays, edited by Robin Blackburn and Alexander Cockburn, the eldest of Claud Cockburn's sons, was to counter the demonisation of the unions, then considered by some the bogeymen of British society. Paul's long chapter detailed every twist and turn of the seamen's strike, starting with Wilson's opening salvo: a TV broadcast on the eve of the strike, pipe in hand, in front of a cosy fire, explaining in a broad Yorkshire accent why it was the government's duty to resist the strike. This, in Paul's view, was a strike brought about entirely by the actions of the employers, who were able to make substantial profits while the seamen earned less than their counterparts in any other European country, except for Spain.

While the government spoke for the employers, and the *Economist*, 'which fights the class war more ruthlessly than any other major British publication', spoke for the government, urging it to face down the unions, who spoke for the workers? Not the popular press, who opposed the strikers in the face of popular support. When the *Daily Mirror* ran a sanctimonious editorial on its front page, the printers' chapel immediately carried a resolution of solidarity with the seamen and donated to the strike fund. The *Guardian* sank fairly low, wrote Paul, but not as low as the *Observer*, where Nora Beloff wrote a long piece claiming 'outside direction' of the strike by Communists and other left-wing extremists, all based on innuendo rather than evidence. By contrast, the *Sunday Times* 'Insight' team spent a week living with the militants, following them everywhere. It named names, and concluded that nothing extraordinary was happening.

The government's intention was to hold down wages. Talk of an incomes policy – keeping prices and wages in some sort of balance – had in reality delivered a wage freeze, while there was no attempt to hold down profits. The Labour government was siding with the employers, while dressing up its bias in pleas for patriotism and the national interest. It was seeking 'not to level out inequalities, but to intensify them', wrote Paul.[5]

The longer Wilson was prime minister, the longer Paul's book was going to take. 'I should warn you that it is going to be pretty sharp, though the attack will be strictly political, not in any way personal', he wrote in his letter to Tony Godwin.

This book is going to be about the kind of politics which Wilson represents and has represented over the last 20 years. More importantly, it will examine how it is that the Labour Party accepted him and his politics as their most popular combination in its history.[6]

The Politics of Harold Wilson was finally published the week before the Labour Party conference, in September 1968. As Paul had promised, it was a sharp attack on Wilson from the left, but also an analysis of the development and decline of socialist theory in the Labour Party since the 1930s.

In the 1964 election, Labour had won with a majority of just four. That election, announced Wilson, would be the start of a New Britain, one 'forged in the white heat of a technological revolution', after the 'thirteen wasted years' of Tory rule. Harold Wilson had then – and to some people still has – a reputation as a leader from the left of the party, not least because of his resignation in 1951 alongside Aneurin Bevan, the founder of the National Health Service, over the introduction of health charges. As Bevan made clear, the service should remain free at the point of access, and he 'would never be a member of a government which makes charges on the National Health Service for the patient'.[7]

Harold Wilson was in a slightly different position. Paul went back through decades of speeches and writings, to Oxford in the 1930s and to 1945, when Wilson began his parliamentary career. He had done well in the post-war Labour government under Clement Attlee, and within two years was president of the Board of Trade, his continued rise seemingly assured. But he was eclipsed by another aspiring MP, Hugh Gaitskell, and by-passed as chancellor of the exchequer in Attlee's second government, in 1950. As Wilson's star faded, he took 'an increasingly oppositionist and Bevanite approach to the conservative policies of the Labour leadership', wrote Paul. It was Gaitskell's first budget that introduced NHS charges for false teeth and glasses.[8] As John Junor, political leader-writer of the *Daily Express*, wrote of Wilson's predicament: 'He is a young man, and he sees quite clearly that in the right-wing of the socialist Party there is no room for him to expand . . . for Mr Gaitskell is there taking up all the room.'[9]

In his resignation speech, argued Paul, you could see that Wilson himself was looking for a compromise. He did not want to resign, but in the end had no choice. 'Whatever the real motivation which drove

Wilson out of the Government in April 1951', wrote Paul, 'no one can doubt that the decision, in terms of his future political career, did him nothing but good.'[10]

Gaitskell continued to take up all the room, becoming leader of the Labour Party in 1955 – a position that would make him prime minister were Labour to win an election. But Gaitskell died unexpectedly in 1963, pushing Wilson back into the running. Later that year, his courting of the left paid off, and he was elected leader, becoming prime minister the following year. The left MPs, including Paul's uncle Michael, were enthusiastic, and the entire party rallied round. There were great expectations after so many years of Tory rule. Even Paul had felt optimistic that night in October 1964, as the votes were counted and a Tory majority of nearly one hundred was whittled down to nothing. 'It was quite impossible for even the hardest revolutionary not to feel a rush of joy and even hope', he remembered some years later.[11]

But the economic situation facing the new government was dire. As he walked into the Treasury on the Friday after the election, James Callaghan, the new chancellor of the exchequer, passed the outgoing chancellor on his way out: 'Sorry to leave such a mess, old cock', said the departing Reginald Maudling.[12] The economic situation in 1964 was so bad that Wilson was forced to deflate and devalue sterling, shelve his nationalisation plans, drop his house-building programme, postpone the raising of the school-leaving age and scrap free milk in secondary schools. As Paul asked, in the face of such a collapse, what was a Labour government for? Wilson had always said he believed in 'pragmatic socialism', and pragmatism for Wilson meant efficiency, which would lead to economic growth, along with everything that could confer.

No one is spared Paul's criticism – not his uncle Michael, nor Norman Buchan and Neil Carmichael, the two MPs Paul had got to know so well in Glasgow; all were on the left of the Party. Nor is Paul's portrait of Harold Wilson an edifying one. He is depicted as not just a pragmatist, but an opportunist and a man very often driven by panic. As Paul concludes, 'What is required is not a new leadership but a new socialist politics, with roots deep in the Labour rank and file.'[13]

Paul knew that the book's publication was sure to cause a stir. 'We have a rule in our family and I'm the only one that ever seems to break it', Paul told the *Sunday Times*. 'We don't attack each other in public. But if you take an interest in politics you keep stumbling over your own family.'[14] Paul's father, his uncle Dingle and his uncle Michael all worked with Wilson, and most of the book was written in the top room of Michael Foot's house in Hampstead. An incredible abuse of hospitality, Paul conceded – but he was sure that to have tempered his criticisms would have been a greater insult to Michael's libertarian spirit than to include them.

He offered the early proofs of the book to Michael, who declined to read them, but he did promise to reply when it was published. 'If he hits back, I shall get absolutely murdered', Paul reflected. This is exactly what happened. In a long review for *Tribune*, Michael pulled the book apart. Although he admitted that disillusionment with Wilson was 'wide and deep', the left in the party and the left MPs supported him at critical moments because they preferred 'the devil they know to the others they know even better'. Michael also defended Wilson's economics against Paul's criticism, even while he admitted that it could have been managed differently, with a very different outcome. Equally, while allowing that parliament needed drastic reform and agitation from outside, 'to toss the whole contraption out of the window is theoretical bunk'.

'The politics of Harold Wilson are an extraordinary mixture of opportunism, improvisation, short-sightedness and resilience. Which is one reason for this book', wrote Michael.

> The politics of Paul Foot are an extraordinary mixture of first-class reporting, primitive Marxism, family wit and fantasy. Which is one reason for this review. Both may recover. The politics of Michael Foot are rejected in all quarters. Which is the reason for the general mess.[15]

It was a half-hour walk from Paul's house in Gondar Gardens to Michael's house in Hampstead. Although Paul had told his readers he had found a quiet space to write at the top of his uncle Michael's house, there was a more profound reason for taking himself there to write. His marriage to Monica was collapsing.

In the early summer of 1968, he moved out and went to stay with his aunt Dorothy in Albert Hall Mansions. His mother, on a short visit from New York, hoped she could help patch things up between them, but this was not going to happen. 'Both were in a terrible state of shattered nerves', she wrote to Monica's mother in Oxford. 'I had not realised that their misery had gone on for some time.' What his mother may not have discovered was that Paul had found his own refuge from Monica with Rosanne Harvey – Rose – whom he'd met at the *Telegraph*. Monica had found out about his affair, and she was furious.

In July, Paul travelled down to Cornwall with his two boys. John was now four and Matt was nearly two. Paul's younger brother Oliver was also there, and he had a way with small creatures. To everyone's delight he found a hedgehog, lured it out of its hole, carried it into the house and set it down in a bath full of water, where the tiny creature uncurled and swam up and down. Paul was happy at Trematon, lazily watching the distant ships from the veranda of the house. There was relief, too, in being with the children without Monica, and not, as he put it in a letter to Rose, perpetually on guard against the next 'deadly shaft'. Ever the optimist, Paul believed that John had reluctantly accepted that his father would not be going back to live with them in Gondar Gardens. Matt was too young to have that conversation.

While Paul was in Cornwall, Monica was on holiday in Wales with married friends. Something of a 'sick scene', Paul wrote in a letter to Rose, because Monica was herself having a very public affair with this same married man, a journalist and TV personality.

The letters to Rose were gossipy, recounting Paul's delight in beating his cousin Win at tennis, getting his legs burned in the hot sunshine, and listening to his father complaining at coming under attack from Paul Johnson in the *New Statesman*. Following a visit to Israel after the Six-Day War, Johnson had described Hugh Foot as a comical figure: 'In the twilight of Britain's pretensions to world power status, this pro-consul without an empire performs the duties of chief clerk to superpowers who would willingly dispense with his services.'[16] This made Hugh Foot laugh, and made Paul want to revisit Jerusalem. World news bubbles through the letters: Mayor Daley and the Democratic Convention in the United States; men walking on the moon; the investiture of the Prince of Wales; the outrageous decision by the selectors to drop Basil D'Oliveira from the England touring team for South Africa.

Eventually, Paul summoned up the courage to write one final letter to Monica's mother, trying to explain or rationalise what had happened to their marriage. He kept it short. His decision had not been taken lightly, he said, and he promised he would continue to look after his sons.

The news of Paul's separation from Monica made the newspapers. Once his divorce came through, he and Rose married at Hampstead register office, in July 1971. During that turbulent year, Monica fired one last dart at Paul. She wrote a piece about a marriage break-up, which appeared anonymously in *Forum* magazine. It was a thinly disguised description, in minute detail, of her relationship with Paul, from first to last.[17] Paul read it, of course. In fact, he could hardly have avoided seeing it, as someone sent an anonymous note to *Private Eye* providing details of where to find it.

Later that year, just before Christmas, Monica also remarried. She had met the radical young journalist Neil Lyndon in 1969; together they made quite a couple. Her friends called him the 'beach boy', in reference to his tall, blond good looks. He remembers her quick wit and her very 1960s fashion sense – Biba, Jean Muir, Foale and Tuffin; and he was not the only one to recognise her style. The Welsh actor Richard Burton remarked on it too when they met at a work function, and the sight of this 'slip of a girl called Foot' reminded him of a meeting he had been at with Michael Foot and local miners in Ebbw Vale. She was, he noted, 'as mini-skirted as a Californian Palm tree. The hem was only slightly below the neck'.[18]

Her marriage to Neil was short-lived. Monica decided to sell Gondar Gardens. She locked Neil out and moved into a commune, where he was not welcome. Monica's sister Mary was so upset by this turn of events that she urged Paul to take the boys, or at least find them a place in a boarding school – not the sort of school that he had been to, but somewhere kinder. But this was something Paul was unable or unwilling to do.

Neil kept in touch with the boys for a few years, and would meet Paul occasionally for lunch to talk about them. But he too finally walked away. The boys eventually moved in with Paul and Rose for a time, when Monica went to work in Bristol for a year, and life was calmer for everyone.

Once the Wilson book had been sent to the publisher, Paul was keen to get on with his book about the Hanratty case. But events forced another change of course. Penguin had been asking for an updated edition of *Immigration and Race*, and this soon became an entirely new book: *The Rise of Enoch Powell*.

On 20 April 1968, Enoch Powell, Conservative MP for Wolverhampton South West, had made a dramatic speech on immigration to a Conservative Association meeting, in which he quoted an anonymous voter who claimed that, 'in this country, in 15 or 20 years' time, the black man will have the whip hand over the white man'. It was a startling and crude thing to say, quite outside the normal conventions of political speeches from members of parliament. How could he ignore this man, Powell asked:

> Here is a decent, ordinary fellow Englishman, who in broad daylight in my own town says to me, his Member of Parliament, that the country will not be worth living in for his children. I simply do not have the right to shrug my shoulders and think about something else.[19]

The indigenous population, he added – by which he meant white people – would be strangers in their own country, unable to find hospital beds for their women to give birth, school places for their children, their neighbourhoods changed beyond recognition. To drive the point home, he quoted the Roman poet Virgil: 'As I look ahead, I am filled with foreboding. Like the Roman, I seem to see "the River Tiber foaming with much blood".'

The speech made the headlines and shook the political establishment. Edward Heath immediately sacked Powell from the shadow cabinet; meanwhile, meat porters from Smithfield Market and dockers from Tilbury poured onto the streets and marched to parliament in Powell's support.

But there was at least one docker who held out against Enoch. Terry Barrett, a shop steward at Tilbury, was a member of the

International Socialists. At a mass meeting of 2,000 dockers, his was a lone voice in defence of black workers. Jim Nichol was there, too, having driven Barrett more than twenty miles to the docks on the back of his moped. He remembers how the dockers jeered and threw pennies at him. 'They made Terry cry.'

On the day of the strike, Barrett stood on the picket line with his own placard handing out a leaflet that Paul had written, and which Terry had signed: 'Who is Enoch Powell? He is a right-wing Tory opportunist who will stop at nothing to help his Party and his class. He lives in fashionable Belgravia and writes Greek verse.' Addressing the occasion more directly, he wrote: 'Again and again, he has argued that the docks are "grossly overmanned".'

How did we get here, asked Paul – and more importantly, how can we stop it? He wrote that his book would 'provide ammunition for a counter-attack'.[20]

Surprisingly, the book was written with Enoch Powell's cooperation. A small item in the *Evening Standard* 'Londoner's Diary' announced that 'Paul Foot, irritant extraordinary and author of one of the most devastating political tomes of recent years, *The Politics of Harold Wilson*, is now turning his attention to that other *bête noire* of the extreme Left, Mr Enoch Powell.' The article continued, 'Mr Foot says this will be a "very quick, short, pot-boiling operation. Part of the mythology about Powell is the belief that he has been consistent and courageous in his views on this issue".'[21]

Enoch Powell immediately wrote to Paul offering help with articles, speeches and information. He was always punctilious. 'I liked him', Paul groaned to his colleagues at *Private Eye* after a long interview. It was a character trait – perhaps a flaw. 'Paul was always wary of meeting people he was writing about', says Richard Ingrams, 'because he did have this regrettable habit of liking people.'

Was there something to like in Powell? Paul's uncle Michael certainly thought so. The two politicians shared dinners at Michael's Hampstead home, where they discussed books and authors, free from political or media intrusion. According to Michael Foot's biographer, he liked Powell 'for his cerebral approach to politics, his love of learning, and especially his feeling for the use of language'.[22] If Paul liked him, it was not apparent in his book.

This was a game of 'Immigration Poker', wrote Paul, in which players had to raise the bid each time they played. What began as an argument about empire and citizenship became one about control, which then devolved into a question of control over numbers – in particular, numbers of black people. Powell's final bid was in favour of repatriation. For a man who had written in his local paper in Wolverhampton during the 1964 election that he would set his face 'like flint against making any difference between one citizen of this country and another on grounds of his origin', this was something of a turnaround.[23] But, in 1964, Powell had not yet started playing the game of Immigration Poker.

Now, just four years later, Powell talked of non-white areas, non-white births, and a country divided: 'The West Indian or Indian does not, by being born in England, become an Englishman.'[24] This, argued Paul, was political opportunism of the lowest sort.

What had induced Powell to change course? Paul quotes another Conservative MP, Lord Lambton, also on the right wing of the Party: 'His speech should not be regarded in isolation', Lambton said, 'but as part of a planned policy, which he has followed since the retirement of Mr Macmillan. Ever since, he has believed sincerely that he was the right man to lead the Conservative Party.' To be leader, to be chosen as the man who understood what people in the country wanted, he would play the immigration card and risk his whole career.

Powell knew how to make a speech, and used each one to great effect. They were prepared in advance and handed, word-perfect, to the press; they contained no vague ideas or sloppy language. He knew how to grab the attention of his audience.

In a speech to the Conservative Political Centre in Gloucester in October 1967, Powell bemoaned the fate of the electorate, who were constantly told they had failed in comparison to other countries. The economy was not growing fast enough, exports were too low, the country was not paying its way. 'A babel of voices dins these unintelligible moral denunciations into the heads of ordinary English men and women, for whom they bear not the slightest relationship to any of the facts of their daily existence.' Powell wanted an end to it, and a return to something simpler: 'Some time – and why not now? – the citizen will put his faith again in the great simplicities and will confound the merchants of mumbo-jumbo.' By the following year, argued Paul, the greatest of these 'great simplicities' was 'the campaign against coloured immigration'.[25]

This was an extraordinary reversal for a man who had believed passionately in the British Empire as a force for good. Powell had served in the British army in India during the 1940s, and argued with Winston Churchill against independence, believing that the loss of India, the jewel in the imperial crown, was a tragedy. But once the people of the empire had taken back their countries, the indivisible whole was broken. For Powell, the Commonwealth, as a group of independent countries, had little significance, and the notion of a common citizenship meaningless. His retreat from Grand Imperialist to Little Englander was complete.

For his book Paul had once again relied on the press cuttings at the Institute of Race Relations library, and picked the brains of everyone who worked there – in particular the librarian A. Sivanandan, with whom he became friends. Originally from Sri Lanka, Sivanandan became a prominent thinker and activist on matters of race, and editor of the IRR's journal *Race*, which he renamed *Race and Class*. 'No one could escape Paul's warmth or integrity', he recalled. The two quarrelled often over politics – in particular, the politics of race and class – without spoiling their friendship.

The book was finished by July 1969. It was short, at 50,000 words, and the editor at Penguin noted it was 'clean text with hardly a footnote'.[26] Despite some production setbacks, it appeared before the end of the year. For its publicity campaign, Paul did the rounds of the BBC radio stations, including the Caribbean Service and Good Morning Africa. He met up with Powell once more on *Any Questions?*, in July 1972. The questions themselves during the recording were uncontroversial, but Paul had one last say on the slogans of demagogues. 'The crucial question', he said, was 'to get on with the discussion about the conditions, housing conditions, old age pensions, the conditions of people who live in this country, white and black, that's the issue.'

Was Powell a racist? The question was reignited when Powell died in 1998. As so often, there were politicians – including Labour figures – who were reluctant to speak ill of the dead, keen in this case to save

Powell from his toxic legacy. In an obituary for *Socialist Review*, Paul named some of them: Tony Blair, who said of Powell that he had 'said things we didn't agree with'; Denis Healey, called him 'an extreme nationalist, but not a racialist'; even Tony Benn, who had called him a racialist in the past, now softened his tone and said that, though he inspired racialists, he 'was not a racialist himself'.[27]

This was odd, Paul thought, because by far the most important thing about Enoch Powell was that he was a racist. And that racism stemmed from his belief in capitalism and empire, 'and with it an incontrovertible belief that the white man was ordained by god to conquer and control the world which was populated mainly by inferior black people'.

8

Who Killed Hanratty?

One day, as Paul toiled in his office at *Private Eye*, the phone rang.

'John here. John Lennon.'

'Ha. Very funny,' Paul replied. 'Now bugger off, I've got a paper to produce here', according to James Hanratty's brother Michael.

Paul had good reason to assume it was a family member having a laugh: such pranks were a Foot family speciality. But the phone soon rang again. It really was John Lennon, and he wanted to know how he could support the Hanratty campaign. Lennon was no doubt taken aback at being treated so dismissively by Paul, but not as taken aback as the waitress in the café around the corner from the *Eye*, who was clearly overwhelmed when Paul walked in with one of the Beatles – at the time the most famous band on the planet.

The late 1960s were Lennon's most political years. In November 1969, in protest at British involvement in the 'Nigeria–Biafra thing, against our support of America in Vietnam and against "Cold Turkey" slipping down the charts', he had returned his MBE to the Queen. He spoke up for peace and against poverty, and paid the fines of anti-apartheid campaigners in Scotland, who were protesting against the tour of the South African rugby team.

He also asked to meet some real worker socialists, and Paul obliged by taking a young electrician called Dave Southern to meet him. Dave was from Newcastle, where he worked in the Parsons factory along with other members of the International Socialists, but happened to be in London for an IS meeting. He clearly thought rather less of John

Lennon than Paul did: 'Fuck off with your peace and love', was his legendary response. Those who knew Dave Southern as a young man say it sounds about right.

Whatever happened with Dave Southern, John Lennon believed 'without a shadow of a doubt' that Hanratty's case had been a miscarriage of justice, and he wanted to help.[1] He visited the Hanratty family at home in their council house in Kingsbury, London – 'just like my auntie's house', he told them – and organised a 'Silent Protest for James Hanratty' with Hanratty's father, at Speakers' Corner in Hyde Park. On 9 December 1969 he called a press conference, and announced that he was planning to make a film about the Hanratty case.

The film, *Did Britain Murder Hanratty?*, was partly recorded at one of the huge public meetings organised by the A6 Committee. The Committee had been Paul's idea. 'I'll show you how it's done', he had told the family, and sat with Hanratty's father Jim every evening for a week planning what they could do. It was an informal affair involving Mr and Mrs Hanratty, their son Michael, Jean Justice, who was an early campaigner for an inquiry into the case, his friend, a barrister called Jeremy Fox, and of course Paul. The MP Fenner Brockway lent his support, as did a host of other people at different times.

The film featured Jim and Mary Hanratty on the platform at Watford Town Hall, and a very young-looking Paul Foot, already the clever public speaker that so many people remember. Paul's speech was clear and persuasive, mocking the prosecution at Hanratty's trial and mimicking their voices. Part of it was devoted to unpicking the prosecution's evidence about Hanratty's whereabouts on the day of the murder – Tuesday, 22 August 1961. Hanratty claimed he had gone to Liverpool that day, and remembered going into a sweetshop on Scotland Road late in the afternoon, where he spoke to a woman behind the counter. That woman was Mrs Olive Dinwoodie. She remembered Hanratty, although she was unsure of the precise day. It could have been Tuesday, 22 August, or it could have been the preceding Monday. It had to be one of the two, because those were the only two days she had worked in the shop that month. Her niece was with her, as well as her niece's friend, and the two schoolgirls confirmed seeing the man who looked like Hanratty in the shop on one of those days.

The problem with the Monday was that several of the prosecution's own witnesses had already given evidence at the committal hearing to the effect that Hanratty had spent the Monday in London. So, 'it must have been the Tuesday', Paul explained to his audience. 'And if it was the Tuesday, if he was in Liverpool in the sweetshop at five o'clock in the afternoon, he couldn't have walked to the car in the cornfield in Slough, Bucks, at half past nine.'[2]

'Could he have got a plane?' Paul asked. This bizarre idea had come from the police. But the plane times didn't work. Perhaps he flew a helicopter? 'He's believed not to fly', Paul mocked the police. 'Although he has many remarkable qualities', he said, 'Hanratty couldn't fly.' Whichever way the prosecution argued the point, they could not deal with the evidence from the sweetshop.

At the end of the film, Jim Hanratty looks into the camera: 'Beyond all doubt, in my mind, I am convinced that my son had no connection to this crime.' Then his mother reads her son's last letter, written to his brother: 'Well, Mick, I am going to do my best to face the morning with courage and strength.' And then he asked a favour of his brother: 'Try and clear my name.' It was almost daylight. 'I have to say goodbye for now.'

James Hanratty was executed at eight o'clock in the morning on 4 April 1962.

The original film still exists on its huge old reels, under Michael Hanratty's bed. For years, the family took it round the country, showing it at meetings organised by the A6 Committee, at universities, in the crypt of St Martin-in-the Fields in Trafalgar Square – anywhere they could find an audience.

Paul's interest in the case began during his time at the *Sunday Telegraph*, when he met Hanratty's parents and his brother Michael at the reburial of Hanratty's remains. He then published his long article in *Queen*, and worked alongside the BBC team making the *Panorama* programme. The publisher Tom Maschler had watched the programme and read the *Queen* feature, and promptly wrote to Paul suggesting: 'There is a terrific book in here.'[3]

To research the book Paul needed documents, and he had them in abundance. All the defence papers had been returned to the family, and these included a copy of the trial transcript, which ran to a massive 600,000 words. There were also the depositions taken after the committal hearing, statements from witnesses – including James Hanratty himself, and various photos and maps. He was able to delve into the media coverage having successfully negotiated access to both the *Daily Mirror* and *Sunday Times* cuttings libraries. Added to this were his own tape recordings of his numerous phone calls with Peter Alphon, and his own notes from the witnesses he had interviewed – although neither Valerie Storie, the survivor of the attack, nor Detective Superintendent Robert Acott, who ran the police investigation, would talk to him.

Letters went back and forth between Paul and Maschler, but Paul was constantly side-tracked – first by the Wilson book, then by the Powell book. The move to *Private Eye* helped, and there was assistance of a different sort from Lord Russell of Liverpool. Langley Russell was an experienced lawyer of some repute, who had raised the case for an inquiry in the House of Lords. In 1965 he had published his own book about what happened on Deadman's Hill.[4] Paul spent a lot of time on the phone asking his advice.

There were other distractions for Paul. He went to see his boys as often as he could, but preferred having them with him, away from Monica and the house at Gondar Gardens. As he had moved out for good, Monica, understandably, took Paul off the electoral register, much to his disappointment. Now he found that, at the end of a lengthy debate in the International Socialists about the organisation's attitude to voting for Labour in the next election, he was unable to vote at all in 1970. 'All those furious arguments in IS – deciding we should Vote Labour Without Illusions – and then finding I haven't a vote to give Labour, illusions or no', he wrote to Rose.

It was a lively time for political debate. In 1970 the International Socialists argued the ins and outs of women's liberation for the first time; and Paul complained to Rose of his exhaustion while preparing for a meeting about Black Power. He had had the good fortune to hear Stokely Carmichael speak at the Roundhouse in 1967, at the Dialectics of Liberation congress, organised by a group of radical intellectuals and psychiatrists, and that experience had sharpened up his ideas about workers' power and black power. 'All of us lucky to be there that morning discovered a new black America, angry, funny, intransigent, determined to be free.'[5]

There was also a ferocious debate about race under way inside the National Union of Journalists. Two years earlier, in 1968, the South African cricket authorities had refused to play against England unless their selectors fielded an all-white team. If Basil D'Oliveira, a black South African cricketer who played for the England touring side, was not removed from the team, as the South Africans demanded, the tour would be cancelled. D'Oliveira was dropped, then reinistated, but the tour was still cancelled. In the summer of 1970, the South Africans were due to tour England again, and in April the Central London Branch of the National Union of Journalists, of which Paul was a member, discussed a boycott of all news coverage of the tour if it went ahead. Paul had been surprised at their success. The resolution then moved to the NUJ's annual conference in Harrogate, where it was heavily defeated. Paul was exposed in the *Observer* as the evil conspirator who had started it all.

A further distraction was an invitation from his father to visit his parents in New York, with an offer that was hard to refuse: his father would pay his airfare. The general election was pending, and his father could see the writing on the wall for the Wilson government, which would almost certainly bring his current job to an end, and with it his tenancy of a beautiful apartment on the corner of Fifth Avenue and East 66th Street, overlooking Central Park. 'I really will have to make a great effort with the book when I get back', Paul wrote to Rose from New York. 'Poor old Maschler will be very cross.'

Tom Maschler was indeed cross, and insisted he must have the copy by the end of July. But July came and went, with no book. In August, Paul wrote again: 'Since it is twice as long and twice as good as anticipated when I promised it, I trust you will take a pretty liberal view of the fact that it has taken less than twice as long as promised!'[6] It was being typed, all 180,000 words of it, and he committed to deliver it on his return to London from Cornwall. Once it was finally in his hands, Maschler telegrammed Paul promising that publication would justify Paul's labours.

The book followed a simple structure. Paul started with the events of 22 August: Gregsten and Storie in their car in a cornfield near

Slough; the intruder knocking on the car window and making them drive away at gunpoint; the murder of Michael Gregsten, and the rape and shooting of Valerie Storie at Deadman's Hill on the A6; and the search for the murderer. The prosecution case against Hanratty followed, and then the defence case for Hanratty – particularly the Rhyl alibi, which Paul had investigated so closely. Then, in an extraordinary final chapter, Paul named Peter Alphon as the most likely suspect for the murder.

Peter Alphon had been questioned by the police soon after the murder because of his weird behaviour in a London hotel. Nothing further happened until two cartridge cases, fired by the gun used in the murder, turned up in yet another hotel – the Vienna Hotel in Paddington. Alphon had stayed there too, and he soon became the number-one police suspect. A consummate self-publicist, Alphon knew the police were looking for him, so he went to Scotland Yard, and before going in phoned the press from a call box outside to announce his arrival and his innocence.

But the case against Alphon collapsed when Valerie Storie failed to pick him out in an identity parade, and the attention of the police turned to another man who had also stayed at the Vienna Hotel – James Hanratty. When Valerie Storie picked him out in a line-up, the police believed they had their man.

Instead of slinking away with relief, Peter Alphon seemed to love the publicity – or perhaps the notoriety – that the case brought, and confessed to the murder repeatedly. For years he continued to make confessions, and then withdraw them, to anyone who would listen – including Paul. The phone calls from Alphon began in 1966, when Paul wrote his first article for *Queen*, and throughout the years of writing for *Private Eye* and the *Sunday Times* he continued to call, until the book was ready for publication. But then he fell silent.

Who Killed Hanratty? was published by Jonathan Cape in early May 1971, and the publicity was as Maschler had promised. There were posters on the front of London's buses and in bookshops. Extra copies were printed, so that one could be sent to each member of parliament, and a good number to the House of Lords, with a letter pressing them to support an inquiry. Replies poured in, with Labour MPs overwhelmingly supporting the call. Conservatives were less keen, although there were some exceptions. Jeffrey Archer MP wrote a note of support for the campaign – a fact that did not stop Paul writing in *Private Eye* about the continuing saga of Archer's expenses at the United Nations Association.[7]

On the night of the book's publication, there was champagne for the Hanratty family at Rose's flat, from where they left for a large public meeting in Rhyl. Three hundred people packed into the Little Theatre and, after the speeches, the family and campaigners heard another possible alibi witness speak out for the first time. Then another witness, a barber in Rhyl, came forward. The case for an inquiry was growing.

Among the glowing endorsements for the book, however, one review struck a contrary note. In the *Sunday Times*, Dick Taverne, a lawyer and the Labour MP for Lincoln, clearly took the view that Hanratty was guilty – and, as Paul noticed, he seemed to be relying on evidence not in the public domain. Had he, Paul asked, been able to look at unseen evidence, available only to those with privileged access in the Home Office? Dick Taverne had been parliamentary undersecretary at the Home Office when the then home secretary turned down the demand for a public inquiry in 1967. Paul demanded the release of all the papers.

The case for an inquiry seemed overwhelming. The home secretary, whose decision it would be, was Reginald Maudling. While Maudling was mulling over his options, he wrote to Paul asking for a note on all the new evidence on the case. Paul replied at length, detailing in a 4,000-word letter everything that had come to light over the intervening years – but to no avail. In October 1972, Maudling turned down the request for an inquiry.

Jim Hanratty was a proud man. He would argue his case at Hyde Park Corner, or stand with a placard outside the Home Office, never giving up the search for the truth about his son. Not many years later, when Jim was dying, Paul would visit in the evenings after work and do what he could to help, calling the doctor and running errands to the chemist. 'Paul idolised my dad', says Michael. 'He was more than a journalist. He became a friend.'

On his deathbed, Jim mourned the failure of the A6 campaign, and urged Paul to continue with it. Although Jim's death knocked the heart out of the committee, Paul kept going, as did Jean Justice until his death in 1990. That seemed to be the end of it, until hope sprang from a number of unlikely sources.

Paul was approached by Janet Gregsten, whose husband was murdered that night on the A6. She too had grown increasingly uncertain of Hanratty's guilt. They spoke on several occasions, before she died suddenly of a heart attack. But out of these conversations Paul became convinced that she had had nothing to do with her husband's death – a claim that Alphon had always made. Then, to Paul's utter surprise, after more than twenty years of silence, Alphon also got in touch – and Paul became less sure of his involvement as well.

In 1992, to mark the thirtieth anniversary of Hanratty's execution, Bob Woffinden and Ros Franey made a film for Yorkshire Television, and another long dossier went to the home secretary.[8] Again, a lengthy wait ensued, at the end of which the home secretary, Michael Howard, passed the buck to the newly formed Criminal Cases Review Commission. The CCRC was set up in 1997 following the successful outcome of the campaigns around several miscarriage-of-justice cases in the 1980s and '90s. In future, this new, independent organisation, with broad powers to reinvestigate, would make decisions about reopening cases, including that of James Hanratty.

9

One Glorious Summer

In 1972, with his reputation as a writer and a journalist riding high and a promising career before him, Paul left *Private Eye* to work for *Socialist Worker*. The pay was terrible, the office space even worse than at the *Eye*, and the hours were long with no alternate week off to write books. Even the circulation was not great. He could have had any job, anywhere in the country. What on earth made him join this small political paper? For Paul, though, when the offer came it was irresistible. He accepted at once.

Well, not quite at once. First, he had to go home and talk to Rose about the massive pay cut and doubling of his hours he was about to take. By then, Paul was settled in Rose's large, rambling flat at the top of a Victorian mansion block just off the Finchley Road in West Hampstead. It was rather old-fashioned, and Paul had to lug scuttles full of coal up the five flights of stairs. But the rooms were huge, and there was plenty of space for the boys to stay to escape the turmoil of their home life.

His sons were now eight and six, and he saw them as often as he could, playing French cricket in the local park until the light faded and they could barely see the ball. At weekends there were games of football on Parliament Hill Fields, with boots in place of goal posts, and the sons and daughters of Paul's friends: Nicholas Deakin and Ken Loach, who were both contemporaries from Oxford, and then Gordon Carr, who worked for the BBC. Paul kept out of Monica's way as much as he could, although occasions like Christmas Day presented their problems. John remembers them as terrible – and when Paul announced that he was going to work on *Socialist Worker* and money would be tight, even the Christmas presents suffered.

There were away trips for the boys, for lunch with Ronald Segal at his country house or to see Auberon Waugh in Somerset, at the grandest of all the houses they visited. They would visit Ditch (Paul's familiar name for Richard Ingrams), and watch the annual *Private Eye* cricket match, with Martin Tomkinson as demon fast bowler – and there was more cricket at Peter Jay's annual match in Oxford. Each summer they would take the train to Cornwall and stay for six weeks with their grandparents at Trematon, on one memorable occasion making the journey on their own. Monica had put the boys on the train. Paul arrived, but then disappeared to buy a newspaper – and failed to reappear before the whistle blew. The train and the two boys left without him.

Matt loved those trips to Trematon. His birthday was in August, just a few days before the birthday of Paul's younger brother Benjie. As many of the extended Foot family as could make it would gather round the long dining table for the celebrations, over which Sylvia would preside.

The plea for Paul to join the tiny staff at *Socialist Worker* in 1972 came from Jim Nichol, who had spent that restless night with Paul and the mouse in Newcastle. From Tony Cliff's sofa, Jim had been drawn into the small IS print shop, working in a corner of a larger print works under Tottenham's football stadium. He was not much of a printer, but did progress to become the paper's publisher and managing director of the company that printed it.

It was a good time to be in London and at the heart of things. 'It was so exciting', Jim remembers. 'The French events. Prague. Enoch Powell. Chicago. Maoism. Vietnam. The place was buzzing.'

The French events of 1968 might have been the high point, but there was much else going on. Students fought police on the streets of Poland, and challenged authority around the world. In Prague, the old regime gave way to a year of intellectual ferment and liberal reforms under Alexander Dubček, until Russian tanks rolled into Czechoslovakia. The mighty US war machine in Vietnam was brought to a standstill by the

Tet Offensive, and half a million American troops came close to defeat. Those who had been attracted to CND in the early 1960s now poured into London's Grosvenor Square to demonstrate against the war in Vietnam in front of the US embassy. At home the women at Ford came out on strike demanding equal pay, and the first stirrings of the women's liberation movement were emerging. When Martin Luther King was murdered in 1968, black neighbourhoods across urban America erupted. In Northern Ireland the Catholic minority took to the streets – as did the people of Mexico, before the police opened fire and killed 500, just before the country hosted the Olympics. The clenched-fist salute of two black American athletes grabbed attention across the world.

This was the year that the old four-page monthly, the *Labour Worker*, gave way to the weekly *Socialist Worker*, at the same time severing its political ties to Labour. Radical and revolutionary socialist ideas were more popular than they had been for decades, and *Socialist Worker* caught the zeitgeist.

When Paul had first edited *Labour Worker* in Glasgow, the print run was in the hundreds, and he liked to joke that the IS membership could fit into one room. The change of name and the move to weekly publication saw the print run grow from a few hundred to several thousand, and the membership of IS grew rapidly alongside it. It went on growing in the years that followed, as the militancy of the students spread, in an unprecedented wave, to workers and trade unionists. The slogan 'Neither Washington nor Moscow but International Socialism', which appeared on the paper's front page, appealed to a layer of young people repelled by both the imperialism of the United States and the Stalinism of the Soviet Union.

These tempestuous times attracted other young radical writers to *Socialist Worker*. One of them, Christopher Hitchens, was so good he was soon promoted to features editor: 'Working to improve these dour pages brought me into proper contact with Paul Foot', he wrote many years later. 'He was somewhat older than me, but his reaction to any injustice was as outraged and appalled as that of any young person who had just discovered that life is unfair.'[1] Hitchens's brother Peter also contributed to the paper, as did the poet James Fenton and the playwright David Edgar. Eamonn McCann was reporting from Northern Ireland; Dave Widgery wrote regularly between his shifts as a GP in the East End of London; and the future film producer Christopher Hird was writing anonymously as T. H. Rogmorton, while he laboured in the City of London.

Paul had given up the editorship of *Labour Worker* in 1966. But he continued to sit on the editorial board, and never stopped writing. Through the years of working on the Wilson and Powell books, and his part-time job at the *Eye*, he pounded out articles on almost any topic, but always with a keen eye on the Wilson government: the corruption of Labour, its lack of interest in political ideas, and the emptiness of its slogans.

Before Paul left for New York in 1970 to visit his parents, and with a general election looming, he wrote a long piece on the record of the Labour government. In 1964 Harold Wilson had promised a minimum income guarantee for lower-paid workers. He had promised to abolish prescription charges, and to build 500,000 houses by 1970. He had promised a Rent Act to protect tenants from high rents. And he had apologised for reneging on Labour's opposition to Commonwealth immigration control, emphasising that there would be no further extension of controls. He had promised that his economic policies would not increase unemployment, and that a Labour government would support trade unions when wages and conditions were under pressure. Every single promise was broken. 'Now, however, there is an election to be won', wrote Paul, 'and Labour must woo its traditional working-class voters to the polls. There has started a slow shuffle to the left.'[2] Forgotten phrases fell from the lips of Labour ministers; old slogans were dusted down. But still Labour lost.

Despite the opinion polls, and despite the recent enfranchisement of eighteen-year-olds, 1970 saw a Conservative victory, and Edward Heath moved into Number 10. Too many disillusioned Labour voters had stayed at home. Following the election, Paul wrote a short pamphlet for *Socialist Worker* denouncing Heath and his cabinet of bankers and businessmen. It was, wrote Paul, a cabinet of the rich, for the rich: 'Eighteen Ministers with 45 directorships, all but three from public schools, four from Eton. Behind the rhetoric of national unity there is nothing in their politics but the slogans of the snob and the racialist.'[3]

It was true that the Labour government had been bashing the unions, but there would no doubt be worse to come. Economic problems would be resolved by screwing the workers. Forget about ordinary wage increases: the drive for increased productivity was going to be ratcheted up. Workers would be expected to work more, for less, in the national interest.

'The fruits of such productivity sacrifices are not enjoyed by the workers. The rich remain rich.' It was all a hoax, argued Paul, 'a class hoax, cunningly packaged, and too often discovered too late.'[4]

Battle lines were drawn. The number of strikes was rising. The long post-war boom was coming to an end, but union membership was relatively high, there were still jobs to be had, and there was a spirit of rebellion within the working class. In December 1970, half a million workers stopped work to protest against the Tories' new anti-union legislation. The next year the number of days lost to official strikes jumped from 3.3 million to 10 million. Including in the unofficial strikes, that figure was 13.5 million. The following year these numbers doubled again.[5] Week after week, *Socialist Worker* reported on the increasingly angry mood. Then the Post Office workers came out on strike.

Beginning in the depths of winter in January 1971, and lasting for forty-four days, the Post Office strike was the largest that Britain had seen since the war, with almost all of the 200,000 postmen and telephonists coming out. The Union of Post Office Workers (UPW) had no strike fund, just a hardship fund for the worst off. Though hundreds of donations, most of them for tiny amounts, flowed in from individuals across the country, and union branches dipped into their funds as other workers supported the strike, it was not enough to keep it going. The UPW's financial difficulties became so severe that mid-way through the strike the banks demanded the title deeds and keys of the union's headquarters.

If the hardship fund could not be sustained, the strike would crumble. 'This was the union's Achilles heel', wrote Paul in a pamphlet about the strike, which was promptly pierced not by the employers or strike breakers, 'but by the Trades Union Congress General Council'.[6]

On 21 February – day thirty-three of the strike – a huge demonstration was held in London against the government's Industrial Relations Bill – a piece of legislation that would severely restrict the right to strike. 'The most popular man on the demonstration was Tom Jackson [the union's general secretary], the most popular delegation that of the UPW,' wrote Paul. Three days later the TUC General Council met, and Jackson asked for financial help in the form of cash rather than loans. He got nothing, as other union leaders mumbled about how difficult things were and looked away. 'When Jackson left the TUC that morning', wrote Paul, 'he must have known the game was up.'

A few days later the postmen and women went back to work for the hollow promise of an inquiry – something they could have agreed to on the first day of the strike. The government was delighted to have inflicted a defeat on such a large union. For the postal workers it was a serious setback, but 'the refusal among workers to be pushed around by the wealthy is stronger now than ever before in history', Paul argued. 'The spirit of the postmen, and of workers everywhere, is far from broken.' He was right: the strikes would continue.[7]

In June 1971, 100,000 workers in Glasgow stopped work for a day and marched through the city centre in support of the workers at Upper Clyde Shipbuilders. The company had gone bust, and the government refused to bail it out. Yards would close, and 6,000 workers would lose their jobs. The workers voted to occupy the yards. More strikes and demonstrations followed, until the chief constable of Strathclyde warned of civil disorder. The government was worried he might be right, and after seven months the money was found to keep some of the UCS yards open.

At the end of the year, it was the miners' turn for a wage demand. Their strike began in January 1972 – the first since their terrible defeat in 1926. Britain was heavily dependent on coal to keep the lights on, and by the following month power supplies were under pressure, and the Central Electricity Generating Board under siege. The government's confidence, high at the start of the strike following their defeat of the postal workers, quickly evaporated, and on 9 February a state of emergency was declared. In the face of government intransigence, public sympathy swiftly turned to the miners – even the *Daily Express* had to admit that the vast majority of ordinary people supported the strike.[8]

Although no pits were working, coal was still available. The largest depot in the country, in Birmingham, saw hundreds of lorries a day queuing to load up, and the pickets from the nearby Staffordshire coalfields were not strong enough to stem the flow. The miners asked for help. Within hours, pickets began arriving from the South Yorkshire and South Wales mining areas. But still the lorries were getting through. Then the call went out across the engineering factories of the Midlands for a day of mass picketing – and they came in their thousands. Huge crowds of miners massed outside the depot, facing down a thousand police officers. Then, over a hill, came a banner; as far as the eye could see, thousands of workers were marching towards the depot. In the interests of public safety, the chief constable closed the gates of the depot to lorries, and the Battle of Saltley Gate was over.

Douglas Hurd, the prime minister's political secretary, wrote in his diary the following day: 'The Government [is] now wandering all over the battlefield looking for someone to surrender to – and being massacred all the time.'[9] As electricity supplies sank dangerously low, a deal was struck with the miners, and the strike was won. Arthur Scargill, the leader of those Yorkshire miners, entered the history books – as did the miners' new tactic: the flying picket.

That year, 1972, saw a dramatic increase in union militancy, the success of the miners encouraging others. In April a series of overtime bans and work-to-rules began across the railways, an all-out strike becoming a possibility. Then the government decided it should use the power it had under the Industrial Relations Act to force the unions to hold a ballot. It was a terrible miscalculation. The turnout for the ballot was nearly 90 per cent, and 85 per cent of those who voted wanted action. If there was an all-out strike, chaos would ensue. Within weeks the government was forced to agree a settlement. A wave of occupations hit the engineering industry in Manchester. Building workers were out on strike across the country, their flying pickets moving from site to site.

And then a dispute began in the docks, where containers were revolutionising the nature of dock work. The dockers were demanding both a pay increase and the unionisation of the container depots. Strikes across the docks had been bubbling up all year, and on 4 July, Midland Cold Storage applied to the National Industrial Relations Court for an order to stop the London dockers from picketing their depot. The order named individual dockers, rather than the union, and instructed them to desist. The dockers refused. The court immediately issued arrest warrants, and on Friday, 21 July five dockers were sent to prison for contempt of court.

To those who were there, what happened next felt like a revolution.

All the London docks stopped work – bringing to a halt 24,000 workers, in docks that stretched over thirty-five miles down the Thames to the sea. Then the docks in Liverpool, Manchester and Hull stopped, and by Monday 40,000 dockers were on strike. There was almost 100 per cent support for the strike across the country.

The dockers were joined in their industrial action by print workers from Fleet Street. *Printworker* – a bulletin founded by IS members but with contacts across the political spectrum and across the print unions – now came into its own. Its editor was Ross Pritchard, one of those young men who had followed Gus Macdonald to London from Glasgow. By then Ross was running the presses at the IS print shop. Paul helped to write the paper.[10] On the evening of Saturday, 22 July, as the national newspaper presses were gearing up to print the Sunday editions, supporters of the *Printworker* were getting dockers into the big printing houses to talk to the stewards, and gradually the presses stopped – first the *Sunday Mirror*, and then the rest falling like dominoes (the sole exception being the *Sunday Times*).

An estimated quarter of a million workers were on strike at some point during those five days. London's Covent Garden and Smithfield markets stopped, as did fish packers in Grimsby, lorry drivers in Liverpool, and steel workers in Shotton and maintenance workers at British Leyland, London bus drivers and ground staff at Heathrow airport. South Wales miners were ready to strike if the dockers were not released, as were engineers in the AUEW. The picket outside Pentonville prison grew, and stayed all day and night, as some 90,000 dockers and other trade unionists brought a whole district of London to a halt. There was even talk from the TUC of a one-day general strike.

Finally, with such overwhelming support from across the labour movement, the government and the courts got their act together. The Official Solicitor appeared from nowhere, and on Wednesday, 26 July the five dockers, who had become known as the Pentonville Five, were released. The Industrial Relations Act and its hated court, the NIRC, had taken a serious battering – and the government was severely damaged.

Just over a month later, on 2 September 1972, *Socialist Worker* announced on its front page that Paul Foot was joining the paper. It would expand from twelve to sixteen pages, and the IS print works would be moving to larger premises at Corbridge Works, in Hackney, which would house a new, grander, faster printing press.

Money for such a move was readily available. Paul remembered going to visit various wealthy individuals who were interested in revolutionary ideas and asking them for donations, and the fundraising was helped by a cheque for £17,000 that arrived through the post with a short note attached: 'I renounce my inheritance and declare my solidarity with International Socialism.'[11]

The print works was already operating flat out. Leaflets were being printed for free for any group of strikers who wanted them, and alongside *Printworker*, there was *Carworker*, *Redder Tape* (for civil servants), *Rank and File Teacher*, the *Collier* and many more – as well as the *Barricades Bulletin* for the civil rights movement in Northern Ireland. The works also printed *Private Eye*.

The *Eye* had outgrown its printers, and in 1972 Paul introduced its business manager to Jim Nichol. It was a contract that made the new IS printshop commercially viable. Although their political views were a million miles apart, they rubbed along in a spirit of good will, the *Eye* even carrying a flyer for *Socialist Worker*.[12]

Martin Tomkinson – who had joined *Private Eye* that year and, at Paul's request, was making his way up and down to John Poulson's bankruptcy hearings in Wakefield – was baffled that Paul had left the *Eye* for the small IS paper. 'Footnotes', his *Eye* column, had scored success after success, and when Reginald Maudling was forced to resign as home secretary in July, Paul had jumped up and down with glee, shouting, 'We've got him, we've got him!' But there were tensions developing, and Paul had had a number of rows with his colleagues about the way the magazine jeered at some of those who Paul supported. One piece in particular, about the 'Loonie Ladies', didn't go down well with him at all. The 'loonies' included the black American activist Angela Davis, held in solitary confinement and on trial for her life in the US, and Bernadette Devlin, the civil rights activist from Northern Ireland who had been elected to parliament as MP for mid-Ulster in 1969. But whatever Paul felt about the magazine, he and Richard Ingrams never fell out with one another. Reflecting back on those times, Richard could see the attraction for Paul of going to work on *Socialist Worker*: 'Things were looking up and there were a lot of people, on both sides of the barricades, who thought a revolution was coming.'

Paul's new column for *Socialist Worker* was called 'Foot Prints', and Footnotes in *Private Eye* quietly disappeared. But some of the stories he had investigated for the *Eye* continued: the shameless waste of public money on the development of Concorde; the antics of Tiny Rowland of Lonhro in buying politicians in Africa; the case of the Clay Cross councillors who had been fined by the courts for protecting cheap rents for local people. His writing remit was broad. He would write about bent coppers in Britain or the spread of political terror in Turkey, and he moved freely between the present and the past: a gas workers' strike prompted an article on the beginnings of their union in 1889.

Paul would also take any opportunity to speak around the country. One day it would be 'Reform or Revolution' at the Conway Hall in Central London; the next, a commemoration for all those who had died on Bloody Sunday in Northern Ireland, speaking with Bernadette Devlin and Tony Cliff. He would often draw huge audiences: 800 people heard him speak at a May Day rally in Islington. But what he really liked was talking to workers – steel workers in Ebbw Vale or Consett, or miners in Wales, where another strike was brewing.

In the run-up to Christmas 1973, Paul interviewed miners at Morlais Colliery in South Wales about the possibility of a strike. 'I'm a high paid miner who's better off on sick pay', he was told by Dafryg Anthony, an underground miner and the chairman of the NUM lodge at the pit. It was, he said, easier for his family when he was sick because his wife would receive a minimum social security payment for her and their children, and the rent would be paid. Their lodge had voted overwhelmingly for an overtime ban in support of their union's pay claim. 'They tell us to think of our country', one miner complained to Paul. 'Well, I don't believe in patriotism. You've got to think of your fellow man, not your country.'[13]

That December, the government declared a three-day week starting in the new year to cut demand for electricity and preserve coal stocks. What this amounted to in practice was a lock-out of all industrial workers for half the week in order to defeat the miners – the cost of which would far outweigh the miners' pay claim. Nonetheless, the miners voted to strike by over 80 per cent in the militant areas of South Wales and Yorkshire, and by 60 per cent even in the more conservative areas. On 3 February 1974, the strike began.

It took just two days for Edward Heath to respond. In a reaction to the increasing union militancy, the prime minister called a general election, asking the country: 'Who Governs Britain?' The answer soon came back: not you. The Conservatives were out, and Labour were back in, with Harold Wilson in power once again – ruling over a minority government, following the failure of the Conservative Party to agree a coalition with the Liberals and Ulster Unionists.

As soon as the election was over an argument erupted inside IS about *Socialist Worker*. Sales had gone up during the election, to a peak of 23,000, which easily put *Socialist Worker* alongside *Tribune*, and ahead of a host of other left-wing papers. But who was reading the paper? And who was it aimed at?

Was it writing for trade union militants well versed in politics? Or was it writing for new readers? The paper took too much for granted, argued Tony Cliff. The sheer density of the words on the page was intimidating. Articles should be shorter, simpler, and 'the more complicated the argument, the simpler the style should be'.[14]

Roger Protz, the paper's editor, agreed that things needed to change, but saw danger ahead. Any attempt to make the paper more 'popular', with more pictures and over-simplified text, could weaken its politics and fracture the paper's relationship with its most important readership – experienced, politically aware militants. Roger had thought Paul agreed with him, but in the end Paul decided to side with Cliff.

At the IS National Committee meeting in March 1974, the argument came to a head. The quarrel had been going on for some time, Paul told the meeting. A lot of workers had joined the organisation in the last year, but the paper did not reflect that. The editor lost the argument and the vote, and then left his job.

Paul had to write Roger's farewell: 'Roger edited *Socialist Worker* ever since it started as a weekly paper in October 1968. Through all that time, he has put the interests of the organisation, the paper and the fight for socialism above all other considerations.'[15] Now he was leaving and a new editor would be elected at the next National Committee meeting.

The new editor would be Paul Foot.

10

Y, Oh Lord, Oh Why

Paul thought his writing for *Socialist Worker* was 'by far the best work I did'. He was inspired by the workers he talked to – 'the people who were fighting at the bottom of the pile'.[1] People like the Clay Cross Labour councillors in Derbyshire who were refusing to impose the increased council rents forced on them by government legislation. The local people, they argued, were just too poor.[2] Paul met the councillors in 1973, and in his article in *Socialist Worker* he named each of them, giving their trade and their union:

> Charlie Bunting unemployed, sacked two years ago for his leading part in a strike at Inghams, a local engineering firm; David Nuttall, GMWU branch secretary, victimised and sacked by a road haulage firm for refusing to carry a letter during the postal strike; Roy Booker, coke worker and a member of the NUM . . .

Furious at this flagrant breach of the law by the council, the Conservative government had sent in auditors to calculate just how much rent had been lost, and demanded it from the eleven councillors. They refused to pay, and were fined; then they refused to pay their fines as well. In response, the Labour Party conference had voted to support them. But then, in early 1974, a Labour government was elected once more. Would it stand by those resolutions? No, came the answer from Harold Wilson: pay your fines.

It seemed that Labour could still win elections, but it was rapidly losing touch with its grassroots members, who were becoming increasingly demoralised. To illustrate his point, Paul told the story of Arthur Affleck, chairman of the joint shop stewards' committee at the Lackenby steelworks in Teesside. He and Arthur had spoken together at a meeting in Ebbw Vale – another of Britain's steel towns – when Arthur bemoaned the state of his local Labour Party. 'Arthur's predecessor as check-weighman at the Lackenby works was a Labour councillor, A. S. Seed, JP, who was chairman of the Eston Urban Council planning committee', wrote Paul. Two other local councillors also sat on the planning committee. The committee argued back and forth over a planning application for a housing development in Cricket Lane. Applications were rejected, and then resubmitted. Finally, planning consent was agreed. Soon after the bungalows were built, all three councillors just happened to change address – to Cricket Lane. Nothing was untoward, it was all just a coincidence, Arthur ironically assured his audience. Apparently, 'they all had insurance policies which matured at the same time'.[3]

Because of the lamentable state of the Labour Party, many people like Arthur joined the International Socialists. Another was Len Blood, an engineer who had become incensed by workers being sold out by union officials time and again in work disputes. In 1976, Len stood as the left-wing candidate for assistant general secretary of the AUEW, the engineers' union. 'Our union isn't democratic enough', he told Paul. 'I'd like to see executive members stand down after each three-year stint and go back to the shop floor. If we don't change the union, we won't change our lives.'[4]

Alongside the long piece about Len's election campaign in *Socialist Worker* was another piece by Paul. Len's son Philip had muscular dystrophy. The photo that accompanied the article showed the slight figure of his wife Sadie, alongside a smiling boy in a wheelchair. For years Sadie had struggled to get a lift installed in their house, so that Philip could get upstairs to his bedroom. He weighed four stone, she just six.

Living with a tragedy in your home is bad enough. But living with a tragedy which the authorities make worse and worse just by meanness is terrible. Did you know the council here spent a few minutes deciding to buy a Rolls-Royce for the Mayor? Four minutes to get £8,000 of our money for a Rolls-Royce for a Mayor – and four years fighting to get £900 for a lift for a sick child.

Paul railed against trade union leaders who sold out their members and, in particular, those who then took seats in the House of Lords. They included people like Richard Briginshaw, general secretary of one of the print unions, who defended his decision on the spurious grounds that he was going to fight for socialism – in the House of Lords.[5] Paul also criticised the Labour Party in general, and the left MPs in particular, uncle Michael included, because they had so little power. When the Labour government agreed to go ahead with closures in the steel industry at Ebbw Vale, Michael Foot's constituency, Paul dug out the speech his uncle had made in the House of Commons when the cuts in steel production had first been proposed by the Conservative government. 'We have a right – we do not come here to beg', Foot had said,

> to demand from the government the assistance which great democratic communities ought to have from this house. If this government will not give assistance to places like Shotton, Ebbw Vale and all the others that are threatened, then the next Labour government will.[6]

If only this had been so.

Paul also weighed in against the media. As the gas workers began a strike, 'The lords and masters of television and the press are using all their powers to win "public opinion" for the government', Paul wrote on the front page of *Socialist Worker* in early 1973.[7] 'The gas men are being pilloried as murderous layabouts who have abandoned all other interests save that of their own greed.' To press home his point, he went back a hundred years to the history of Will Thorne, the Beckton Gas Works, and the formation of their new union. Unfortunately, the fire which had formed the union was soon doused. Thorne himself became a member of parliament, and the leadership of the union passed into the hands of men who would not fight, until the lesson was learned all over again in the 1970s.

❧

Each year the union leaders gathered at the Trades Union Congress, where 'by day the resolutions come and go. Congress deplores this . . . totally rejects that . . . demands the other', Paul wrote of the gathering in 1975. But by night, 'as the booze flows even more lavishly than usual, the serious business – the horse-trading on votes, resolutions and TUC General Council positions – is under way'.[8]

At Congress that year, the presence of Ricky Tomlinson livened things up. Tomlinson is now a well-known actor, but was then a building worker who had come along for a debate on the plight of the Shrewsbury pickets – a group of building workers, including Tomlinson, imprisoned after a strike in 1972. Tomlinson asked if he could speak, as a fraternal delegate, an honour that had been bestowed at the same Congress on an American trade unionist. But the committee that decided these things turned him down. He could not address the delegates; he could only listen from the gallery to what others had to say about him. He was furious. 'I gave them fifteen months of my life', said Tomlinson. 'I thought they might give me fifteen minutes of theirs.'[9]

In the summer of 1972, Tomlinson was just one of thousands of building workers out on strike for better pay and shorter hours, and an end to the system of self-employment known in the building industry as 'the lump'. In North Wales, where he lived, the strike was well organised and well supported, but up the road in Shrewsbury things were more difficult, and the unions there put out a call for help. On 6 September a Welsh contingent drove into the area in an assortment of cars and coaches, and descended on the unorganised sites. At first, they were greeted by the son of the contractor, armed with a twelve-bore shotgun. The pickets disarmed him, made the gun safe, and handed it to the police. From Shrewsbury they moved on to Telford New Town, and a site run by one of the country's largest building companies, McAlpine. They talked to the workers on the site, and even got involved in some scuffles. But in the end the site stopped, and its workers joined the strike. For two long days the police were at every site they visited, but no one was arrested. Then the pickets went home.

Months later, on 14 February 1973, twenty-four men from North Wales were arrested, including the strike committee, and charged with conspiracy to intimidate others while picketing in the Shrewsbury area – a charge considered so severe that it carried no maximum sentence.

The builders appeared in court in groups of six later in the year, and at the end of the first trial, just days before Christmas 1973, three builders were sent to prison: Des Warren for three years, Tomlinson for two years, and John McKinsie Jones for nine months.

Of all the workers on strike in 1972, why go for the building workers? And why in North Wales? Because, argued Laurie Flynn in a special pamphlet for the campaign to support the builders, they were a relatively weak section of workers. But there was another factor in play. The Telford site the pickets had shut down was run by McAlpine, which had very close links to the police in North Wales. It also had the ear of the Tory government.[10]

In *Socialist Worker*, Paul compared the Shrewsbury pickets to the Tolpuddle Martyrs. In 1837, George Loveless, a leader of the Dorset farm workers, had called for the men of Britain to take a stand: 'Rally round the standard of Liberty, or forever lay prostrate under the iron hand of your money-mongering taskmasters!' It was no different in December 1973. From the dock at his trial, Tomlinson said,

> I hope the trade union movement and the working class of this country will act now to ensure that another charade such as this will never take place again, and the right to picket or strike will be defended even at the cost of great hardship or individual freedom.[11]

Just weeks before that TUC meeting, Tomlinson had finally been released on parole. Paul and Jim Nichol were waiting outside Leicester prison when he appeared, dressed smartly in a pin-stripe suit, and trim – he had been on hunger strike for thirty-one of his days inside.[12] Even now, Tomlinson is not bitter, but he is angry. 'They picked on people living in Wales, all those they jailed were from Wales, but the pickets during that strike came from all over. McAlpines is the link.' Tomlinson fought to clear his name, and that of his fellow pickets, from the day he was released from prison. Eventually he succeeded. All the Shrewsbury pickets had their convictions quashed by the Court of Appeal in 2021 – forty-eight years after the verdicts.

After his release Tomlinson went back on the sites, and Paul followed him to North Wales, where they were rebuilding the Pontin's holiday camp in Prestatyn. 'We were living in the chalets and Paul came and stayed', he remembers. 'We were rough, tough building workers and him with his plum voice. He was dead at ease with us. I remember hearing him speak at a meeting soon after I got out of prison. He had that wonderful knack of bringing comedy into it. He could be very funny.'

The mid 1970s was a tough time to be a militant on the building sites, or in any union. The employers ran blacklists of trade unionists, and MI5 ran spies. Telephones were tapped and post was monitored. At the *Socialist Worker* print shop in Hackney, letters to the paper would arrive carefully bundled together with the post for other left-wing organisations in other parts of London. Either Special Branch were useless, or they didn't care.

In his articles for *Socialist Worker*, Paul wrote about the trial of anti-apartheid activists in South Africa, and about Rachmanism among London's landlords. He covered the Watergate scandal in America, and the rights of the Palestinians. He detailed the iniquities of the Prevention of Terrorism Act, which followed the Birmingham and Guildford bombings, and the Protestant workers' strike in Northern Ireland. He wrote about the takeover of Africa by Tiny Rowland of Lonrho, who had bought up cheap national enterprises being sold off by the departing imperialists.[13] And whenever he could, Paul returned to Reginald Maudling, denouncing his decision as home secretary to expel the radical German student leader Rudi Dutschke from Britain – and exposing his complicity in yet another scandal, surrounding the building of a hospital in Gozo, Malta.

He also returned whenever he could to Enoch Powell.

Powell had not let up since 1968, and in 1971 the Conservative government gave in to the pressure with a new Immigration Act. Two years later it came into effect, and directly affected the Windrush generation. These migrants from the Commonwealth had come to Britain as citizens, with the right to live and work in the UK, and to bring their families. But the 1971 Act distinguished between the 'new' and the 'old' Commonwealth. People coming to Britain from the 'old'

– or white – Commonwealth, like Canada, Australia and New Zealand, would still be allowed to come, because their parents or grandparents were British. The restrictions in the Act only applied to the 'new' – or black – commonwealth, the West Indies or East Africa, for example. Yet the workers who had come since 1948 had done so because there were jobs, and those jobs needed filling, argued Paul in *Workers against Racism*, a short pamphlet published by IS as the law came into effect. 'No one in his right mind prefers a winter in Birmingham to the blue skies of Jamaica. But in Jamaica there was no work, and in Birmingham there was work.'[14]

Now that the economic growth of the post-war years had stalled, these workers were no longer welcome, and those already in Britain were blamed for society's ills:

> Tories, who for generations have denied the existence of a shortage in housing or schools, suddenly discover that there are not enough houses or schools and use the statistics of their own shameful record to blame the black workers. Yet their arguments touch a sensitive nerve among white workers who are only too aware of the shortages around them.[15]

Workers were arguing among themselves, wrote Paul, about how to share the crumbs rather than who controlled the cake.

One of the things Paul understood was that racism in the white working class was a real problem. In this, he drew on his experience of a strike at Courtaulds's Red Scar plant in Preston, in the mid 1960s. The plant employed thousands of workers, including hundreds of Asian and Caribbean workers, in their rayon mill, where the machines never stopped, the noise was appalling, and the air was thick with the stench of chemicals. The local union branch of the TGWU negotiated a 50 per cent increase in workload for a meagre 3 per cent increase in wages. All the workers rejected the deal. But on 24 May 1965, management of the section where the Asian and Caribbean workers were concentrated announced the introduction of the speed-up, to start immediately. In response, the workers downed tools. The local trade union official said he could do nothing unless the men went back to work. The workers refused to return. The strike was therefore unofficial, and the rest of the plant was dissuaded by the union from doing anything to support the strikers – the white workers kept working. The strikers were further infuriated when the union official told the local paper that the issues in the strike were racial.[16]

The strike ran on for three bitter weeks, until the black workers returned to work, beaten. A few weeks later, the same speed-up was introduced for the rest of the plant.[17]

Paul's original report on the strike was written for the Institute of Race Relations, which had been such a help when he had written *Immigration and Race* and his book on Powell. During the strike, Paul visited the plant in Preston, and the report shows his forensic approach. He analysed exactly what had happened, carefully establishing what had been said and done, and by whom. He took nothing at face value.

How should the black working class react to such racism in the workplace? By organising separately, concluded A. Sivanandan at the Institute of Race Relations. This was an issue that Sivanandan and Paul quarrelled about, 'mostly on my position that the white working class and its unions were racist', reflected Siva many years later, 'and that the struggles of the Asian and Afro-Caribbean working class had to be autonomous, to begin with'.

'Ideologically, Paul held that the race struggle should be subordinated to the class struggle, that the Black working class would be free when the whole working class became free after socialism's victory.' Sivanandan did not agree. In a long editorial in *Race Today*, he had argued that the trade union movement had blunted the edge of political consciousness among the white working class, too concerned as it was with the effects of exploitation rather than its causes. Whereas for black workers, for whom exploitation was inseparable from racial oppression, 'their economic struggle is at once a political struggle'. To ask them to join the trade union movement 'is to ask them to abnegate their political consciousness and to play down their political role'.[18]

They argued, but did not fall out, remembered Sivanandan: 'We became closer precisely because of that difference, as comrades would, even after my controversial editorial. I think we respected each other's integrity and understood that our paths would be different but would come together at the rendezvous.'

That editorial was written in 1973, a year of turmoil at the IRR, where black activists like Sivanandan and Darcus Howe wanted to shift the organisation's focus away from the purely academic to something more radical and interventionist. Paul and Darcus, who would become the first black editor at *Race Today*, also became friends and political comrades. Their children were at the same school, Beckford Infants, whose head teacher was the Caribbean novelist and poet Beryl Gilroy – the first black school head in Britain. Paul would have admired the way she instilled a love of words in the children in her care. Paul's son Matt remembers how, one Christmas, she persuaded Paul to dress up in red gown and snowy white beard as Father Christmas.

While Paul and Darcus Howe no doubt argued, they had much to share. Darcus was the nephew of C. L. R. James. The Caribbean was a constant point of reference in the Foot family. In 1973, Paul's youngest brother Benjie was the tour manager for Bob Marley's first trip to Britain, organising his band's appearances at the Speakeasy Club in London. Benjie knew Chris Blackwell, the founder of Island Records, who had worked for his father when he was governor of Jamaica. But Benjie's days in the job were probably numbered when he told Marley that he did not think a new song he had written was hit material. The song was 'No Woman, No Cry'.

Marley's music might not have been such a draw for Paul, but West Indian cricket certainly was. So it was no surprise that, when the West Indies played England in 1976, Paul was there, in the front row. Four of them went. Paul, John Deason, the International Socialists' industrial organiser, and Paul Holborow, another IS organiser, all sloped off one Saturday from a meeting of the IS National Committee. It was an important meeting, and their presence was expected. But they made their various excuses about other important things they had to do, and meetings they had to attend. They were joined at Lord's by Geoff Ellen, who worked as a subeditor on *Socialist Worker*. A brilliant shot hit the boundary fence and landed at their feet. 'We knew the camera had caught us', remembers Paul Holborow. 'We looked at each other like naughty schoolboys.' In their defence, it was an important test match. The West Indies had lost the series in Australia the previous year, and the England batsman, Tony Greig, had patronisingly said they would make the West Indies team grovel. But after their test defeat in Australia, the team had worked at a new style of play. They thrashed England: two draws, including that match at Lord's, and three wins. It was the beginning of the ascendency of West Indian cricket, and Paul loved every ball and every stroke.

Powell was not the only person stoking anti-immigration politics at this time. The National Front had grown on the coattails of his speeches, using both violence and the electoral system to recruit to their organisation and expand their influence. In June 1974, both the National Front and a counter-demonstration had been given permission by the police to march to Red Lion Square, albeit at slightly different times. As the counter-marchers came down a narrow street and turned into the square, a pitched battle with the police broke out, erupting into mayhem. Police on horseback weighed in, and the Special Patrol Group gave it their best. A lot of people were injured, and within minutes the lifeless body of Kevin Gately, who had been on the counter-demonstration, was carried out of the crowd to a waiting ambulance by the police, one holding onto his arms, another his legs.

'When you get police diving in with truncheons and horses and somebody is killed in circumstances like this, I would call it murder', said the march organiser the next day. 'Murdered by the police', ran the caption on a poster published by *Socialist Worker*, above a photo of a baton-wielding policeman at the demonstration. Overnight it was stuck up on walls all over London. Somehow, a copy ended up in the hands of Robert Taylor, the Conservative MP for Wandsworth, who brandished it in the House of Commons. What, he demanded to know, was the home secretary going to do about it?

The police duly came knocking. Paul, as editor of *Socialist Worker*, and Jim, as its publisher, were both cautioned. They quickly found lawyers, because this was a serious case: the police were talking about criminal libel.

'We had used a photo of a policeman wielding a baton and seeming to hit someone', says Jim. 'Of course, we were saying it was *a* police officer, not *this* police officer. We should have thought about that.'

Then something strange happened. Serious though it was, the case simply disappeared; they heard no more. Jim thinks that Michael Foot, who was now a minister in the second Wilson government, had intervened. Another possible explanation might have been the presence of a police spy in the ranks of the demonstrators, whose cover needed to be protected. An inquiry into the demonstration, led by Lord Scarman, exonerated the police. Kevin Gately died, and no one was responsible.

That same week in June, when the police visited concerning the poster, was a bad one for Paul and Jim. They also heard that an order had been issued seeking their committal to prison for contempt of court for a story that had appeared in *Socialist Worker* two months earlier.[19] 'Y, oh Lord, oh Why', ran the curious headline over Paul's article about Janie Jones, a woman who provided escorts to wealthy men. She was on trial for blackmailing her rich clients – a charge that relied on those same rich men coming to court as witnesses. While her name was all over the reporting of the case, the judge had decided that the men would be referred to in court as Mr Y and Mr Z.

'For some reason', wrote Paul 'no one is allowed to know who the rich men are.' But Paul named them. Mr Y was, in fact, Lord Y – Lord Belper; and Mr Z was Michael Morris, who described himself as a property developer but was, according to Paul, a 'swindler of some notoriety', a man who had been found guilty of fraud over the collapse of his bank.[20]

Paul decided to name them because a sharp-eared journalist sitting in court had heard the judge admit that he did not in fact have the authority to compel the press not to publish the names. Janie Jones was cheered by Paul's intervention. As the judge was explaining to the jury the 'art of the blackmailer', she got up and shouted: 'I am not a blackmailer. This is not a court of law, this is a joke.' The judge ordered her out, and as she was taken down to the cells below, she shouted again: 'You are biased, judge. Thank God for Paul Foot!'[21] When they were called to give their verdict, the jury unanimously acquitted her of blackmail. But the judge still sent her to prison for a shocking seven years on the much lesser charges of controlling prostitutes and attempting to pervert the course of justice. And he added costs and fines for good measure.

The judge, fuming about Paul's article, referred the matter to the director of public prosecutions, and the case of *R v Socialist Worker* was heard at the High Court later in the year.

The night before the trial began, Paul sat his children down and explained that he might not be coming home. The matter was considered so serious that the judge might send him to prison. Eight-year-old Matt could not believe it. In his childish hand he wrote Paul a letter telling him exactly what he thought: 'I am going to give you a bet that you won't go to prison', he wrote, '10p the amount of money you have to give to me if I win. Love Matty.' His aunt Jill, Michael's wife, also wrote to Paul, wishing him well. Jill Craigie was a staunch feminist, and was no doubt shocked by the way the court was so protective of men. She wrote: 'If you have broken the law – IF – then there is one law for women and another for men.' She couldn't resist a little jab at Paul: 'Are you, by some miracle, basing your plea on the feminist argument? Strangely out of character for a Foot if so.'

Paul had reason to worry. 'He could have probably been hanged 200 years ago', Stephen Sedley jokes. What neither Paul nor Stephen Sedley, who represented *Socialist Worker* in the case, knew at the time was that there was unease about going ahead among those whose decision it was to prosecute. In a letter to the attorney general, the deputy director of prosecutions explained his doubts 'as to whether a judge has power to make an order prohibiting the publication of the names of witnesses. The Director is not as convinced but does feel that the point is capable of argument either way.'[22] They might just lose. In a further letter, having checked what the judge had said by looking at the shorthand note of the proceedings, the case against Paul looked even thinner: 'It appeared that [the judge] had made the observations that he did about not having jurisdiction over the Press.'[23] The Labour attorney general, Sam Silkin, had no such doubts, and prosecuted the case himself.

In his statement to the court, Paul made his thinking plain:

> I regarded this trial of Miss Jones as a glaring example of the unfairness of protecting rich and disreputable witnesses by such informal agreements, particularly when contrasted with the absence of anonymity for less well-connected witnesses in rape and other cases.[24]

The judges sided with their fellow judge, and found Paul and *Socialist Worker* guilty. Was Paul really in danger of going to prison? 'I think the judges would have been wary of making a martyr out of a journalist', is Sedley's view today. Instead they were hit with fines. The sums were not so serious – £500 each; but as they lost, and therefore had to pay the opposing side's costs, the amount owed was huge: Silkin's fees were enormous.

Jim Nichol had set up a defence fund before the case came to court, when people had, with good reason, been shocked that a Labour government was trying to send journalists to prison, and his fundraising proved successful. This was just as well, as he and Paul were in and out of the courts like yoyos.

The following year saw a libel action brought by Clive Jenkins, the leader of the white-collar ASTMS union, which had members in the insurance business. Jenkins's union, like the electricians' union led by Frank Chapple, was at the time offering cheap holidays in Spain to union members, just as its fascist leader General Franco was garrotting his opponents. In response, *Socialist Worker* had some fun with a newly created British Airways advertisement, which offered to 'Fly Me' to all the new and exciting destinations the airline was offering. 'You know me', it read.

> I'm in the insurance business. I give talks to employers' organisations for large fees. Well I'm in the travel business as well. I'd love to take you to Spain, a country ruled by my fellow TUC council member Franco Chapel. What about it? Fly me, I'm Clive.[25]

Jenkins failed to see the funny side.

It was decided that Paul would defend himself, and Stephen Sedley would once again represent the paper, considerably reducing their potential costs. But the judge this time was Melford Stevenson, a notoriously conservative judge, who clearly decided he liked *Socialist Worker* even less than he liked the union man. Paul sat at the front of the court, at a special table for people who were not represented by a barrister, and next to him sat Peter Cook, the publisher of *Private Eye*, who had come to lend moral support. 'He probably did for us', says Stephen Sedley. 'Every time the judge pulled a hostile face, Peter Cook mimicked it to the jury. It became a farce.'

In those days libel trials were heard by juries, who decided both whether there had been a libel and, if so, then decided the level of the fine. The jury also had little liking for *Socialist Worker*, and Jenkins was awarded £1,500 in damages, plus his costs.

Once again, Jim had to pull out the stops to raise the money. It soon flowed in – particularly from members of ASTMS who disliked their own union leader. Sedley thought they had cast-iron grounds for an appeal. But weeks went by, and no instructions appeared. So he phoned the solicitor for *Socialist Worker*, only to discover that 'so much money had poured in from haters of Jenkins, there was enough money to pay all the libel damages and costs and enough for the next two actions as well'.

By June 1975, just fifteen months after he had taken the reins, Paul decided he had had enough, and resigned. He wasn't an editor. He admitted as much himself, even if he loved writing for the paper and would continue to do so.

As editor, Paul's week would begin early on a Monday morning over a fried breakfast in a café near the print shop in Hackney, where he would tear holes in the daily papers, extracting ideas for that week's edition. It was work Paul enjoyed. He didn't even mind the late nights on a Tuesday, working to get the paper finished and downstairs to the plate makers and the printers. Wednesdays were the problem.

'We would work late, eating those terrible take-out kebabs, and on Wednesday mornings we would get a lie in, and Paul would get criticised by the Executive Committee', remembers Peter Clark. Laurie sat opposite Paul in the office. He says that Paul used to come back from that weekly session looking harangued and defeated.

The editorial team was small. Some came for a short time, some stayed for years, some worked part-time, and some were contributors. Duncan Hallas, at the time a member of that Executive Committee, would appear in the office on Monday mornings, ready to write the leaders. Paul had a certain fondness for him. Duncan, he later wrote,

> would grab himself a disgusting coffee, light up an infernal cigarette,
> bark out a few testy comments about the state of the world, and then,
> grabbing a biro or even a pencil, would scribble out in longhand an
> impeccable editorial, not a word out of place. He was the most coher-
> ent socialist I ever knew whether he was writing or speaking.[26]

Another member of the team was Peter Clark, who spent his days busily taking down and typing out the strike reports from around the country. 'It's where I learned to write, in the boiler room of the strikes', he remembers. 'Geoff Ellen would turn my copy into something readable.' He filled the back pages, where a mainstream paper would have sport, each week trying to squeeze in extra stories, cutting them for length, edging them onto more pages of the paper. Geoff Ellen was the paper's cricket-loving subeditor, and he stayed for years, working alongside the long-suffering Peter Marsden. The former editor, Roger Protz, had been able to lay out a paper and had clear design ideas, which made *Socialist Worker* more readable than the other revolutionary papers of its time. Paul had none of that technical skill, so the burden of physically putting the paper together fell on Peter's shoulders.

David Widgery had written for the paper for several years – sometimes as a doctor under a pseudonym, sometimes under his own name. He was thrilled to be contributing to a socialist weekly, and he had very clear ideas of his own. 'It did seem possible and essential to find new forms of socialist journalism', he later wrote, 'to make *Socialist Worker* almost a sort of political billboard on which people who were not used to writing could feel they had the right to paste up their ideas in public.'[27] No doubt there was a yawning gap between David's vision of a 'political billboard' and Tony Cliff's vision of a 'workers' paper'. But David did not flinch from the idea of getting workers to write for the paper. In his column 'Under the Influence', he persuaded car makers, miners, sheet-metal workers, dockers, bus drivers and teachers to share their love of books. They wrote about *The Jungle*, by Upton Sinclair, Howard Fast's *Spartacus*, and *The Floating Republic* – an account of the Spithead Mutiny. They loved Oscar Wilde and Robert Tressell, Sean O'Casey and Tennessee Williams. 'A strike report is fascinating', remembers Nigel Fountain, 'but 'Under the Influence' was the real interest.' Nigel was on the staff, and edited the letters pages, among other things. He also travelled round the country with the band of *Socialist Worker* journalists, including Paul, to the writing schools that were held in the industrial towns, intended to turn workers into writers. 'After ten minutes people wanted to talk about stories and poetry, not "my strike".'

None of it was easy. Just before Christmas 1974, David Widgery wrote to Paul complaining about a story Paul had spiked. 'I am not complaining about you not bothering to make the slightest effort to contact me', he wrote. 'I am complaining about your political judgement.' And on it went, paragraph after paragraph. But there he was the next Monday morning, looking sheepish. He had a deep commitment to the paper and to trying to make it work.

Paul remembered hearing Widgery speak at the IS conference in 1973, about *Socialist Worker* – how and where it was produced, who wrote for it, the process of production, what a miracle it all was. 'His words, full of wit, came tumbling out, it seemed, almost by accident and yet in perfect order, and the whole hall was lit up in vicarious enthusiasm.' Paul had a particular love for David's use of language. 'He was the only person I ever knew who used "proletariat" unselfconsciously, as though it came from the chorus of a popular rock band.'[28]

A few months later, a second letter arrived. 'As someone who believed with all my instincts in the changes proposed by Paul and Cliff last summer', wrote Widgery, 'and accomplished with such turmoil, I feel pretty cynical about the rather small result of such a destructive episode.' What annoyed David more than anything was the interference of the political full-timers who served on the Executive Committee, and their appointed advisory committees.

> Their pressure will inevitably be towards a more narrowly 'political', homogeneous and frankly boring paper with even greater scepticism about imaginative writing, moral expression, humour, first person description, genuinely polemical writing . . . all those forms which have characterised the most successful working-class journalism in British labour history.

David had resigned.

Remembering those letters years later, after David had died, Paul had a longer perspective on what had happened:

> We can look back now and easily trace how the enthusiasm and inspirations of the early 1970s were snared in Wilsonian pragmatism. While the Tories were in, lots of workers listened eagerly to

calls for revolution. When Labour won in February [1974] and then confirmed their position a few months later, the mood changed. All our moods changed too.[29]

Paul missed David, and not just for his writing. 'He had a terrible temper, but none of his invective was ever ill-considered. That was the worst of those editorial board meetings. His criticisms cut like knives because they were (at least partly) justified.' He missed something else, too. 'At times, lying in bed at night with the SW pages rolling round in the darkness, I would yearn for some plain good prose, something which people would enjoy reading for its own sake, even if the line was slightly dubious.'[30]

11

Vote for Foot

'Dear brave Hercules, what a "socialist" policy this is.' *Socialist Worker's* front page at the start of 1976 ran an open letter to Harold Wilson from Jack Cummins, a widower and engineer from Bolton. He described the life of his young daughter Alison, aged just eight, who was dying of a rare disease. Jack had been turned down for attendance allowance to pay for a nurse to care for Alison. Not long before, his wife had also been refused the same allowance for the same illness – and her letter of refusal had arrived in the post the day after they had buried her.

Jack was a fighter, as was his daughter. 'You slash the living standards of the sick', he wrote, 'the elderly, the one-parent families, all the sections of the community who need help most but who you look upon as fair game because of their inability to hit back.'[1]

By 1976, the great strikes for higher pay and better working conditions of 1972 and the militancy that defeated the Tory government in 1974, had given way to something very different. The Labour Party had fought the 1974 election on a manifesto that promised 'to bring about a fundamental and irreversible shift in the balance of power and wealth in favour of working people and their families', wrote Paul in a short *Stop the Cuts* pamphlet.[2] Now the Labour government was slashing public spending. It had been, in the party's own words, 'blown off course' by an economic recession not of its own making. Michael Foot talked of an 'economic typhoon' and 'a plague' of inflation and unemployment. This, argued Paul, was nonsense. The crisis was not caused by the weather in the Pacific or an outbreak of illness. 'The causes of the recession are human causes.' And the remedies were human remedies. To illustrate his point, Paul picked out one name: Edward du Cann.

Du Cann was a senior Tory MP, chairman of the prestigious Commons Public Accounts Committee, a director of Lonrho, and chairman of Keyser Ullman, the biggest fringe bank to collapse in the 1974 banking crisis, owing millions. He had made a fortune out of the orgy of profit-making that had preceded the crash – but when asked about the economic crisis, his solution was to cut public expenditure. He believed the culprits were 'non-productive workers' – people who worked in hospitals and schools, drove buses and trains, emptied the bins and delivered the post. All were a drain on the public purse. The crassness of this idea drove Paul to fury.

While cutting public spending, the Labour government was busily reducing tax for companies. Paul quoted the *Economist*, which lauded the chancellor, Denis Healey, as the businessman's friend, who had 'emphatically paved the way for higher profits and investment . . . profit is a clean word again.'[3] 'All over the city of London, everywhere rich men gather together,' Paul wrote, 'they are grinning at their success in persuading the Labour Government to cut the workers' standard of living.' Don't leave politics to the politicians, exhorted Paul – no one voted for these cuts. 'They are imposed by a weak, shambling government in the interests of a reckless and greedy class.'

The pamphlet was published for the Right to Work campaign, which toured workplaces, unions, towns and cities up and down the country. It also organised marches, the first of which was from Manchester to London. The march began on Saturday 28 February 1976, with a rally addressed by Harry McShane, the secretary of the Scottish Unemployed Workers' Movement in the 1930s. Harry was there to make a speech and wave off the eighty, mostly young, unemployed workers at the start of their long walk. They slept overnight in church halls, took baths with the Yorkshire miners, and were greeted by 4,000 people in a great rally in the Albert Hall when they made it to London. Harry McShane had travelled south by more conventional means, and was once again on the platform, alongside Paul, Ricky Tomlinson, and the campaign organiser John Deason.

The rally was held in the afternoon, and Paul's two boys were there with him. Soon after they were all together again, as Paul drove Rose and the boys to Skegness, which 'Is So Bracing', according to the tourist board's advertising slogan for this popular seaside resort on England's chilly east coast. It was also home to the Derbyshire Mine Workers' Holiday Camp, which was, as the name suggests, a holiday resort – a bit like Butlins or Pontins, but for coalminers and their families, with accommodation available to other groups. Paul had been there before, with Gus Macdonald and the Young Socialists. This time the International Socialists had booked for their members and their families over the Easter weekend in 1976.

The Foot boys loved it. There was five-a-side football, competitive sport of every sort, and Leeds IS beat Marnham Colliery 8–2 in the football final. There was also a bar the size of a football pitch. Peter Heathfield, the president of the Derbyshire Miners, addressed the assembled socialists, and Paul spoke on the poet Shelley's revolutionary politics. He had studied Shelley at school, and then in 1974 discovered a very different Shelley in the pages of a magnificent new biography by Richard Holmes: Shelley the atheist and republican, the Leveller and feminist.[4] The confluence of poetry and revolutionary politics was a gift.

All Paul's talks were something of a performance. They required practice and preparation, and would include carefully crafted jokes and funny voices. A pile of books would have their pages marked in advance for quotation. His notes, by contrast, were scrappy, on pages of A4 torn in half, which he kept, slipped inside a relevant book, to be recycled for the next occasion. His Shelley notes eventually ran to dozens of pages, with repeated page numbers, no longer decipherable in any coherent form.

The talk on Shelley would grow into a book. It also set the pattern for future talks during what became an annual IS trip to Skegness. The following year, Paul talked about Tom Paine and *The Rights of Man*, and in 1978 about Toussaint L'Ouverture, the Black Jacobin leader of the Haitian Revolution. These were followed by Louise Michel and the Paris Commune, and John Reed, the author of *Ten Days That Shook the World* – one of the best books about the Russian revolution, according to Paul. Reed was exactly the sort of journalist Paul admired, 'a war correspondent, a class war correspondent' in the US, before he went to Russia.

He was nervous, remembers his son John, before these big set pieces, which was quite unusual for someone for whom public speaking was such a pleasure. John noticed something else as well. Paul sometimes had company on those long walks along the beach when he was supposed to be practising his speeches. 'We began to realise there were women at Skegness', he remembers.

Rose only went that first time. In the following years, Paul would take the boys along with John Rose, one of the *Socialist Worker* journalists, stopping on the drive up for a curry at Boston in Lincolnshire. After that, they would have to survive on the large quantities of terrible food that were the staple at the camp.

Between the Right to Work rally in the Albert Hall in March and the Skegness holiday camp in April, Harold Wilson had unexpectedly resigned as prime minister. He claimed this had been long planned, but there was gossip about plots against him by the South African intelligence services. After a hotly contested vote within the Parliamentary Labour Party, James Callaghan took over as prime minister. In the first round, Michael Foot led the field, ahead of five other contenders – Callaghan, Roy Jenkins, Tony Benn, Anthony Crosland and Denis Healey. After winning the final vote, Callaghan continued with the same policies as Wilson. But there were a series of by-elections ahead, and the International Socialists decided they would stand candidates – not with the aim of winning seats, but because an election is a good time to be making political propaganda. If the campaigns were successful, perhaps they could stand as many as fifty candidates in the next general election.

The first two by-elections were in Newcastle upon Tyne and Walsall. Paul travelled up to the Midlands to support Jimmy McCallum, the IS candidate. Nigel Fountain was helping to run the campaign, and he remembers Paul and Jimmy speaking at one meeting in a local infant school, balanced on tiny chairs, with next to no one in the audience. At the end of the meeting two West Indians approached Paul. 'We know you', they told him, and Paul asked which strike or meeting they were talking about. But they had recognised him from earlier than that – at a cricket match between small boys in Jamaica. Finally, the penny dropped: 'I bowled all day and couldn't get either of you out!' As Jimmy was a friend of Paul's, the two men agreed to vote for him.

It made little difference to McCallum's vote, although he proudly remembers that, of all the by-elections in which the International Socialists stood candidates, he got more votes than anyone else. Using his newspaper skills, Nigel produced a local give-away edition of *Socialist Worker* for the election. As he distributed copies, a BBC reporter asked him why the IS candidate was standing as a *Socialist Worker* candidate. 'Are you going to become the Socialist Workers Party?' he asked. 'Yes', replied Nigel, 'that's what we will be doing.' He knew no such thing. But he was right: the International Socialists soon became the Socialist Workers Party.

The debate about the name change took place at that year's IS conference. Paul, Jim Nichol and Tony Cliff agreed with the idea of the International Socialists becoming a party, but favoured the name the Socialist Party, rather than the Socialist Workers Party. The latter won the day, and in the pages of *Socialist Worker* Cliff explained the change as a shift from propaganda to action – although the Socialist Workers Party, he wrote, had 'no illusions of grandeur, we are still in the fourth division'.[5] Inside the organisation, the perspective, for some, was much bolder: the organisation would double its size by Christmas, the circulation of *Socialist Worker* would reach 50,000, and the number of workplace units touch one hundred. This was all rather optimistic.[6]

To mark the launch of the party in January 1977, Paul wrote a new pamphlet, *Why You Should Be a Socialist* – almost a short book, at just under a hundred pages, and echoing John Strachey's 1938 pamphlet of the same title.[7] Strachey's pamphlet sold 349,000 copies in nine editions, 'and did as much to enthuse a generation with socialist ideas as Blatchford's *Merrie England* had done before the First World War', Paul explained in *Socialist Worker*.[8] This was the pre-war Strachey – Strachey the Marxist; the man who explained the causes and meaning of fascism; the man who savaged the leaders of the Labour Party and exposed the bankruptcy of social democracy. Not the post-war Strachey, the Labour politician of the 1950s and 1960s who became the very person his younger self had ridiculed.

'The thirty years dream is over', Paul began the pamphlet. 'Since the end of the Second World War, people have imagined that things will get better. Now they are not getting better. They are getting worse.' His opening lines made grim reading: British people were eating less meat, less milk, fewer eggs. Council house rents were rising. The cost of electricity was set to double. In the previous two years, 5 million more people had fallen below the government's poverty line. 'There is plenty of beef, butter, cheese; plenty of milk and eggs. There are plenty of hungry people. But somehow the hungry and the food do not meet.' In the pamphlet's pages, Paul rehearses the familiar arguments about where wealth comes from, who controls it, the waste of resources on things like advertising. He revisits some of the arguments he had used in *Stop the Cuts* and, having analysed the problem, gets to the crux of the matter: What to put in its place?

In a word, it was socialism – socialism built on three principles. The first was the social ownership of the means of production, the factories, the machines, the chemical plants and printing presses, the pits, the building materials – everything that produced wealth. 'If the means of production are owned by society as a whole, then it becomes impossible for one group of people to grow rich from other people's work.'[9] The second was equality: 'The rewards which people get out of society for what they do should not differ just because their abilities differ.' It is a notion that is often ridiculed because people are not the same. Of course they are not, Paul argued. Equality simply means the rewards should not differ. The third principle was workers' democracy – not the conventional, parliamentary style of democracy but something infinitely more dynamic, with one caveat: accountability 'of the representative to the represented'. This meant discussion and argument, as well as elections: 'Far more elections than there are at present, and at many different levels.'[10]

Could it work? People were not instinctively greedy, he argued. And the way things were at present did not guarantee that the rich were always decent, or clever, or capable of taking the best decisions. There were plenty of examples of the opposite, of people with 'the ability to bluff, bully or bribe their way to greater riches'.[11] But how can this ideal society come about? Although the Labour Party was committed to socialism – which was written into its constitution – the words of the party and the actions of Labour governments were miles apart.

Paul made his way through the history, and concluded that the Labour Party had changed from the campaigning organisation it had once been – an organisation that owned newspapers and published millions of leaflets – into a machine for pulling in the vote. Its focus had become parliament alone. The problem with this was that there was 'no prospect whatever of the class with property abandoning that property just because a parliament says so'. That required a different strategy. The working class had the power to change society. 'They can rock capitalism back on its heels, but they will only knock it out if they have the organisation, the socialist party, which can show the way to a new, socialist order of society.'[12] 'We socialists are not fanatics or time-servers', Paul concludes:

> We are socialists because we see the prospect which life holds out for all working people. We want the commitment of workers who laugh and love and want to end the wretchedness and despair which shuts love and laughter out of so many lives. Society *can* be changed, but only if masses of working people abandon the rotten shipwreck of the 'leave it to us' reformers and commit themselves to change from below.[13]

As copies went on sale, Paul set off on a speaking tour across the country. He travelled to Glasgow; to Liverpool and Bootle in the north-west – including a meeting at noon for workers at the shipbuilders Cammel Laird in Birkenhead; to Lowestoft in the east; to Gloucester and Cheltenham in the south-west; and to dozens of workplaces and colleges in between. The *Sunday Times* caught up with him in Islington. At that meeting, their reporter wrote,

> A man at the back stood up to say: 'I've got this uncle, and he's always saying you can't have a revolution without violence.' Foot had an easy way out of that question: 'I've got an uncle who is always saying the same thing.'

Then, for the reporter's benefit, Paul added after the meeting: 'I've learnt a lot from him. But I've often got to be rude about him in my speeches now.' He was not going to dinner with his uncle Michael as often as people thought he did. Paul would be forty in 1977, the *Sunday*

Times concluded. 'He's going to spend his 40th year preaching revolution, practising his leg glance, and starting a book on Shelley.'[14] Thirty thousand copies of *Why You Should Be a Socialist* were printed, and sold out in just six weeks.

The by-elections continued throughout 1977, and the new Socialist Workers Party stood in all of them, including Stechford in Birmingham, where Paul himself was the candidate.

The midlands had been hit hard by government cuts, and, as Paul wrote in *Socialist Worker*,

> we are standing to build an alternative to Labour. We aim to search out and bring together all those people in Birmingham who are fed up with years of Labour betrayal and who want to take part in a fight back against the Social Contract, the cuts, unemployment, racialism and every other aspect of a corrupt society.[15]

Paul threw himself into the campaign. He had just arrived in Birmingham when he bumped into an estate agent who immediately offered him an office for the duration of the election. From this base, the local SWP members toured the vast working-class housing estates looking for *Socialist Worker* sales and votes, knocking on the doors of homes and pubs. As Sheila McGregor, the local organiser, recalls, 'It was quite tough, and we had to go out in groups. Those were scary times.' They were scary because the National Front was also standing in the election. But Paul was not to be put off. Going door to door might pull in votes and get people talking, but he also needed publicity. He called a press conference and denounced corruption in Birmingham public life. The *Birmingham Evening Mail* reported him saying it was so rife that 'it makes the Poulson scandals look like "cheating at a vicarage whist drive".'[16] Sure enough, a few days later the same paper reported on its front page that the chairman and managing director of the largest construction group in the midlands was one of four top building executives facing corruption charges.[17]

The radical vote, such as it was, was split between the SWP and the International Marxist Group. As Tariq Ali, then a member of the IMG, remembers, it would have made sense for them to have had one united candidate. But it was not to be; neither organisation would countenance it. But Tariq would not stand against Paul, although he was the most obvious candidate in an area with a substantial Pakistani population. He was probably the most famous Pakistani in Britain at the time, and his speeches during the campaign attracted great crowds of Pakistani workers, which secured the IMG more votes than the SWP.

One candidate or two was not going to make that much difference. The vacancy had arisen because Roy Jenkins, the incumbent Labour MP, who had held the seat with a 12,000 majority, had gone off to be president of the European Commission. But the popularity of the Labour Party was on the wane. And Margaret Thatcher was the new leader of the Conservatives, with her eyes firmly on the prize.

The Tory snatched the seat from Labour – and the National Front, with slightly under 3,000 votes, beat the Liberals into third place. By comparison, Paul's 377 votes and the IMG candidate's 494 (just 2.5 per cent between them) suggested the radical ideas of the early '70s were making little significant progress. More by-elections followed, but the numbers of votes gained by the SWP candidates continued to be poor. The plan for fifty candidates at the general election was dropped. By the following year, the policy had been wound up.

In these election campaigns, however, the National Front was just getting into its stride.

12

Honey on the Elbow

In the summer of 1976 Eric Clapton, one of the best-known musicians in Britain, stood on stage and ranted for Powell: 'Vote for Enoch Powell . . . Stop Britain becoming a black colony!'

Red Saunders, the photographer and director, was outraged. He sat down and drafted a letter to the music press. 'What's going on Eric?' he wrote. 'Own up. Half your music is black.' And, in a reference to Clapton's latest hit, 'Who shot the Sheriff, Eric? It sure as hell wasn't you!'[1] Co-signing the letter was Roger Huddle, a friend of Red's and a graphic designer in the *Socialist Worker* print shop. At the end, they asked anyone interested in a movement against the racism poisoning rock music to write to Rock Against Racism, care of the SWP's Cottons Gardens address. The letters poured in in their hundreds.

Rock Against Racism club nights soon followed, as did their zany publication *Temporary Hoarding*. David Widgery interviewed Johnny Rotten of the Sex Pistols for *Socialist Worker*: 'The Tories, the NF, the Queen and me.'[2] Soon after, RAR adopted the Pistols' famous slogan: 'NF = No Future, No Fun'.

During the late 1970s, the racist poison of the National Front was spreading thick and fast. Its members were marching in places as dispersed as Blackburn, Southall, Walsall, Rotherham and Grays. A terrifying level of violence was spreading, too. One morning, Jack Robertson arrived at the *Socialist Worker* print shop in Cottons Gardens to find the entire building ablaze. It had been fire-bombed. Just up the road, in Dalston, the Centerprise Bookshop also went up in flames.

In the pages of the literary magazine *Books and Bookmen*, while reviewing a book by Martin Walker on the National Front, Paul spelled out the scale of the problem. 'During the great racialist onslaught of the summer of 1976', he wrote,

> so carefully orchestrated by the *Daily Mail*, the *Sun*, Enoch Powell and the National Front, racialist outrages increased in every area where black people live. In literally hundreds of cases, many of them unreported, black people were attacked, and their homes were petrol-bombed. That is what the rise of the National Front means in practice.[3]

In one small area of East London, the Bethnal Green and Stepney Trades Council documented over a hundred vicious racist attacks that occurred between January 1976 and August 1978. The local black population, mostly Bengalis, as well as West Indians and Somalis, were harassed by the racists. They smashed their windows, pushed petrol-soaked rags through their letter boxes, painted racist slogans on their front doors. They attacked people with knives and stones in their homes, or as they left for work. They attacked children on their way home from school. And while this violent mayhem was happening, the BBC lifted its ban on giving the National Front airtime, because they were 'campaigning constitutionally for seats in Parliament'. Standing in elections, local and national, had added a sheen of respectability to their activities, and was garnering the National Front large numbers of votes and seats on local councils. It would never have happened under the old order at the Corporation, grumbled Paul.[4]

Paul was not happy with Martin Walker's book, in which Walker referred to his National Front friends. The racialists 'do not want a society where argument and reason prevail', he wrote. 'They want the rule of the dictator and the bully.'[5] There was only one way to deal with them: they had to be confronted head-on.

When the National Front planned a march in London's Wood Green in April 1977, the counter-demonstrators were out in large numbers, ready for a fight. And they were out again four months later when the Front marched in Lewisham. Paul knew something about the background to the Lewisham march. In *Socialist Worker* he described a police raid on a house in Childeric Road, New Cross, in the early morning of 30 May. The police had smashed down the front door with an axe, and gone on a rampage, 'overturning furniture, ripping open drawers, and turning black people out of their beds'. Across south-east London sixty young blacks were arrested that day. It was, according to the police, part of its anti-mugging campaign. Paul had heard a different account of what happened. Outside the magistrates' court, a policeman in conversation with a bus inspector had explained that this was 'Operation PNH – police n****r hunt'.[6]

So, when the National Front chose to march to Lewisham in August, starting out from New Cross, there was as much anger with the police as against the Front. A crowd of thousands gathered in a counter-demonstration, and the NF was confined to the back streets, where, under police protection and a hail of missiles, they eventually abandoned their march. But by the end of the day, after the racists had been escorted away, the demonstration turned into something else: a running battle between the police and the young, local and very angry black population.

Not long after, Paul had his own run-in with the police – not on the streets, but in the pages of the in-house magazine for Britain's police force. 'Panellist on Radio's *Any Questions*, TV pundit, editor of *Socialist Worker*', the article in *Police* began, 'Paul (Hanratty was innocent) Foot worked hard for the glorious Shrewsbury Two, spurred no doubt by memories of his own suffering schooldays at Shrewsbury Public School.'[7] The cause of this extraordinary outburst? A mass picket outside the Grunwick film-processing laboratory in north-west London, where a long-running dispute had led to weekly pickets supported by large numbers of socialists and trade unionists.

The dispute had begun quietly enough in August 1976, with a simple demand for trade union recognition. But by the summer of 1977 it had become a battleground for trade union rights. Against the workers stood the police, who had no love of the pickets – or, more specifically, their supporters: 'They ensure that, come what may, people will be arrested as grist to the martyr's mill, police helmets will fly and the time-honoured cry of "police brutality" will echo down the corridors of the Police Complaints Board.' And there, in a photo next to the article, circled in bright pink, is the face of Paul Foot.

Except that the picture doesn't look remotely like him. The photo had been taken on the Grunwick picket line – and, while Paul was often there, on that particular day he was not. The magazine had to apologise and give Paul space for a written reply defending the strike and the mass picket. 'What would your members have done in such a situation?' he asked. 'You want a free trade union and the right to strike for policemen. Why? Because you know that any trade union organisation is useless unless it has the right to strike, *and to make that strike effective*.'[8]

The Grunwick strike lasted for nearly two years. Many of the company's poorly paid, mostly female, mostly Asian workforce had stood up for their right to belong to a trade union. They had almost no industrial clout, as they printed people's holiday snaps. And they worked for a belligerent and overbearing master called George Ward, who refused to negotiate, and within days had sacked all those on strike. He was helped by employees who continued to work, but critical support came from the NAFF, the National Association for Freedom – a group of rich industrialists and ultraconservatives whose limitless funds were used to help Ward fight the unions through the courts. On the other side, Brent Trades Council did everything they could to support the strike. But the most important support came from workers at the local Post Office, who put themselves on the front line by voting to keep the company's mail marooned at the Cricklewood sorting office. For a company run entirely by the postal service, it was a disaster. It was unable to get its post in or out of its factory, until one Saturday night when the NAFF was let into the plant, took out the mail sacks, and used a network of volunteers to drive Grunwick's post to hundreds of country post boxes.

On Monday, 13 June 1977, the police arrested eighty-four out of one hundred pickets. This was a publicity disaster for the police, and galvanised support for the strike. George Ward decided to bring his workers in by bus – and there was only one way to stop a bus: a call went out for mass pickets. Through late June and July, the numbers on the picket line grew, as thousands of trade unionists made their way to the narrow streets around the plant. The police were there in numbers, the Special Patrol Group was on call. Hundreds were injured, and hundreds more arrested – the Labour MP Audrey Wise and the Yorkshire miners' leader Arthur Scargill among them.[9]

The strike was debated in both houses of parliament, and the national press worked itself into a lather of fury against the unions. At the *Sun*, on 1 July 1977, a blank space appeared instead of an editorial condemning the strike. The printers refused to print the paper at all if the editorial was included.

In response to the arrests and violence, the unions called a day of action for Monday, 11 July. Eighteen thousand people massed on the picket line, and the Grunwick boss was on the verge of defeat.

Later in the year, as Paul looked back on what had happened, he argued that the national trade union leadership had done everything it could, at this crucial moment, to undermine the strike. They supported the strikers – Paul quoted Len Murray, TUC general secretary: 'We're with you all the way'; and Roy Grantham, general secretary of APEX, the strikers' own union: 'The strikers are fighting nineteenth century conditions. Their case is one of the strongest I've ever seen'; and Tom Jackson, general secretary of the postal workers who were blocking the post from being delivered: 'If we can't win at Grunwick, then we can't win anywhere.' But these men were terrified of the mass action, and of losing control over events. Crucially, they got the mail moving again. The UPW, the postal workers' union, threatened their own members with expulsion from the union – a threat that could have led to the loss of their jobs – if they did not lift their ban on handling Grunwick's post. The Cricklewood postmen were in tears as they gave the news to the strike committee. Meanwhile, APEX threatened to withdraw their union membership unless they stopped the mass pickets.

In early November, 8,000 supporters massed on the picket line facing 4,000 police in one last bid to bring the factory to a halt. In response, police waded in, and managed to get a busload of strike-breakers into the plant. A senior police inspector jeered at the pickets: 'You've lost, and you know it.' He was right; the strike was lost – and the pickets knew it, including Paul.

In his article reflecting on the strike, Paul quoted Jayaben Desai, one of the most prominent of the strike leaders. Her image, showing

her dressed in her sari and cardigan, dominated every national newspaper and media outlet: 'Official trade union action is like honey on
the elbow', she said. 'You can smell it, you can see it. But you can never
taste it.'[10]

Rock against Racism, the Anti-Nazi League, clashes with the National
Front, the response of young black people and Asian communities to
the assaults – all of these were bringing a new, younger, more diverse
readership to *Socialist Worker*. The paper looked tired and out of date,
and it needed a new direction. The Central Committee agreed that Jim
Nichol would become the editor.

Paul had tried editing *Socialist Worker*, and had given up. He was
a journalist, not an editor. Jim was no editor either, nor even a journalist; but he did have ideas, and he knew how to get things done and, he
reflects, 'Paul and Laurie thought I could achieve something they
couldn't, and together we could transform the paper.'

Jim took over during a firefighters' strike that began in November
1977, then ran through Christmas and into 1978. There was strong
public support for the strike, which only increased when the government announced it would draft in the army. But it ended in a rotten
deal, no better than the one that had been rejected at the start, and
Paul spelled out the myriad ways in which the union officials had
themselves dampened down their own strike and then sold it out: 'The
firemen were quite prepared to take on the government, the employers, even the TUC. They were beaten not by any of these – but by their
own leaders.'[11]

In February 1978, the 'new' *Socialist Worker* was officially launched.
Inside, Paul had a regular column, as well as writing feature pieces;
Eamonn McCann wrote the television column; Chris Harman contributed one on Marxism made easy; and Nick Pitt, the sports journalist,
had the most innovative column of all: 'This Sporting Life'. Laurie was
the features editor, and new faces were pulled in from other parts of
the SWP organisation.[12]

Writers from outside the office were welcomed, too. The SWP
branch inside the Desoutter engineering factory, just up the road from
Grunwick, wrote about Dadaism. Workers at the Lucas plant at
Fazakerley, who made components for the motor industry, wrote

about the closure of their factory, as retold by the Prophet and the Pharaoh: 'And there was a gnashing of teeth and a tearing of boiler suits . . .'[13] Dave Batley, a member of the NUM at Wath Main colliery in Yorkshire, dealt delightfully with the sell-out of the miners' claim, written as a play: a tragic farce in six acts. And Paul recruited a new journalist to the paper, a young man called Alan Gibbons, who was amazed to find himself interviewing musicians like Tom Robinson, then an icon for Gay rights and anti-racism, who would go on to play at the Victoria Park Carnival – the brainchild of Jim Nichol, and organised by Rock Against Racism and the newly formed Anti-Nazi League.

Launched the previous November, just as Jim was taking the reins at *Socialist Worker*, the Anti-Nazi League was another of his bright ideas, bringing together many of the disparate organisations campaigning against racism on the narrow issue of defeating the new nazis of the National Front. Paul Holborow became its national organiser, and Peter Hain, who had organised the Stop the Seventies rugby tour against the South African rugby team, joined him as press officer. Ernie Roberts, an engineering union official and soon-to-be Labour MP, acted as its political scout, signing up dozens of Labour MPs and several trade union general secretaries. 'Ernie Roberts's role was very important', remembers Hain. 'He started with Audrey Wise, then recruited Neil and Glenys Kinnock.' The roll-call of famous names across politics, sport and the arts just kept on growing.

The Carnival was huge. Its organisers thought it would be a success if 10,000 turned up. No one had imagined it might attract an 80,000-strong audience; the idea of starting with an anti-racism rally in Trafalgar Square, and then marching five miles to Victoria Park in the East End, seemed like madness. But they did so, with banners, floats and flags, passing on their way the pubs where the National Front hung out.

'Magic!' was the single word on the front page of *Socialist Worker* the following week, accompanied by a photo of Tom Robinson on stage and a crowd stretching as far as the eye could see. The four centre pages contained nothing but photos – no text except for the names of performers: Poly Styrene, The Clash, Steel Pulse, Sham 69, 90 Degrees.[14]

Two weeks later, on election night, a young machinist called Altab Ali was stabbed on his way home, and died in the street in Whitechapel, his neck pierced by a knife. By the following day it was clear the National Front had been humiliated in the local council elections.

The Carnival editions were the first of a series of *Socialist Worker* specials, all with dramatically different front pages than the usual diet of political news. A month later, a special edition for the 1978 World Cup being played in Argentina – then a military dictatorship – caused some political grief. 'Enjoy the goals but remember the jails', was the front-page headline, over a Phil Evans cartoon of a blindfolded dissident tied to a goalpost. Inside, there was sports news on the teams, alongside the politics of the countries they played for. Some members had called for a boycott, but the *Socialist Worker* journalists thought differently. Jim Nichol knew its readers would watch anyway, boycott or not.

A celebration of the fiftieth anniversary of women winning the vote followed a week later, with the masthead *Socialist Worker* printed in purple, and a cat with green eyes dominating the front page. Inside, the articles were almost all either written by women or about women's struggles. They told the story of the working-class women in the Lancashire cotton mills who had campaigned for the vote in 1905. In an interview, Connie Lewcock, then eighty-four, described her campaign for suffrage among the miners of Northumberland and Durham, and their help in burning down Eshwinning railway station when the militant phase of the suffragette campaign began.[15]

Paul took up the story of the militants. Despite the eight occasions between 1870 and 1912 when MPs had tried to pass bills in parliament giving votes to women, the Liberal government would not pass any of them into law. The campaign for the vote had grown in size and militancy, and politicians were heckled whenever they spoke in public. Meanwhile, posh houses and letter boxes were being set on fire, every window in the department stores of central London was broken, and 'Votes for Women' was carved in acid on golf greens. The government reacted by sending the women to prison, and force-feeding them when they went on hunger strike in protest. The final indignity was the introduction in 1913 of the Act – widely known as the 'Cat and

Mouse Act' – which allowed women on hunger strike to be released until they were fit, and then rearrested, repeatedly.[16]

In his article, Paul also challenged the muddled thinking about supporting the women's campaign. 'It is fashionable today', he wrote, 'among socialists and revolutionaries to denounce the suffrage movement.' Two of the Pankhursts, Emmeline and Christabel, ended up supporting the First World War, and 'all sorts of crackpottery'. But, he argued 'those who concentrate upon them cannot see the trees for the bark.' The suffrage agitation had beckoned a generation of women out of the gloom, and, with courage and ingenuity, they had wrested the vote from a reluctant ruling class.[17]

By then, *Socialist Worker* was doing well. The Carnival edition had a bumper print run, and paid sales of over 27,000 copies. But the paper achieved a level of public recognition way beyond its sales. 'Paul brought it that profile', says Jim. 'It had a huge profile in the media and in the unions.'

But hot on the heels of the women's edition of the paper came the SWP annual conference. As it turned out, none of the editorial team had prepared for the opposition to their efforts that had been brewing. The paper was mauled by the delegates. They disliked the World Cup special, and they criticised Paul's political line on the suffragettes. A conference resolution declared that the paper had lost its way. It was the death-knell for their efforts, and Jim's position as editor was now on the line. The Central Committee tried a compromise, keeping Jim as editor, but appointing Chris Harman as political editor. That was never going to work as the paper would effectively have two editors. Paul and Laurie made it clear that if Jim went, they would too. Their joint letter of resignation was written on 18 July 1978: 'We wanted a break not with our politics – but with the style and language in which they have in the past been presented', they wrote. 'We had scarcely begun to make the changes which we believed were needed.'

What were they to do? Jim continued working for the SWP for a while, and then retrained as a lawyer. Laurie left to join the team at *World in Action*, making investigative television documentaries with Gus Macdonald and Ray Fitzwalter. Alan Gibbons fled back home to Liverpool as the paper's northern correspondent, then retrained as a primary school teacher and started writing children's books. Paul, meanwhile, had by this time worked on *Socialist Worker* for six years. His arrival in 1972 had been at the high point of a great political upsurge. In 1978 things were very different, and less than a year later Margaret Thatcher would become prime minister, inaugurating a long era of economic neoliberalism. The welfare state was to be cut at every opportunity; the trade unions defeated and hobbled.

With the passage of time, an understanding of the wider changes that had taken place in the second half of the 1970s became clearer. Twenty years later, Paul wrote to Tony Cliff, giving an account of how they had misread the political movement at the time. Rather than understanding the political collapse that was taking place around them – the downturn in political struggle – they had become entranced by the Right to Work campaign, the firemen's strike and the Anti-Nazi League. Confused by the situation, they had turned on each other, and came close to tearing the whole organisation apart.[18]

13

The Ditto Man

Paul was forty when he left *Socialist Worker* in 1978, and he had neither money nor a job. So, he went back to *Private Eye*, and, as he put it, 'hovered about'. Richard was, of course, very pleased to see him. 'I remember him taking me for a walk through Covent Garden', he later remembered, 'and telling me that Jeremy Thorpe was about to be arrested. He wanted to predict that this was going to happen. It is not every day that the leader of a political party is charged with conspiracy to murder, so any story to this effect was sensational, not to say fraught with risk.'[1]

Jeremy Thorpe, the Liberal MP for North Devon, was a great friend of Paul's uncle John. He was charismatic – a favourite with the younger Foot children because he was funny and such a good mimic – and always easy to spot in his trademark trilby hat. He had risen through the ranks of the Liberal Party in the 1960s, until he became its leader in 1967. By 1978 the party was doing well in parliament, with Labour increasingly relying on their votes to keep the government going. But Thorpe also harboured a dark secret: he was a homosexual when homosexuality was a criminal offence.

The story of Thorpe and his relationship with Norman Scott had had its first outing in the pages of *Private Eye* in a short diary piece by Auberon Waugh. He described an incident on Exmoor, in Devon, when Norman Scott was found weeping beside the body of his Great Dane, after the dog had been shot dead. 'Information about this puzzling incident has since been restricted', he wrote. 'My only hope is that sorrow over his friend's dog will not cause Mr Thorpe's premature retirement from public life.'[2] Three months later, Andrew Newton, an airline pilot, stood trial, accused of shooting the dog. In his evidence at Newton's trial, Norman Scott claimed that Newton had intended to kill him as well as the dog, but at the crucial moment the gun jammed. All of this the *Eye* reported, as well as Newton's conviction and Thorpe's resignation as leader of the Liberals, which followed soon after. But a much murkier story about Thorpe was bubbling under the surface.

On the same day that Newton's trial began, Harold Wilson had announced his resignation as prime minister, much to the surprise of the media and most of his Labour MPs. A couple of days later Wilson rang the BBC and asked that they investigate the activities of South African intelligence in British political life. The director general's office rang Gordon Carr, a friend of Paul's, and gave him the job. Gordon started work, following up on the various hints and clues that Wilson had given him; there was a limit to what an outgoing prime minister could say, as he was covered by Privy Council rules. But one avenue of enquiry led to North Devon.

'My team went down there and traced Norman Scott', Gordon remembered, 'who said, this is all to do with my affair with Jeremy Thorpe.' His team continued digging, until the story took an unexpected turn. A document was leaked to Gordon that had originated in the attorney general's office. He had one chance to look at it, at midnight, for just fifteen minutes. He met his mole on the Thames Embankment, and speedily read the entire document into his tape recorder. It was not until the next day that he realised what he had read. 'I played the tape back and was astonished. It was recommending that there was enough evidence to prosecute Thorpe for conspiracy to murder. My editor went white.' The document had been written by Chief Superintendent Michael Challes, a senior policeman in the Avon and Somerset police, responsible for investigating Scott's allegations. There the story was to end for Gordon. Ian Trethowan, the director general of the BBC, would not countenance broadcasting anything. 'He got really angry, said it was scandalous rubbish, we're not touching this, forget it.' And he insisted the document be destroyed. 'I rang Paul and told him: you'll have to do it.'

Paul knew what a sensational story it might turn out to be, and he and Gordon decided to feed it slowly, bit by bit, into the *Eye*. All through the first months of 1978, as they laboured on improving the pages of *Socialist Worker*, Paul was also writing the Thorpe story for the *Eye*. He began in February and continued in all three March editions, more in April, and again in June. Finally, on 21 July, just as he was leaving *Socialist Worker*, Paul predicted the arrest of Jeremy Thorpe. 'In a seemingly vain attempt to stave off the inevitable', wrote Paul,

> the Director of Public Prosecutions, Mr Tony Hetherington, appears to have ordered yet further police inquiries into the Norman Scott affair.
>
> Mr Thorpe was interviewed by the police but didn't endear himself to them. He is known to police investigators as 'the ditto man'. He answered every question with the one word: 'ditto' (believed to be a reference to an earlier reply that he had been told by his advisers to say nothing, nothing at all).

Peter Bessell, who had also been a Liberal MP and a close confidant of Thorpe, was by contrast very cooperative. In his statement he told the police of his conversations with Thorpe in the mid '60s, when Thorpe had admitted he had a sexual relationship with Scott. Scott was now pestering him, and Bessell offered to help sort out the problem. But nothing would shut Scott up. Thorpe told Bessell that Scott would have to be 'done away with'. Several mad plans were hatched. David Holmes, former deputy treasurer of the Liberals and a friend of Thorpe's, went looking for a hit man. Meanwhile, another friend stumped up the necessary cash for 'election expenses' – money to be spent on anything but. Paul wrote:

> These are just a few of the extraordinary coincidences and revelations which Mr Tony Hetherington has been studying in recent days. Life is not easy for him. No one, least of all Hetherington, wants to start off a scandal the like of which British politics hasn't known for half a century.[3]

Thorpe immediately issued a writ. A week later he was charged with conspiracy and incitement to murder.

Before the case came to trial, the government called a general election, for 3 May 1979. Thorpe stood once more as the Liberal candidate for North Devon, as if nothing was amiss. Auberon Waugh decided to stand against him as the Dog Lover's candidate. 'I found myself', he wrote in his autobiography, 'genuinely indignant at the suggestion that murder was to be reintroduced as a means of political advancement.'[4] He did not go to Devon to canvass because the courts, in response to a request from Thorpe's lawyers, had banned him from publishing his Dog Lover's manifesto. On election day, Waugh received 79 votes, while Thorpe received over 23,000, despite the lurid press accounts of sexual abuse, financial crookery and attempted murder. He lost to his Conservative adversary.

Five days later, Thorpe's trial began. Gordon Carr was back on the story – and so was the whole of Fleet Street. The press benches at the Old Bailey were packed. 'Then, in one of the most dramatic moments of my life', remembered Gordon, 'the jury came back – not guilty.' Everyone was taken by surprise. 'All over Fleet Street one heard the noise of tearing paper as "background" stories, written in the expectation that the defendants would be convicted, were torn up', wrote Waugh, who had sat through the entire trial.[5] In Gordon Carr's studio there was the sound of tapes being unwound and shredded. His film was to have been transmitted that night. 'We were all ready to go. It was two years' work down the drain', he said. 'The thing that did it was Peter Bessell. He'd been offered £50,000 by the *Sunday Telegraph* on condition that Thorpe was found guilty, and the Defence said, how can you possibly depend on his evidence because it's tainted.'

The story reconfirmed Paul's popularity as a journalist, and the work began to roll in. He wrote regularly for the *Eye*, the Thorpe story becoming something of a passion. He appeared on *What the Papers Say*, Granada Television's media programme, and *Any Questions?* on BBC radio. He was also recruited by Bruce Page, the editor of the *New Statesman*, to write regularly for its 'London Diary' column.

Paul had written for the *New Statesman* before, including a long article about a trip to Portugal he had taken after he resigned as editor of *Socialist Worker* in 1975. He had gone with Rose to see for himself how the revolutionary events that had begun the previous year were unfolding.[6] Wherever he went, Paul looked for the good news: the Lisbon clinic that was providing free healthcare, which had been built and fitted by the shipyard workers from Lisnave; the residents' committees solving the dual problem of empty houses alongside homelessness; the Committee of Consumption in Setubal, in charge of food distribution. He cheered the fact that *República* was run by an elected workers' commission. Here was 'the glimmer of an answer' to the outrage of production for profit – though it was only a glimmer: 'The commissions and cooperatives are not in power.' Even as Paul wrote his article, that glimmer was fading. He had seen it for himself: the spare parts withheld, investment denied, orders cancelled. After 25 November – the date of a failed rebellion of army paratroopers – came the imprisonment of army officers, the sacking of editors, the raids on farms, and 'the foul stench of repression'.

A return to more conventional government was being advocated. Surrender was Paul's word – to parliaments elected at long intervals, and industrialists and bankers not elected at all. This, he wrote, was the declared aim of Mario Soares, leader of the Portuguese Socialist Party, ably supported by the Portuguese Communist Party. In the pages of the *New Statesman*, Paul urged the workers and farm labourers, with the active assistance of socialists everywhere, to press on with their revolution: 'to take control of the state and establish in Portugal a genuine socialist democracy'. He was simply dreaming. The events of 25 November were the beginning of the end of the revolution. Four years earlier, in a long article in *Socialist Worker*, he had warned that this would be the ending if the revolution was not pushed to a successful conclusion, and he quoted Goethe to reinforce his point:

> You must rise or fall.
> You must rule and win
> Or serve and forfeit,
> Suffer or triumph,
> Be anvil or be hammer.[7]

Alongside his political journalism for the diary column in the *New Statesman*, Paul also wrote occasional pieces on poetry and books. In

October 1978, he issued an appeal for a first edition of Olive Schreiner's *Trooper Peter Halket of Mashonaland*, which included a photo of a public hanging: 'a few louts from Rhodes' army are standing under the hanging corpses. They look half-bored, half-triumphant.' Twelve readers got in touch.[8] He also reviewed Wendy Parkinson's *This Gilded African*, her biography of Toussaint L'Ouverture – a book he found disappointing compared to C. L. R. James's *The Black Jacobins*, which firmly tied the Haitian uprising to the Revolution in France. There was one aspect of the book that Paul was enthusiastic about. On its back cover, Parkinson had included Wordsworth's poem *Toussaint*, a poem, Paul commented, 'not often quoted in schools – it is not about daffodils. It is about Toussaint L'Ouverture and the indissoluble bond between his great rebellion and oppressed black people everywhere, from Johannesburg, to Bulawayo, to Brick Lane.'[9]

In the critical weeks of the general election campaign in April and May 1979, Paul wrote a series of articles about the press and the way they conducted themselves to the Conservatives' advantage, with their consistent red-baiting. The *Daily Mail* had named forty-three Labour MPs as extremists, based on dubious evidence, showcased beneath a front-page headline, 'Labour's Danger Men', accompanied by comparisons between Labour's Manifesto and the *Communist Manifesto*. Even if this was directed at the Labour left, in Paul's estimation they had never been weaker, and their influence on Labour's Manifesto was negligible. The *Mail*'s diatribes were aided by those in the *Sun*, and those Paul called the Labour renegades, 'a number of tired and discredited gentlemen who have taken the familiar road from youthful conviction to middle-aged reaction'. Lord George Brown came to mind, writing anywhere and everywhere of his hope for a Tory victory.

Ten days before the election, the National Front planned an election meeting in the town hall in Southall, West London – an intentionally provocative act given Southall's large Asian population. Local community groups tried in vain to persuade the council to ban the meeting. When this was refused, a peaceful sit-down outside the town hall was planned instead, with shops and businesses closed in protest – a plan the community shared with the police.

When the day came, thousands of police arrived in the centre of Southall, shutting it down. The Special Patrol Group were once again on duty, and mayhem and violence followed. Paul would later quote a policeman caught up in that day's events: 'We went wanging down there, jumped out of the van and just started fighting . . . it was a great day out, fighting the Pakis. It ought to be an annual fixture. I thoroughly enjoyed myself.'[10]

Blair Peach died that day, killed by a single blow to the head. It had been 'staved in', wrote the independent pathologist, by something more solid than a police truncheon.[11] The police's own raids on the lockers used by the SPG turned up illegal weapons and a shortlist of names, all in the Special Patrol Group. It was, Paul wrote in *Socialist Worker*, no surprise. 'Killing is just a routine matter for the SPG.' They had killed Kevin Gateley in 1974, and two Pakistani workers in Bradford in 1973. They had been in action on the Grunwick picket line. And when they were not on picket or demonstration duty, they patrolled areas of London looking for 'criminals' – areas that just happened to be where most black people lived.[12]

The Asian population of Southall turned out in their thousands to march in Blair Peach's memory: 'Blair Peach Zindabad', the mourners chanted in Gujerati – 'Long live Blair Peach.'

In his obituary for *Socialist Worker*, Paul recalled a similar killing a hundred years earlier, when Alfred Linnell had joined a demonstration for free speech in Trafalgar Square. He was standing 'unarmed and unsuspecting' by the side of the crowd when a posse of police, who had orders to keep the square free of demonstrators, charged straight into him, breaking his neck with their horses' hooves. Tens of thousands of socialists, Irish republicans, radicals, feminists and working people joined one of the greatest demonstrations London had seen. The streets were lined with sympathetic crowds all the way to Bow cemetery. 'In Southall, as in Trafalgar Square 100 years ago', Paul wrote,

> the police were driven on by a contempt for the demonstrators –
> 'black scum' as one mounted officer so politely put it. We march at
> his funeral not just in sympathy with the people who loved him, nor
> just out of respect for all he did for us, but in anger.[13]

All those years ago, William Morris wrote a song to commemorate Alfred Linnell, and its words were printed in a short pamphlet published by the Anti-Nazi League, setting out the details of the funeral march that would accompany Peach's coffin from Southall to the cemetery in East London, where he had lived and worked as a teacher in a special school in Bow. The march would be silent, with teachers walking at the front, and banners left at the cemetery gates:

> Not one, not one, nor thousands must they slay,
> But one and all if they would dusk the day.

The Conservatives won the general election with a huge majority, and Margaret Thatcher became prime minister. It was the end of an era.

Three months later, on Thursday 16 August 1979 at 9.32 in the morning, Paul's third son was born. Unusually for Paul, he recorded this personal detail in his *New Statesman* Diary. 'It's a boy. Big and beautiful', the midwife had announced. On closer examination, thought Paul, 'the bundle she carried showed that both adjectives were singularly inappropriate.'[14]

While he was phoning friends and family with the news, Rose was lying in bed, in Paul's words, bruised and battered. It had been a huge effort, a long birth that had ended with a caesarean. Privately, he knew Rose was both happy and relieved, because she had been pregnant before. That baby had died in the womb, and Rose had gone through the excruciating experience of a still birth.

This baby would be called Tom: 'after Tom Paine, Tom Wooler (a contemporary of Paine, and publisher of the *Black Dwarf*) and Tom Mann (leader of the London Dock strike in 1889)'. He arrived just in time: in his next London Diary, Paul announced it would be his last column. He had been made an offer he couldn't refuse.

14

Poetry and Revolution

Paul loved poetry. From a very young age he had learned to recite poems out loud at his grandfather's house in Cornwall, and no doubt Shelley was in the mix. But Paul's experience of Shelley at school began badly. He had kept his small, dark blue textbook, *Shelley* by A. M. D. Hughes – an anthology which contained no poems inspired by the poet's political ideas. As far as he was aware, Shelley was interested only in skylarks, clouds and Greek gods. Things did not improve in his final year, when he had to work through another edition of Shelley, this one edited by Isobel Quigley. She was a Tory, and someone who had no qualms about editing out all of Shelley's ideas: 'No poet better repays cutting; no great poet was ever less worth reading in his entirety.'[1]

Things were not so different at Oxford. Shelley had attended the same college as Paul. On the way to the football changing rooms, he would pass the white marble statue of a naked and drowned Shelley, borne aloft by lions and angels. He asked the dean about the statue and the descriptive plate alongside it, which stated that Shelley had been at the College in 1811. 'How is it', Paul asked, 'that Shelley was only here for a year?' He was drowned, came the reply. Which was true – but that happened eleven years later. The real explanation was that Shelley had been expelled from the college for writing a pamphlet, *The Necessity of Atheism*. He had sent copies to various bishops and religious scholars in Oxford, and was quickly given his marching orders. His father cut him off without a penny.

Paul was thirty-seven by the time he realised what a wonderful poet Shelley was. To keep up his spirits while he was sick in bed, Rose had given him Richard Holmes's recently published biography. It was to prove a revelation.

Shelley was indeed the finest of poets, Paul wrote in a long review of Holmes's book for *International Socialism Journal*.[2] But he was also a relentless enemy of all irresponsible authority and power, especially the power that came with wealth. He was an atheist and a republican, who sided on every occasion with the masses, when the workers and the first trade unionists rose against what the poet called 'the pelting wretches of the new aristocracy'. The genius of the poetry was inextricably entwined with Shelley's convictions, inspired by the French Revolution and the writings of his mentor, the philosopher William Godwin. Women are equal to men, Godwin had written in *Political Justice*, religion is superstition, riches and poverty unnecessary evils. But the society Shelley lived in was very different from the vision of liberty, equality and fraternity offered by the French Revolution. In Britain, political repression was the order of the day; there were troops in the cities and spies everywhere. Publications were censored. Meetings were banned. There was an endless war with France and, following a failed rebellion in Ireland in 1798, the repression of an entire population.

The great revolutionary poets of the French revolution – Samuel Taylor Coleridge, Robert Southey and William Wordsworth – were becoming conservative with age, defending the regime they had once denounced. Wordsworth no longer felt as he had as a young man in revolutionary France: 'Bliss was it in that dawn to be alive, / But to be young was very heaven!' Now Shelley mocked the ageing poet in 'Peter Bell the Third': He was 'Dull – oh, so dull – so very dull!'

By contrast, Shelley was very much engaged with the radical ideas of the age of revolution, and when he was just nineteen travelled to Ireland with the names of the remnants of the United Irishmen in his pocket, courtesy of William Godwin. He took with him his *Address to the Irish People*, which he distributed around Dublin, pinning it up in coffee shops, posting it to anyone whose name he could find. But once Shelley saw for himself the full horror of Irish poverty and destitution, and started to meet those republicans, he wrote a new pamphlet,

Proposals for an Association – an association that would organise for Catholic emancipation and the repeal of the union. He sent the pamphlets to Godwin, who had a fit, writing back to Shelley to tell him to forget all this nonsense and to sit back and await progress. But Shelley refused to wind up his association, and Godwin feared the worst: 'Shelley, you are preparing a scene of blood!'[3]

Paul wanted to understand *this* Shelley. The poet who could write of 'An old, mad, blind, despised and dying king' in his poem 'England in 1819'; who asked, 'Who made terror, madness, crime, remorse', in *Prometheus Unbound*; who got to the roots of inequality in 'Song to the Men of England': 'The seed ye sow, another reaps; the wealth ye find, another keeps'; who understood, in *Queen Mab*, 'War is the statesman's game, the priest's delight, the lawyer's jest, the hired assassin's trade'; who asked in *The Revolt of Islam* – in 1817 – the great feminist question: 'Can man be free if woman be a slave?'

After reading Holmes, Paul started working out his own ideas about Shelley, first during his talk at Skegness in 1976, and then at the first of the SWP's Marxism weekends the following year – and, in 1981, in his book *Red Shelley*.

To write, he needed books. Of course, he used London's libraries; but he preferred, like his grandfather Isaac and his uncle Michael, to collect his own. The post would regularly bring booksellers' lists, and Paul knew the location of every secondhand bookshop in greater London. An invitation to speak almost anywhere around the country offered the delightful prospect of a side trip to a shop, where one or two – perhaps even three or four – books might be found.

On one sunny Saturday, Paul was in Manchester speaking at a *Socialist Worker* writers' school. With time to kill before the session began, he persuaded a young Geoff Brown to take him to the local secondhand bookshops. 'Paul found a couple of books about Shelley and explained something about Shelley's politics to me', remembers Geoff. But then, perhaps pumped up by his youthful radicalism, Geoff suggested that Paul's habit of book collecting was a bit bourgeois – an obsession with owning things. Paul rather sheepishly agreed, and hid his books away for the rest of the day.

It is very hard to break a habit of a lifetime, however, and Paul remembered the incident in a piece he wrote some years later. Having reflected on the matter, he realised Geoff was not right at all. The point about public ownership and planning is that it releases capital for producing things that people need and want – it does not lead to the abolition of private possessions. 'For people who think and who value ideas there is no replacement for books', he wrote. 'There is a peculiar advantage in owning books, since they can be marked, stored away in shelves and in the mind, and returned to again and again when a new idea or argument comes along.' Over a lifetime, he acquired a vast collection.[4]

As he started his marathon of reading on Shelley, Paul came across an essay by Geoffrey Matthews that cut through much of the literary criticism, arguing that, to understand his poetry, the reader had to deal with the whole of Shelley – 'his science, his politics, his theories of literature, his medical record'.[5] He wrote to Matthews, and then, quite out of the blue, met him. Paul received an invitation to join a small group of Shelley scholars and enthusiasts at the first ever Shelley conference, held at Gregynog, a rambling old house, miles from anywhere, and an outpost of St David's University in Wales where the conference organiser, Kelvin Everest, worked. Everest was amazed when Paul said he would come – and not just to join in their discussions, but to give a paper of his own. It was there that Paul met Matthews, as well as Judith Chernaik, whose book on Shelley's lyrics he had already found in one of the secondhand bookshops in Hampstead.[6] The group soon became friends: Judith and her husband, Geoffrey and his wife, Paul and Rose. 'From all these talks and the long discussions which went on late into the night a very different Shelley emerged to the prototype "beautiful and ineffectual angel",' wrote Paul in the *New Statesman*. 'Here was the restless, republican, revolutionary Shelley who has been banished from examination papers for one and a half centuries.'[7]

There was one small hitch. At the conference Paul had learned about the influence on Shelley of Erasmus Darwin, founder of the Lunar Society of Birmingham, and an inventor, botanist, scientific thinker and man of words and poetry. A *New Statesman* editor, presuming the reference to him in Paul's article was a typing error, decided to split the name into two, and so the article described the influence on Shelley of both Erasmus and Darwin. Paul had some fun in the diary: 'I have a great respect for Christopher Hitchens, so I have been making inquiries', he wrote. 'As far as I can see, Erasmus's influence on Shelley was negligible. Charles Darwin (the person normally thought of as 'Darwin') was restricted in his influence on Shelley by being only 12 when Shelley died.'[8] Christopher Hitchens was the editor of the piece.

Paul learned so much at the conference that he felt he had to rewrite much of his manuscript, enlisting the help of everyone he could to finish it. Rose trawled the archive for old communist and socialist newspapers which might have mentioned Shelley; his aunt Jill dug into her feminist archive; Janet Montefiore, then an English literature lecturer at Liverpool, researched exam papers; and Geoffrey Matthews read the final manuscript. 'You have not erred on the side of pedantry', he wrote back.

Geoffrey, like Paul, was a Marxist and a revolutionary, having joined the Communist Party in the 1930s, and the emancipating ideas of Marx had inspired his criticism and scholarship. He also had an astonishing knack of simplifying even the most complicated passages. Paul read his essay on Shakespeare's *Othello* in some excitement. 'The most important feature of Othello', began the essay, 'is the colour of the hero's skin.' Suddenly, for Paul, the play became a drama about real people in real society. 'Othello is not a vaguely timeless story of jealousy', wrote Geoffrey, 'but a modern instance of a black man's love for a white woman.'[9]

Paul's book on Shelley was published by Sidgwick & Jackson, whose offices were in Museum Street – a row of rickety old houses and shops near the British Museum. Jane Birdsell, at the time a secretary at the publisher, enjoyed working on the book. It was her task to cross the road to the British Museum's reading room and check Paul's quotes and sources; he always wrote at such a furious pace that there was no time to check everything as he went along.

Red Shelley was published on 7 May 1981. It is not a biography in the conventional sense, but a book about the ideas central to Shelley's thinking: his republicanism, atheism and feminism, and the radical politics of the Levellers. The longest section is devoted to the argument that runs through so much of Shelley's prose and poetry: How could change come about, through reform or revolution?

Following publication, the *Guardian* carried a long extract devoted to Paul's chapter on religion, and the book was widely reviewed.[10] For *Tribune*, Brian Sedgemore revealed that he too had been in Skegness in 1976, where he was lecturing the Derbyshire miners while Paul was delivering his first talk on Shelley. Sedgemore noticed the socialists and, intrigued, went along to listen. 'There was an unexpected buzz in the room. The performance, like the book, which has just been published, was mesmeric, and such as to make the reading of Shelley's works an urgent necessity.'[11] The *Listener*, a BBC publication, reviewed it enthusiastically, as did Marilyn Butler in the *London Review of Books*. Butler praised its emphasis on Shelley's place in the world in the years after his death, 'his underground influence as a political educator and his special reputation among Chartists, Fabians and other progressives'.[12] The *Telegraph* was less keen – where was Shelley's vegetarianism, the reviewer asked. And Richard Holmes, in *The Times*, found it 'too tub-thumping, simplistic, ill-humoured, narrow'.[13]

Radio programmes followed the book's publication. *The Late Show* and *World of Books*, but also the rather wonderfully titled *Poetry and Revolution* for BBC radio, with Christopher Hill and Tom Paulin, among a host of others with whom Paul was keen to discuss poetry.[14] They talked of Shelley and Byron, John Clare – the poet of the enclosures – and William Blake, the English Revolution, *Paradise Lost* and John Milton. They discussed war and Northern Ireland, and finished with Tony Harrison and his poem *V*, written after the miners' strike. Terry Eagleton explained how revolutions unleash the unconscious and a quickening of energy.

Other events included one in June 1985, on the anniversary of Shelley's drowning, when Paul was invited by the local Labour Party to Windsor Girls' school. Shelley had lived down the road, at Marlow, and they wanted to celebrate his radical ideas. Kelvin Everest and Judith Chernaik were also there, as well as Marilyn Butler. Butler talked eloquently of the politics of the romantic poets, which had mostly been written out of the story by her fellow academics. Mystical claptrap, she said, had replaced what the poets were actually saying. Paul was in awe: 'The combination of scholarship and commitment was intoxicating.' And all of this was in a constituency with a huge Tory majority. 'As the man said, if winter comes, can spring be far behind?'[15]

Paul also made an hour-long television programme, *The Trumpet of a Prophecy*, broadcast on Channel Four in 1987. Featuring extracts from Shelley's poems and essays, voiced by a talented group of actors including Josette Simon and Art Malik, the programme began and ended with Paul talking about one of Shelley's most famous and most misinterpreted poems: 'Ode to the West Wind'. Often described as a nature poem, and considered a safe bet for school anthologies, it was not about nature at all, Paul told his audience. It was a poem about revolution, about the revolutionary ideas that were blowing across the Atlantic from America: scatter my words among mankind, Shelley urged, as if they were 'the trumpet of a prophecy!' It was one of the poems Shelley wrote with a new collection in mind following the events of August 1819.[16]

On 16 August 1819, a great demonstration for parliamentary reform gathered in St Peter's Field in Manchester. Thousands of men, women and children travelled from across the north-west to hear the speakers, including the famous radical orator Henry Hunt, call for political and economic reform. As the meeting began, the crowd was attacked by the local yeomanry and cavalry, who rode into the crowd slashing right and left with their sabres, killing seventeen people and injuring hundreds more.

Shelley was living in Italy when news reached him of the massacre at Peterloo. Boiling with indignation, he wrote the ninety-two verses of *The Mask of Anarchy* – 'one of the great political poems of all time', according to Paul.[17] The poem is different in both style and language from his other longer poems. Written in short, sharp stanzas, like the popular ballads of the time, it is easy to understand and easy to learn. It starts with a description of a masquerade, in which Shelley tears into the Tory government and its ministers:

I met murder on the way –
He had a mask like Castlereagh.

Castlereagh was the foreign secretary, and the butcher of the Irish rebellion of 1798; Lord Sidmouth, who wore the mask of hypocrisy, was home secretary; and fraud was Lord Eldon, a judge. These men represented the chaos, horror and violence of the hideous class society of the time that Shelley detested. Their leader was the ghastly spectre of Anarchy: 'I am God, and King and Law'.

Against anarchy Shelley pitches a woman – his agitators are often women – who asks three questions: What's wrong with society – what is slavery? What would you put in its place – what is freedom? And how will you get from slavery to freedom? Freedom, Paul pointed out, is economic freedom, the strongest idea of all in the poem. Shelley calls for another demonstration, 'a great assembly of the fearless and the free', and, in his famous last stanza, calls on the people to

Rise like lions after slumber,
In unvanquishable number –
Shake your chains to earth like dew
Which in sleep had fallen on you –
Ye are many – they are few.

It is a call that has echoed around the world and over the centuries.

In the months that followed, Shelley's output was prolific. By the end of the year, he had written his radical pamphlet *A Philosophical View of Reform*, and sent it to England for publication with a collection of popular songs, including 'Ode to the West Wind'. Shelley hoped to publish them together in a single volume. He sent them to his friend Leigh Hunt, who calculated that any of these popular songs and any single line of the *Philosophical View of Reform* would be instantly prosecuted under the array of repressive laws. He ignored all of Shelley's repeated requests to find a publisher for them. No one read any of this outpouring of political writing during Shelley's lifetime. *The Mask of Anarchy* was not published until 1832. *A Philosophical View of Reform* waited another hundred years.

Yet, for Paul, this short work stood alongside Paine's *Rights of Man* and Mary Wollstonecraft's *A Vindication of the Rights of Woman*, as well as the pamphlets of Jeremy Bentham and Robert Owen, Marx and Engels. Those three-and-a-half months at the end of 1819 were, Paul thought, 'perhaps the most sustained and prolific period of fine writing in British literary history'. Besides all the material he sent to London, Shelley also wrote his 'Letter on Richard Carlile', 'one of the greatest essays in support of free speech ever written in our language'; *Peter Bell the Third*, his long satirical poem about Wordsworth; and a substantial slice of *Prometheus Unbound*.[18]

Eventually, in 1990, *A Philosophical View of Reform* was published together with its accompanying songs, just as Shelley had intended. Redwords, one of the publishing imprints of the Socialist Workers Party, collected these texts as *Shelley's Revolutionary Year*, with an introduction by Paul.

Another milestone was a performance, devised by Judith Chernaik, to celebrate the bicentenary of the death of Mary Wollstonecraft and the birth of her daughter Mary, who became Mary Shelley. She wrote, and actors performed, an imagined conversation between the mother and daughter. Paul recited *The Mask of Anarchy*, Mary Wollstonecraft's biographer Claire Tomalin spoke about the feminist pioneer, and the evening ended with a clip of Boris Karloff playing Frankenstein, from the 1931 film of Mary Shelley's famous book.

Shelley had read all of Mary Wollstonecraft, and wrote in both his poems and essays about her ideas: the one-sidedness of many marriages, the degradation of prostitution, the potential exhilaration of sex, the very idea of women's liberation. In *Rosalind and Helen*, he described the battered and brutalised wife whose children, when they heard their father's footstep on the stair, would grow pale:

> The babe at my bosom was hushed with fear
> If it thought it heard his father near;
> And my two wild boys would near my knee
> Cling, cowed and cowering fearfully.

Shelley knew from his own experience that 'Love withers under constraint'.[19] And he wrestled with the answer he found in the idea of free love:

> True love in this differs from gold and clay,
> to divide is not to take away.[20]

But there was a problem with all of this. In the introduction to his book, Paul quotes a drama teacher at Hampstead School who approached him after his first attempt to speak about Shelley, who put her finger on it when she asked him why Shelley was 'such a shit to his women?'[21] Paul could not answer her then, but in his chapter on Shelley the feminist, he wrestled in his turn with the gap between theory and practice.

The demand for Paul as a speaker did not slow in the years that followed, and at every opportunity he would urge his readers and his audiences to read Shelley for themselves. As he told his first audience at Skegness in 1977, 'the whole purpose of this meeting is to get you to go home and get hold of a copy of *Queen Mab*, and read in particular those central cantos'. Read 'Ode to the West Wind', Paul would plead. Read *Prometheus Unbound*.[22]

Written in the early months of 1820, *Prometheus Unbound* was perhaps Shelley's most difficult poem. But for all that, it was a poem of revolution – specifically, according to Geoffrey Matthews, the English Revolution.[23] A figure from Greek mythology, Prometheus is the subversive symbol of resistance, chained to a rock and tortured for his defiance of the tyrant Jupiter. Asia – one of Shelley's female agitators – comes to his rescue, and seeks out Demogorgon, the people-monster (from *demos*, the Greek for 'the people', and *gorgon*, the Greek for 'monster'), to aid her in her quest. With the people-monster, the emerging working class, on her side, Asia can challenge Jupiter. But how to rouse Demogorgon to fight? At this point the reader really has to follow Paul's argument in *Red Shelley*.[24] It is, says Judith Chernaik, heady stuff, and the best approach is to sit with the poem in one hand and *Red Shelley* in the other – or, perhaps, the poem in one hand and Paul talking the reader through it in one ear, in the recording of his Skegness talk 'Shelley and Revolution'.[25]

Go straight to Act 2 Scene 4, Paul urges. Act 1 is extremely difficult to read, but Act 2 gets the reader right into the action: Asia goes down into the cave, where she provokes Demogorgon to go with her to challenge Jupiter. As soon as Jupiter sees Demogorgon, he senses that this is not the people as he knew them, but the people inspired by the vision of a new society, confident and determined to destroy the old tyranny. 'In this the most wonderful of all his poems', wrote Paul,

Shelley worked out the contradiction which dogs so much of his straight political writing. Reform, the poem concludes, is impossible without revolution. The forces of wealth and power in England in 1819 would not, in the foreseeable future, concede that wealth and power. They could easily contain the movement for reform for as long as that movement confined itself to the 'enlightened few'. The only power which could not be contained was the power of the people, organised, united and confident in revolutionary action.[26]

The bicentenary of Shelley's birth in 1992 happened to be a general election year. In his *Mirror* column just before election day in April, Paul asked his readers, 'Do you really want another five years of this?'[27]

He spelled out the price people had paid since 1979 when the Tories had come to power: the collapse of council house building; the fall in the value of the state pension; cuts in the number of NHS hospital beds; the decline in spending on state schools; cuts in subsidies to British rail; the increase in the number of company cars, at vast cost to taxpayers; the doubling of unemployment; the explosion in unearned as compared to earned income. The whole page was liberally spiced with the names of the rich who had benefited. In a strap along the bottom of the page ran two lines from 'England in 1819', in which Shelley described the Tory government of his day:

Rulers who neither see, nor feel, nor know
But leech-like to their fainting country cling.

The year was a busy one for Paul. He was on form again at that year's SWP Marxism meeting, repeating his Shelley talk. Bill Keach, an American Shelley scholar and Marxist, was there, along with around 500 others – twice the size of any other audience Keach had seen during the Shelley bicentenary. Paul quoted long sequences from *The Mask of Anarchy* and 'Ode to the West Wind' from memory. 'I have never heard Shelley's verse more impressively spoken. I was inspired', he recalled.[28]

The year 1992 was not an easy one for a celebration. In Keach's words, it was a year of 'grinding disorder'. It was marked by worldwide economic crisis; civil war in the former Yugoslavia; the re-emergence of religious and nationalist fanaticism and fascism; famine in Somalia and other parts of Africa, Asia and Latin America; threats of war in the Middle East; violent urban uprisings and riots of the kind Shelley feared, but saw as unavoidable, in Los Angeles and Britain. It was also the year when the Super Nintendo was first released for sale in the UK. Paul's son Tom, then just 12, was bribed to learn *The Mask of Anarchy* by heart. Paul promised to give him 50p a verse, for ninety-two verses. For that, he had to be able to quote each verse and the verses that preceded it, until he could recite the whole poem. He readily agreed, because that would be quite a sum of money, and Tom was very keen to get his hands on a Nintendo. Paul gave him the slim volume of *Shelley's Revolutionary Year*, and Tom got to work. It was a good investment. Thirty years later he can still remember the poem, or most of it, and still plays his Super Nintendo.

Tom used to believe his father's attitude to making him learn poetry was a way of trying to get him to like literature. There were other poems and other poets, and lots of Shakespeare. It was all for money, and often learned when they were on holiday in Cornwall. All that money, Tom remembers, went straight to the arcade. Now, though, Tom thinks it was less about literature and more about politics: the spreading of revolutionary ideas. 'Socialists have a duty to their children to bribe or bully them to learn the poetry which carries revolutionary ideas through the centuries', Paul wrote in the introduction to *Red Shelley*. A good start, he suggested, was *The Mask of Anarchy*, working through to the last verse of 'Ode to the West Wind', and reinforcing it with the irresistible message of the *Philosophical View of Reform* – to rise, finally, like lions.

15

Look in the Mirror

One evening in June 1979, Paul took a call from the *Daily Mirror*. Would he, they asked, join Mike Molloy, the paper's editor, for dinner? They had met before, at a *Private Eye* lunch, and had got on immediately, so the call was not all that surprising. What followed was.

Would Paul come and work at the *Mirror* on investigations, Mike asked. No, Paul said, he would not. His rationale was that he disliked being told what to do, and he knew what it was like to fight for space on a national newspaper. He had no such problems at the *Eye*. But, he added, partly as a joke, if he had his own space every week, that would be quite a different matter. 'I was fishing really', he was later to remember; he thought it would never happen. 'After all, Mike, I am a Trot', he added.[1] But Mike liked the idea, and offered him the job.

Molloy believed, like so many before and after him, that he could cure Paul of that particular political delinquency. He rang the *Mirror*'s owners, Reed International, to inform them the paper was taking on a revolutionary. They had no problem with the decision, but their managers were soon tearing their hair out. With his freelance contract came a certain level of salary. 'It was a good salary', remembers Mike, and Paul was taken aback. His last regular pay cheque had been the appallingly low wages paid out at *Socialist Worker*. 'Oh no, God no, that's too much', he replied. Mike had to explain that he couldn't turn it down because it was something the union had fought for. Just in case he was going to continue to resist, Mike sent Joe Haines to talk to him. Haines was a leader writer of great skill – a small, taciturn man and, it turned out, from the same school of Glasgow journalism as Paul. He too knew the Buchans and the Carmichaels. 'I was on about the same salary, so I told Paul that he was letting the rest of us down. If he refused to accept, it made it more difficult for us.' He soon complied.

Mike Molloy explained that there were also expenses – and an office – and a car. At that point, Paul flatly refused: 'I am not having a car.' A month went by. Then Paul announced that he was coming in to talk about the car. Molloy's hopes were raised – only to be frustrated once again. Could he, Paul asked, have a pass for the underground instead? Mike rang the managing editor.

'Foot wants a Tube pass.'

'Tell him to fuck off, we don't give Tube passes', came the reply. 'Tell him to put it on his expenses.'

Paul was amazed. Can I do that, he asked. 'You can do anything you like', Molloy told him.

Glasgow had produced quite a collection of journalists for the *Mirror*. Not only Joe Haines and Paul but also Alasdair Buchan, who had been just a young boy when Paul was in Glasgow. He had followed Paul to the *Record*, and was now a feature writer at the *Mirror*. John Pilger was also writing for the *Mirror*. Paul was not entirely on his own, but his first day at the office was a lonely affair.

'I sat there all afternoon paralysed by delight and terror', he later wrote.

> Delight that such an unlikely dream had come true, terror as to how on earth I was to find the stories to fill the page. The answer, which now seems obvious but then was unheard of, was: from the readers of the *Daily Mirror*.[2]

When his column appeared for the first time, on 10 October, there was a little box at the bottom that read: 'If you have something you think I ought to investigate let me know at the *Mirror*', and the phone number. 'This was, I think, the first time a national paper had openly solicited information from whistle-blowers, grasses and finks', wrote Paul about that decision, 'and provided a name (and a photograph) with which they could communicate.'

There was a certain level of razzmatazz to accompany the announcement of Paul's arrival. 'Britain's top investigative reporter in the *Mirror* TODAY', the paper announced, with Paul's photo and the new logo, 'Paul Foot Reporting', alongside the main masthead on the front page.³ The same appeared the following week, and for three further weeks there was a strap along the bottom of the front page. Molloy had no intention of under-selling his new appointment.

His first column covered all the bases: a corrupt policeman, a worker fighting for compensation after working with asbestos and breathing in its killer dust, a quote from a politician – Margaret Thatcher for this first column – and a 'Spot the Judge' competition. Paul listed the contestants for a vacancy in the Family Division of the High Court. There were three who were eminently qualified in the way that nominees usually are (sitting judges, QCs or Treasury counsel) and a fourth, who was not a QC, not already a judge or Treasury counsel – but the sister of the attorney general, Michael Havers. It was she who got the job. Lord Harris, a Labour peer, was appalled to have judges denounced in this way. His letter, published in the *Mirror* the following Saturday, described Paul as an extremist, a judge-hater, a police-detester and an enemy of democracy. Paul would have some fun with that.⁴

The *Mirror* was based at Holborn Circus, in a swanky 1960s office block riddled with mousetraps. Lorries trundled in with newsprint and out with newspapers. Hatton Garden was across the road, where, tucked among the jewellery shops, were Jewish cafés and Italian delis which became Paul's favourites. The secondhand booksellers' carts on Farringdon Road were a short walk east. To the south was Fleet Street and the St Bride Institute, where Paul would sometimes play ping-pong with Joe Haines and Angela Pitts, or hunt for more secondhand finds in the Dickensian bookshop. In the opposite direction was the Marx Memorial Library, on Clerkenwell Green, where Paul would escape to prepare his talks and pamphlets.

The promised office was small, with just enough room for a standard-issue metal desk, two chairs, a couple of filing cabinets and a view across the roofs of Chancery Lane. It was small, but grand, because it was an office of his own. Other feature writers and the City desk shared offices on the same floor. The open-plan newsroom and the editors' offices were on the floor below. Below that was the no-go area for journalists, where the copy was laid out on the stone. Paul's office soon became two, when a secretary arrived with an answering machine for the nights and weekends. Then a second secretary was recruited, and another journalist arrived – Angela Pitts joined Paul's team from the newsroom. Then I arrived as the third journalist. When Angela left, Bryan Rostron joined, and finally Bridget Whelan.

Besides the endless phone messages, there were soon fifty or sixty letters a week and, in those days, printed copies of Hansard and the Register of Members' Interests, which Paul read avidly for interesting bits and pieces. The company's own research showed how popular Paul's column became: read by about 12 per cent of *Mirror* readers – or, as Paul pointed out, about a quarter of a million people each week. The column quickly fell into a routine: page eleven, five stories, each no more than 400 words, often much less; one or two stamp-sized photos of the people he was writing about, or occasionally a building; eye-catching headlines, and always a joke – perhaps an irreverent competition, or a quote, often at the expense of a politician, or of himself: 'Why Foot got the boot'.

Paul had been due to speak to boys at William Ellis School, North London, where his son Matt was a student. He had been invited to speak on 'the urgent need for socialism in our time'. But the invitation had been hastily withdrawn because, he was told, there would be an unfortunate clash with another visitor who was coming at the same time. 'My inquiries reveal that this other visitor is her Majesty the Queen. Since I gather she is not speaking on the Urgent Need for Socialism in Our Time, I cannot understand what all the fuss is about.'[5]

Stories for the column came from all directions: people he knew, stories he had worked on for the *Eye* or *Socialist Worker*. Among the letters from readers were a lot of 'my gas fire doesn't work' complaints, most of which Paul could do nothing about, as well as the occasional 'I can't get an erection' plea. Those he could pass to Marjorie Proops, the *Daily Mirror*'s agony aunt.

In late November, he ran a sad tale of a woman and her dying child, and the damp and squalid conditions in which the family lived. They had made it close to the top of the rehousing list at Wandsworth Council when it was run by Labour, but once the Tories took control the list had been revised and Mrs Parkins found herself way down at number 230. In the same week, the council announced the sale of an entire block, emptied of its tenants and refurbished with new central heating – paid for by the taxes of the local people of Wandsworth. Two days later, the story made it to the news pages. Wandsworth Council suddenly had three flats available for the Parkins family, and the sick toddler would be moving to a newly decorated, centrally heated flat close to the hospital that cared for him. Paul's page was proving a success.

To round off the year, and Paul's first three months at the *Mirror*, he notched up his first front page, about a Tory plan to deal with strikers by cutting benefits and stopping hardship payments to their families. The information came from a leaked Treasury briefing. The architect of the plan was Sir Keith Joseph, the industry secretary. The memo was addressed to Sir Geoffrey Howe, the chancellor. Families with disabled children or invalid parents would be hardest hit.[6]

Paul's column always went past the careful gaze of the *Mirror*'s lawyers. Hugh Corrie was skilled in the arts of avoiding the libel laws. With a difficult story he would work with Paul until he was sure they were in the clear. But one story in particular caused them both a great deal of anxiety.

It came to Paul through Phillip Whitehead, the Labour MP for Derby North. They had been at Oxford together, so when the MP sent Florence Siddons to see Paul, he listened carefully to what she had to say. Florence's sixteen-year-old granddaughter Lynn had been murdered in 1978. Florence believed, with good reason, that her murderer was still at large. Lynn had been stabbed to death while she was out walking with a friend called Roy Brookes, who was then just fourteen years old. Roy had confessed to the murder, was charged, and then withdrew his confession. At his trial he told the court that he and Lynn had been surprised on their walk by his stepfather, Michael Brookes, who attacked Lynn with a knife, urging his stepson to take part. The judge clearly believed Roy, and so did the jury. Roy Brookes was acquitted. Yet the Derbyshire police – no doubt, in Paul's words, sulking after the acquittal – refused to reopen the case.

At first, Paul was reluctant to tell the story. He explained the laws of libel to Florence, and said there was nothing he could do. But the case would not go away, and he struggled with how best to write it. The story was argued through with Hugh Corrie, until they felt confident that the article was libel-free. The proofs were then sent up to *Mirror* chairman Tony Miles.

'He yelled that we had taken leave of our senses and were hell-bent on ruining the *Daily Mirror* forever.'[7] So Paul and Richard Stott, who was then the paper's features editor, went through the whole argument with him again. Miles agreed to publication – because, in Paul's view, he recognised a good story when he saw one.

'Who killed Lynn Siddons?' appeared across two pages on 8 April 1981. But nothing happened. There was no writ from Michael Brookes, and no writ from the Derbyshire police. But there was no new investigation, either. Over fifteen years, Florence Siddons kept up her campaign, and Paul would return to the story, both in the *Mirror* and in a long account in *Unsolved*, a popular crime magazine.[8] Eventually, in August 1996, Michael Brookes was convicted for the murder of Lynn Siddons.

Mike Molloy had made it clear from the start that Paul could not use his column as a platform for the Socialist Workers Party, and Paul had agreed. It would be a page (it very soon became a page) that would take the side of the poor against the rich, Labour against Tories, wrongly convicted prisoners against the judiciary, and so on. But the agreement about the SWP didn't really affect what Paul wrote. When he described, in June 1980, how a story had come from 'my friends in the Royal Group of the London docks', he was talking about Eddie Prevost, a member of the SWP. It was a story of humbug on a grand scale.

Lord Carrington, the foreign secretary, had been pressuring the British Olympic Association and the leaders of British sport to sign up to the boycott of the Moscow Olympics in protest over the Soviet invasion of Afghanistan. And it just so happened that, down at the docks, there were 1,500 tons of engineering – two entire chemical factories – stacked up on the quayside, waiting to be loaded on a Russian container ship destined for the Urals. Eddie Prevost was working on the Russian ship.

'I was on my way home and listening to the radio. And thinking, these athletes have been preparing for this for four years. I thought, you bastards, and rang Paul', Eddie says. Paul did the rest. He sent a *Mirror* man to get a photograph of the huge pile of metal on the quayside, and rooted around in the financial details of the companies involved.

The directors of the bank that had organised the financing of the deal included the son of the former Tory prime minister, Alec Douglas-Home, and the son of Lord Carrington. The syndicate of banks that provided the money included Barclays, of which Lord Carrington was himself a director when the deal was signed. Meanwhile, wrote Paul, 'the Olympic athletes are expected to make the biggest possible sacrifice to appease everyone's indignation over the Afghanistan invasion'.[9]

The political restraint only affected what Paul wrote for the *Mirror*. He could continue to write for *Socialist Worker*, speak at SWP meetings, and visit Skegness or the Marxism conference. In March 1980, he spoke at the grandly named 'Debate of the Decade'. The debate was the inspiration of Peter Hain, a former Liberal who had organised the Stop the Seventies tours against the South African rugby and cricket teams, and was now in the Labour Party. He remembered the debate that Tariq Ali had organised in 1968 between *Black Dwarf* and Michael Foot, and hoped for something similar: an exchange of socialist ideas between the Left in the Labour Party and parliament, and the more radical left outside them. The hope was that a strategy of cooperation would emerge to cope with what were clearly going to be difficult times ahead as the Thatcher government built up steam.

Two-and-a-half thousand tickets were sold, and the venue was fully booked days in advance. Peter Hain was chairing, with Paul as the main speaker for the revolutionary left and Tony Benn the main speaker for the Labour left. Benn, then an MP in Bristol, was joined by Stuart Holland, the MP for Vauxhall, and Audrey Wise, who had been an MP in Coventry. The revolutionaries included Hilary Wainwright and Tariq Ali.

A year into Margaret Thatcher's government, what should the left do faced with an ascendant Tory Party, a world recession, increasing unemployment, cuts to public spending, and the terrible legacy of the previous Labour government? 'We have a Tory government rampaging through the country, slashing and stabbing at whatever they can, and we have a rotten opposition to it', began Paul. 'Whenever you see a Labour spokesman in parliament attacking the Tory government, they get the same reply: You did it too.'[10]

Why had the last Labour government been so awful? Paul found part of the answer in Tony Benn's recent volume, *Arguments for Socialism*, which he had reread to prepare for the debate.[11] In its pages Benn had described how the immense power of bankers and industrialists, in Britain and worldwide, had been used to bring direct pressure on the last Labour government: 'The power of bankers and industrialists', exclaimed Paul. 'Let's add to it, judges, civil servants, police chiefs, army chiefs, [who] are able – we hear from somebody who was there at the time – to halt and reverse the policies of the Labour government.'

What was needed now was more radical extra-parliamentary activity, alongside radical socialist policies and a joint fight against the Tories, argued Paul, 'against the union bill, against the cuts, yes, united activity to get those troops out of Ireland and those political prisoners out of the prisons there.'

But do not join the Labour Party, he appealed to his audience. 'Don't go back in there, comrades, because one more time of a Labour government elected with even more radical promises than the last one, but able to deliver even less, will land us all in troubles that none of us have even imagined.'

Peter Hain remembers Tony Benn leaning across and whispering, 'He's very hostile, isn't he!' 'I felt, well, he was entitled to put that view, that's why he was there. Paul was challenging parliamentary socialism. I also remember Paul saying, "Peter Hain, I wonder where he will end up?"'

The good thing about the debate, according to Tariq Ali, was that they were arguing with an intelligent Labour left. The far left and the Labour left could exchange ideas, and did not simply rant at one another.

During the debate, to push home his point about organising from below, Paul had said there was more 'socialism in a strike committee at Stocksbridge working out the hardship fund than in all the plans of the Labour Party'. He had been to Stocksbridge and Rotherham to report on the steel strike, and could remember the thrill he had felt as he sat in the strike headquarters one cold morning.[12]

The strike had begun in January. It was the first national strike in the steel industry since 1926, and it continued through the day of the debate and on into the first week in April. There was an immediate demand for a pay increase in response to rapidly rising inflation – the price of gas for people's homes was going up by 29 per cent, inflation was running at 22 per cent. But the real issue in the strike was the fear of redundancies and plant closures. At Rotherham, the shop stewards had taken over the running of the strike from the union officials. They had organised themselves, including the women workers, to stop the movement of steel, travelling to ports around the country including Hull and Grimsby. Before their very eyes, wrote Paul, the workers could feel themselves changing. When they were at work in the plant, Tom Bartholomew told him, they talked about the same things every day: 'Sex, booze and sport.' But during the strike, on the picket line, in their cars and vans, it was very different:

> People start talking about the government, about the Labour Party, about the union, about how we're going to change the world. I've got four kids all under ten. I feel that one day I'll be telling those children's children what it was like being in the Great Steel Strike of 1980.[13]

It might have been a great strike, but it was not a great outcome. The government and British Steel had been well prepared, and after thirteen weeks the union leaders signed a deal for little more than had been offered at the start. Then the government appointed Ian MacGregor as the new chairman of British Steel, and a savage rationalisation programme began. By the end of the year the steelworks at Consett, Corby and Shotton had all closed, and along with them had gone 20,000 jobs. Between 1979 and 1981, just short of 70,000 jobs in steel disappeared. After four years at steel, Ian MacGregor was appointed chairman of the National Coal Board.

There had been talk at the debate of a shift to the left among the Labour Party membership. The previous year, Michael Foot had been elected as leader of the party over Denis Healey, in a clear success for the left. People were also joining in considerable numbers, encouraged by Tony Benn's decision to stand as deputy leader. His campaign had given the left focus, both inside and outside the Labour Party, and great crowds were turning out to hear him speak – 2,000 in Newcastle, 4,000 in Leeds. It was a new radicalism, after the dismal years of the Wilson and Callaghan governments, and people wanted to be part of it.

Within a year of the debate, Tariq Ali had resigned from the International Marxist Group and applied to join the Labour Party. What had caused such a dramatic about-turn? Tariq argued that the combination of Benn's campaign to move the Labour Party to the left, the better to resist Thatcherism, combined with the departure of the Gang of Four, from the right of the party, to form the new centrist Social Democratic Party (SDP), changed the terrain inside the Labour Party. Socialists needed to be part of the campaign for a broader vision of socialist politics, and that meant being in the Labour Party. Tariq predicted that Benn's campaign might even make itself felt beyond the party, in the wider working-class movement.[14]

Paul was not unsympathetic to this argument. Benn's campaign had 'awakened and excited more socialists than has anything or anyone from the Labour Party for decades', he wrote in *Socialist Worker*, in the run-up to the Labour conference in 1981.[15] He was enthusiastic that, on the campaign trail, Benn had openly attacked the previous Labour government: 'On nuclear weapons, on Ireland, but above all on his dream of a democratic and egalitarian society, he speaks with a messianic fervour which shines up strongly against the dull clichés of the Labour leadership.' If Benn lost, the result would be profoundly disappointing for all socialists.

But differences between them remained, particulary in, as Paul put it, 'the different ways we talk about socialism in order to get it'. The Labour Party was still an electoral machine. It would continue to adapt its policies and its leaders in the direction that would give it the greatest chance of electoral success. Paul's article appeared as the Labour Party gathered in Brighton. At the end of the conference the result was announced: 49.6 per cent for Tony Benn, 50.4 per cent for Denis Healey. Benn had lost by the narrowest of margins.

Two months later, at a by-election in Crosby, Shirley Williams – one of the original Gang of Four – took the seat from the Conservatives for the SDP. Hundreds of people had turned out to hear Tony Benn speak for the Labour candidate, but the votes had not been forthcoming. The great turn to the left had not spread to the electorate. It was an extraordinary upset. Crosby was a safe Conservative seat, where Labour had been closing the gap at each election until now. Shirley Williams took it with 28,000 votes, compared to just 5,000 for Labour.

Paul was not surprised. The left might have advanced within the Labour Party, but that was not reflected in the wider movement. 'So savage has been the downturn in working class confidence, so deep the defeats on unemployment over the past three years, that the people who vote Labour as a class have shifted to the Right.'[16] Voters were too nervous and afraid to vote for anything more than what seemed safe and moderate: Shirley Williams rather than Tony Benn.

These defeats were a challenge to both the Labour Party and the left within it. If they were to have a hope of winning the next election, they would have to do a political U-turn. This opened up a cruel choice for Tony Benn and his supporters. 'If they stick to the political course which they have set themselves they will lose the electoral support which makes the election possible', wrote Paul. 'On the other hand, if they abandon that political course, they throw away all they have gained in the hearts and minds of the people they have inspired.'[17] What was needed was a break with electoral politics, he argued. But he qualified that thought: he was advocating a break with the obsession with elections to bodies which could not deliver the goods, not a break with elections themselves.

'I got your long letter just before Christmas and I have crawled away for a few hours to try to do it justice', Paul began in a new pamphlet, *Three Letters to a Bennite*.[18] Written in a style quite unlike anything else he had written, the pamphlet is an imagined exchange with someone who had done what several members of the SWP were doing, and Tariq Ali had recently tried to do: resign from a revolutionary organisation to join the Labour Party.

It begins by covering familiar ground: the inspiration of Tony Benn's campaign; the state of the working-class movement; the Tories, unpopular in the polls after two years of rising unemployment and prices, but full of self-confidence; the Labour Party tearing itself apart.

Then the imagined response comes: you're just against elections. No, Paul replies in his second letter, I'm not. I want democracy in every field of public life. The idea that everyone should vote 'didn't come from the reforming consciences of the rich'. It came from the clamour of voteless people. That is how we change society. 'Change does not just happen, and it certainly doesn't just come because one day Tony Benn might be prime minister at the head of a left-wing Labour government. It comes when people fight for it.'[19]

The two letter-writers needed to be working together, Paul argued, in the same organisation. And there was no chance the Labour Party would let him join. 'My application alone would probably cost you a dozen more defections from the Parliamentary Labour Party to the SDP and another couple of points drop in the opinion polls.' The movement needed to be the other way. 'Come to us', were his final words to his imagined correspondent.[20]

Paul and Tariq met to discuss their differences, taking their children to the park, sitting to talk with only one eye on the children. Although he disagreed with him, Paul thought Tariq's resignation from the IMG was a courageous decision – even if the Labour Party rejected his request to join. And Paul admitted to Tariq that when he attended the Labour Party conference, he often felt that if he was there as a delegate, rather than as a reporter, in that hall packed with trade unionists, he could destroy the Labour right and their pathetic arguments. 'I was touched', Tariq remembers. 'Paul was thinking of the role he could play. And rightly so. His fear was that he would become an opportunist. I told him he was tougher than that.' As their fathers chatted, the two children wandered off. Rose suddenly appeared out of nowhere. 'Typical' was her one word. She picked Tom up and left. 'It is true that we took our eye off the kids, but not for long.'

Paul and Tariq had known each other since the early days of *Private Eye* in the 1960s, and their long chats were often about personal matters, not politics: Monica's rather public affairs; their childhoods – Tariq's was happy, and he was dismayed when Paul told him he could not remember a warm embrace or kiss from his mother; their women friends – Paul rather envied Tariq's relationships with political women.

❧

As Paul's short pamphlet was being published, events on the other side of the world drastically altered the course of British politics.

The Falkland Islands are about as far south as you can go before you get to the Antarctic. Eight thousand miles from Britain, they were an outpost of the old Empire – ignored, but not quite forgotten. In an effort to save money, the British government was planning to withdraw its one naval vessel from the area, and was proposing to end the right to British citizenship of many of its 1,800 inhabitants.

Then, on Friday, 2 April 1982, Argentinian troops invaded the Islands. Margaret Thatcher immediately called an extraordinary sitting of the House of Commons. She announced that, as Britain's sovereignty had been breached, a taskforce would be readied. Michael Foot, as leader of the Labour Party, supported her decision on behalf of the Labour opposition. The fleet left port two days later.

Tam Dalyell, the Labour MP for West Lothian, was appalled. No meeting of Labour MPs or the National Executive had had any opportunity to discuss the Labour Party's position. It was a fait accompli. He was angry with Michael Foot, but even more angry with Thatcher.

For a month, nothing happened. There was little to report as a vast fleet of aircraft carriers, frigates and destroyers sailed south. In the United States and at the UN, a diplomatic shuffle commenced to try to resolve the Argentinian government's claim to what it called the Islas Malvinas. All the while, Margaret Thatcher ratchetted up the British rhetoric. Britain declared a two-hundred-mile exclusion zone around the Islands, and threatened to sink any ships found either within it or sailing towards it.

And then, on Sunday, 2 May, HMS *Conqueror* sank the Argentinian cruiser *General Belgrano*. 'Gotcha!' ran the infamous headline in the first edition of the *Sun*. The lives of 368 Argentinian sailors were lost. The Argentine navy retaliated against HMS *Sheffield*, and another twenty-one sailors, this time British, were killed. The deaths continued until the war ended in June, the Islands once again secured for Britain.

Why did Margaret Thatcher and her war cabinet give the order to sink the *Belgrano*? Was it to scupper a peace plan, which was being hammered out that very day between Peru and Washington, acting on behalf of Argentina and Britain? That was the astonishing charge made by Tam Dalyell. For months he pestered the government with questions. But whenever he managed to elicit a reply, the responses from government ministers were so contradictory that the mystery only deepened. Was the *Belgrano* a threat, closing in on the British taskforce? Or was it positioned miles away, sailing in the opposite direction? When did HMS *Conqueror* get the *Belgrano* in its sights – the day it fired its deadly missiles, or the day before, or even the day before that? What did the government know of the Peruvian peace proposals?

Paul went to Lima to find out. There he met Peru's foreign minister at the time, Dr Javier Arias Stella, who had been one of the politicians in the diplomatic shuttle between Peru and the US secretary of state, Alexander Haig. With Haig in Washington was the British foreign secretary, Francis Pym, who had flown into Washington for the weekend, announcing as he arrived that there would be no further military action. Stella told Paul his government believed that, over the weekend of 1 and 2 May 1982, they had hammered out a deal. They printed and bound it ready for signature and prepared the Peace Room at the presidential palace, inviting the British and Argentinian ambassadors to the signing. The Argentine president held a press conference to tell the world what they were doing.

Then news suddenly came through of the sinking of the *Belgrano*. The peace went down with the ship. Stella told Paul: 'From that moment war was certain. All our efforts were – how can I put it – sunk.'[21]

For a year, Tam Dalyell had fought a vigorous campaign to find out why the *Belgrano* had been sunk when it was outside the total exclusion zone. If it had not been sunk, he believed, there would probably have been 'no *Sheffield*, no *Altlantic Conveyor*, no *Ardent*, no *Antelope* and no *Coventry*' – all the British ships which suffered loss of life during the war.[22] It was a serious charge, wrote Paul, that deserved a serious answer.

Paul's article in the *Mirror* in May 1983 coincided with the first anniversary of the sinking, and with a decision by Margaret Thatcher to call a general election. The following week, Paul was back on the attack. He had seen a report that Reuters had sent out at the time the Peruvian peace plan was being prepared, followed a few minutes later by a report from Downing Street saying they knew nothing of the reported negotiations or agreement in principle. 'Nothing?' asked Paul. 'Hadn't the Foreign Secretary been negotiating all day? Surely something must have filtered through?'[23] Neither the Foreign Office nor Thatcher's spokesman were much use to Paul. They just kept repeating that it was 'nonsense' to suggest any connection between the sinking and the peace plan.

Tam Dalyell tried again in the House of Commons. Both Thatcher and her minister of state at the Foreign Office, Cranley Onslow MP, insisted they had known nothing of the plan until after the *Belgrano* was sunk. According to Onslow, 'there was no treaty'. 'There was a treaty', wrote Paul. 'It was bound in red leather. It is still in the Peruvian Foreign Office where Mr Onslow can go and see it.'[24]

What of Francis Pym? Perhaps he and the officials in the British embassy in Washington could 'speak up for themselves', suggested Paul. Pym duly obliged. The following day, the *Mirror* published a long reply in which he dismissed Paul's articles as an absurd theory. He had met Alexander Haig for a two-hour meeting followed by lunch, but Haig's outline of the peace proposals had been brief. Any suggestion that he should have phoned London was 'a travesty of the truth'.[25]

What about HMS *Conqueror*? One of the questions that seemed so difficult to answer was when exactly the submarine had picked up the *Belgrano* on its radar. In their answers, government ministers had at the time been falling over themselves to sow confusion. But it seemed safe to conclude that it had happened thirty hours before the sinking – long before the decision was taken by the war cabinet to sink the ship. There was a way to end the speculation, wrote Paul: publish the ship's log.

For readers not keeping up with the story in the *Mirror*, Paul wrote a long piece for the *New Statesman*, setting it out in even more detail. He didn't have the answers he had sought, but he did understand the significance of the event:

The sinking of the *Belgrano* was, at best, a crass blunder, based on false information, which made a laughing-stock of Pym's negotiations. At worst, it was, as Tam Dalyell suggests, a desperate fling to force the other side back from a peace treaty which could have sunk the Tory leadership.[26]

There was one other important outcome of the Falklands War. Thatcher's popularity, and that of her government, had been at a low ebb before it began.[27] But just a year later, in the general election of June 1983, she successfully increased her majority by a whopping 101 seats.

Both Paul and Tam Dalyell continued to ask questions about the *Conqueror*'s log and the derailed peace plan, and Tam Dalyell continued to call Thatcher a liar (for which he was suspended from the House of Commons).

Paul and Dalyell had first met in Scotland in 1962. The young reporter on the Glasgow *Daily Record* had asked the newly selected Labour candidate for West Lothian: 'How on earth is it that the West Lothian Labour Party with six coal mines in the constituency can choose somebody from Eton as their candidate?' It was a question Tam would not forget.[28]

They would work in tandem again, demanding answers from those in power, when a plane was blown up over the small Scottish town of Lockerbie.

In that brief period in 1979 between leaving *Socialist Worker* and arriving at the *Daily Mirror*, Paul had found himself mercilessly cutting a long story about the death of Helen Smith that had arrived at *Private Eye*. Helen, a young British nurse, had died in mysterious circumstances in Saudi Arabia. Her father, Ron Smith, had travelled to Jeddah to identify her body, where he had poured out his story to Jack Lundin, then working for the local *Arab News*. Lundin wrote it up for the *Eye*.

His 'Letter from Jeddah' began by setting out the official version of what had happened. Helen had been to a drinks party, and fell to her death from the sixth-floor balcony of a flat belonging to a surgeon at the hospital where she worked. A Dutchman had died with her. The authorities said it had been a ghastly accident.[29] Ron did not believe a word of it. When he went to identify his daughter's body, the idea of just looking at her face was not going to cut it for this

The Foot family in 1938: front row from the left, Dingle and his wife Dorothy, Eva and Isaac (Paul's grandparents), Sylvia and Hugh, holding Paul; standing from left, Christopher, Sally, Michael, Anne (wife of John), John holding Kate, Jenny

Paul, fourth left, with his mother's family, the Tods: his maternal grandmother sits front left, his father front right

Second Lieutenant Foot and the Jamaica regiment on parade before the governor, Paul's father

*Paul at eight years old with his
cricket team in Jamaica*

*Paul with his mother and sister
Sarah on the beach in Jamaica*

*Paul, third left, and Gus Macdonald, third from the right, and
the Young Socialists in Skegness in the early 1960s*

Richard Ingrams and Paul in their Oxford days, with Brahms

Paul calling for an inquiry into the Hanratty case at Speakers' Corner, Hyde Park

Paul speaking at an anti-apartheid rally in Trafalger Square, 1970, with Reg Prentice MP (seated)

Paul and Ricky Tomlinson outside Leicester prison, with Marlene Tomlinson and Jim Nichol

Paul in front of a vast crowd in Newcastle upon Tyne during the 1984 miners' strike

Paul speaking up for his fellow members of the National Union of Journalists

Paul with Arthur Scargill, Dennis Skinner MP and Sylvia Pye, chair of National Women against Pit Closures, as Scargill and Peter Heathfield fight to clear their names, August 1990

Paul speaking in defence of the Bridgewater Four

What a mess! Paul and a meringue, much to the amusement of his friend Malcolm Blair

Paul with his political mentor Tony Cliff

Paul on sticks with, from the left, his sons Matt, Tom, John and daughter Kate

Paul with his partner Clare recovering at home from his aneurism

ex-policeman. He demanded to see her injuries and, when he did so, he knew there was something wrong with what he was being told. Why were there no obvious fall injuries? Why was her arm raised, as if to protect her face? Why were her thighs bruised on the inside? He demanded an autopsy.

Ron was particularly unimpressed by the officials he met at the British consulate in Jeddah. They seemed more interested in protecting their good relations with the Saudis than finding out how his daughter had died. Relations deteriorated so much that, on one memorable day, Ron punched the British consul in the face.

Paul was intrigued by the story; he had a sneaking regard for this man thrust into events over which he had no control: 'Every now and then', he wrote, 'an individual bucks the system; manages to worm his way into the very joints which make it work; and intensely annoys the people in charge of the machinery. Such a man is Ron Smith.'[30] The *Mirror* gave Paul an extraordinary amount of space, over two days in September 1980, to tell the Helen Smith story in her own words. Her father had given Paul exclusive access to her diary, which he had retrieved from her room at the nurses' home, and which he had until then been keeping to himself. 'These were Helen's secrets', Ron told Paul. 'And I didn't want them bandied about. The diary shows a little of the life Helen was leading – and being encouraged to lead. I think it was that style of life which led to her being murdered.'[31]

Paul became so caught up in the story that even the school holidays were no bar to searching out witnesses. 'I was meant to be on holiday', he later wrote, 'but on 11 August, taking my son Matthew who was recuperating from an operation, I drove to Brinkworth.'[32] Matt recalls it vividly. 'I remember it because I'd had three operations on my stomach. On our way, we visited an aunt in Wiltshire, a classic opportunistic use of family time, and then Paul crashed the car. He was talking and not looking.'

Paul continued to write about the case in the *Mirror*, but it was in *Private Eye* that he kept up the pressure, issue after issue, month after month, often in the prime spot on the opening inside page. It had become, wrote Paul, 'a running serial – a serial of a living story, which excited the imagination of the *Eye's* readership.'[33] In July 1982, the *Eye's* circulation rose for the first time to an extraordinary 200,000.

Of the stories that appeared – about the failings of the Foreign Office, the paucity of evidence from the enquiries both by the Yorkshire police and the police in Jeddah – it was the saga surrounding the inquest into Helen's death that exposed the difficulties Ron Smith was up against. It took months for him to get Helen's body back home, and when it was finally returned he made two requests – the first for a post-mortem, the second for an inquest. But the West Yorkshire coroner refused the inquest request outright, claiming he had no jurisdiction. The matter went to court, and then to appeal. Simon Brown QC, the high-profile barrister representing coroner Philip Gill, argued that bodies would be coming in from everywhere if such requests were agreed to. Nonsense, retorted Stephen Sedley for Ron Smith. He called Brown's argument 'the case of the peripatetic necrophile'. 'It doesn't conform with anything in real life . . . Experience provides not a single instance of anybody bringing in a corpse capriciously anywhere to get an inquest.' It was so absurd it should be dismissed.[34] And the Court of Appeal agreed.

It was Richard Ingram's idea for Paul to write a book about Ron Smith's story, however difficult that might be. Ron was, by his own account, a cantankerous bastard, and not a man who was easy to work with. He would latch on to facts in his favour and dismiss those that were inconvenient to his version of events. He would call Paul endlessly, at any hour of the day or night. He was, to put it mildly, demanding. But Paul accepted the challenge, so long as he had the final say.

The plan was to write the book in 1981. Paul found a publisher who wanted to take the book on; but ultimately, as the story kept changing, the publisher pulled out. A new publisher was found, but then the inquest was denied, then agreed after the appeal. The story continued to run on. Finally, in November 1982, the inquest began. To their credit, the jury returned an open verdict, not one of accidental death. They had accepted that Helen had fallen but, were unable to decide whether she was the victim of a crime.

Paul picked over the failings of the inquest at length in the book: the coroner's failure to call a number of witnesses, the refusal of other witnesses to appear, the coroner's summing up of the evidence. At the end of it all, the mystery remained unsolved. Why, asked Paul, did it take three-and-a-half years for the inquest to be held? And why did all the authorities at home and abroad strive so mightily to prevent it?[35]

The book reads like a whodunnit: a thrilling account of one man's long and lonely fight – a David and Goliath story, Ron Smith against the British establishment and the secretive Saudi state. He had fought with the Foreign Office, the coroners, and the gutter press, most of which had pilloried him. Gradually, he proved his case.

The Helen Smith Story was published at last in March 1983. For four years, *Private Eye* and the *Daily Mirror* had kept up a relentless barrage of stories. Every national paper had covered the three weeks of the inquest; not one of them reviewed the book. 'Not one single newspaper or magazine published one single review of this book!' Paul wrote in a scornful note inside a copy. 'Can this be a coincidence or are they all in the pay of the Foreign Office?'

16

The Enemy Within

The year 1984 was dominated by the miners' strike. It began on Monday, 5 March, and until Monday, 4 March 1985, the overwhelming majority of Britain's 200,000 coalminers were on strike. They were fighting for their jobs, and in many cases fighting for a way of life in pit villages that stretched from Kent in the south, up through the backbone of England and into Scotland, and west into Wales. For that whole year, the government, the police, the courts and the media fought a dirty war against the miners, replete with violence, misinformation and political duplicity. Thousands were taken to court and fined, nearly two hundred were sent to prison, many were evicted from their homes, an entire community went hungry – and there were even some deaths. It was, in Paul's words, 'as tough and crude a class battle' as had ever been waged.[1] There were two sides to this battle, and Paul was clear from the start whose side he was on.

The National Coal Board and the miners had been skirmishing for months about closures. There had been stoppages in Scotland and a national overtime ban. But it was the sudden announcement at the beginning of March 1984 that Cortonwood colliery in Yorkshire would close that suggested the Coal Board was upping the stakes. It knew, as did the government, that the miners would have to react. To ensure that they did, the closure of another twenty pits was announced just six days later.

By then, the miners at Cortonwood were already on strike, and the strike was spreading fast – across the Yorkshire coalfield and on into

Durham and Kent, Wales and Scotland; but not to Nottinghamshire. A majority, but not all, of the Nottinghamshire miners voted against a strike. The historical solidarity of the miners in 1926, and in the 1972 and 1974 strikes, was compromised from the start: 165,000 miners joined the strike, but 30,000 did not.

The government was prepared. In fact, Margaret Thatcher and her transport minister, Nicholas Ridley, had been planning her revenge against the miners for bringing down the previous Conservative government for years. Ian MacGregor had been installed as chairman of the National Coal Board; coal stocks had been piled high. The closure was announced in spring; summer was imminent, and demand for coal would dip. The police had been reorganised and retrained as strike-breakers.[2]

Thousands of police were drafted into the coalfields, and plain-clothes officers infiltrated the picket lines. The police had been given a free hand to stop miners moving around the country. Their behaviour was often excessive, sometimes cruel – even absurd. In the first month of the strike, Staveley Town football club, in Derbyshire – a club from an area where the miners were on strike – was due to play a Central Midland Football League match in Radford, Nottingham, where the miners were still at work. As the Staveley Town team drove down the M1, they were stopped by the police and accused of being pickets. The eleven men produced eleven pairs of boots, eleven football strips, the phone number of their manager and the location of the ground they were travelling to. No matter, the police turned them back. The club protested to the police, who denied in writing that any police car stopped them on that day.[3] This was just one of hundreds of stories about the strike and the harassment of the miners that came to Paul, mostly from miners themselves.

The courts were just as bad as the police. A miner on his way to appear before magistrates was arrested and locked up in a police van. When he failed to appear, the court was told by the police that they had no idea where he was. In another case, the magistrates imposed such draconian bail conditions on a striking miner that he was prevented from going anywhere near his own pit – which meant he was unable to live in his own house. It was of no interest to the magis-trates, and he and his girlfriend had to move in with their respective parents. Magistrates convicted a miner from Cortonwood of threatening behaviour, and fined him £100 plus £90 costs. The prosecution then asked for additional costs to cover the expense of two policemen who had travelled from Surrey to give evidence: a total of £230.90. No lawyer was aware of an order for police witness expenses being made in any other case, going back for years. Paul reported on all these cases, all of which were heard in the Nottingham courts.[4]

The National Coal Board behaved just as cynically. A striking miner in Nottingham, who lived in a Coal Board house, received a letter from his estate manager threatening him for having people to stay who were not immediate family. Who were these strange guests? Were they pickets? No, they were not. They were the miner's son, a soldier in the Royal Fusiliers, on leave from the Falklands, and his friend, another Fusilier.[5]

The volume of stories reaching Paul continued to grow. Then, in June, an anonymous package arrived. It contained a sheaf of letters that contradicted Thatcher's claim that she could not intervene in a dispute between the Coal Board and the miners. 'The Government has been secretly masterminding the handling of the miners' strike', Paul wrote, as he unveiled the contents of the letters, which included one from the prime minister's own private secretary at No. 10 to his counterpart at the Ministry of Transport, Nicholas Ridley's department. It was dated 16 April, and printed in full on the front page of the *Daily Mirror* on 6 June.[6] It set out the details of an enhanced offer to be made to the railwaymen to stop them striking at the same time as the miners. A second letter, from John Selwyn Gummer, then chairman of the Tory Party and minister for employment, described how it was 'critical' to avoid the risk of the militants on the railways making 'common cause' with the miners. The government's offer to the rail unions was accepted: their overtime ban was called off, and the 'second front' against the government had been outmanoeuvred.

The following day the leak was discussed in the cabinet, where Thatcher insisted: 'Government spokesmen should be robust in dismissing any criticism founded on the leak of documents in the *Daily Mirror.*'[7] Questions were raised in the House of Commons because, as Michael Foot put it, 'The Prime Minister had lied to the House.'[8]

Paul had added a note at the end of his article to protect the sender of the documents, whom he did not know and could not identify: 'All copies and negatives of them have been destroyed.'[9] He was making a serious point. A few months earlier, the *Guardian* had run a story about the arrival of cruise missiles in the UK, also based on documents from an anonymous source. The government was outraged and, appealing to national security, demanded their return. The *Guardian* believed – mistakenly – that it was protected from prosecution by the law, but the courts soon disabused them of this idea. 'Instead of saying they had burnt the thing long ago', which Paul thought they should have done, the *Guardian* pathetically admitted they still had them, and handed them over. A lowly clerk called Sarah Tisdall was arrested, and in March 1984 sent to prison for six months.[10]

Paul was outraged by the *Guardian's* behaviour. 'The people who break cover and say, "I'm not going to continue with this because I'm doing something wrong," are a goldmine, the jewels in the crown. And you do not sell them out.'[11]

From the start of the strike, Paul had been at odds with much of the liberal media over the question of the ballot. The strike had spread quickly, until most of the pits across the country were out – except for Nottingham. It was in effect a national strike, called by each of the mining areas, but without the NUM having collectively balloted for a national strike. That issue of the ballot bedevilled the union from the start. The government used it as a stick with which to beat Arthur Scargill, and pessimists in the media believed the failure to ballot had undermined the strike's legitimacy. The truth was, Paul argued, 'that actions spoke louder than ballots'.

What were the miners supposed to do? Go back to work while their union organised a ballot, and then come out on strike again? What if the ballot was lost? Were the miners' leaders expected to stand by while the government and the National Coal Board picked off the pits one by one, and two by two, until they had laid waste to the British coal industry? 'The sheer size and breath-taking solidarity of the mass strike was the fact, and the suggestion that the action should have been put at risk by a ballot was an argument that could be sustained only by enemies of the miners' union.'[12]

Paul was irritated by those journalists who were mealy-mouthed about the strike, predicting nothing but gloom and doom, and he pointedly named the *New Statesman* and the *Observer*. 'When I am approached by the new pessimists and asked anxiously if I think the miners will win, I reply that I have no idea', he wrote. But

> what is absolutely plain as a pikestaff, undeniable, written large in recent history is that the miners *can* win, and that if they do, they will change the whole political and social climate. What they need least of all in their struggle are 'well-informed' moaners and wimps on the left, who are so uncomfortable in their own pessimism that they try to paralyse everyone else with it.[13]

The right-wing media were united in their opposition to the strike, condemning the miners at every opportunity. They had little regard for the facts, which they simply made up if it suited their purpose. In May, two months into the strike, a front-page headline in the *Evening Standard* read: 'Sabotage!' The story claimed that five lorries had had their wheel nuts loosened, causing two of them to crash. The newspaper blamed the strikers, quoting the police and the Coal Board, who both did the same. But what were the facts? The haulage company explained to Paul that a vehicle had broken down and, because it could not be repaired immediately, the driver had disabled it by removing the wheel. What about the other lorries, Paul asked, the ones with loosened wheel nuts that had crashed? Not true: it had never happened. 'There was no vandalism of any sort whatsoever', according to the company. The 'Sabotage!' reported by the *Standard* was pure invention.[14]

At the centre of this media furore, as each newspaper tried to outdo its competitors, was NUM leader Arthur Scargill. In that same month of May, the *Sun* planned an offensive front page, with 'Mine Führer' above a photo of Scargill snapped giving a Hitler-style salute. The *Sun* printers, angry at such an odious attack, refused to handle it, and the paper appeared instead with an extraordinary front-page statement within a blank space: 'Members of all The *Sun* production chapels refused to handle the Arthur Scargill picture and major head-line on our lead story.'[15]

The *Daily Express* was no better. That month, it also ran a front-page lead story about Scargill, ostensibly written by the NUM leader himself, but which was in fact by the paper's editor, Sir Larry Lamb.[16] Paul was incandescent. 'It was a vile, desperate, below-the-belt lunge of hatred in the middle of a miners' strike', he wrote, 'which should have buckled long ago, but hasn't.'[17]

Paul had known Scargill since his days as president of the Yorkshire miners, and spoke to him often during the strike. 'He is a little too proud of himself, perhaps', he wrote in the same article, but not averse to friendly criticism. Scargill would not listen to Paul's arguments when it came to the question of Polish coal. During the strike, the British government was spending millions importing coal from Poland and South Africa. The miners wanted to keep it out of the country, and Scargill had been to Paris to talk to the international trade unions in the hope that they would assist. In South Africa they appealed to the unions not to handle coal destined for Britain, but in the case of Poland – then still a part of the Soviet bloc – Scargill was not calling on the Polish unions not to handle coal: he was asking the Polish military government to stop exporting it.

'Many weeks ago, long before the strike, I criticised Arthur Scargill for his public defence of the Polish government', wrote Paul. 'I asked him to consider the government's attitude to trade unions and the fact that what [General] Jaruzelski says today, [Norman] Tebbit says tomorrow. He has had his answer. Polish coal will flood in.'[18] And that is exactly what happened.

There seemed to be no limit to the resources the government was prepared to pump into defeating the miners. Nigel Lawson, the chancellor, admitted in July that the strike had already cost the government over £300 million. It was, he said, 'a worthy investment'. By the end, estimates of the cost ran as high as £5 billion. At enormous expense, 10,000 police had been drafted into the coalmining areas – partly to boost numbers, but also because it was thought that police who were not local might be less sympathetic to the miners' cause. Pickets across the coalfields were doing whatever they could to avoid the police and to stop working miners from scabbing, coal and coke lorries from moving, and steel from leaving the smelters. And then there was Orgreave.

❧

Orgreave was a huge coking plant near Rotherham that supplied the Scunthorpe steel mills. On 23 May, convoys of lorries started leaving the smelter under police escort. The miners responded with picket lines, but ended up engaged in running battles with the police. These rose in intensity until June, when Scargill joined thousands of miners and, with many others, was arrested and charged with obstruction. On 18 June 1984, Scargill called for one big push – a mass picket big enough to stop the lorries and the plant through sheer force of numbers. He would be there himself, alongside 8,000 pickets.

It was a sunny day, and the miners were in T-shirts, jeans and trainers. They had had an unusually easy time getting to the site, only to find they were facing 5,000 highly organised police, hundreds of them in specialist riot gear, others with dogs, and more still on horse-back. The police had come prepared for something far more serious than stopping the lorries.

What took place that day came to be known as the Battle of Orgreave. It was the most violent confrontation between strikers and police throughout the strike. Footage showed police horses charging into the crowds, wielding long-handled batons, and blood-ied miners being hauled away under arrest. Not even Scargill was safe: there were photos of him collapsed on the ground and being helped up and into an ambulance. He too, he said, had been attacked by the police.

That evening, Assistant Chief Constable Tony Clement went on television to set the news agenda for the day: the police had come under attack; they were the victims of violent rioters, and Arthur Scargill had not been hit by anyone, but had slipped down a grassy bank. Not so, said Paul. He spoke to two miners who saw Scargill being hit on the back of the head by the police, and collapsing. They helped him up, and lifted him off the road and then up a bank, where he was sitting when the assistant chief constable arrived and called an ambulance. Paul spoke to a total of six miners, all from different areas, who did not know each other – and all said Scargill was attacked by the police.[19]

What happened in the terrifying ordeal that day, both for the miners and those who lived in the village of Orgreave, was the oppo-site of what had happened to the miners at Saltley Gate over a decade before. This time, no Birmingham engineers appeared over the brow of the hill. And if one person understood perfectly the lessons of that day at Saltley Gate in February 1972, it was Margaret Thatcher. To bring the unions under control, she knew that the battle would have to be taken to them: out to the pits and the factories, not, as she wrote in her autobiography, 'in the debating chamber of the House of Commons'.[20]

More than ninety miners were arrested at Orgreave, and fifty-five charged with riot. Leon Brittan, then the home secretary, announced publicly that miners convicted of riot should be sentenced to the maximum term in prison for that offence: life. Yet not one miner was convicted. It transpired that the police colluded with each other in writing up their statements, made up their evidence, and lied outright. When this was revealed in court the trials collapsed. The South Yorkshire Police had to pay out a small fortune in compensation for the arrests.

Violence was nothing new to the strike. David Jones, a Yorkshire miner aged just twenty-four, died picketing at Ollerton in Nottinghamshire on 15 March. Joe Green was hit by a scab lorry at Ferrybridge in June. But there was, for Paul, another sort of violence – the violence of poverty.

'They buried Paul Womersley yesterday', he wrote in the news pages of the *Mirror* in September.

> In the old Coal Board houses in Upton, you need coal to heat the rooms and the water. Almost every striker has stocked up for the winter from the tips of the old Upton colliery. There's high grade coal to be found there if you dig deep and hard enough. Paul Wormsley didn't stand a chance. The rain had loosened the slurry and he was suffocated to death under a ton of it.[21]

He was just fourteen years old.

Paul travelled to Upton for his funeral, organised by the women of the village, the local Miners' Wives Support Group. These were the women who had been cooking for the miners and their families from the start of the strike. 'Many older miners were ashamed to accept what they saw as charity', Edie Woolley told Paul. 'We told them it wasn't charity, it was solidarity. People gave not because they're sorry for us, but because they support us.' They packed up food parcels, provided nappies, and were on permanent alert for visits from bailiffs and the electricity board. They ran around the streets intercepting the vans that arrived to cut off the supply to the miners unable to pay their electricity bills, and chased the bailiffs away. The government had reckoned neither with the ingenuity of these women nor the sheer optimism of the strikers.

Much later, Paul would recall that day in Upton. He had bumped into a miner and asked him about the wretchedness of the strike. The miner beamed back, a grin that spread from ear to ear. 'I've enjoyed it', he told Paul. Of course, he and his family had very little money, and of course they were worried by the cold. But life was different. The daily grind had gone. The miners were making their own decisions – about picketing, about welfare, about how to respond to the political ebbs and flows of the strike. They were not waiting for someone else, some high-up somewhere, to do it for them. They were in charge of their own destiny.

'There was change all about', Paul wrote. 'People were changing. In the strength of their collective action, they felt a new confidence in themselves and the people around them. Ideas and prejudices which had been grafted into them like barnacles were suddenly blasted away.'[22]

Throughout the strike, Paul was also writing a column for *Socialist Worker*. The idea had been suggested to him the previous year by Chris Harman, the paper's editor. 'We'll like it', Harman had said, 'but that's not the point. It will do you good.'[23] Paul agreed. It did do him good, and he went on writing the column for years.

But if he and Harman were rubbing along together, it did nothing to quell Paul's irritation at the way the paper and the party were dealing with the strike. The front pages of *Socialist Worker* were devoted to the strike; week after week, the paper spoke up for the miners, urged others to support them, and denounced the lack of leadership from the TUC and the Labour Party. But there was something missing. There was an air of telling workers what should be done, rather than participating in what was being done. In fact, Paul became so fed up he wrote a short letter to the paper's staff, arguing that they could do better.

'Dear Comrades', he began.

> I have just read this week's SW from cover to cover. As far as I can see, apart from a small story on page 2, there is not a *single living experience* reported from a *single* coalfield. Everything about the strike (except for letters, and they aren't very descriptive either) is comment, written from the office, or from other industries.

He had a simple solution: 'Shouldn't almost all of you be *in the coalfields* almost all the time?'

He had been prompted to write the letter after speaking at a miners' rally. Afterwards, he chatted to several of the miners and picked up four or five new stories for his column. Surely the journalists on the paper could do the same? 'There is a lot of picketing – not to mention hundreds of stories from the coalfields about the *life* of the strike.'[24]

Paul was not the only one feeling critical. A cartoon in *Socialist Worker* in July 1984 summed up the arguments taking place within the SWP at the time. Tim Sanders had drawn a tin of baked beans flying through the air and knocking off a policeman's helmet.[25] Should the party's support go to the pickets, the most militant of the strikers? Or to the families, the women and the kitchens who were keeping the strike going by feeding it? Money for pickets or money for beans? It was a serious row. At one national meeting, Paul criticised the entire SWP central committee for the way they were running the party's intervention in the strike. Matters were resolved. The party took heed. Perhaps there had been too much focus on the militants rather than the wider campaign of support for the miners.

Paul spoke at miners' rallies as often as he was invited. In June he was at a vast open-air rally in Newcastle – one of the best meetings of his life, he thought – speaking to 5,000 miners and their families: 'They were full of confidence and pride. It was marvellous.'[26] Then he spoke with Tony Cliff to the Bentley miners and their families in Yorkshire; in August he would speak alongside Scargill and Denis Skinner MP, in Sheffield.

In that same month of August a sequence of events began that would tie the NUM up in legal knots, leading the High Court to impose massive fines on the union and appoint receivers to run its finances. The person who kick-started that chain of events was a working miner called Ken Foulstone, a man who was proving very popular with the media. During his many television appearances in the summer of 1984, Foulstone's constant refrain was that the laws of the land must be upheld. 'This causes some hilarity in the village of Harley', wrote Paul later in the year, 'where his ex-wife lives with her three grown-up children.'²⁷ One of his children, Stephen, then aged eighteen, remembered his father arriving home when he was about eleven with a suitcase full of items, all stolen from an historic building called Cantley Hall, in Doncaster – a haul that included a pair of white porcelain Meissen doves. Foulstone was so taken with these doves that he photographed them, and Stephen kept the photo as a memento.

Soon after, Foulstone left his wife and children and, with his second wife, opened an antique shop in Nottinghamshire. When Paul rang him about the doves and the picture now in his possession, he had no explanation for how his son had a photograph.

Paul was helped with the story on Foulstone by Phil Turner, a reporter on the *Rotherham Advertiser*, and also a member of the SWP. He tracked down the caretaker of Cantley Hall, who confirmed the burglary and recognised the missing doves. The police also confirmed the burglary, and told him no one had yet been arrested for the crime. After the strike, Paul was called as a witness at the trial of Ken Foulstone for burglary. He was acquitted of that particular charge.²⁸

Chris Butcher was another of the working miners popular with the media during 1984. Nicknamed 'Silver Birch' by the *Daily Mail* (because of his shock of grey hair; Scargill preferred to call him 'Dutch Elm'), Butcher claimed he wanted to bring back democracy to the NUM. 'Perhaps he should start by having a proper vote at his own pit, Bevercotes', wrote Paul. Elections for officers had been held in June, and all those elected, including Butcher, were working miners. The striking miners were all defeated, some by as little as two votes, even when they had held office for years. Immediately after the vote, complaints started to pour in from striking miners: the police had prevented them from getting to the vote. Over fifty complaints were lodged, and new elections were ordered.[29] Chris Butcher did not stand.[30]

Men like Foulstone and Butcher needed help to organise the working miners, and one of those who stepped forward to give them a hand was David Hart, described by Paul as 'an imbecile property tycoon and right-wing fanatic'.[31] But Hart had the ear of Margaret Thatcher and Ian MacGregor, and he was authorised to establish and fund a National Working Miners' Committee from among the strike-breakers. He drove across the coalfields in his fancy car, inviting the favoured few for meetings at Claridge's – then the poshest of London's hotels.

The inside story of the formation of the committee came to Paul from Brian Copping, a working miner at Houghton Main colliery near Barnsley, who at the start of the strike had wanted a ballot. He joined the Committee thinking that was its purpose, and sat through several meetings with Hart. But he soon realised that it was turning into something else entirely – an anti-trade union organisation. He objected strongly to the idea, and told his story to Paul.

On their own, the miners could not win. The railwaymen were bought off in the early months of the strike. The steelworkers had been defeated two years earlier. The dockers came out, went back, came out again, and went back again. But there was one group that could bring the working pits to a standstill: the pit deputies who were members of NACODS, the National Association of Colliery Overmen, Deputies and Shotfirers. These men worked underground as supervisors of the work in the coal seams, and they were responsible for all safety and explosives work. No seam could be worked without them.

In August, the Coal Board ordered the NACODS men to cross the NUM picket lines or face the sack. Ian MacGregor then made matters worse by telling the BBC that NACODS had agreed to this, when they had done nothing of the sort. It was a move of considerable stupidity. NACODS had never been on strike, but they were hostile to the closure of the pits. Peter McNestry, general secretary of the union, rang Paul to complain about MacGregor – and Paul rang the coal board: 'We hope to meet NACODS shortly to discuss this', they told him.[32]

In September, NACODS balloted its members on the pit closures and the order to cross picket lines. With a turnout of 90 per cent, 82 per cent voted to strike, starting in late October. 'For many, many months now British newspapers have been howling for a ballot over the miners' strike', wrote Paul in a Media Watch column in the *New Statesman*. 'Last week, they got a ballot which produced a sensational result. How did [the media] respond?' The *Daily Mirror* and the *Guardian* did all right, he judged, but

> pride of place for bias and distortion . . . must go, as so often, to Murdoch's *Times*, for its glorious headline: 'Pit hopes still alive despite deputies 82% vote for strike.' The word 'hopes', of course, is not an objective one. It depends who is doing the hoping.[33]

The NACODS strike was due to start just as the decline in coal stocks was becoming critical. Margaret Thatcher was concerned enough to be considering sending in troops. If the strike went ahead, no working pit would be able to continue: there would be a total stoppage. The trickle of miners returning to work would end. In response, Thatcher made it clear to Ian MacGregor that he was to settle with NACODS. In the end he did enough, and the union buckled.

In that same week at the end of October, news hit the headlines that the NUM had sent its chief executive officer, Roger Windsor, to Libya to try to persuade Colonel Gaddafi to support the miners by ending the export of oil to Britain. 'The Poisonous Embrace' was the *Mirror's* front-page lead, as a photo of Roger Windsor and Gaddafi was relayed around the world.[34] After the killing of PC Yvonne Fletcher outside the Libyan embassy in London earlier in the year, and the expulsion of Libyan diplomats and severing of diplomatic ties that followed, this was seen as a step too far. The fury of the government and the media against the NUM was now without limit.

Such humbug, wrote Paul. The government condemns the NUM for their recent 'Libyan encounter' while the government meets with the Libyan government all the time to discuss trade. A senior Libyan minister came to Britain in October 1981 to meet Ian MacGregor when he was chairman of British Steel. On and on the meetings went, between officials and some of Britain's largest companies, and the Libyan state. Millions of pounds' worth of business had been achieved, 'more than will come from Libya to the National Union of Mineworkers'.[35]

As autumn wore on into winter, the courts continued to wreak their havoc on the NUM. Meanwhile the Labour Party, Neil Kinnock and the leaders of the TUC continued to offer warm words but no action – that is, when they were not vocally condemning the strike and its violence, as the police ran riot in pit village after pit village. The miners had no other strategy than to fight on for as long as possible. All through the last months of the year, the strike continued to hold. It would all be over by Christmas, predicted the media and the government; but it was not. It continued into the biting cold of January and February 1985.

Support for the strike endured, and Paul continued to speak at meetings around the country. He was off to Rotherham in January, then joined Tony Cliff at Easington colliery in County Durham, and the two spoke together again at a huge meeting in Pontefract in mid February. Paul was full of stories about the strike – about the evidence concocted by the police against striking miners, and the bias of the media. Both he and Cliff talked of the magnificent contribution to the struggle of the miners' wives.

But poverty and hardship were sucking the life out of the strike, and driving the miners back to work. On Sunday, 3 March, the NUM called a delegate conference and voted to end the strike. They had been out for a year, but had to accept it had all ended in defeat. There was no deal with the Coal Board, no surrender. The miners simply picked up their banners and marched back into the pits, heads high. And there, in the pits, their optimism slowly died in the daily grind of work deep underground.

Paul returned to Newcastle for a May Day rally in 1985. In June the previous year, at the most optimistic moment of the strike, he had spoken to 5,000 miners and their families at their rally. Now there were just 120, and their mood was 'sad, low, rudderless', he wrote in *Socialist Worker*.[36]

The miners' strike was the longest mass strike in British history. Thatcher's government was stopped in its tracks for a full year. But the price for individual miners was high: a year without wages for everyone on strike; thousands injured; nearly a thousand sacked; 200 sent to prison; and two killed on picket lines. And still the pit closures went ahead. This meant not just the 20,000 jobs that were already slated to go – they were just the beginning of the end of coalmining in Britain.

Paul could see that the consequences were far wider than the mining industry. 'The end of the strike led to a collapse of aspirations and morale among its supporters', he wrote. 'Neil Kinnock, who had been attacked in almost every Labour Party in the country for his weasel words about the strike, suddenly became "the only hope".'[37] But not much of a hope: Labour still lost the election in 1987.

The end of the strike left a bitter taste. But, wrote Paul, 'we must remember that the strike fell short of its aims not because it happened nor because it was led by extremists nor because a ballot wasn't held but because the other side was better organised and better prepared than ours was; and that therefore next time we must be better prepared.'[38]

The person who had been best prepared was Margaret Thatcher. During the strike, she described the miners and their leaders as 'the enemy within'. Writing about her in *Socialist Worker* as the strike ground to its end, Paul explained something of her political touch:

Mrs Thatcher's real skill comes from her deep sensitivity to the ebbs and flows in the fortunes of her class. She is a class general who knows no sentiment in the struggle. She is a new-fashioned two-nation Tory who understands the simple truth, which evades too many of us: that class confidence comes out of class strength, and that her class can win only if the other class loses.[39]

17

Pamphleteer

The miners' strike ended in March 1985, and once more Paul drove up to Skegness for the Easter weekend. It was, he admitted in his *Socialist Worker* column, one of the nastiest seaside towns in Britain. 'The weather is usually cold and wet. The journey to the place is interminable. The countryside is tedious beyond belief and even the beaches are bleak. Am I mad?'[1] Yet he had been making this trip to the SWP's annual Easter weekend get together for ten years, and he never tired of it. 'It is probably the only place on God's earth where people are queuing at 8.30 in the morning waiting for the bookshop to open ... Nowhere else is the ballroom a place for non-stop political meetings 12 hours a day.' Nothing much changed from year to year, but when 2,000 like-minded people gathered to argue, debate and play games, Paul felt at ease. 'For once I don't feel an oddball because I'm a member of the SWP. At Skegness suddenly everyone is a Trot.'

The miners' strike was topped and tailed by these trips to the Lincolnshire coast. At the start, in 1984, he was there to talk about George Orwell's book, *Nineteen Eighty-Four*. Paul had first read Orwell at Oxford, and recognised in him the 'implacable enemy of class society, of inequality, of empire, of what he called the Blimps who ran Britain.'[2] Paul claimed he had read everything, or almost everything, Orwell had written. For his Skegness meeting there was a mountain of material to quote, and plenty of political debate to be had. But the book itself hardly got a look in. In his speech, Paul ran through Orwell's early life, his school days at Eton, his years in the Burmese police, his early works. But his focus was on *The Road to Wigan Pier* and, by contrast, *Homage to Catalonia*. When reading *The Road to Wigan Pier*, he said,

> You get a real feeling of the conditions that workers lived in. The dreadful conditions in their houses, the dreadful conditions in the places that they worked. You get a real feeling of the warmth and decency of working-class people, as opposed to the people among whom Orwell had moved up to that time. But you get no feeling at all, throughout the whole book, of their strength and their power; no feeling of the collective action which can change these conditions.[3]

To write the book, George Orwell had been to Wigan to live among the miners. In 1936 he was off again, this time to Spain, in support of the Republican cause in the civil war.

Paul had read *Homage to Catalonia*, the book Orwell wrote on his return from Spain, as a young man. 'I remember twenty-four years ago', he said,

> as the President of the Oxford University Liberal Club, picking up this book, and just on the third page reading this: 'It was the first time that I had ever been in a town where the working class were in the saddle. Practically every building of any size had been seized by the workers and was draped with red flags or with the red and black flag of the Anarchists; every wall was scrawled with the hammer and sickle and with the initials of the revolutionary parties; almost every church had been gutted and its images burnt.'

Paul read out the whole description – how every shop and café had had been collectivised, even the bootblacks; how the waiters and the shopkeepers treated their customers as equals, and tipping was forbidden; the more familiar forms of speech that were used; the absence of private motorcars, which had all been commandeered. 'In outward appearance', wrote Orwell, 'it was a town in which the wealthy classes had practically ceased to exist', and it made him feel uneasy. 'All this was queer and moving. There was much in it that I did not understand, in some ways I did not even like it, but I recognised it immediately as a state of affairs worth fighting for.'

Orwell's description of his experience at the front, fighting the fascists with the militia was, Paul thought, some of the finest revolutionary writing in English literature:

> However much one cursed at the time, one realised afterwards that one had been in contact with something strange and valuable. One had been in a community where hope was more normal than apathy or cynicism, where the word 'comrade' stood for comradeship, and not, as in most countries, for humbug. One had breathed the air of equality.[4]

Here, for Paul, was the contrast to *The Road to Wigan Pier*. Orwell had seen the working class in action, and in control, and written a very different book.

There was something else that Orwell had discovered in Spain. He was shocked by the role of the Communist Party. The CP had fought the fascists, but it had sided with the liberals against the socialists and the revolution. 'The thing that struck him', Paul said, 'and struck him all the way through the rest of his life, almost every day of it, was this business of the Communist Party allying themselves with the counter-revolution.' That was the explanation for what followed. 'It was impossible really to appreciate all the things that Orwell later wrote unless you understand that fact. How deeply he was enraged by the role of the Communists in Spain.'[5]

It became his preoccupation, and almost no one else's at the time. He believed the destruction of the Soviet myth was essential to any revival of the socialist movement in Britain. It was this myth that Orwell set out to destroy in his two satires on the totalitarian state – first *Animal Farm*, then *Nineteen Eighty-Four*.

That day in Skegness, Paul urged his audience to read Orwell. If they hadn't read *Homage to Catalonia*, then they should feel ashamed, he said. But if they had read *Nineteen Eighty-Four* and *Animal Farm*, but had not read *Homage to Catalonia*, that was a catastrophe.

When Paul and the others left *Socialist Worker* in 1979, Peter Marsden stayed to run the SWP's publishing projects. He built up quite an industry recording almost all of the Skegness and Marxism talks, which he sold as cassette tapes, reprinting many as short pamphlets.

In 1981, for example, on the anniversary of the peasants' revolt, Paul's talk at the SWP's Skegness Easter weekend, about the high hopes and terrible defeat of Wat Tyler and the peasant armies in 1381, was published within weeks as 'This Bright Day of Summer'.[6]

It was the story of a tremendous victory by the English peasantry against the king after the introduction of a poll tax, followed by a terrible and bloody defeat as Richard took his revenge. Very few had died in the rebellion – perhaps a hundred; but thousands died in its defeat, including Wat Tyler himself. 'Serfs you have been and serfs you shall remain', Paul quoted King Richard's reply to the men of Essex, who were slaughtered in their hundreds.[7] Their bondage would be even viler than before, he told them, as an example to anyone who might dream of following in their footsteps.

Would it have been better, Paul asked, as so many historians have argued, if the peasants had stayed at home? Not at all, and for good reason.

> For Richard, as he spoke those words, was whistling in the dark, and he *knew* he was whistling in the dark, because he and his nobles had seen the strength and the potential of the risen people, and he wasn't going to risk that in any circumstances again.

'Nothing concentrates the minds of the hereditary landlords and capitalists', Paul said, 'quite like the memory of Wat Tyler.'

Three years later, the Orwell talk was also prepared for publication by Marsden, although it never appeared.[8] Perhaps the talk included too many digs at the SWP line, too many jokes at the party's expense, about its language, about Central Committee documents. Whatever the reason, it was typed up and ready to go to the printers, but was never sent.[9]

The miners' defeat was still raw by the time Paul returned to Skegness in 1985. But the comrades who gathered there discussed it in a series of meetings in front of what Paul described as one of the most politically sophisticated audiences in the country. His own talk that year was about A. J. Cook, the revolutionary miners' leader, during one of the great moments of the trade union movement in Britain: the general strike of 1926.

Cook was a working miner who became a socialist, then a communist, a union activist and a vocal advocate of class war. In 1924 he was elected secretary of the Miners' Federation, and immediately announced his intention of speaking in the coalfields every weekend. 'This was one of the most extraordinary agitations in the history of the British working-class movement. Old miners today still remember the impact of those huge meetings', wrote Paul in the pamphlet taken from his talk.[10]

What was it about the man that made him so electric and compelling a speaker? He was described by Beatrice Webb as a man of no intellect and not much intelligence, but as not without personal attractiveness: 'an inspired idiot, drunk with his own words, dominated by his own slogans'. This quote reappeared in the *Guardian* during the 1984 strike, whose industrial correspondent applied it freely to Arthur Scargill.[11] It was true, explained Paul, that Cook could be inarticulate. But he was also enormously popular, because he was speaking *for* his audience, not *to* his audience.

Cook had seen the struggle with the mine owners coming. It began on 30 April 1926. When the miners were locked out, a general strike was called, and lasted for nine days before it was sold out in a deal between the TUC and the government. The miners were left to fight on by themselves for another seven months, before the owners lifted their lockout and imposed their pay cuts. The miners were starved back to work.

The parallels to the 1984 strike were clear in the reporting of the 1926 strike:

> The early confidence and enthusiasm; the importance of the communal kitchens; the emancipation of the women. Again, and again, the *Sunday Worker* pays tribute to the 'astonishment' of the miners' leaders and supporters at the role of the women in the pit communities . . .

Here Paul echoed his own column in *Socialist Worker* about the 'exhilarating and exciting' phenomenon of the women in 1984.[12]

> Then there were the bad things: the flooding of the coalfields with police from outside forces; the mass arrests; the discrimination against miners' families by the Board of Poor Law Guardians (the equivalent

of the DHSS[13]); the revenge of the judges and magistrates – and of course the press, which Cook described as 'the most lying in the world'.

The defeat of the miners and the failure of the general strike heralded the great depression of the 1930s, and a mindset in the TUC and the leadership of the Labour Party that talking to government was what mattered, rather than talking to their own members.

As with his talk on Orwell, the plan for publication ran into difficulties. During the 1926 strike Cook had led from the front, drawing his strength from the support of the miners. When the strike was defeated, he lost their support and his strength. Paul quotes Robin Page Arnot, a contemporary of Cook, who wrote that, when he lost that support,

> he lost the ground on which he lived and moved and had his being. Today his faults are forgotten or forgiven amongst the older miners who tell the younger men their recollections of past days; and still in every colliery village there abides the memory of a great name.

Paul liked that epitaph because, he wrote at the very end of his pamphlet,

> It seems to me that one of the important tests of socialists' behaviour is how we relate to, and how we criticise, great working-class leaders who can lead their class in the heat of the struggle, impervious to the most awful onslaught from the other side. Of such leaders Arthur Cook was undoubtedly one.

The pamphlet ended there. But Paul's talk and his original copy had ended differently. The last line had read: 'And Arthur Scargill is undoubtedly another.' The line was deleted.

Peter Marsden described getting a 'blast' when the SWP's publications committee read the draft. Perhaps they felt that Paul was a little soft on Arthur Scargill. 'He's not dead yet', warned Tony Cliff, who wanted to see changes to Paul's draft.

At issue was a sensitive argument about legitimate criticism of trade union leaders. The danger for socialists, Paul argued, was not being insufficiently critical of trade union leaders, like A. J. Cook after 1926 or Arthur Scargill after 1984, but being too sectarian towards them. 'As we try to steer our tiny socialist craft through the same sort of stormy waters, what dangers loom up ahead?' he asked. On the one side was the huge rock of Reformism, to which socialists are lured by the prospect of defeating a vicious Tory government. On the other side was the rock of Sectarianism.

> As we pull the tiller over, we had better beware . . . the voices which beckon us away altogether from the real, living working-class movement, which becalm us in eddies and pools where other socialists are sailing around in smaller and smaller circles . . . Sectarianism is the hiding place for socialists who refuse to accept that they must be part of the working-class movement, or they are finished.[14]

Just such an attitude, Paul felt, was strong within the SWP: 'In times like these', he continued, 'it seems to me, sectarianism is if anything an even greater menace for small socialist organisations than is accommodation to reformism.' That paragraph was also excised.

Peter Marsden tended to agree with Cliff. In his letter to Paul, he argued that during the strike the struggle itself was pulling socialists to the left, and Kinnock's rightward drift was against the stream. But the climate had changed radically since the strike ended, and now the pull was to the right. 'Phone me if you agree to [the deletions]; phone Cliff if you don't.'[15]

The deletions were made, and publication went ahead.

Tony Cliff responded by writing his own account of A. J. Cook for *International Socialism Journal*, with no reference at all to Paul's talk or his pamphlet.[16]

Over the course of his life, Paul wrote a lot of pamphlets. He agreed with George Orwell, who had written in 1943: 'We live in a time when political passions run high, channels of free expression are dwindling, and organised lying exists on a scale never before known. For plugging the holes in history, the pamphlet is the ideal form.'[17]

Altogether, Paul wrote eleven short pamphlets and another three longer ones, co-wrote another, and wrote introductions to at least three more. Some were designed to plug the holes, in particular the pamphlets of the 1980s, on Wat Tyler, George Orwell and A. J. Cook.

Others were more agitational – the self-explanatory *How to Fight the Tories* in 1970, after the election of the Heath government, for instance; and *The Postal Workers and the Tory Offensive* from a year later, following the sell-out of the postal workers' strike. Some were more explanatory: *Unemployment: The Socialist Answer*, which Paul wrote in Glasgow in 1963, and *Workers against Racism* a decade later. And there were those that were clearly directed at the debate of the day: *While Tories Shriek . . . Socialism Has an Answer* was a reprint from *Socialist Worker* in January 1979, in the run-up to the election that Margaret Thatcher won (this one must certainly take the prize for worst title). *Three Letters to a Bennite* followed in 1982, as Paul and the SWP tried to stem the tide of people leaving to join the Labour Party.

The first of the longer pamphlets, *Why You Should Be a Socialist*, appeared in 1977, when the International Socialists relaunched themselves as the Socialist Workers Party at a time when Labour's popularity was declining in the Wilson and Callaghan years. The second, *The Case for Socialism*, was published in 1990, after the fall of the Berlin Wall. That event threw up a larger question: Had the people of eastern Europe not rejected socialism? Paul argued they had not, because those regimes never were socialist. The very word needed rescuing.

While most of these pamphlets were published by the SWP, in a variety of guises, there was just one written for a commercial publisher. In the late 1980s, the publishing house Chatto & Windus brought out a series of 'Counterblasts', in which, according to the publishers' description, Britain's finest writers and thinkers confronted the crucial issues of the day 'in the best tradition of pamphleteering'. It was music to Paul's ears. His contribution, *Ireland: Why Britain Must Get Out*, published in the summer of 1989, began with a simple proposition:

> There is a solution to the problem of Northern Ireland. There is a way out of the endless cycle of killing and terror. It is for the British government to cut its connection with the state of Northern Ireland, and to get out of Ireland.[18]

It was a bold and direct opening to a short, tightly argued polemic.

The central problem, he argued, was partition of the North from the South. 'Ireland is England's oldest colony', he wrote. He rattled through the Act of Union between Ireland and Britain (1800); the demand for independence and Home Rule (1910); the ferocious campaign against it in the name of religion and support for partition (1912); the acquiescence by the nationalists that half a loaf was better than none (1914); the lone voice of James Connolly, insisting that half a loaf poisoned by religion was worse than no loaf at all; the failure of the Easter Rising (1916); and the creation of a Protestant state for a Protestant people (1921).

'The carnival of reaction was about to begin', he wrote. In the North, Catholics were driven out of their jobs and their homes. Council borders were gerrymandered to ensure no political representation for Catholics. Northern Ireland became a Protestant state with a Protestant police force, and an economy dependent on subsidies from Britain. It lasted for fifty years before the dam burst in 1968. Then successive British governments and prime ministers – Edward Heath, Harold Wilson, James Callaghan, Margaret Thatcher – tried ineffectually to bring about some minor political changes. No one even discussed cutting Northern Ireland loose.

'My proposal is very simple: the British government should declare that it intends to withdraw its troops from Ireland forever; and that it will no longer sustain a separate state in the North of Ireland.' The government should set a date and convene an international constitutional conference to plan the withdrawal, and agree 'what contribution Britain should make to a new, united Ireland'.

He anticipated the outcry. But, he argued, there could be a positive outcome: 'In the shock of the sudden collapse of the Old Order, the positive sides of the people of Ireland of both religions could well prevail over the narrow superstitions which have kept them at each other's throats for so long.'[19]

The reason the British government clung limpet-like to the Orange state could not be the fear of a bloodbath, although that was always raised. Such a fear had not deterred Britain leaving India, where there was a mighty bloodbath. More likely, Paul reasoned, the fear of defeat, of appearing to be beaten by the IRA, was too much to countenance. But that, Paul pointed out, was nothing more than political paralysis.

It was a paralysis that would run on for years.

18

Baldric's Cunning Plan

There was one other event in that long year of the miners' strike which would profoundly affect Paul's own future. 'I was bought last Friday', he wrote in a furious piece in *Socialist Worker* in July 1984.

That Friday evening, he had watched *Newsnight*, followed by the cricket, and then gone to bed, no doubt as happy as a lark. The West Indies were playing brilliantly against England in the third test at Headingley, a test and series they would go on to win. Next morning, he turned on the news and found that he, along with about 7,000 others, had been bought 'by a bloke who hands over a banker's draft for £113.4m'.[1] That bloke was Robert Maxwell, who bought the entire Mirror Group, including the *Daily Mirror*, the *Sunday Mirror*, the *Sunday People*, the *Daily Record*, *Sunday Mail* and *Sporting Life*, with a combined newspaper circulation of 31 million copies a week. The *Mirror* alone was then selling over 3 million copies a day – second only to the *Sun*.

There was one initial obstacle to Maxwell's purchase, and that was the previous owners' commitment not to sell the entire Group to a single bidder. In the event, however, they did. The other obstacle was the Labour Party.

The *Mirror* was the only national newspaper committed to the Labour Party, to which it had always lent its support at election time. In 1984 its leader, Neil Kinnock, was opposed to the sale to Maxwell. Department of Trade inspectors had once described Maxwell as 'utterly unfit to run a public company', as Paul put it – in more robust language than that of the inspectors themselves, who talked about 'stewardship'.[2] But Maxwell had ensured that he had the support of Michael Foot, who persuaded Kinnock to drop his opposition. Michael should have known better. In 1964, he had been persuaded by Robert Maxwell to write a campaign biography of Harold Wilson. It was not an onerous task – there were not many words, it was mostly photos and cartoons. But after its publication by Maxwell's publishing company, Pergamon Press, Michael had some difficulty getting his fee paid – an early warning, perhaps, of what was to come.[3]

Within days of his arrival, Maxwell summoned Paul and John Pilger to his penthouse suite at the top of the Mirror building. Pilger remembers that, as they arrived, one of Maxwell's sons was on his way out, followed by a booming voice: 'He's worried I'm going to sack him. So are you two, I suppose.' Neither had any idea what Maxwell planned, and they were not particularly interested in playing Maxwell's mind games. Instead, they sat in silence for what seemed like an eternity, until Maxwell finally said, 'Let's have a drink. One of you do the honours.' Neither of them moved.

'We were expected to do his bidding', says Pilger, 'or perhaps we would be sacked. He often played games like this with underlings and visitors.'

Maxwell was full of praise and bonhomie. 'Humbly, he assured us that he would not interfere in anything we did', Paul told Stephen Glover.

> When I insisted that this pledge must be total – that he must keep out of all my operations even when he thought he had a story for me – he waved his assurance – 'of course, of course'. I explained that this made the issue quite simple for me because I had my own space. 'Yes, Paul,' he said, sharply, pretending to joke, 'I regard you as a space imperialist.'[4]

Before the meeting was over, Maxwell had also guaranteed that neither of them would ever be sacked. 'You have my word', he said. Which of course he did not keep. Eighteen months later, John Pilger was fired.

The *Mirror*'s main competition was the *Sun*. In the 1960s the *Mirror* led the tabloids, with a circulation that peaked at 5 million copies a day. But once Rupert Murdoch bought the *Sun* and took it downmarket, the *Mirror* slowly lost out until, by 1978 Murdoch's paper was taking pole position. By the time Maxwell arrived, he was obsessed with Murdoch, who had beaten him in the purchase of the *News of the World* in 1969, and the *Sun* and *The Times* in the years that followed. The circulation war between their daily tabloids was their new battleground.

But Maxwell's innovative management style did nothing to stop the *Mirror*'s decline in circulation, and with it the loss of revenue. He tried everything to compete with the *Sun*, including pin-ups and competitions, and could not resist publishing endless photos and stories about himself: flying food aid into Ethiopia during a famine, visiting the injured in hospital after the Bradford football stadium fire. He even believed that he had a hand in the game during the miners' strike: 'Scargill to Ballot Miners on Final Offer', was the front-page headline in September 1984, when no such plan existed.[5]

As he told the print unions when he first arrived, his attitude to business and unions was a simple one: 'There can only be one boss and that is me.'[6] No union was immune during the Thatcher years. At the end of a bloody dispute in Warrington, the *Today* newspaper was already being printed by non-unionised workers. Meanwhile, Rupert Murdoch was fighting his own battles with the print unions at the *Sun*, *The Times* and the *News of the World* – demanding they sign a no-strike deal and end the closed shop. They refused, and in January 1986 Murdoch organised the exodus of his entire operation to Wapping, with no unions.

At the *Mirror*, negotiations lasted for months. Printing was disrupted, copies were lost. At the end of it, over 2,000 out of 6,500 jobs were axed, printing was moved out of London and, more to the point, beyond the reach of the Fleet Street print agreements.

A year after that first dismal meeting, Paul was back in the penthouse to discuss his contract again. Maxwell wanted to meet not just Paul but also Rose, and Mike Molloy and his wife Sandy joined them to make up the numbers. The meeting was worse than anything Paul could have imagined.

In a long letter, he described how the four had gone upstairs together, and, after Mike had opened the champagne, waited for the Great

Entrance.[7] 'I think he perfects these entrances, at the proper moment when his guests are suitably intimidated by the wait and the revolting imposing furniture he has moved in there', Paul wrote. After shaking hands and sitting them all down in a row on a sofa, Maxwell asked Rose if she was interested in her husband's work. Rose was rather taken aback, but managed to ask in reply, 'What do you mean – for the *Mirror*?'

It had probably never occurred to him that Paul had numerous other papers he could and did write for, and always at least one book in progress and another in the queue. He was not dependent on the *Mirror*, and certainly was not going to be dependent on Robert Maxwell. Maxwell then launched into a terrific tirade against Paul's page. It was, he said, too narrow, too one-sided: injustice affected every level of society, not just 'shop stewards'. He continued to rant in a similar vein:

> He kept coming back with a sort of contemptuous sneer to 'shop stewards'. He *had* read the column that day, so he seemed to be refer-ring to the piece about Tom Clarke and the Barnoldswick strike; but then he switched to some case which had got stuck in his mind about a copper who had been wrongly convicted and said that I would never touch such a case, because it favoured a policeman.

Paul could feel the hair on the back of his neck begin to rise. He told Maxwell he would have to take him as he was, because he was inter-ested in the people at the bottom of the pile. If there was any injustice for people at the top, the rest of the media could assist them; it wasn't Paul's job, or Paul's inclination. What struck them all as they sat there was that Maxwell was quite unused to someone who argued back. 'People just agree with him and do his bidding. He seemed to recoil from the argument, almost as if I'd struck him.'[8]

Maxwell also wanted to know about the letters that Paul received, which he considered part of the 'assets' of the company. He thought they might contain stories that Paul would not use because of his poli-tics. Paul told him he was quite happy to make the letters available, knowing, of course, that this was all utter nonsense. No one else on the paper was remotely interested in the reams of letters that arrived in Paul's office.

After a great deal of beating about the bush, Paul's contract was finally renewed. What to make of it all? 'Rose thinks', he wrote, 'and I'm sure she is right, that it is an attempt to impose himself on me, and to try to frighten the column to the right.' Paul would not comply. Instead, he stuck a list of Maxwell's friends to the office wall and resolved not to concede an inch. Maxwell may have been 'utterly vile', but 'as long as the space is mine to fill, I think it would be madness to chuck in the towel.'[9]

Maxwell's threats were not entirely idle. There was an occasion when a gamekeeper had written to Paul about Lord Forte and his grouse shoot. Knowing that Forte was a great friend of Maxwell, and that as soon as you put the story to Forte he would call Maxwell, Paul knew he had to have the story sewn up, and was prepared to deal with Maxwell asking if this was true. 'He can't quite say he won't publish it just like that.'[10] Richard Stott, the *Mirror* editor, was likewise prepared, and recounted in his memoir how Maxwell never took Paul on. He tried once – over the exposure of one of his friends – but was frustrated by a Baldric-like cunning plan cooked up by Stott. 'We told him the story had been watered down considerably – that we could have accused his mate of much worse. We couldn't actually, but it worked.'[11]

Paul was not scared of provoking Maxwell, either. In early 1989 Maxwell had sacked twenty-three members of the NUJ campaigning for union recognition at his publishing house, Pergamon Press. After several months on strike – they stayed on strike for years – Paul joined them on the picket line at Headington Hall in Oxfordshire, which was both the headquarters of Pergamon and Maxwell's home. Noticing a security camera, Paul abandoned the picket and started denouncing Maxwell to the camera. Someone told Maxwell, who invited Richard Stott to pop up to see him. 'Your mate is taking the piss out of me', he thundered. 'He's picketing my offices and he bloody works for me. He should be fired.' Stott pointed out that firing him would play into the hands of Maxwell's enemies. Stott remembered the moment's hesitation before Maxwell continued: 'Tell your mate he's bloody lucky he's got a merciful and compassionate publisher.' It was, wrote Stott, 'a rare example of Maxwell wisdom'. Stott was out of the door before Maxwell could change his mind.[12]

The same summer of 1985 that Paul and Rose were forced to sit through the painful meeting with Maxwell, Paul's mother died. Paul spoke, as he so often did at family funerals, but hated it when the vicar described her as a lady for the people: Paul thought she was a snob. She was not, in Paul's experience, the perfect mother, but he was sometimes proud of her, and her grandchildren adored her. She was, remembers Matt, 'an amazing grandmother. She had all the grandchildren for all the holidays and took us on adventures. She was also a terrible driver.'

The stories kept on coming. If he could not quite fit them all into his *Mirror* column, Paul had a new outlet in the *London Review of Books*.

The attraction of the *LRB* was the sheer length of their articles. They liked Paul because, according to Mary-Kay Wilmers, one of the founders, who would go on to become the *LRB*'s editor, he always told a story. He was also the sort of journalist who got angry. 'Once you have a writer like that', remembers Wilmers, who had known Paul and Monica since their Oxford days, 'you see a story and you ask him if he wants to do a piece.' His writing was also cliché free – although, she adds, they always cut out the bit at the start or the end where he had added his thoughts about the SWP line.

Jeffrey Archer and the three suits was the sort of story he wrote for the *LRB*. Paul had first written about Archer for *Private Eye* in the 1960s. Since then, he had followed Archer's chequered career, until 1985, when he was elected as deputy chairman of the Conservative Party. Then Paul and Bryan Rostron, who was working with him on the story, wrote to Archer asking him about a rumour circulating in Fleet Street: Had he been arrested for stealing three suits in Toronto, Canada? No, came the reply from his solicitor, 'Mr Archer has never been involved in any such incident.' The denial was unequivocal and, at least for the moment, that appeared to be the end of it. But some stories never go away.

Two years later, Archer was back in the news, embroiled in a famous libel trial against the *Daily Star*, involving prostitutes and money and his fragrant wife. Someone chose that moment to send Paul a copy of a shoplifter's report from a store in Toronto, dated 18 November 1975: the names and the details matched Jeffrey Archer.

At great expense to the *Mirror*, Paul hopped on a plane to Toronto and sought out everyone connected with the case. All confirmed verbally what had happened, and then clammed up. Not one of them would put anything in writing. His only success was with the assistant attorney general of Ontario, who said, 'Of course it was Jeffrey Archer.'

In a long letter to Archer, Paul and Bryan asked again about the suits. This time, Archer dealt with the matter himself. 'I was not involved in any such incident', he wrote on his headed notepaper. Confronted with this absolute denial, Richard Stott could not publish. They were left with the rest of the stories they had, which still made a good article, but they knew it was missing something.[13] It had been an expensive effort. 'A thousand quid of *Mirror* money had gone down the drain', wrote Paul, 'but those were the days when the *Mirror* spent money on assisting journalists rather than sacking them. We crept away, licked our wounds and determined never to forget.'[14]

So, when Paul was asked to review fellow journalist Michael Crick's book *Jeffrey Archer: Stranger than Fiction* for the *LRB*, he was jubilant. Finally, he had the chance to indulge his 'most bitterly regretted journalistic failure'. Here, once again, was the story of the trip to Toronto, the three suits, the arresting store detectives, and all the rest of them. Crick got more out of the witnesses, but in the end was kinder about Archer's explanation that it was all a misunderstanding. That did not cut it for Paul:

> He is not an amiable rogue at all, but a nasty hypocritical charlatan whose economy with the truth, Thatcherite politics and ability to write sentimental trash make him a paragon of the age of avarice, fit only for the House of Lords.

Or, as it turned out, fit only for prison. Archer had lied during his libel trial, and in 2001 he was sent to prison for perjury and perverting the course of justice.

Nor was Jeffrey Archer the only Conservative MP who got Paul's attention. The Department of Environment, where Nicholas Ridley was secretary of state, had agreed that the Earl of Scarborough could build a golf course on common land at Maltby, Yorkshire. Paul wanted his readers to know that the Earl of Scarborough's sister was married to Nicholas Ridley's brother, Viscount Ridley – a fact raised in the House of Commons by the Labour MP Kevin Barron.[15]

Ridley was outraged. He had not personally handled the application. It had been passed, as it should have been, to his junior minister to deal with. This explanation was included in Paul's article. Two weeks later, Paul returned to the story: 'My view is that people have a right to know these things. They also have a right to know the Minister's response' – and he told his readers he had received a writ.[16] That was more than enough for Ridley. Paul had now compounded the problem by repeating it, and made it worse by the mere fact of telling his readers about the writ.

The stories about Conservative MPs appeared week in and week out in his *Mirror* column, interspersed with stories about Conservative councillors and councils and their outrages and misdeeds. Occasionally he would have a go at a whole bunch of them at the same time.

'Who cares about state schools?' Paul asked, as the Conservative government's education reforms hit parliament. Not one of the changes would increase the funding of the schools where the vast majority of Britain's children were educated. The Cabinet certainly did not care about state schools because, in Paul's estimation, fifty-two out of fifty-four ministers' children over the age of eleven went to fee-paying schools, compared to just 8 per cent of British children generally. How did Paul know? Because his team had been rooting around for weeks to find out.[17]

For security reasons, such private information about ministers was not readily available. Paul took no notice. People he had known from his own private-school days and his years at Oxford were inveigled into disclosing bits and pieces of the story. Conservative constituency chairmen and secretaries, business acquaintances, local journalists, editors, anyone the team could think of, were contacted, and gradually the picture came together.

Richard Stott agreed to run an entire page, without even a small ad. or two to distract from the content: a line-up of the entire cabinet, each with a photo, with their children if possible, and their children's schools and fees, with the name of the school omitted if the children were still attending. Margaret Thatcher starred, of course: two children, Carol, who went to St Pauls, with fees of £3,000 a year, and Mark, who had been to Harrow, at £7,750 a year. Also appearing was Kenneth Baker, secretary of state for education: two daughters, at Roedean and Westminster, and a son at one of the handful of unnamed schools, with fees of £6,200 a year. The rest of the cabinet were there too: another nineteen names. All the top schools got a mention – Eton more than once, along with Radley and Marlborough. Only one minister, Nigel Lawson, chancellor of the exchequer, had two daughters at a state school in West London.

Politics was a constant theme in Paul's column, injustice another. In December 1986, he told his readers he would be sending cards to thirteen innocent people, wrongly incarcerated for life for murder. 'I firmly believe that all thirteen have spent a total of 144 years in prison for crimes someone else committed.'[18] The first six would go to the six Irish men convicted in 1975 of the Birmingham pub bombings, in which twenty-seven people had lost their lives. They had confessed to the crime after traces of nitroglycerin were found on their hands. In court they recanted their confessions.

The positive traces of nitroglycerin had been found through something called the Griess test, carried out by Frank Skuse, a Home Office forensic scientist. Granada Television's *World in Action* programme had commissioned two independent forensic scientists to re-run Skuse's test, using the same formula he had used. This showed that the positive result could have come from lots of things other than nitroglycerin, including playing cards. Immediately after the programme aired, the Home Office moved the goal posts. The television programme had made a mistake, it said. The formula they had been given by the laboratory where Skuse worked was not, after all, the correct formula. He had used 0.1 per cent of caustic soda, not 1 per cent.

'Six men's freedom hangs on this decimal point', wrote Paul.[19] And no, the Home Office would not share with him any of the papers on which it was relying for its interpretation of the formula used by Frank Skuse. It had, however, launched an urgent inquiry into the case. The inquiry had been running for sixteen months.

Paul had been interested in Frank Skuse from his days on *Socialist Worker*, and had returned to the subject several times in the *Mirror*. But the person who had really dug deep into the case was Chris Mullin, who had worked on the *World in Action* programme. His book, *Error of Judgment: The Truth about the Birmingham Bombing*, had been published earlier, in 1986, and reviewed by Paul for the *LRB*.[20]

The next four Christmas cards would go to the young people convicted of bombing pubs in Guildford and Woolwich in 1974, where five people had died. Again, there were confessions, and again the confessions were recanted in court. In this case, though, there had been a unique development. An IRA active service unit had been arrested after a siege at Balcombe Street in London in December 1975. One of the men arrested admitted that he had taken part in the Guildford bombings, and that the four imprisoned had nothing to do with it. The Home Office had set up another urgent inquiry. This inquiry had been running for four months. There was a book on this case too, *Trial and Error* by Robert Kee, also published in 1986, and a Yorkshire Television programme, *The Guildford Time Bomb*, broadcast the same year. Pressure on the Home Office was growing on all the Irish cases. It was now clear, to some at least, that Irish people had been rounded up and stitched up in response to the IRA's bombing campaign.

The remainder of Paul's cards would go to the men convicted in 1979 of the murder of newspaper boy Carl Bridgewater. This was different from the intensely political Birmingham and Guildford bombing cases – the victim was a child, and the men convicted of his murder were a band of local criminals. But there were elements shared with the other cases, including corrupt policemen and false confessions. It was a case to which Paul devoted his energies for years.

19

Who Killed Carl Bridgewater?

In early 1980, a letter arrived in Paul's office at the *Mirror*.

> Dear Mr Foot,
> My son, along with three other men, has been found guilty of
> murder – a very horrible murder of a newspaper boy named Carl
> Bridgewater from Staffordshire. My son is the youngest of the
> accused, Michael Hickey. He is innocent beyond doubt. Indeed so
> are the other three accused . . .

The writer was Ann Whelan, Michael Hickey's mother. In November
1979, her son, his cousin Vincent Hickey and two other men, Jimmy
Robinson and Pat Molloy, were convicted of killing Carl Bridgewater
at a farmhouse in the west Midlands. Carl was thirteen years old, and
each afternoon after school he delivered the local paper, cycling
around the area where he lived in Wordsley, Staffordshire. His body
was found slumped on the sofa in the sitting room of Yew Tree Farm.
He had been shot in the head at point-blank range with a sawn-off
shotgun.

It was the sort of crime that made the headlines: 'Guilty! The Cruel
Killers of Carl the Newsboy' ran the *Mirror*'s front page at the end of
their trial in 1979, just weeks after Paul had arrived at the paper.[1]
Initially, Paul was not convinced by the letter. What mother would not
protest her son's innocence? It was some months before he went to
Birmingham to meet Ann and her husband, Fred. He listened long

and hard. Whatever they said, he became convinced of the men's innocence, and in October the following year the first of many articles
about the case ran in his column. Over the next twelve years, he estimated that he wrote another thirty articles on it for the *Mirror* alone.

Carl Bridgewater was murdered on 19 September 1978, and for weeks
the Staffordshire police pulled in and questioned every suspect or
local robber they could track down. Then they had a piece of luck. On
30 November, an armed robbery at a farm less than an hour's drive
from Yew Tree Farm led the police to Michael, Vincent and Jimmy.
They all denied any involvement, and each of them had an alibi. But
the most incriminating evidence against them came from their
co-accused and drinking companion, Pat Molloy. Pat admitted to the
police he had been at Yew Tree Farm with the others, but said he was
upstairs when he heard the gun go off.

There were further apparent admissions of guilt. It was claimed that
Jimmy Robinson had told Tex Ritter, a fellow prisoner while he was on
remand, that he had killed Carl, but that it was an accident. Meanwhile,
Brian Sinton told the court that Michael Hickey had confessed to him
while they were in prison that he was the one who had pulled the trigger. While there was no forensic evidence against the four men, there
were eyewitnesses to cars coming and going, gossip about who had
said and done what in the four friends' drinking place, the Dog and
Partridge pub in Selly Oak. Most of the alibi witnesses for the four
became confused about what they had seen and when.

The jury declared them guilty. Pat Molloy was convicted of
manslaughter, and received twelve years. Michael, sixteen at the time
of the crime, was sent to prison for an indefinite term at Her Majesty's
pleasure. Vincent and Jimmy got life, with a recommendation they
serve twenty-five years. 'They're all lying, mum', shouted Michael in
the court as he was taken down to the cells.

Paul's first article for the *Mirror* told the story of another murder,
at the farm next to Yew Tree. Soon after the four were found guilty,
Hubert Wilkes, a seventy-year-old farmer, was shot dead at point-
blank range by Hubert Spencer. There was no doubt about what had
happened here: Wilkes's thirty-four-year-old daughter and Spencer's
wife Janet were in the house at the time.

Hubert Spencer's name had cropped up in the police investigation of Carl's murder. A witness told the police that, as he drove home on the afternoon of the murder, he had seen a blue Vauxhall Viva turn into the drive of Yew Tree Farm, its driver wearing a dark blue uniform. Spencer drove a blue Vauxhall Viva, and wore a blue uniform for his work as an ambulance officer at a hospital in the west Midlands. And he knew Carl Bridgewater – they had lived in the same street when Carl was ten. He also owned a shot gun. But if the police had been interested in Spencer at the outset, they soon forgot about him when they arrested the other four.

Paul devoted his column in November 1980 to the 'strange coincidences' linking Hubert Spencer to Carl Bridgewater.[2] He spoke to Spencer's wife Janet, who did not believe her husband had anything to do with the Bridgewater murder. However, she did confirm that the two men had been discussing Carl Bridgewater just before Spencer blew out Mr Wilkes's brains.

In the freezing cold of February 1983, Michael Hickey decided to take matters into his own hands. After persuading his cousin to go with him, Michael and Vincent climbed onto the roof of Long Lartin prison and, with the support of other prisoners, stayed there for twenty-one days, alongside huge lettering they had painted on the prison roof: 'SPENCER KILLED CARL'.

It was this protest that convinced Paul to listen to Ann Whelan's pleas for him to write a book about the 'Bridgewater Four', as the four convicted men would become known. Paul had been reluctant. His book on Helen Smith was only just out, and he knew from the book on Hanratty just how much time and effort it would take to change the verdict of a jury in a celebrated case.

Later that year, Michael made another foray onto a prison roof, at Gartree in Leicester. He was on his own this time, after he and Vincent had been separated and kept in different prisons. He was also better prepared. He had put on five jumpers, two pairs of long johns, three pairs of jeans and four pairs of socks under an oversized pair of trainers. He had string and scissors, bin liners, cardboard and a bed sheet on which he had written in large letters: 'SPENCER KILLED CARL. WE ARE INNOCENT.' He went up in November, and nothing could have prepared him for the cold, the rain and the wind. He stayed up there all winter, a total of eighty-nine days, supported by his fellow prisoners (and some prison officers) who attached food parcels each day to one of his long bits of string. The experience ruined his health forever.

Ann Whelan became Paul's eyes and ears in trying to find the evidence that proved the innocence of the four. But what he also needed was a lawyer to work alongside him. His other ally would be Jim Nichol, his old friend and comrade. After his departure as editor of *Socialist Worker*, Jim had decided to study law. He was then taking his articles at Seifert Sedley, a firm of solicitors with a strong left-wing reputation, whose offices in Dyers Buildings were two minutes away from Paul's office at the *Mirror*.

Throughout 1983 and 1984, the articles in the *Mirror* continued; Paul's obsession became the butt of jokes in the editorial offices. The journalists and subeditors would wind him up by calling out to him: 'Here comes the man who supports the murder of newspaper boys! Watch out if any newspaper boys are around!' When he submitted his columns, the editor would chide him, 'Oh Christ, you're not doing this again, are you?' Paul ignored them all. For him, the repetition was crucial. Despite the joshing, the *Mirror* was supportive of Paul's campaign, stumping up an enormous sum of money to buy the complete transcript of the original trial, all 1,500 pages of it, at a cost of £7,000. Out of it he and Jim were able to glean all sorts of details. Here, on record, was exactly what was said by each witness and each police officer. Gradually, Jim pulled together a submission to the Home Office for a review of the case.

Tiny details could make a huge difference. Michael and Vincent had been together on the afternoon of the murder, first at a friend's flat and then at a garage buying a car. Besides the owner, there was, according to Michael, a 'large Greek man' sitting in the garage office. It seemed of little importance at the time of the trial, and the alibi was dismissed by the judge, who concluded that the visit to the garage had happened the following day. Paul and Ann visited the Bristol Road Garage, and learned from the proprietor that his father-in-law was a Greek Cypriot called Mr Tsokalides, who had been living in Birmingham in 1978 and visited the garage from time to time. Jim flew to Cyprus and found Mr Tsokalides, who was indeed rather stout. Jim followed up every detail until he was sure that the 'large Greek man' had been sitting in the garage on the afternoon of 19 September 1978 – the day of the murder – and not the following day.

Paul wrote the main draft of *Murder at the Farm* during a hectic and sleepless month in January 1986 in the Whelans' flat. Ann was the best researcher Paul could have had. She had copies of every document, and was a walking encyclopaedia of every detail of the case. In June of that year, Paul sent the final copy of the text to his publishers, who scheduled its release for 19 September, the eighth anniversary of the murder. And then, in July, Ann found Brian Sinton.

Sinton had been the key witness against Michael, telling the court that, while they were in prison, Michael had confessed to pulling the trigger because Carl Bridgewater was crying. Now Sinton told Ann that everything he had said at the trial was a lie. He would not go public, but he did agree to talk to Paul. So, from a phone box in Barnsley, he repeated his story. He told Paul how he had been put up to it by two prison officers. He thought at the time that Michael had been involved in the murder, and that he deserved what he got.

Paul was about to go on holiday, so they agreed Sinton would come to the *Daily Mirror* on 28 August, after Paul had returned. And, sure enough, when he reached his office towards the end of the month, there they were: Brian Sinton and his wife June. After Sinton repeated his story again, Paul took him round to Jim Nichol's office, where he made and signed a statement, and a press conference was organised.

On 3 September 1986, just three weeks before the book's publication date, the story broke in the *Daily Mirror*. 'Exclusive: I Lied about Carl's Killer', ran the front-page headline.[3] The story ran on to page two, and the centre pages, where the *Mirror* began its extracts from Paul's forthcoming book. It made that night's television news, and very soon the home secretary ordered a police inquiry.

That winter it was Paul's turn to stand around in the freezing cold, in the roads around Yew Tree Farm, contributing to an hour-long documentary for Thames Television, broadcast in March 1987, which focused on the unreliability of the prosecution case and, once again, the possible involvement of Hubert Spencer.

Six months later, on 15 October 1987, a handwritten note on a small sheet of blue Home Office–headed notepaper was delivered personally to Paul at the *Mirror*:

> Dear Paul Foot,
>   I am writing to let you know that after looking carefully at all the information available, I have decided that the case should be referred to the Court of Appeal. The case will now be treated as an appeal by the men to the Court of Appeal.
>   Yours, Douglas Hurd.

Paul pinned the note to his office wall, where it remained until he departed the *Mirror*.

Jim Nichol would now get paid by the courts, and could devote his time to the case. He had access to documents he had never seen before, and resources that allowed him to investigate the alibis properly. He had started by taking over as Michael's solicitor. By the time of the appeal, he was also representing Vincent and Jimmy, and the family of Pat Molloy, who had died in 1981. Despite his admission and his silence at the trial – he had been advised not to give evidence by his lawyers – Molloy had protested his innocence from the start. He claimed he had made the confession because the police had shown him a statement signed by Vincent Hickey, in which Vincent named Molloy as one of the killers. No one had believed him because, in fact, Vincent had not signed any statement to the police. Once the trial was over, Molloy had written a flurry of letters expressing regret for his role in what had happened. In one letter, sent to Ann Whelan in June 1981, he expressed his hope that he would be able to prove they were all innocent. Two days later, on 12 June 1981, while playing football in the prison exercise yard, Molloy collapsed and died.

A powerful legal team was assembled for the appeal, including Stephen Sedley, who had reviewed Paul's book on the case for the *LRB*, representing Michael – even though Sedley no longer practised criminal law. Everyone was optimistic. The appeal lasted through Christmas and into the new year. The prosecution conceded nothing.

A crucial moment came when Brian Sinton was called to give evidence. He was not the sort of person who could easily stick to one version of events. After the press conference the previous year, he had ended up back in prison, where he was visited by the police. He immediately retracted what he had told Ann, and then repeated to Paul and Jim. Then he retracted the retraction. What would he say when he took the witness stand at the appeal hearing?

> Q. You will remember, I am sure, giving evidence at the Michael
>   Hickey trial?
> A. Yes.
> Q. You remember you said he had confessed to you?
> A. Yes.
> Q. Was it true that he did, or was it a lie?
> A. It was a lie.[4]

A huge sigh of relief went around the defence team. The prosecution battered away at him, but on the one central fact he would not shift. Michael had not confessed. He, Sinton, had lied.

Having lost such a key witness, the prosecution changed tack and turned their fire on Ann, the person who had tracked down Sinton, and then Paul. When she was called to the court, Ann was kept in the witness box for the best part of three days, as they tried to show that the witnesses she had approached had changed their minds because of her pestering and bullying. She was reduced to tears. 'She was treated by the court as if she was a common criminal for setting up Sinton', remembers Stephen Sedley.

Then it was Paul's turn. He was cross-examined by Jeremy Roberts QC, who was, according to Stephen, a model cross-examiner, impeccably polite and patient. He would go on and on until he got the answer he wanted, without ever being unpleasant or rude. In Paul, he met his match.

'Paul had an answer, a very polite answer, for everything', Stephen remembers. 'Jeremy got nowhere with him. Until finally he picked up a criticism Paul had made of the attorney general and something he had or had not done, and Jeremy very loftily said, Are you aware that attorney generals have consistently done this? Paul replied, then the attorney generals have been consistently wrong . . . It was a King Kong versus Godzilla moment. And Jeremy couldn't get any further with him. It brought him to a standstill.'

Tex Ritter, the other prison informant, was also called to court. At the original trial his evidence had been that Jimmy Robinson had confessed. What was now known was the extent of Ritter's lying and cheating. Doctors, psychiatrists and probation officers described him as a pathological liar. Jim Nichol remembers reading, in answer to a question from a police officer, about the lengths he had gone to to con a man out of a very small amount of money, Ritter had replied: 'There is one born every minute. It is a challenge to me every time.' Like Sinton, Ritter had also benefited from his evidence at the trial. He was released from prison with a Royal pardon, specifically for his information in the Bridgewater case. At the appeal, he stuck to his original story.

The appeal ran for forty-six days, making it the longest-running criminal appeal in the English courts – but all to no avail. On St Patrick's Day, 17 March 1989, the judges read out their findings: 'We entertain no doubt whatever but that Hubert Spencer had nothing whatever to do with the killing of Carl Bridgewater.'[5] The judges accepted that Michael and Vincent had been at the Bristol Road Garage on the day of the murder, but only *after* they had committed the murder. On, Tex Ritter, they said: 'We have come to the clear conclusion that on this occasion Ritter can safely be relied upon as a witness of truth.'[6] There was, wrote Paul, an audible gasp in the court.

Brian Sinton's evidence was more difficult for them to dismiss – so they simply placed no reliance on it. But just in case that might lead to the conclusion that Michael was innocent, they dealt that idea a quick blow. They relied on the 'bits and pieces' of evidence at the original trial. 'We have come to the firm conclusion that upon the totality of the evidence' Michael was involved.[7] The appeal was dismissed.

'The frustrating thing about that first appeal', says Stephen Sedley, 'was that we proved Michael's alibi and the judges wouldn't have it.'

Everyone was dejected and exhausted. 'It was over', Paul wrote. 'We all gave angry interviews and pushed our way through the shouting throng outside. Ann was in tears and so were the rest of us.'[8]

At home, Paul's son Matt suggested he give in. He had done what he could. 'He was furious. It was the only time he was ever really angry with me', he remembers. Paul was not for giving in. His next *Mirror* column was devoted once again to the case, focusing on the three Appeal Court judges, alongside their photos. They were nothing but 'men of straw', Paul wrote. The Court of Appeal should have above its door: 'Abandon hope, all ye who enter here.'[9] He was angry, but in the office at the *Mirror* he tried to cheer everyone up: 'Something will turn up. It always does.'

A year later, a letter arrived at the *Mirror* from a retired prison officer. Frank Gibson was working at Pentonville prison in London on the morning the Court of Appeal judgment was broadcast on the radio. Listening to the broadcast with him was Tex Ritter, back in prison once again. 'My Christ, they believed me!' he shouted. And when Mr Gibson asked him if he had told the truth in court, he shook his head, indicating he had not. For good measure, Ritter added: 'Paul Foot is making a fortune out of this – why shouldn't I?' Gibson agreed that Paul could run the story in the *Mirror*, and he too made a statement to Jim Nichol.[10]

As in the past, the publicity generated by one story led to more. A week later another letter arrived at the *Mirror*, this time from the Reverend Andrew Morton. He had studied languages, and having been given a copy of Paul's book had compared the language of Molloy's confession with Molloy's prison letters. Morton concluded: 'the confession is not Molloy's. It was made up by more than one person.'[11] Once again, Paul published the story in the *Mirror*. Jim Nichol went to other language experts, who all agreed with Morton. Off went another petition to the Home Office. Another long wait. Another rejection.

Then an extraordinary thing happened. The BBC had been preparing a drama about the case, *Bad Company*, broadcast over two evenings in May 1993. It had an illustrious cast including Jonny Lee Miller playing Michael Hickey, George Irving as Jimmy Robinson, and Susan Wooldridge as Ann Whelan. Paul Foot was played by Angus Deayton. Following the broadcast more letters of support poured in, including one from a man called Tim O'Malley:

Dear Mrs Whelan

I was the foreman of the jury at your son's trial in 1979. I am completely convinced of Michael's innocence, and indeed all four of them. I have felt this for some time, and I wrote to the Home Secretary (copy enclosed). The TV drama moved me very profoundly and was the motivation for me to write to you. I want to do all I can to help your cause.[12]

What impressed Jim Nichol about O'Malley's letter to the home secretary, written a year earlier, were the doubts he had expressed about the language of Molloy's confession:

My gut feeling at the time of the trial was that there was something odd about the confession, but I could not put my finger on it. It all seemed factually sound. It was only when I read reports recently of language experts examining it that the penny dropped. My father was Irish and so I am familiar with the ways in which the Irish use the English language in their own way. It was not a confession of an Irishman. I cannot prove it. I just feel it. I feel that without the confession the case against the men cannot be sustained.

Paul was immediately on the phone, and Tim O'Malley agreed to go public. Alongside Paul's reporting, Jim Nichol was now using every legal wheeze he could think up to keep the case in front of the home secretary (it was now before its fourth home secretary) and the public. The case was debated in parliament, and the BBC's *Rough Justice* programme made an hour-long special.

In the fifth and last edition of Paul's book, *Murder at the Farm*, he described how he was at home one day when the phone rang:

Strange, hysterical and strangulated noises emerged from the receiver. There was, it seemed, a maniac on the line shouting and screaming about the pain in his back. It took me several seconds to decipher the words: "We're back! We're back! We're back man!" It was Jim Nichol in a state of high disorder.[13]

'Miracles can happen. Pigs can fly', Paul told his *Guardian* readers. 'And Michael Howard can make the right decision.' The home secretary had agreed the case would return once more to the Court of Appeal.[14]

One of the great conundrums of the case was the claim by Vincent that he had never signed a statement, although Pat Molloy always said he only made his confession because he was shown a statement signed by Vincent. In 1997 more documents were released, and Jim decided to have one more go at sifting through the originals to see what he could find.

There is a forensic technique – an ESDA test, using an electrostatic detection device – which measures the imprints in a piece of paper. If, for example, you write on a notepad and then tear off the sheet you have been writing on, the imprint of your words will appear on the sheet below. An ESDA test can reveal the imprint, even if the paper is old and the imprint light. The real expert in this field at the time was Robert Radley. He had tested the handwritten copy of Molloy's confession before, but by 1997 the technology had improved, and as Radley reran the test he made out the words, 'I, Vincent Hickey'. What Radley was looking at was the standard caution which runs at the top of a witness statement. And there, at the end, was a signature: 'Vincent Hickey'.

What if Molloy's claim was true? Had he been shown a statement, which implicated him? Not one written by Vincent, but one forged by police officers. What Radley was looking at that day was a forged confession, written in the very distinctive handwriting of DC John Perkins – the most corrupt of policemen in a corrupt police squad.

The results threw the prosecution lawyers into turmoil – and then panic, when the Home Office's own expert said he agreed with Radley. Molloy *had* told the truth. He had been tricked into making a confession. It was no longer worth the paper it was written on, and the prosecution knew it.

Vincent Hickey was in Durham prison when he was woken early one morning in February 1997 and told to get a move on. He had no idea where he was going, or why he was put in an ordinary prison van and not the Category A van usually used for convicted murderers like him. All day he travelled south, until he was taken into a cell in Brixton prison where he was surprised to find Michael Hickey: 'The last time I'd seen Michael was on the roof of Long Lartin in 1983', he said.

They were up early again the next morning and taken to court, still not knowing what was going on. Jimmy Robinson joined them, and Jim Nichol. Within minutes they went up into the court, and heard for themselves that the prosecution had thrown in the towel. There was uproar.

The nightmare was over. They were granted bail until the full appeal hearing could take place, and they were out, into the enormous space of the great hall at the Court of Appeal, where everyone with business in the courts – lawyers, journalists, witnesses, cleaners, security guards – was standing on the benches, and on tiptoes up the stairs, trying to get sight of the three men, clapping and cheering. They then moved to the steps of the Court in London's Strand, amid scenes of chaotic jubilation. The story ran on every news channel, and photos from outside the court appeared in every national newspaper. 'Framed' was the *Mirror*'s pointed front-page headline.[15]

Eighteen years in prison, accused of the worst of crimes – the murder of a child – takes its toll. Michael, who had refused parole because he would not leave prison a guilty man, and had taken to the prison roofs twice to protest his innocence – was in a state of nervous collapse. The scars inflicted on all of them ran deep.

The appeal hearing would still go ahead, in April. The new evidence would be heard. When the judges finally published their reasons for overturning the convictions in July, it was a damp squib, like knowing the result of a football match in advance.

Paul wrote a new chapter for the fifth and final edition of his book, published in 1998. It told the story of those final months: the Molloy statement, the release of the men from prison, and the appeal. It then looked back on what had happened over those long years:

> A courageous woman set out to overturn a unanimous jury verdict
> in a famous murder case. At the outset she had no support save that
> of her mother and her husband, she had no money, no property, no
> experience of public life and her office was her council flat. Her one
> resource was her indomitable determination.[16]

It had begun as an investigation, but it became a campaign, in which Ann was supported by Paul and numerous others: first and foremost, her husband Fred, who, in one last, cruel twist of the knife by the Home Office, had been sent to prison himself while the appeal was pending, for taking cannabis into the prison for Michael. Then there were the lawyers, and the actors in *Bad Company*, who formed the core of a campaign committee; the numerous other newspaper and television journalists who stuck with the story for so long; the *Mirror* editors Mike Molloy and Richard Stott; the MPs who supported parliamentary motions on the case; and the other families, in particular Vincent's mother Anne Skett. All of them had kept up the pressure.

The repetition – those endless articles in the *Daily Mirror* – had kept Vincent's hopes alive. 'They were little gems that would bloom on the page', he said, long after his release.

Paul should have the last word: 'By the way, who killed Carl Bridgewater? In the answer to that question the massed ranks of law and order, police officers, Home Office bureaucrats, Crown prosecutors and High Court judges show not the slightest interest.'[17]

20

A Rattling Good Yarn

Paul was slogging through a pile of letters from his *Daily Mirror* readers late one night in 1986 when he came across a long letter written by Fred Holroyd, a former captain in military intelligence. It was an account of an injustice suffered by a former colleague and now friend of his, Colin Wallace. It took Paul hours to read through that first missive, but by the time he had finished he was convinced that, if half the document was true, it told an extraordinary story.

'Colin Wallace has a fantastic story to tell', Paul told his *Daily Mirror* readers, 'so fantastic that official spokesmen everywhere fall over themselves to deny it.'[1]

In the 1970s Colin had worked for a special army unit in Northern Ireland whose job was to wage 'psychological war' on terrorists on both sides of the political divide. But after the Labour government was elected in 1974, he noticed his instructions were changing. Instead of working against those perpetuating the violence, he was working against the elected government. In a secret operation called Clockwork Orange, he was asked to leak false stories to make the Labour government look out of control, or even as if it were controlled by communists, as well as smearing the private lives of prominent Conservative politicians who favoured power-sharing in Northern Ireland. This was work that Colin says he refused to carry out. 'We were there to fight terrorism, not to take part in this political nonsense', he told Paul.[2] As a result of his intransigence, he was drummed out of his job, and out of Northern Ireland.

Colin and his wife Eileen eventually moved to England, where they settled in Arundel, Sussex. Then, in 1981, Colin said he was framed for killing his friend Jonathan Lewis. He would spend six years in prison. 'That's what Colin Wallace says', Paul wrote in his column. 'It is fantastic. But is it true?'[3]

Paul was fascinated by the story, but he realised very quickly that he simply did not have enough space in the *Mirror* to do it justice. He would need to write another book. Macmillan agreed to publish but, because of its sensitive nature, kept the project a secret. Only two people knew – Phillipa Harrison, the editor who commissioned it, and Lord Stockton, Alexander Macmillan, the publisher's owner, who said he would back Paul 'to the hilt'.[4]

To write the book, Paul would need to know a lot more about Colin, a man whose life was steeped in the beliefs of Irish Protestantism and loyalty to the British crown – a position that was diametrically opposed to Paul's. To find out more, Paul went with Colin to visit what remained of his family and the people he had grown up with. Paul was a little nervous. These were Orangemen, former B Specials and Paisleyites, after all.

In 1968, Colin had been recruited as an assistant public relations officer for the army in Northern Ireland, working in the press office of the Lisburn barracks, not far from Belfast. He was a civil servant, but with an equivalent army rank of major. For good measure, he was also a reservist in the Territorial Army and the B specials – the heavily armed special Protestant-only police. He expected Lisburn to be a fairly routine posting, but all that was about to change.

In October of that year a civil rights demonstration in Derry, demanding political rights for the Catholic population, was savagely broken up by the Royal Ulster Constabulary. From there, the violence escalated, and in 1969 the government sent troops first into Derry and then to Belfast, when whole streets in that city went up in flames. This was followed up with a policy of internment: imprisonment without trial. In this incredibly volatile period, the press office in which Colin Wallace worked in Lisburn was expanded. For them, Colin had a distinct advantage over many of the new recruits: he knew both the area and the people.

As the political situation deteriorated, the burgeoning intelligence sector had set up a new office called Information Policy – something of a euphemism for an office that specialised in disinformation, or black propaganda. Colin worked alongside the new unit, until, in 1974, he officially joined it, and was given a new and very different job description.

That year, Colin was called to a high-level conference with senior MI5 officers to discuss an initiative intended to meet the security crisis and stem the rising tide of sectarian killings. Its code name was Clockwork Orange. The initiative's stated purpose was to expose the personal vulnerabilities of the commanders of paramilitary organisations, both Republican and Protestant. Pieces of information came to Colin from a variety of sources, much of it from London, and the stories he put out were mostly, but not always, true.

The unstated purpose of Clockwork Orange, however, was to misrepresent what was happening in London. Dismayed by the election of Wilson's Labour government, all kinds of extreme right-wing organisations emerged in 1974 that had influence within the intelligence services. The strong thread that ran through the notes that Colin kept from that period was the idea that the Labour Party was then under the influence of the Communist Party, perhaps twenty or thirty Labour MPs being secret Communists. Allegedly among them was Harold Wilson himself, as well as Paul's uncle Michael. Most of these 'facts' about the Communist Party and Labour were historical nonsense, as Paul knew. But the stories served a security service obsession with the idea that the Labour Party in general, and Harold Wilson in particular, were at the beck and call of the Russians. If Wilson himself was a Communist and Soviet agent, it was only a short step to believe he was also a covert agent for the IRA.

Colin's unit circulated forged election leaflets and curious pamphlets, one apparently written by three Labour MPs – Denis Healey, Tony Benn and Stan Orme – all of whom had been brought into the government in 1974. It purported to be one of a series entitled 'The Labour Movement', and was sub-headed 'Imperialism – Crisis – Revolution' – an unlikely title for anything written by anyone in the Labour Party, even in the 1970s. As Paul pointed out, 'the fact that the three men could never have combined to write anything at all never bothered their detractors for a moment'.[5] Authenticity was not an issue. The pamphlet was never meant for savvy British journalists, but was instead intended for foreign journalists visiting Northern Ireland, particularly those from the more conservative American publications. The overall purpose was to discredit Wilson's leadership, in the hope of replacing it with another government more acceptable to the reactionary minds who were supplying the information.

The 'ultras' in the security service did not stop at smearing Labour politicians; they were also concerned about the leadership of the Conservative Party. Labour had formed the government in February 1974, but it did not have a parliamentary majority, and another election was highly likely. Colin's sources were hoping Edward Heath would be deposed as leader, and replaced by someone more to their liking.

To find a way through the deteriorating situation in Northern Ireland, Heath, as prime minister, had decided to bring Catholic politicians into the government in the province. But, while power-sharing might satisfy the minority Catholic population, for the Protestant fundamentalists it was seen as a betrayal. In May 1974, the policy was dealt a mortal blow when the Ulster Workers Council, a self-appointed group of extreme Unionists, organised a strike across Northern Ireland, centred on the energy supply industry. 'The strike was perhaps the most successful major industrial action in the history of the British Isles', wrote Paul. 'The one and only demand of the strikers, the end of power-sharing, was unconditionally conceded.'[6] Within two weeks of the strike, power-sharing was dead. The Executive collapsed and the prime minister of Northern Ireland resigned, all to be replaced by direct rule from London.

If the smears against the Labour Party were about communism, in the Conservative Party they involved allegations of homosexuality. 'All sorts of fantasies were circulated', remembered Paul. At both *Private Eye* and *Socialist Worker*, 'especially the former, anonymous phone calls reported to me news of a "new set of pictures of Heath and his Swedish boyfriends"'. Yet, as Paul remembered, 'when the pictures were asked for, or the names of the callers demanded, the phone went dead. The regularity and frequency of these calls, however, all of them pretending to come from left-wing sources, left some of the muck sticking.'[7]

By September 1974, all the information coming to Colin concentrated on politicians, not paramilitaries. What exactly was he doing, he wondered. That month, he told his handler he no longer wanted any part in Clockwork Orange, and he returned to work as a press officer for the army.

Back in his old job, he continued to write briefings about the situation in Northern Ireland, and one of them in particular came to haunt him. This was a memorandum about TARA, an extreme loyalist group, and the man who ran it, William McGrath, who worked in a Belfast children's home called Kincora. In his briefing, Colin detailed allegations of abuse and assaults in various children's homes in Belfast that had begun in the late 1950s, and the apparent lack of interest on the part of both the Belfast Welfare Authority (and its successor, the Eastern Health and Social Services Board) and the police. His document was circulated in November 1974 to the head of Information Policy, and to army intelligence and police headquarters.

Six weeks later, Colin was banished from Northern Ireland. Called to an interview in London, he was told he was not going back because his life was in danger. He did not believe a word of it, but he was given no choice.

In January 1975, Colin returned briefly to Lisburn to tidy up his affairs and say goodbye to his colleagues, along with almost every leading journalist in Northern Ireland, who gathered at a farewell party for him. Robert Fisk, a journalist he knew well who was then working for *The Times*, could not attend. So, on his way to the airport, he drove past Fisk's house and dropped off a copy of one last document – something he had done dozens of times before. This package would be his downfall.

Back in England, Colin was interviewed by two RUC officers about his contact with Fisk and the information he had passed to him. Someone, not Fisk, had picked up the envelope and handed it to the police. Colin was immediately dismissed – a decision upheld by the Civil Service Appeal Board, which offered him a deal if he resigned. 'I was just chucked out', he told Paul.

And I was now pretty sure the only reason was that I had refused to continue with their political dirty tricks and that they had to find some means of discrediting me in case I blew the whole story to Fleet Street.[8]

Colin took a job as an information and liaison officer for Arun District Council, in Sussex. In 1979, the council entered a team for *It's A Knockout* – a popular BBC light entertainment programme that involved teams from across the United Kingdom competing in races – usually in ridiculous costumes, performing ludicrous antics. The Arun team made the final, which would be filmed locally in July 1980. On the Arun organising team was a young woman called Jane Lewis. For months, she and Colin worked alongside each other, and soon they became close. When the competition was over, Colin organised a surprise dinner party to celebrate her birthday and thank her for her hard work over recent months. A number of local dignitaries and the local chief of police were invited, as well as Jane's husband Jonathan, who was in on the plan. But Jonathan never turned up.

When his body was found in the river Arun, Colin became a suspect. Nothing linked Colin directly with Jonathan's death, but when questioned by the police his first instinct had been to lie about meeting Jonathan earlier that evening. Jonathan had asked to meet Colin because he wanted to challenge him about his relationship with Jane, and it was only when it became plain that the police knew that the two had met that Colin admitted to it.

Jonathan had died from drowning. The first post-mortem suggested nothing suspicious about his death. Then, just four days later, Ian West, a Home Office pathologist, carried out a second post-mortem and noticed a small bruise at the base of Jonathan's nose. This, he claimed at the trial, was evidence that Jonathan could have been knocked out by a karate blow. Based on this, the prosecution claimed that Colin, with his army training, had knocked Jonathan out before the dinner, dumped his body in the boot of his car, and later that evening driven the body to the river Arun, where he had slung his friend into the river.

On 20 March 1981, Colin was convicted of manslaughter and given a ten-year prison sentence.

✥

In January 1980, not long before the death of Jonathan Lewis and Colin's subsequent imprisonment, the Dublin-based *Irish Independent* published a front-page article exposing the child abuse at Kincora. Sixteen boys had come forward to make statements against McGrath and his co-workers, and when the home was searched, incriminating forensic evidence was found.

At their trial, in December 1980, all three men from Kincora pleaded guilty. But questions remained. Why had the abuse at the home gone on for so long? Why had so many complaints been ignored? And why had the police or welfare department not become involved earlier?

As a result of the political pressure, two inquiries were held into Kincora. The first was led by Sir George Terry, the chief constable of Sussex – the same force responsible for the investigation into Jonathan Lewis's death. Colin wrote to the inquiry team – and to the RUC, the MoD, the attorney general, his MP and his own solicitor – repeating over and over the same question: Is the inquiry concerned about a cover-up at Kincora, or is it only concerned with the homosexual offences themselves? If it was looking into a cover-up, Colin had information. If the inquiry was interested only in the homosexual offences, he had no relevant information, and for him to disclose classified material would have laid him open to prosecution. He did not speak to the Terry inquiry team.

The second inquiry was led by a retired judge, William Hughes. Once again, Colin was approached, and once again, for the same reasons he had given the Terry inquiry, he declined to take part. There was, however, one rather unexpected outcome. While he was in prison, Colin had been put in touch with Fred Holroyd, another man forced out of the army in Northern Ireland because he crossed his intelligence masters. His life, like Colin's, had been turned upside down by his experience in the mid 1970s. Over a period of several months, Fred visited Colin in Lewes prison, and together they collated a huge 200-page dossier about their careers, what had happened to them, the Clockwork Orange project, attempts to discredit the Labour government, the Kincora boys' home, and Colin's wrongful conviction. They attached to it a vast array of relevant documents.

On 1 November 1984, Fred sent the dossier to the prime minister, Margaret Thatcher. The following day, Downing Street acknowledged receipt. Colin was assured by those working for the Hughes Inquiry that the crucial documents in the dossier had been forwarded to Judge Hughes. So he was shocked to read in the inquiry report that no progress had been made on the issue of the cover-up. He was even more shocked at the suggestion in the report that the memo he had written on TARA back in November 1974 was being dismissed as a forgery.

Paul tried to find out from the RUC which forensic experts had examined the TARA memo, but no answer was forthcoming. So, at the *Mirror*'s expense, he commissioned two leading experts, both of whom concluded that there was no evidence of forgery.[9] 'The cover-up was complete', wrote Paul. 'Wallace was a Walter Mitty, he had fabricated documents to shore up his story, and two police inquiries had dismissed his concerns about a cover up over Kincora.'[10]

Once again, help came from an unexpected source. In 1987, Peter Wright, a former spy, wrote his memoirs, in which he alleged that the ultra-right in the intelligence services had plotted against Harold Wilson in 1974. Suddenly, there was confirmation from inside MI5 of what Colin had been claiming for years. The government had tried to prevent the publication of Wright's book, *Spycatcher*, in Britain, but they had been unable to stop its publication in Australia and Ireland, from where copies were brought into Britain in travellers' luggage. Paul's brother Oliver brought him a copy, and a family photo shows Michael Foot reading it avidly.

In that first article for the *Daily Mirror* about Colin Wallace, Paul had asked a rhetorical question: It is a fantastic story, but is it true? No, came the reply from the *Independent* newspaper in September 1987, it is not.[11] The article, written mainly by David McKittrick, a long-established and respected Northern Ireland correspondent, dismissed Colin as a fantasist, not only professionally but in relation to details of his private life. If he could not be trusted to tell the truth about himself, how could he be trusted on anything else? In more than a thousand words, beginning on the paper's front page and taking in the whole of page four, McKittrick picked apart Colin's claims: 'A profile of him in a South of England newspaper', he wrote, 'describes him as a graduate of Queen's University Belfast, but the university says he does not hold one of their degrees.' On it went: not a member of the Widgery Tribunal, not recommended for decorations, not a parachutist.

On every point, Paul challenged the article. He rang McKittrick and asked which 'South of England' newspaper he was quoting from. The paper was the *Bognor Regis Observer*, a small-circulation weekly newspaper in a small town in Sussex. Paul asked McKittrick how he had got hold of a tiny clipping about Colin in a Bognor Regis newspaper. 'There was a long and embarrassing silence. At the end of it the journalist muttered, "I can't remember."' But Paul had spoken to the journalist who wrote the original story, and established that the information about Queen's University had come from someone within Arun District Council, not from Colin – someone with access to Colin's CV, which referred to his training of cadets at Queen's as part of his military duties.[12]

And how about Colin not being a parachutist, as he claimed? That short piece had been written by John Ware, not David McKittrick. As Paul discovered, the records held by the British Parachute Association had gone missing. But the international records still existed – and sure enough, they included Colin's licence. For good measure, Paul even spoke on the phone to the major-general in the Parachute Regiment who had jumped with Colin.

Further confirmation of Colin's story came from Clive Ponting. He had headed up the legal department at the Ministry of Defence during the Falklands War. He had got into trouble, and very nearly went to prison, for leaking papers to Tam Dalyell MP about the sinking of the *Belgrano*. In the summer of Colin's release, Ponting had given an interview to *Channel 4 News* about a meeting he had had with two MI5 officers in 1983, in which they had discussed 'the Wallace problem'. 'There was never any suspicion that Wallace was making these stories up or that it was totally unfounded and very easy to rubbish', Ponting told the programme.

> It was very much a matter that, OK the story was being contained at the moment because he was in jail, but that in a few years' time he

would be back out again and could be expected to start making the allegations again and then that would be a serious problem.[13]

Paul signed the contract for the book on Colin Wallace in the summer of 1987. Just weeks later the article in the *Independent* appeared, and for a brief moment the whole project was threatened.

> The publishers argued, with some reason, that if the *Independent* allegations were accurate, I and they might be made to look foolish with a book which boosted a couple of hoaxers and Walter Mittys. When the articles were examined thoroughly, the publishers too determined to proceed.[14]

Paul worked on the book throughout 1988, often writing at Colin and Eileen's home. And Colin spent time at Paul's, helping to thread the story together. Paul had taken over one room of his flat as his writing space. Colin was impressed: 'You couldn't see the floor, it was covered in papers, a mass of documents he'd collected together.' But Paul could locate any document he needed. 'He'd know it was in the third pile on the left.'

There were other stories about Northern Ireland that occupied him during that same year. The first was the case of John Stalker, the assistant chief constable of Greater Manchester Police, who was drafted into Northern Ireland in 1984 to head an inquiry into a possible shoot-to-kill policy being operated by the Royal Ulster Constabulary. Stalker understood he was investigating possible criminal offences committed by policemen, and that he was there to establish the truth. So he ignored the advice of a Belfast community leader who told him to 'get in and get out' as quickly as he could: 'Tell the Government what they want to hear – that the RUC are a fine brave force.'[15]

In his first report, Stalker found that the police had been operating a shoot-to-kill policy for terrorist targets, rather than arresting them. He then asked for access to a secret tape recording that would tell him what really happened when another two young men, Michael Tighe and Martin McCauley, were shot by the police in a ramshackle old hayshed. But while he waited, Stalker was suddenly suspended on a spurious charge of consorting with criminals – or, more specifically, a man named Kevin Taylor. Here was another smear campaign, cooked up to close the book once more on what was happening in Northern Ireland.

As Paul explained in the *Daily Mirror*, the list of people who had associated with Kevin Taylor was long: Cecil Franks, solicitor and Tory MP for Barrow; Lynda Chalker MP, then minister of transport; David Trippier MP, minister of state at the Department of Employment; and Fred Silvester, Tory MP for Manchester Withington. All had attended events hosted by Kevin Taylor, because Taylor was the former chairman of the Conservative Party in Manchester.[16] An internal police inquiry concluded that Stalker should face disciplinary charges – not for meeting Taylor, but for the unauthorised use of police cars. The Manchester Police Authority rejected the suggestion of disciplining Stalker by thirty-six votes to six. 'Only the Liberals – on the fence as ever – voted for them', wrote Paul.

Stalker should have been reinstated to the Northern Ireland inquiry, Paul argued. And 'there should be another even more searching inquiry into how he came to be accused, suspended and smeared in the first place'.[17] But Stalker was not reinstated, and he never returned to Northern Ireland. He resigned from the police a few months later.

The other story that preoccupied Paul related to an event that had taken place in Gibraltar on Sunday, 6 March 1988. That Sunday, at 4.45 p.m., the Ministry of Defence issued a statement: 'A suspected bomb has been found in Gibraltar', it read, 'and three suspects have been shot by civilian police.' That same week, Paul presented an episode of Granada Television's *What the Papers Say*. The show began simply enough, with Paul reading out the headline stories in the eleven national newspapers the day after the shooting: three terrorists had planted a 500-pound bomb on Gibraltar; the bomb had been defused; in a shoot-out, all three terrorists had been shot dead by the Spanish police. There were variations in the details, but all eleven ran the same story. All eleven, announced Paul, had got their facts completely wrong. The reason Paul new this was that, just a day after the shooting, the foreign secretary, Geoffrey Howe, had announced in the House of Commons that, despite the earlier statement from the MoD, there was no bomb in Gibraltar, of 500 pounds or of any size.

Immediately after the shooting, a slew of false news stories appeared in British newspapers. But where did they come from? Paul pointed the finger at the security services, who had a direct interest in getting their version of events out fast, true or not. Paul had Colin Wallace on hand to explain the importance of getting in first: once the papers have printed one version, the damage is done. Even when the true facts come out, the original story is the one that sticks in the public's consciousness.[18]

By the end of April, the controversy over what had happened in Gibraltar was reaching its peak, with the broadcast of *Death on the Rock*, a documentary produced by Thames Television. Their team interviewed every eyewitness they could find to the actual shooting – and, crucially, asked if they had heard a warning before the shooting began. Did those who were killed have their hands up in surrender when they were shot? Were more shots fired when they were already on the ground? The response was official uproar. Both the government and the media attacked the programme, as well as its producer Roger Bolton and its key witness Carmen Proetta. She was unreliable, they claimed, because she ran an escort agency for rich Arabs – 'The Tart of Gib', as the *Sun* tastefully described her – a claim that was malicious as well as unfounded, and ended up in the libel courts.

The story that gradually emerged was that the three dead IRA members, Sean Savage, Mairead Farrell and Daniel McCann, had been tracked across Spain by the local police, who handed them over for further surveillance to the British security services at the border. There was a bomb in a car in Spain, but not in the white Renault that one of the team had driven across the border and parked in the street in Gibraltar. He was joined by the others, who had crossed the border on foot. Under constant surveillance, because MI5 and British military intelligence had known about the plan for months, they were tracked as they returned to the border, again on foot. But before they got there, they were shot in the street by the British SAS.

If that was what had happened, why had the three been allowed into Gibraltar in the first place? Why were they not stopped at the border? Why was one of them allowed to drive a car onto the Rock? Didn't the whole story stink, asked Paul, of what the *Daily Telegraph*, in a moment of blinding clarity, described as 'a trap'?[19]

By the time the inquest opened later in the year, the entire story had changed again. 'Chaos, chance and cock-up was the main theme of the inquest', wrote Paul in *Rock Bottom*, a *Private Eye* special. The new version of events was never tested, and no Spanish policeman was called to give evidence – presumably, Paul wrote, because the Spanish police would not want to publicly disagree with MI5's version of events.

Under pressure, Thames Television had set up its own independent inquiry into its programme. It was chaired by Lord Windlesham, a former Conservative minister in Northern Ireland. His report praised the Thames team, and cleared the programme of any charge of exaggeration or falsification. What followed was more rage and hysteria from the media and politicians. 'With the facts as we now know them, including all the revelations that have come out in the Windlesham inquiry, what can be said about the shootings themselves?' asked Paul. MI5 had spent months tracking the three members of the IRA. They had been followed to the border, and were let in, precisely because they were being lured into a trap. The shooting had all the hallmarks of a carefully planned operation, not a rash reaction to unanticipated events: 'The likelihood is that there was always a plan to shoot the terrorists in the street.'[20]

'*Rock Bottom* is an attempt to analyse the killings and the subsequent campaign of disinformation by the Government and its supporters in the press', wrote Ian Hislop in a short introduction. 'It is not an apology for terrorism but a piece of investigative journalism, a distinction increasingly lost on a government obsessed with secrecy and censorship.'[21]

'It was bloody good', he reflects. No other paper or magazine had the sort of journalist who could do what Paul did, 'because he was fantastically good at detail, both human and forensic. He could do the DNA and firearms and so on, but he could also do why these people might not have done it. He wrote news like it was fiction, everything was story.'

Paul rounded off 1988 with a BBC radio programme: 'You can tune in to my (rather biased) view of the year', he told his *Mirror* readers. 'I can't guarantee you'll enjoy it, but I can guarantee the Prime Minister won't.'[22]

Paul was given an entire half-hour in which to criticise the Tory government. He began with the government's tax cuts and the benefit changes in that year's budget, and continued with the increase in homelessness, the sale of council houses, and the collapse of council house building. He detailed the string of disasters that had begun the year before: the explosion on the Piper Alpha platform, with 164 dead; the Clapham rail disaster (34 dead); Zeebrugge, where the *Herald of Free Enterprise* had capsized (193 dead); and the King's Cross fire (34 dead).

With the radio programme completed and his last *Mirror* column for the year written, Paul packed up and set off for Cornwall with Rose and Tommy, to spend the Christmas holiday in their flat overlooking the sea at St Ives. Within a few days he was back in London. He was under some pressure, and deadlines loomed. His Chatto pamphlet about Ireland was late, and his editor, Carmen Callil pleaded with him just before Christmas finally to deliver it. *Rock Bottom*, the Gibraltar pamphlet for *Private Eye*, was due at the printers, and then there was the Wallace book to get on with, his *Mirror* column was soon to restart – and, besides all of that, the Bridgewater appeal was about to resume.

The deadline for the Wallace book suddenly took on a new urgency. In early 1989, the government was busily pushing through parliament a new, tighter, broader Official Secrets Bill, which would make it risky for any journalist who talked to a source in the security service. The view of Macmillan's lawyers was that, if and when this Official Secrets Bill became law, the book would be in clear breach, and it was due to become law in May 1989. In early January, Paul met Adam Sisman, his new editor at Macmillan, at the Nosherie, a Jewish café near the *Mirror* building – one of Paul's regular haunts, which served an endless supply of chicken soup and salt-beef sandwiches. Sisman was there to persuade Paul that it was just about humanely possible to get the book published before the deadline – but Paul would have to finish the manuscript by the end of March; it would take another month to get copies into the shops. When they met, the book was still only half-written.

Operation Weasel, Sisman's code-word for this highly secret project, was under way. No one was to talk about it over the phone. All copy had to be delivered by hand, not by post or messenger. Paul had warned him, 'Some very weird things will happen before this is out.'[23] There was good reason for the caution: the smaller the number of people involved, the smaller the number at risk of prosecution, if that ever arose.

In the first week of April, Paul delivered his finished manuscript to Sisman's home, and the circle of people in the know widened, though only slightly. Eileen Wallace typed the manuscript, and Macmillan's typesetter worked from her discs. The production manager was brought into the loop, as was the printer. Publication of *Who Framed Colin Wallace?* was planned for 9 May.

A handful of individual copies of the book were distributed discreetly. The *Daily Mirror* was given one so that it could carry a long article on publication day. The day before publication, Lord Stockton gave two copies to former prime minister Edward Heath. He also invited Paul and Colin to the House of Lords to meet Merlyn Rees, Roy Jenkins and David Owen, all of them politicians with an intimate involvement in the politics of Northern Ireland. Paul and Colin went from there to meet two Labour MPs, Tam Dalyell and Ken Livingstone. Paul also gave a copy to Richard Ingrams: 'another RGY', he wrote inside – another rattling good yarn.

Bookshops were sent unordered copies, marked as only for sale on 9 May, and with a note inside apologising for the secrecy and asking them not to return the unsolicited order.

No review copies were sent. No advance press release was issued. On the morning of publication day, journalists were invited to a press conference at midday at the Savoy Palace Hotel. Lord Stockton joined Paul and Colin to speak up in person for freedom of the press and against the powers the Conservative government was taking for itself.

The new Official Secrets Act came into force two days later.

Gradually, the reviews started to appear. Robert Kee asked a number of pertinent questions in the *Spectator*. 'A story of gunpowder, treason and plot', was R. W. Johnson's take on the book in the *London Review of Books*.[24] Richard Ingrams was forthright in the *Observer*: 'One might have more sympathy with the intelligence services', he wrote, 'if their underhand methods were shown to get results. But all the evidence from Peter Wright, Colin Wallace and others suggests a gang of incompetents and loonies doing their best to sabotage the efforts of the sane.'[25]

Private Eye was also asking pertinent questions. Why had invitations for Paul to appear on both Channel 4's *After Dark* and BBC's *Start the Week* been withdrawn? Was the old anti–Colin Wallace pressure still being applied?[26] But it was the *Independent* review that must have seemed most satisfying to both Paul and Colin. In it, Godfrey Hodgson dealt head-on with the earlier article in the same newspaper by David McKittrick: 'I find [Paul's] rebuttal devastating', he wrote.

> The fact is that there is now a considerable body of independent but convergent testimony to the central proposition: that in 1973–5, faced with rampant IRA violence, power-sharing and near-insurrectionary Protestant strikes in Northern Ireland and with the energy crisis, the miners' strike, the three-day week and the imminence of a Labour government, a clique of MI5 officers, in moral panic, set about discrediting virtually all British politicians who did not share their view of the world.[27]

Harold Wilson had told journalists the same, and Peter Wright had confirmed it. And so, from a different point of view, had Clive Ponting, who worked for the Ministry of Defence at the time, and Anthony Cavendish, of MI6, who was told something similar by his friend, the head of the secret service, Maurice Oldfield. Cavendish himself reviewed the book for the *Sunday Times*. He had met Wallace, and had duly been warned against him, just like everyone else:

> I believe him and the story which Foot has now documented. I have always believed that the intelligence services (in themselves a sort of freemasonry) could, both by using the old boy network and claiming national security interests, get anything done, or achieve any result in this country.[28]

The book, he said, would be an irritant to the government – and it was. Tam Dalyell, who also reviewed the book, for the *Scotsman*, started asking questions in the House, as did Ken Livingstone, who had referred to a draft book by Fred Holroyd in his maiden speech in 1987 and had demanded a full inquiry.

The probing and questioning paid off. Just six months later, in January 1990, Archie Hamilton, minister for the armed forces, in a written answer to Wallace's MP, explained that some papers had come to light, and the government now admitted that, when Colin Wallace's post had been established, 'it was proposed that its duties should include responsibilities for providing unattributable covert briefings to the press'. He had also been required to make 'on-the-spot decisions on matters of national security during interviews', and these briefings 'may have included disinformation'.[29] The government, he said, would review the decisions of the Civil Service Appeal Board in an inquiry led by David Calcutt QC.

The change of government position happened just in time for the publication of the paperback edition of the book, in March 1990. This would prove to be a particularly good month for Paul, who was named Journalist of the Year in the *What the Papers Say* awards – and for Colin, whose complaint against the *Independent* was upheld by the press regulator because it contained 'unsupported allegations'.[30]

Paul summed up the government's new position thus:

Colin Wallace, who had been portrayed by Ministry spokesmen, newspapers and policemen as a Walter Mitty figure who was always dressing up in uniforms, making up fantastic spy scenarios and killing men, was suddenly revealed as the man who had told the truth while officialdom lied. There *had* been a secret job description for him at Lisburn. There *had* been a psychological operations unit which did deal with disinformation. Colin Wallace *had* been involved in all of this. He *had* been involved in a project called Clockwork Orange. At least four junior Ministers, a Secretary of State and even the Prime Minister had told the House of Commons at one time or another in the previous six years that none of these things were true.

From this flowed a simple question, Paul continued, which all the media and a host of MPs started to ask simultaneously: 'If Colin Wallace was right about the way he was sacked from his job in 1975, might he not be right about the reasons why he was sacked? Was he right about Clockwork Orange? Was he right about Kincora?'[31]

◈

Once again, Jim Nichol was persuaded by Paul to take up Colin's case. He and Colin went together to meet David Calcutt QC, where they discussed Colin's job, the circumstances of his dismissal and resignation, and what had been said, and by whom, at his Civil Service Appeal Board hearing. The secret job description for the Clockwork Orange project was central to Colin's argument – and there, in David Calcutt's hands, was the long-contested document, which had at last been handed over by the Ministry of Defence. 'The thing about Colin', says Jim, 'is that he has a photographic memory.' Colin described to Calcutt what the original had looked like – the way it was typed out, the numbering used on the opening page, the number of pages, the size – A4 – of the paper. Calcutt was holding a single, rather small sheet of paper. Jim remembers the silence that followed. As they prepared to leave, Calcutt made one last comment: 'I have not lost sight of what you said about the job description.'

By August 1990 his enquiries were over. Then, quick as a flash, there was a leak to the *Sunday Times*. It predicted that Calcutt would find in Colin's favour. 'The whole business has not been handled terribly well', an MoD source told the paper. 'But whatever he might think, it has been a cock-up and not a conspiracy.'[32]

Anticipating such a response, Calcutt, who had been asked *not* to prepare a written report but simply to express his conclusions, did precisely the opposite. His report was very short and to the point, and was written because, if it had not been, he said, it would leave matters 'open to misrepresentation.'[33] Colin Wallace, it maintained, had been wrongfully dismissed from the army in Northern Ireland for two reasons. First, the MoD had spoken privately to the chairman before the hearing, which he said probably affected the outcome. He had been nobbled, in the plain language that Paul preferred.[34] Nor had the MoD explained the full range of Colin's work to the Board. The job description problem had come full circle. It had not been shown to the Appeal Board and, as David Calcutt was well aware, it had not been shown to him either.

There was one more outstanding question: What about Colin's conviction for the killing of Jonathan Lewis? He had said from the start that he had had nothing to do with it. He knew he looked guilty, but insisted he was not. Had he been framed for that, too?

A miscarriage of justice was familiar territory to Jim Nichol. And then, in the surprising way in which this story constantly unravelled, he watched a television documentary that included an interview with Home Office pathologist Ian West. *Facing South*, made for the south of England station TVS, asked Dr West how he formed the view that Jonathan Lewis was killed by a karate blow to the nose. 'I talked to a karate expert', he explained. 'It was nothing to do with the British army or British police.' 'The American security services?' asked the interviewer. 'Yes', came West's reply.

For the appeal hearing, Jim Nichol assembled a number of experts who would challenge the blow-to-the-nose theory that had been the basis of the prosecution's case at trial. Adrian Sugar, a consultant with particular experience in head and facial injuries, did not accept the karate-chop theory, and neither did his colleagues. No one knew of any such case. In his evidence at the appeal, Ian West agreed that he had never seen it either.

The three Appeal Court judges accepted that the most likely scenario was that Jonathan Lewis had been knocked unconscious on the riverbank, and not in Colin Wallace's home. The body had never been in the boot of his car. Colin's conviction was quashed.

'It was clear to me from the outset that Jonathan Lewis had been mugged while on the riverbank', says Jim Nichol. 'And I believe Colin was being watched by the intelligence service. When someone like that was done over in Northern Ireland, people kept a watch, perhaps retired officers, perhaps police officers, perhaps people in the intelligence service living in the area. How else do you explain the "American" who gave Ian West the idea of the karate chop? How else do you explain David McKittrick getting that tiny item from the *Bognor Regis Observer*?'

Jim's reading of events found further support many years later, when it was revealed to the Northern Ireland Historical Institutional Abuse Inquiry that the security services had been in contact with McKittrick on a weekly basis in 1987.[35] Although there was no evidence the intelligence service had been directly involved in framing Colin Wallace, they may have taken advantage when an interesting story reached their ears.

Paul was not at all surprised that the conviction was quashed. Nor, he thought, were the readers of *Private Eye*, who had been reading about the case since March 1988. In all, Paul had written thirty-four items for the *Eye* about Colin Wallace. By the time the appeal began, there was very little left of the original case – yet the prosecution barrister still claimed Wallace was guilty, and demanded a retrial. The judges said no.[36]

Colin was exonerated, and so was Paul. He had been under extreme pressure while writing the book – not just because of the tight time-frame, the denials from the Ministry of Defence, the threat of the new Official Secrets Act, the attacks by other journalists on his integrity, but because of Colin himself.

'Nothing terrifies a journalist as much as an accomplished deceiver', Paul wrote in the introduction to *Who Framed Colin Wallace?* 'Colin had been a professional deceiver, paid for his abilities as deceiver by the British Army, and unrivalled in his field.'[37]

21
To Divide Is Not to Take Away

Of all the deadlines jostling for Paul's attention in early January 1989, Jim Nichol was most concerned about the Bridgewater appeal.

He rang Paul to discuss it. 'He's not here', Rose told him. 'He's left.' When would he be back, Jim asked? He wouldn't be, Rose had to explain. When she said Paul had left, she meant he had left her. Jim was, unusually for him, lost for words. So Rose helped him out: he should try calling Paul at the *Mirror*, or he should speak to someone called Clare Fermont. Jim couldn't believe it. He had always prided himself on knowing what was going on in his friends' lives, and he knew Clare. But he had no idea about her and Paul. Or their secret affair, which, it seemed, had been going on for years.

Paul and Clare had first met in the early '80s, and bumped into each other again during the miners' strike – kindred spirits on the question of the SWP's intervention in it. From the start of their affair, Paul was clear: he was married, and he would not be leaving his wife. Clare was perfectly happy with that – she had been part of a couple, and was not interested in being in a couple again. But the occasional walk or the odd meal together soon turned into the odd night together, and gradually the opportunities seemed to increase.

Such a long-running affair inevitably had its complications, and the mechanics of the deceits eventually got the better of Clare. She thought being on her own seemed a better option, and she met Paul at a restaurant and explained that she didn't want to continue. He was upset, but off she went, thinking that was that.

Paul wrote her a long and emotional letter, full of romantic, Shelley-like language. Shelley's belief in free love, what he called true love, appealed strongly to Paul:

> True love in this differs from gold and clay,
> That to divide is not to take away.[1]

Clare's name was, after all, so similar to that of Claire Claremont, Mary Shelley's stepsister, who almost certainly had a brief affair with Shelley. Paul always had a special sympathy for that Claire.

But the letter never arrived. Paul was in the middle of writing the Wallace book, and was spooked: Had someone in MI5 got hold of it? Might events spiral out of his control? He wrote it out again, and this time it did arrive, and the two of them began a long and painful discussion about what to do.

Clare remained adamant throughout: she was not asking him to leave Rose, she could not bear the guilt and the cliché of being responsible for ending his marriage, taking him away from Tom. Paul would agree. And then he would insist he only had one life. 'In truth, those conversations got a bit boring', she says. 'I thought it would have been better if he had left and then had a think about it. But he had never lived on his own. He'd always had someone.' It was not going to happen that way.

In Cornwall for Christmas, Paul was distracted, and Rose asked what was troubling him. He told her about his affair, how he was in love with someone else. Rose asked him to leave – immediately.

Paul and Rose had been together for twenty years, and their son Tom was then ten years old. Paul was racked with guilt, which was of no great help to Rose. Clare told him she would understand if he did go back. He thought about it, he even talked to his friends about it, but he stayed.

Following the break-up, Rose had fewer visitors: there were no more suppers, no more of Paul's wide circle of friends or the people he was writing about. Tom remembers how shattering it was for his mother when Paul left. It was strange for him, too; there was no one else in his class at school whose dad had just walked out. 'Afterwards my relationship with him did get better', Tom remembers.

Some of the couple's friends were appalled by Paul's behaviour towards Rose, and cut him off. 'He got very thin', remembers his son John. 'He felt very guilty and just worked himself into the ground. He had to do a lot of freelance work to earn some money.' Money was an issue, not least because Paul had promised Rose that she would not be worse off. He simply transferred his wages from the *Mirror* to her, which left him without a regular income.

Clare knew that it was going to be tough when Paul moved in, but she had no idea just how tough. 'That first year was very difficult for him', Clare says now. 'We spent a lot of time walking round Springfield Park and playing tennis.' Paul was as competitive as ever, never seeing any reason why Clare, or a child – even if they were only ten – should be allowed to win. There was a new sport, too: golf. Paul had left behind a stylish flat in upmarket Hampstead and moved to Clare's rather modest house in Stamford Hill. In Hackney at that time there was a small pitch-and-putt golf course along the Lea Bridge Road. It was rough, with eighteen holes and next to no facilities, but plenty of users: taxi drivers, shift workers, local people. At weekends it was somewhere for Paul and Clare to take Tom, who soon learned to outplay his father.

Before Paul moved in with Clare, he had shared a secret with her: besides his three sons, John, Matt and Tom, he had a fourth son, not much younger than Tom.

Whatever Grey Gowrie might have thought about Paul's unease about women when they were at Oxford together, it was something Paul quickly grew out of. He liked women, and during the years he worked on *Socialist Worker* in the 1970s, he had affairs, some short, some long, with a number of women. Although he must have known there was always a risk, when he first heard from one of his women friends that she was pregnant, he was both surprised and angry, and retreated from both the mother and the child. He was terrified that Rose would find out.

The mother of his son was not expecting much, but she was deeply hurt by his angry response and his refusal to navigate any sort of relationship with his son. Put simply, she says 'he could have been a better dad'. Paul did meet his son, at the request of the young teenager, in the

1990s. But too many years had passed, or there was too much ambivalence on Paul's part to make up for those missed years.

Tom would eventually find out when, after his father died, a friend told him she had been at school with his half-brother. Tom had no idea what she was talking about. So she told him what she knew, and Tom arranged for them to meet. 'It was weird when someone who looked just like me, is tall and thin like me, turned up. We had a very nice day walking up and down beside the Thames.'

Paul's Counterblasts pamphlet, *Ireland: Why Britain Must Get Out*, was published at the beginning of June 1989. Shortly after its publication, Paul and Clare set out for Dublin with a box of the pamphlets in their luggage, and an appointment with Paul O'Brien, a long-standing friend in the SWP, who was then writing his own book about Shelley in Ireland.[2] Together the three drove north to Belfast for an SWP public meeting in the Conway Mill, where Paul would be sharing the platform with another old SWP friend, the journalist and political activist Eamonn McCann. It was something they had done before, not least on a memorable occasion twenty years earlier when, at the very start of the Irish civil rights movement, they had agreed to do a meeting in Kilburn, London, at which not a single person turned up.

This time it was very different: hundreds came to hear them. But before they could begin, Clare remembers the tramp, tramp of feet on the stairs as a contingent from Sinn Fein arrived – some of whom were probably also in the Provisional IRA. Its members rarely, if ever, came to SWP meetings, but this was a critical moment. The Republicans had published a book about the history of socialism and republicanism in Ireland, and there was talk of ending the armed struggle. They wanted to hear what was being said by the socialists. There was a buzz in the room – and both speakers were on good form. Paul's pamphlet sold well – unlike his book on Colin Wallace, which was not popular in the North, Eamonn explains, because the political journalists felt it was their territory, while the Unionists saw Colin as a traitor and the Republicans saw him as a part of the British state.

After Belfast, Paul and Clare took off for a holiday along the west coast, where they were planning to play golf and take in some political sightseeing. Before their trip, Clare had given Paul a copy of *Partners in Revolution*, about the founding of the United Irishmen in the 1790s, the internationalism then sweeping Europe, and the efforts made by the French to help overthrow English rule in Ireland. On the holiday Paul steeped himself in the story of Wolfe Tone and Robert Emmet, as Clare drove them around, in and out of the bays and ports that appear in the book and play a role in the story: Bantry Bay, Enniscothy in Wexford and Killane. 'Wonderful', Paul wrote on its last page, in a note dated 26 June 1989.[3]

Tucked inside, he kept his notes for a Marxism meeting that he was to speak at on his return to London. The meeting, on the influence of the French Revolution on Ireland in the 1790s, began with a joke about *Desert Island Discs*. Although he was never invited to appear on the BBC radio programme, Paul wondered what records he would choose if he were. *I'm a Gnu*, by Flanders and Swann, was guaranteed a slot. He loved singing along to it with a car full of small children. Perhaps something from Gilbert and Sullivan. The 'Internationale'. And an Irish rebel song – one of the songs he would sing with his sons on the long drive down to Cornwall. His preference would be *Kelly, the Boy from Killane*, sung by The Dubliners. And in his speech he took the part of a pompous BBC producer: No, no, you can't have that, it's banned. No political Dubliners.

Paul quoted the third verse in full, carefully written out in his notes for the talk:

Enniscorthy's in flames, and old Wexford is won
And the Barrow tomorrow we cross,
On a hill o'er the town we have planted a gun
That will batter the gateways of Ross!
All the Forth men and Bargy men march oe'r the heath
With brave Harvey to lead in the van;
But the foremost of all in that grim gap of death
Will be Kelly, the boy from Killane.

Ireland in 1789 had a population of 4 million Catholics, discriminated against by half a million Protestants. There were demands for parliamentary reform, for representation, manhood suffrage and equal constituencies. The United Irishmen was formed in October 1791, by both Catholics and Protestants, to fight for those demands.

The uprisings it organised, in 1796 and 1798, were defeated. The Barrow River had been crossed; the town of Enniscothy had gone up in flames; the uprising in Wexford, led by brave Harvey Bagnall, was successful, if short-lived. The gateways of Ross, however, had stayed closed – and two centuries later the consequences were still being felt.

The song was not banned by the BBC, but a ban was politically quite logical, explained Paul to his audience, because if that gateway to Ross had been battered, the struggle in Northern Ireland would have been won long ago.

22
The Hired Bravos

It was all change at the *Daily Mirror* in the early months of 1990. Out of the blue, just after Christmas, Robert Maxwell rang Roy Greenslade, then the managing editor of Rupert Murdoch's *Sunday Times*, and asked him if he would like to edit the paper. Roy was surprised by the offer, as he was not aware there was a vacancy.

Maxwell had tired of Richard Stott, and had persuaded him to take over at the *Sunday People*. It was a weekly, rather than a daily, with a smaller circulation than the millions sold by the *Daily Mirror*. It also came with an irresistible upside – a potential management buy-out. Stott would have a paper of his own, and slip out of Maxwell's reach.

Roy Greenslade and Paul already knew each other. Roy was married to Noreen Taylor, one of the *Mirror*'s most prominent feature writers, and the three of them lunched together at the Nosherie. But Roy's memories of Paul went even further back. In the mid '70s, while Roy was a student at Sussex University, he had heard Paul speak alongside a young Welsh MP called Neil Kinnock. They were debating their approaches to socialism: gradualism versus radical change. Paul spoke first, and likened gradualism, the idea that you could just creep up on socialism, to a one-armed bandit: pull the lever and wait for four apples in a row. 'You could pull it a hundred times,' Paul had said, 'and never get four in a row. But that's what they wanted to do, these pretend socialists.' The wonderful trick in Paul's performance, Roy realised, came when it was Kinnock's turn to speak. 'As he spoke, Paul would pull an imaginary lever. The students adored it', he says. 'I liked him long before I met him.'

When Roy arrived at the *Mirror*, he inherited a scoop: 'Scargill and the Libyan Money', ran the front-page headline in huge letters on Monday, 5 March.[1] Inside, there was an editorial signed personally by Robert Maxwell, and seven further pages of detail, gossip and colour. During the miners' strike, the story claimed, Arthur Scargill and Peter Heathfield, president and general secretary respectively of the NUM, had taken money from Libya and used it to pay off their personal home loans.

Paul had been enthusiastic when Greenslade first arrived. He had bounded into his office full of cheer the first time a black face appeared on the front page of the *Mirror* – that of Frank Bruno, at his wedding, with his new wife resplendent in a vast white wedding gown. And he was back there a few days later, as Roy made the final preparations for the publication of the Scargill story, telling him that the story was not true. 'He knew we would go ahead', Roy remembers, 'but warned me that we had got it all wrong. I told him about the signed statements we had, and that we couldn't get Scargill to say anything.'

The story ran all week across the front pages, and endless pages inside. There was even a Roger Cook television investigation being broadcast at the same time, creating a perfect media storm. If it was true, the two men were finished. If not, surely, they would sue? Arthur Scargill did not sue; as a matter of principle, he would not sue. But the NUM did ask Gavin Lightman, a leading barrister, to head an inquiry, and until that was over there was little that Paul could do or say. He believed the facts would prove him right.

Just as the Scargill story was breaking, Paul was once again named Journalist of the Year in the *What the Papers Say* awards, and 'Journalist of the Year' was added to the masthead on his page every week for the next year.

When Lightman concluded his inquiry, publishing his findings on 3 July 1990, Paul could finally speak out. In the pages of the *Mirror*, he reminded his readers of the story he had told in 1984 of the battle of Orgreave, when Arthur Scargill was knocked to the ground by the police. Now, Scargill's driver Jim Parker was claiming that the police had not pushed him over, but that Scargill had slipped and hit his head on a log. Paul was amazed. He had been to Yorkshire in 1984 and interviewed six witnesses who saw Scargill being hit over the head with a policeman's shield. 'I also collected pictures which showed him being carried unconscious to a green verge', Paul wrote. 'There were no logs to be seen there.'[2]

The inquiry had dismissed the story about the Libyan money being used to pay off the home loans as nonsense, as neither man had had a home loan at the time. But Lightman had then opened another can of worms: What had happened to money sent to the NUM from the Soviet Union, he asked. Once again, the *Mirror* ran with the story. The allegations kept coming, and the NUM's executive felt so beleaguered that it decided to sue its own leaders.

Socialist Worker campaigned in defence of Scargill and Heathfield against the renewed attacks and smears. Each week it gathered scores of names of trade union branch secretaries and shop stewards, officials and general secretaries, who agreed that the endless stream of allegations were 'a crude attempt to break the tradition of fighting trade unionism'.[3]

In August that year, on a stiflingly hot night, 800 people packed into Sheffield City Hall to hear the two men defend themselves and their record. 'We have done nothing wrong', Peter Heathfield told the audience. 'We have not pinched a penny-piece, we have misappropriated nothing.'[4] Paul was there, too. He had interrupted his summer holiday to fly over from Ireland to speak at the meeting. The *Mirror*'s scoop, Paul charged, was cheque-book journalism of the meanest kind. Roger Windsor, the NUM's chief executive officer at the time of the strike, had been paid £80,000 for his story, and Jim Parker, Scargill's driver, £30,000. Imagine, Paul told the rally, that he had written a story like this about two Tory MPs who had paid off their mortgages out of funds they had raised for charity. Suppose an inquiry found that one MP did not have a mortgage and the other had paid his mortgage off long before the charity money had even been raised. 'My feet wouldn't have touched the ground. I'd have been fired and nobody would have ever believed a word I'd written ever again about Tory MPs or anything else.'[5] Paul was loath to criticise his own paper. It paid his wages. But he knew he had to be in Sheffield. It was, he said, the most important meeting he had ever spoken at.

For over a year, Scargill and Heathfield were hounded by the media, the police and the courts. Of the legal actions, prosecutions and investigations launched in July 1990, all were abandoned, dismissed, or settled in favour of the two miners' leaders. Charges brought against them by the NUM Executive were discontinued. Charges brought by the body that oversaw the statutory duties of trade unions, the Certification Officer, were thrown out. A Fraud Squad investigation was dropped. The Commissioner for Trade Unions' investigation never went anywhere. Finally, in the last official investigation into the story, the Inland Revenue found unequivocally in the NUM leaders' favour.[6] But the episode seriously damaged the two men, and hurried along the demise of the NUM – even if the continuing pit closures were doing the main work on that front. The whole trade union movement had been damaged by the affair.

A few days after the Sheffield meeting, Paul's father died at the age of eighty-two. He was buried in Cornwall, with a Palestinian flag draped across his coffin, and the family gathered again for a more formal memorial at the Methodist Church in Westminster Central Hall, dignified by the presence of the high commissioner of Cyprus. Michael Foot read from Gibbon's *The Decline and Fall of the Roman Empire*. John, Lord Foot, read Clemence Dane's Second World War poem 'I've just been down to Plymouth', where, in spite of the bombs, 'The boys and girls of Plymouth / Were dancing on the Hoe'. Paul and his brother Oliver read tributes; there was Cornish music and the singing of Blake's *Jerusalem*.

There were other deaths to remember in those years. Simon Guttmann, an anti-Zionist Jew who saw the aftermath of the Russian Revolution close up, fought the Nazis in Germany and his native Austria, and detested all imperialism and racism, had died in January 1990 at the age of ninety-nine. Paul remembered meeting him in the 1960s at the Report photo agency, when he was already seventy-four. He was, for Paul, a hero: 'probably the most infuriating, obstreperous and cantankerous working-class hero there has ever been', he wrote in his obituary.

> On the only too rare occasions when he could contain his fury to sit
> and talk, he would explain how the power and passion of a strike is
> far better portrayed in pictures than in words, and how, if we ever
> once treat a single strike as routine, we are finished.[7]

On a good day, he also served the most beautiful Viennese coffee.

Another hero was C. L. R. James, the Caribbean writer and intellectual, who had died the previous year at the age of eighty-eight. Paul loved cricket, and so the author of *Beyond a Boundary* occupied a special place in his pantheon of heroes. It was his understanding of 'the dialectical significance of the game of cricket in general and of West Indian cricket in particular' that so endeared him to Paul. That and *The Black Jacobins*.[8]

The two had first met in 1963 in Glasgow, where Paul collected him from the railway station and took him to a very small meeting of the Young Socialists, where James spoke about the African National Revolution. But Paul could not resist wondering why someone whose chief hero in history was Lenin, was so resistant to one of the central tenets of Leninism: the need for organisation. Even when he was 'politically shipwrecked with a handful of bickering emigres', Lenin disciplined himself for the creation of socialist organisation. But on the few occasions Paul had the chance to argue with James, and 'tried to get an answer to this conundrum', he 'never got one that even started to satisfy me'.

Harry McShane, who Paul also met in Glasgow, and who had had such a profound impact on his political thinking, had died in 1988. At ninety-six, he was only a shade younger than Simon Guttman. 'The commonest jibe of reactionaries against revolution is that it is an infatuation of youth', Paul wrote in his obituary for *Socialist Worker*.[9] 'When people get old, we are constantly told, they drop the silly idealism of their youth. They become "old realists". Not Harry. He had become a revolutionary Marxist in 1908, and died a revolutionary Marxist eighty years later. 'We all know that great men and women don't make history, but we also know that working-class history would be a mean thing if it were not enriched by great men and women.'

The late 1980s were a time of considerable political turmoil, particularly in eastern Europe. After the collapse of the communist regimes in Poland and Hungary, Czechoslovakia and Romania, and the dismantling of the Berlin Wall in November 1989, *Socialist Worker* organised a weekend of meetings and debate to discuss the future of socialism.

Over 2,000 people came to hear Paul and Tony Cliff, together with speakers from across the old Eastern Bloc countries, debate. Paul followed it up with a new pamphlet, *The Case for Socialism*, the point of which was to

> rescue socialism from the awful caricature which has been made of it in Russia and Eastern Europe; to remember what the point of socialism was when it was first put forward; to restore to it its democratic essence; and to hold out a real socialist alternative to the defeatist apathy that now paralyses the left.[10]

It was an argument he had been having since the 1960s.

Britain was also caught up in its own turmoil. In 1990, Margaret Thatcher was on her way out, to be succeeded by John Major; she had been defeated by the hated Poll Tax and her back-stabbing colleagues. 'It All Ends in Tears', ran the *Daily Mirror* front page on 23 November 1990, over the iconic photo of a tearful Thatcher being driven away from Downing Street for the last time.[11] That same day, a new strap appeared across the bottom of Paul's page in the *Mirror*, as the paper promoted the publication of *Words as Weapons*, a collection of Paul's writings.

The book was a collection of his journalism from the past decade, taken from the *Daily Mirror*, *Socialist Worker*, the *London Review of Books*, and numerous other publications. The selection, made by the writer Mike Marqusee, was broad, and included some of the pieces Paul had written about the people who had inspired him: Shelley, of course, and Mary Shelley, William Godwin, the South African writer Olive Schreiner (his Introduction for Virago of their reprint of her book *From Man to Man*), George Orwell, and the American journalist John Reed, whose account of the Russian Revolution, told in *Ten Days that Shook the World*, 'shook me to pieces', he wrote. He also included pages from *The Case for Socialism*, which quoted Friedrich Engels's simple words at Marx's graveside in Highgate, North London, that 'mankind must first of all eat and drink, have shelter and clothing', before it can pursue anything else in life.

'I write this, half-watching early-morning television on 17 January 1991', Paul wrote in the *London Review of Books* in February that year.

A BBC nincompoop in battledress, safe in his bunker in Riyadh, is reading out jingoistic nonsense from Henry V, and now Margaret Thatcher regales us with the horrors of Saddam's attack on Iran, an attack she supported. The air is thick with chauvinist drivel. When the dead are stretched out, and the hideous cost of this crazy war is counted, the blame must be allowed to stop at the *Sun*, the Prime Minister and his exultant predecessor.[12]

As soon as the ground war in Iraq began, Jack Robertson, an SWP comrade, and a small group of journalists in London asked Paul to speak at a meeting against the war. They suggested that the journalist John Pilger be invited as well. Then Edward Pearce, a columnist at the *Sunday Times*, was added to the line-up. Jack got together with another group of angry journalists at the *Guardian*, including the cartoonist Steve Bell, and booked Conway Hall in Red Lion Square. Hundreds turned up. Together, they called themselves 'Media Workers Against the War', and following the meeting they issued a brief statement:

> As workers in the media, we are opposed to the war for oil in the Gulf. We are also revolted at the obvious pressures which are being put on journalists to present a one-sided view of this conflict; to ignore the slaughter of the Iraqi people; and to hide the extent of the opposition in Britain to the war. We therefore agree to support the campaign against the war and the censorship of information.

The most obvious case of censorship was the decision by the BBC to cancel a planned programme on the Iraq Supergun affair. All sorts of programmes were taken off air because they might offend troops in battle, but this one, Paul argued, could not possibly offend them. Paul had the inside track on the programme, and spelled out for his *Mirror* readers the main points it would have made: Gerald Bull, a Canadian gun designer, had been contacted in 1988 by the Iraqi government to build a vast artillery system – a system that included the biggest gun in the world. But before he signed the contract, Bull had sought approval from the US and British governments, which he was obliged to do. The barrels, breach and recoil mechanism were made by British companies. Now one of his guns was pointing at British troops.

The only people who might be embarrassed by the programme, Paul thought, were the British government, which 'now pretends' it was always hostile to Saddam Hussein.[13] And if anyone doubted the story, the *Mirror* ran it as a World Exclusive on its front page. Underneath a photo of another huge gun barrel was the headline: 'It's aimed at our troops.'[14] The supergun first made the news in April 1990, when Customs and Excise turned up at Teesport on the north-east coast and impounded huge gun barrels destined for Iraq. The seizure created something of a political storm. At the time there was a ban on arms sales to Iraq and Iran; while one gun, the Supergun, was stopped, two others had gone to Iraq, and were ready to be fired. The critical question, Paul asked his *Mirror* readers, was whether the government, while pretending to enforce an arms embargo, was in reality encouraging British firms to cash in on Saddam's insatiable appetite for arms?

It was not just the BBC. Across the board, television programmes were scrapped, interviewees stood down, articles spiked. But there was resistance, too. Besides the Media Workers, there were Artists Against the War, Poets Against the War and even Lawyers Against the War. 'Only a decision by the Lord Chancellor to cut our fees could have produced such numbers', Stephen Sedley wryly observed, as 275 lawyers packed into a meeting at Gray's Inn.[15] Against them all was another group, more powerful still, and named by Edward Pearce with sardonic delight: 'Editors *For* the War', made up of all those influential media people lining up to voluntarily censor everything that came their way. Not a single newspaper had taken an anti-war stance, not even the *Guardian*, Paul pointed out. The paper had appeared to be against the war before it started, but 'threw up its hands at the first sound of gunfire'.[16]

Media Workers Against the War was a grassroots movement. There was a weekly organising meeting, chaired by Paul, which attracted huge numbers every Monday evening, including Tony Benn MP, an NUJ member. Steve Bell provided the cartoons: 'I spit on this war', proclaimed his bellowing camel. Posters and stickers were produced, as well as a bulletin. 'You can't publish this', Paul objected, as he looked in dismay at the proofs for the first edition, riddled with typos and spelling mistakes. They ignored him. 'Fight the censors', it proclaimed, above news from around the country. The second bulletin looked better.

The war was a gift for Paul in his *Mirror* column. He detailed the endless trips to Baghdad by Tory government ministers – Tony Newton at Social Security, William Waldegrave at Health, John Wakeham at Energy, and David Mellor at the Treasury – with a photo of Mellor sharing a sofa with Saddam.[17] At the other end of the scale, Paul told the story of a young woman whose fiancé had departed for the Gulf with the Royal Corps of Transport. His barracks at Aldershot had kindly forwarded his summons to court for non-payment of his Poll Tax. The local (Conservative) council had sent 550 similar summonses to the barracks.

A second Media Workers rally was planned for early March, described by Edward Pearce as a memorial meeting for the 150,000 who had died. The war was short and devastating, and by then it was already over. But the rally went ahead, with a Vietnam veteran over from America, and Bernie Grant, the Labour MP for Tottenham, speaking alongside the journalists. As Paul told the assembled crowd, one of the war's consequences was that words themselves had become distorted. 'Collateral damage' was how the media now described a massacre; the word 'stability' was used to describe chaos; 'liberation' was in reality military law.

Paul, who had received a death threat by phone at the *Daily Mirror*, had been pilloried for his stance by fellow journalists. But he knew where he stood and who he stood alongside: 'The people who are against the war now are the people who were against Saddam Hussein all along.' He quoted Shelley's *Queen Mab*:

War is the statesman's game, the priest's delight,
The lawyer's jest, the hired assassin's trade.

Shelley had also had the editors in his sights all those years ago, the

hired bravos who defend
The tyrant's throne.[18]

23

The Great Crook

_____

On Guy Fawkes Night in 1991, Robert Maxwell was found dead in the sea somewhere off the coast of Tenerife, close to his yacht, the *Lady Ghislaine*.

The *Mirror* was in mourning. The next day's headline, with no hint of irony, lauded 'The Man Who Saved the *Mirror*'. Page after page followed, devoted to the life and times of the great man.[1] 'The giant with a vision', said the editorial. 'The great charmer', gushed columnist Anne Robinson. On and on the tributes ran – from his wife Betty, from regular readers of the *Mirror*, from the footballer Peter Shilton. To honour such a man, it was announced that Maxwell would be buried on the Mount of Olives in Israel, with President Chaim Herzog among the mourners.

Three weeks later, cracks began to appear in this rosy story, and news began to circulate that the company was in serious difficulty. To bail himself out of his financial predicaments, and his dubious flotation of Mirror Group Newspapers earlier in the year, Robert Maxwell had looted the *Mirror* pension scheme. The man who saved the *Mirror* turned out to be a crook, who died as the whiff of scandal surrounding his companies was becoming a stench. He had made a straight choice between the Mount of Olives and Wormwood Scrubs, mused Paul, as the scale of his looting became clear.

Richard Stott was once again in charge at the *Mirror*. Maxwell had tired of Roy Greenslade as editor, and, as the Iraq War ended, they had agreed that Roy would leave. The *Mirror* journalists called a meeting, and voted 139:0 for a resolution regretting his departure, and noting with dismay that he was leaving because of 'proprietorial interference'. Paul was sorry to see Greenslade go. But he was happy to see Stott back. Realising the proposed buy-out at the *Sunday People* was just another of Maxwell's broken promises, Stott was more than happy to have his old job back. Now he was in charge, with no chairman breathing down his neck, and he ran the paper as he thought fit, with the willing and enthusiastic support of his staff.

'Millions Missing from *Mirror*' ran the front-page headline on 5 December. Money was missing from the company accounts, but a staggering £426 million was missing from the Maxwell and Mirror pension funds. The Board of Mirror Group Newspapers – discredited, culpable – wanted to keep a lid on the details of what had happened on their watch. But Stott was not having it. This was the *Mirror*'s story, and his *Mirror* would lead on it. He wasn't prepared to wait for the rest of Fleet Street to tell the world what was going on; the *Mirror*'s readers and the people who worked there had a right to know, warts and all.

That day, Stott called the first of numerous staff meetings. 'We had been mugged', he told them.² Day after day, the revelations grew. How had Maxwell done it? Why did the Board not resign? What had they been doing while Maxwell siphoned off his millions right under their noses? Lawyers appeared, earning eye-watering amounts per hour, to try to explain to an increasingly belligerent audience what had happened, and what might happen next. Staff might not have read the small print in the past, but now everyone became a pension expert.

Paul was not in the pension scheme. Not long after Maxwell arrived at the *Mirror*, he had told Paul that, because he had achieved the grand age of 51, he was too old to join, and suggested he put his money in Equitable Life instead – which, it turned out, also got into financial difficulties. But not being in the *Mirror* scheme did not stop Paul speaking at the meetings, or writing in his column, about the way it had been run. He knew a thing or two about pension funds – in particular the controversy surrounding the miners' pension scheme in the early 1980s, when Scargill and the miners' union trustees were embroiled in a fight with the Coal Board trustees on where they should invest the scheme's billions of pounds. At stake was the power of the City of London, its bankers and accountants, on the one hand, and the workers who contributed, on the other. Scargill told Paul what he would have done: 'I wanted to buy Theakstons Brewery and the *Daily Mirror*. My members drink one and read the other. Look how well they've both done ever since.'[3]

As the *Mirror* pension scandal grew, there was no shortage of stories, nor of leaks: 'Strange things are happening at the *Mirror* these days', Paul wrote in his column. 'Not least the arrival in my office of documents about the spending habits of Robert Maxwell.' In 1989, £1.7 million of company money had gone on trips in his private jet – £261,000 of that to pay for the plane when Maxwell was not even in it.[4]

Paul was jubilant – not because Maxwell was dead or the pension fund empty, but because the editors took control: 'We had a wonderful year, there was a democratic spirit because there was no one in charge, no corporate control.'[5]

There were other important stories for Paul that year, not least the corruption surrounding the Al-Yamamah weapons deal between the British government and Saudi Arabia, and an endless stream of revelations about the sale of arms to Iraq – a story which would run for years. There was also outrage from Paul and the editor when the Press Complaints Commission upheld a complaint from the Economic League. 'Who are the members of the PCC which this week upheld a complaint against me and the *Mirror* from the black-listers of the Economic League?'[6] 'Profs and Toffs', ran the headline, because the Commission, which had taken over from the Press Council the previous year, was now made up of lords, ladies and professors, with just a sprinkling of editors and directors. At the old Press Council, he explained to his readers, you could go along and argue your case. The old Press Council included members of the public. Neither was true any longer.

The *Mirror* had run its exclusive, by Paul and Bryan Rostron, six months earlier. Over three days and several pages, including a front-page exclusive and two editorials, the paper had exposed the shambolic blacklists compiled by the League. Robin Cook MP was among the famous and not-so-famous names the League claimed were subversives. Besides Labour MPs, there were trade unionists, journalists, civil rights campaigners, and a large number of building workers.

The Tory government, emboldened by the election result and with John Major as prime minister, was still carving its way through the trade union movement. On 13 October 1992 it took on the miners for one last time: 30,000 jobs would go, and dozens of pits would be closed. The decision was controversial, even among the Tories. The *Mirror* denounced it as a massacre. Pages and pages were devoted over the next few days to the devastation this would wreak across the country – the poverty and unemployment, the broken lives in the mining communities and the country in general. Michael Heseltine, the government minister responsible, was dubbed an 'unctuous creep'.

In his column, Paul got to grips with the economic argument: the government's claim that the decision to close pits was a result of market conditions was simply not true, he argued. When electricity was privatised three years earlier, a fossil-fuel levy was raised. This tax accounted for 11 per cent of everyone's energy bill, and was used to subsidise the nuclear power industry. If it had been used to subsidise coal, not one miner's job would have gone, coal could have been given away free, and the industry would still have made a profit. It was not a market in any real sense, he wrote, but 'a market run by fanatical millionaires whose only energy policy is revenge against the miners for booting the Tories out of office in 1974.'[7]

The *Mirror* gave unconditional support to the miners, calling on its readers to march in their support, and included in its edition on Tuesday, 20 October a centre-spread designed as a poster: 'Coal Not Dole, the Right to Work . . . for All Our Futures.' The poster appeared in front windows across London.

On the day itself, the paper ran lists of coaches leaving from the pits; stories of miners and their families on their way to London; a map of the route for the demo; and news that the Grimethorpe colliery band had taken a 'rest day' to beat a Coal Board ban, and would play on the march. As the paper announced, the *Mirror*'s own journalists would lead a second march from the *Mirror* building in Holborn to join up with the main march in Central London. Richard Stott stood on the steps of the building to see them off, headed by the *Daily Mirror* NUJ banner, and proudly published their photo in the paper the next day.

Paul's page that week was devoted to those who had jumped aboard the gravy train of electricity privatisation. There they were, the twelve company chairmen, with their photos: James Porteous of Yorkshire Electricity: paid £68,280 in 1989–90 (before privatisation), paid £204,088 in 1991–92 (for ten months); James Smith of Eastern Electricity: paid £68,368 in 1989–90, and £242,818 in 1991–2 – and so on.[8] For good measure, Paul also listed all the other people, particularly former Tory ministers now sitting in the House of Lords, who were also doing very well out of the energy companies, as well as all the serving Tory MPs on the payrolls of the banks, PR companies, stockbrokers, lawyers, accountants and estate agents who had made money from the public purse through electricity privatisation.

That weekend there was to be another demonstration. The TUC, often a little late to the party, was holding a rally in Hyde Park on Sunday, 24 October. On an extraordinary day, the *Mirror* journalists were there again: 'My warmest greetings and thanks to all the miners and supporters who mobbed us as we carried the *Mirror* NUJ banner on the vast march last Sunday', Paul wrote in his column. 'As we came down Park Lane, hundreds of marchers swarmed round us to shake hands, clap us on the back and applaud the *Mirror* for joining the miners' fight for jobs. "We don't want another Tory rag," they shouted. 'No, we don't', Paul added.[9]

That jibe about a Tory rag was not a throwaway, but a warning. Everything was about to change at the *Mirror*. David Montgomery had been seen in Holborn: the Board had found the man they thought could save them. Montgomery was a Rupert Murdoch man – former editor of two of his News International titles, the *News of the World* and *Today*. It was, Paul said, a boardroom coup. The discredited Board members had clung on, supported by the big banks, in particular NatWest, wrecking the paper along the way by pushing up the price. *Mirror* readers were being asked to pay for Maxwell's fraud, claimed the *Sun*. That year, the circulation gap between the two papers had started to close. After the price hike, it widened, and would never close again.

For the first time since Maxwell's death, the editorial floor rebelled, holding a series of meetings on the newsroom floor, refusing to accept Montgomery as their new proprietor whatever the assurances about jobs and union recognition. Richard Stott twice persuaded staff to go back to work and get the paper out. On the second occasion, they did so only after Montgomery had made a series of promises, and Richard Stott had appeared, like some latter-day Neville Chamberlain, waving a piece of paper with Montgomery's pledges.

The sackings began three weeks later.

For six months, staff fought every job cut and redundancy, as Montgomery got rid of everyone associated with the union, and what he called 'the old *Mirror* culture'. There were demonstrations and pickets of the building, and endless meetings on the newsroom floor. Union members begged Labour MPs to come to the aid of this Labour-supporting newspaper, only to find themselves stabbed in the back by George Galloway, then the Labour MP for Glasgow Hillhead, who welcomed Terry Pattison's 'retirement' in an early day motion, when Pattison had just been sacked. Galloway could not forgive Pattison for being the man behind the Scargill–Libyan money story.[10] Paul was furious. That was yesterday's battle. Today's battle was with a union-bashing management, and Galloway was lending them his support. Paul rang the House of Commons and asked as many Labour MPs as he could reach to take their names off the motion. But, by the end of March, the industrial battle was lost, the union was crushed, and Paul knew it. The *Mirror* he had joined in 1979 had gone.

Paul's departure was spectacular. To prove a point about freedom of the press, he devoted his entire column to the bullying of his own management, the people discredited by their association with Maxwell who continued to sit on the board, and the raft of journalists from the Tory-supporting *Today* newspaper who were now working for the *Mirror*. Much to Montgomery's annoyance, Paul also detailed the eye-watering share options Montgomery had been given by the board: 1,475,409 shares, to be precise.

But the bulk of the page was dedicated to the people who had been driven out. Just three weeks after Montgomery arrived at the *Mirror*, one hundred casual journalists had been locked out. No one bothered to forewarn them; their passes were simply cancelled, preventing them from getting through the front door.

Two editors lost their jobs. First, Bill Hagerty, editor of the *People*, and, two days later, Richard Stott. In the weeks that followed, thirty-three journalists went. Paul named each one and the jobs they had done. But the sackings that hurt most were those of the NUJ officials,

Trevor Davies and Irvine Hunter – two of the best subeditors on the features desk. Management decided the two roles – subeditor and NUJ official – were incompatible. When they refused to resign their union posts, their contracts were terminated. The union was decapitated. The people who stepped into their shoes as union officials were also terminated. And on it went.

'All is gloom and fear', Paul wrote.

> No one knows where next the axe will fall. Last Friday the corridor where I work echoed to the sound of sobbing. One secretary (27 years) asked me: 'What have I done wrong?' Nothing. None of the people sacked did anything wrong. They were sacked because they did not 'fit in'. But who does?[11]

Paul's column was passed by the *Mirror*'s lawyers, and was submitted to the new editor. David Banks refused to publish it, and asked for another. Paul stood firm: this was his column. The editor stood firm: he would not publish it.

Two days later, on Friday, 26 March, the day his column should have appeared in the *Mirror*, Paul stood on the steps of the Holborn building and gave out copies of his page to people going into the building, and to an array of journalists and news media outside.

Paul had decided he was at the end of the road: he would not be able to continue at the *Daily Mirror*. But he would not go quietly. He would let people know why he could not continue. He had contacted Roy Greenslade and persuaded him, without any difficulty, to help put the page together and lay it out. 'We did it really quickly. There was such passion when we were doing it. Paul was delightful, just like Tigger. He kept saying, "Yes, this is it! Yes! Yes!" And we caught his enthusiasm.' He was amazed that Paul wasn't miserable. 'He'd just been fired. But he turned it into something else. It was probably the perfect example of Paul's inner agenda, recognising where power lay and how to expose it. Exercising press freedom against the press. It was utterly brilliant.'

David Banks was beside himself. 'You have really gone beyond the bounds of reasonable behaviour', he wrote to Paul. 'I suggest you take some compassionate sick leave and seek advice.' And, just to ram the message home, he put out a press release: 'Paul Foot has been offered sick leave so he can have a period of rest.'[12] In their personal replies to readers, David Montgomery and Charles Wilson went further, criticising Paul for his 'uncritical support for Robert Maxwell' – a particularly stinging accusation.

His final *Mirror* page was reproduced in the *Journalist*, the *Press Gazette* and *Socialist Worker*, where he was at pains to explain why he had continued to work for a monster like Robert Maxwell but could not go on any longer under David Montgomery. At first, he had thought it was about censorship. As long as Maxwell did not touch his page, it was worth keeping the column going. Silence about Maxwell's own activities was worth the freedom to expose others, and to sustain the relationship he had with his working-class readers. What in fact changed was the appalling union busting. 'When it was clear the union for the moment was crushed', it was time to go. 'When the editor, who is a ferocious defender of free speech, wouldn't publish the page and then told the world I was off my rocker, there didn't seem much point in hanging around.'[13]

John Foster, general secretary of the NUJ, joined Paul on the steps outside the building, and drily observed that Paul was getting all the professional help he needed – from his union. Foster himself had been banned from the building because he had been attending union chapel meetings, some of which had broken the new editor's rule that no meeting could be held without his express permission, under the threat of dismissal. Management displayed Foster's photo at the entrance to the building, on the wall behind the security desk. 'Doesn't look much like you', he was told by the security guys.

The remaining members of the NUJ chapel at the *Mirror* – the people who a few short months earlier had so proudly carried their banner on the miners' demonstrations – put out their own statement: 'We applaud Paul's principled stand but are heart-broken at losing a wonderful colleague and a superb journalist. We look forward to the day when he can return.'

Richard Stott was appalled by events. 'It was a squalid end to a column that had been unique and one of the finest investigative pages Fleet Street had ever produced. To end it by a third-rate Montgomery man suggesting Foot was ill, said just about everything that needed to be said about Montgomery's regime.'[14]

24

Back to the Honeypot

Paul's departure from the *Mirror* made the news bulletins and the national newspapers. But the photo of him standing outside its Holborn headquarters dishing out copies of his page, grinning from ear to ear, obscured the very real problem he faced. What was he going to do now?

What he wanted to do was to get on with writing his book about the vote. But there was not much money in writing books; finding a new source of income was a more pressing concern. The NUJ would help with his impecunious position by fighting for a financial deal from the *Mirror*, and to that end John Foster gathered together a group of ex-*Mirror* journalists and took the company to court. It was a long battle, with endless meetings, documents and legal arguments. Finally, after two years of toing and froing, and at the door of the court, Mirror Group Newspapers gave in and settled, and each of the applicants received a substantial payout.

The new *Mirror* chief executive, David Montgomery, presented members of parliament with a window into his attitude to the *Mirror*'s staff when he was asked to appear before a House of Commons Select Committee on Employment. He was clearly proud of what he was doing, claiming that he had changed the *Mirror* for the better, getting rid of its 'strident, abusive tone'. 'The place has been cleaned up', he claimed, 'and it is being reflected in our newspapers'. All of this was clearly too much for one Conservative MP: 'If you are putting yourself forward as the voice of the working man', Oliver Heald told Montgomery, 'it is a bit rich if at the same time you are following appalling, old fashioned employee relations which went out with the ark.'[1]

In the meantime, Paul had persuaded the *Mirror* to agree that he could at least keep his files. One Sunday, when few people were about, he arrived at the *Mirror* building with his son Matt and the SWP's print-shop van. They were not planning on packing up the files: far easier to just wheel them out, filing cabinets included. From Holborn they drove them straight to the offices of *Private Eye* in Soho. Paul had come full circle, returning like the proverbial bee to its honeypot.

Ian Hislop had taken over as editor of *Private Eye* from Richard Ingrams in 1986, and he had been trying for years to get Paul back. 'I thought it might be a long process', he remembers. 'He'd got his own page and good resources. I got nowhere, but he did put things my way.'

But as soon as David Montgomery took over at the *Mirror*, Hislop knew he was in with a real chance. He ran a spoof *Daily Mirror* front page in the *Eye*:

> A weeping Lance-Bombardier Paul Foot, 87, looked back to the old days of camaraderie when they all stood shoulder to shoulder against the onslaught of Montgomery and lost. 'Field Marshal Bob was a bastard,' he sobbed. 'But at least he wasn't a Fascist.'[2]

'I never stopped thinking I would get him. I always hoped I would get him.' And he did.

There were many good reasons why Ian was glad to have Paul back. Bryn Estyn was one. Bryn Estyn was a children's home in North Wales. In the original story, written by another journalist at the *Eye*, Gordon Anglesea, a senior policeman, had been accused of sexually abusing boys at the home. The accusation cost them dearly. Anglesea began libel proceedings against the *Eye*, along with the *Observer*, Harlech Television and the *Independent on Sunday*, which had all run variations of the same story. The legal costs were enormous.[3] There was not much Paul could do about that. But after Colin Wallace, after Kincora, Paul's instincts were good. He covered the continuing story for the *Eye*, as ever more horrors poured out of North Wales, but no further writs came in. Eventually a public inquiry was called. For Paul, this was good news. He liked public inquiries, as they richly rewarded his dogged approach. The story was often buried in the detail, and most other journalists would get bored after the opening day or two (it was the same with trials), and only turn up again at the end, or when forewarned that something exciting might happen.

The transcripts of the Waterhouse Inquiry into child abuse in North Wales were readily available, everything was disclosed, and Paul could cover the inquiry from London. But he still went to Ewloe in Clwyd for a few days to follow what was happening. For eighteen months the tribunal listened to hundreds of witnesses describe the unimaginable scale of physical and sexual abuse over a period of twenty years in up to forty residential homes. It shone a light into the darkest recesses of power in police stations, as well as council and government offices. And it exposed the age-old inclination of people in power, Paul wrote in a lengthy feature for the *Mail on Sunday* magazine, to protect their own backs at the expense of children, 'trapped like animals in a cage for the gratification of their keepers'. This was the opportunity 'for the abused children of yesteryear to answer their tormentors back'.[4]

In the inquiry report, finally published in 2000, an entire chapter was devoted to Gordon Anglesea – but it came to no firm view for or against him.[5]

Paul was far less sanguine about another inquiry which he covered at the same time – the Macpherson Inquiry into the 1993 murder of black teenager Stephen Lawrence. He tried, with some difficulty, to keep track of developments, but unlike the North Wales inquiry, the transcripts were not readily available – they required payment of a hefty fee, or a visit to the inquiry office – and there were constant arguments about disclosure, conducted by lawyers behind closed doors, so facts often became known only by accident.[6]

Stephen's death was described at his inquest as a 'completely unprovoked racist attack by five white youths'. Yet, in the murder's immediate aftermath, no arrests were made, even though several witnesses came forward. For years Stephen's family fought for justice for their teenage son. What on earth had been going on in the police investigation?

In 1999, Paul picked over what the Macpherson report called the 'fundamental and fatal error' of not arresting the suspects as soon as their names became known. But the report provided neither an index nor a chronology, so this 'fundamental' failure could not be properly understood.

In his article, Paul set out in detail what had happened in the hours and days after the murder: the five white youths in a red Vauxhall Astra seen laughing at the police cordon on the night of the murder; the roll-call of those five names, Neil and Jamie Acourt, David Norris, Gary Dobson and Luke Knight, as they were given to the police over the next two days by different witnesses; the bungled surveillance by the police of the Acourt home as bin bags of clothes were carried out – the police on duty had no camera. Macpherson also referred to the 'evil influence' of Clifford Norris, a South London drugs and arms dealer, and father of suspect David Norris, and was amazed that he was not arrested. The report identifies this fact as 'unexplained and incomprehensible'.

'These adjectives are absurd', wrote Paul. 'A highly comprehensible explanation was repeatedly urged on the inquiry' – because Norris's 'evil influence' was over the police in south-east London. Yet here it was left as 'inexplicable' and blamed on 'poor old bumbling Inspector Knacker and his institutional racism'.[7]

Why was Clifford Norris not called by the inquiry? Why were witnesses who had named names to the police not called? Why was the police officer who had direct contact with Norris not called? 'Until these questions and many others like them are answered', wrote Paul, 'the sections in the Macpherson report about collusion and corruption are – how shall we put it? – inexplicable and incomprehensible.'

These were not the only inquiries Paul put his mind to during the mid 1990s. There was also the Scott Inquiry into arms sales to Iraq. Following the Teesport seizures of the supergun in April 1990, Customs and Excise had made several arrests. Among them were three directors of Matrix Churchill, a Midlands company working on the project; Chris Cowley, a scientist who had worked in Baghdad for Gerald Bull, the designer of the gun; and Peter Mitchell, the managing director of Walter Somers, also in the West Midlands, where the gun barrels had been forged. Eventually, the charges against both Cowley and Mitchell were dropped and, free of the threat of prosecution, Cowley had a story to tell.

'When he came to see me, he was anxious to disclose information about the whole Supergun scandal', Paul wrote in his introduction to *Guns, Lies and Spies*, Cowley's own account of his incredible story.

> At the centre of the British part of this operation were the intelligence services, a small group of high-placed Tories, including at least one Minister, civil servants in the DTI and the Ministry of Defence, big businessmen 'with intelligence connections' and their bankers. This group was entirely unaccountable. They made up the laws they honoured, and dishonoured ones they didn't make.[8]

Cowley's story, Paul had to admit, had seemed a little fanciful.

Then, in November 1992, the three directors of Matrix Churchill were dramatically acquitted of selling arms to Iraq illegally. Their defence was that they had been encouraged to break the arms embargo by the government itself. Suddenly Cowley's story seemed much less fanciful. An inquiry was demanded, and began hearing evidence in June 1993. How was Paul going to find the time to follow such a complex and intriguing investigation?

Serendipitously, Tim Laxton appeared in his office. Tim had decided to go along to the inquiry and listen – then a friend put him in touch with Paul. Between them, they wrote for every issue of *Private Eye* through 1993, and well into 1994. They detailed the evidence of every civil servant and minister, of the questions asked and not asked.

While they waited for the official report to be published, and while the events surrounding the arms sales remained a live issue, Ian Hislop decided to get their version of events out first. They might be waiting months for the report, he reasoned. It turned out to be years. So, in November 1994 another *Private Eye* special issue was published: *Not the Scott Report*.[9]

To take the reader with him into this complex story, Paul began in 1990, with one of the government ministers involved – an old favourite, Nicolas Ridley. Senior officials in his department had brought him some bad news: 'At Teesport, in the north-east', Paul wrote, a large gang of customs officials had 'seized' several enormous crates of goods bound for Iraq. Inside the crates were huge steel sections of what purported to be pipes for transporting petrochemicals. The awful truth was that they were not pipes at all but parts of by far the biggest gun ever made in Britain for export or for anything else. Ridley's immediate problem was that for ten years his department had assured the British public over and over again that no 'lethal equipment' was being exported to either Iraq or Iran.[10]

Between 1988 and 1994 there were twenty-four occasions when parliament was assured by government ministers, and by Margaret Thatcher herself, that the old guidelines were still in place. One minister, William Waldegrave, signed twenty-six letters to MPs declaring the government had not changed its policy on defence sales to Iraq or Iran, when he knew full well that it had. In his final report, eventually published in early 1996, Sir Richard Scott effectively accused Waldegrave of lying to parliament.[11]

The truth was that the guidelines had been rewritten after the Iraq–Iran War in the hope of expanding arms sales once again, but no one in government could admit it – because, if the guidelines were to be changed, they had to be referred to parliament. There was no reference to parliament, and so, as Paul explained, the change simply never happened.

The problem went deeper than the odd minister being, as Alan Clark had put it during the Matrix Churchill trial, 'economical with the *actualité*'. It was the relationship between the arms manufacturers, civil servants and government ministers that bothered Paul. It was so cosy that 'no one can be quite sure who runs the country or who runs the arms companies, or if some people do both'. A good example was David Hastie. Hastie worked for British Aerospace, where his job was to sell Hawk jet fighters, until he was seconded to the Ministry of Defence in 1988. A good opportunity for selling the Hawks would be an arms fair held in Baghdad in 1989 – but, as a civil servant, he was not allowed to go. He flew there anyway. As he got off the plane, he was seconded back to British Aerospace, and as he left the fair, he was returned to the civil service. It was a political farce. Paul compiled a long list of other arms dealers and manufacturers who had been going through the same revolving door, circulating in and out of the arms companies and the civil service.

The report of the Scott Inquiry was eventually published in early 1996. On the eve of publication, Paul had been persuaded by his old friend Christopher Hird to appear in a television special. *Scott of the Arms Antics* carefully re-enacted moments from the inquiry, with Rory Bremner as John Major, the prime minister who saw nothing and knew nothing, and Alison Steadman performing her Margaret Thatcher impersonation. Self-satisfied civil servants debated the government's guidelines for arms sales over whiskies at their club.[12]

The *Eye* special was well worth the effort. *Not the Scott Report – Thatcher, Major and the Merchants of Death* won the Orwell Prize for journalism for Paul and Tim Laxton. Paul told Tim to keep the trophy, which Tim appreciated. But, for Tim, Paul's lasting gift was the art of good writing. Quoting Orwell, he had told Tim that good prose 'should be like a windowpane, so you can see right through it'.[13]

Four days before Christmas 1988, a fireball smashed into the small Scottish border town of Lockerbie after a Pan Am jumbo jet exploded in mid-air, killing all of its 259 passengers and crew, and another eleven people on the ground. It was the biggest air disaster in British history – but it was no accident.

Tam Dalyell was one of the local MPs, and he pleaded with Paul to take an interest. Paul was happy to oblige, not least because people were already contacting him at the *Mirror*. The questions that needed answering were straightforward enough: how did the bomb get on the plane? Who put it there? At which airport was the bomb placed on the plane? Each was simple to ask, but profoundly difficult to answer.

For a year, most British journalists, like government ministers, accepted that Iran had commissioned the bombing in retaliation for the shooting down by an American warship of an Iranian Airbus, in which 290 people had died. The narrative was that Syria had been commissioned to organise the bombing, and that the bomb was fed into the luggage either at Frankfurt, on the Pan Am feeder flight, or at Heathrow. Then politics took a turn against Saddam Hussein and Iraq. Operation Desert Storm was gathering speed, the Americans wanted

Syria on side, and President Bush declared out of the blue that 'Syria took a bum rap on this'. The case which had been so carefully put together was quietly but firmly junked. Now Libya was to blame.

Remnants of baby clothes found around the bomb originated in Malta, and two Libyans who worked for Iranian intelligence in Malta were identified as the most likely suspects. To complete the story, it was claimed that the bomb had been put on a plane in Malta destined for Frankfurt. It was then transferred to a plane headed to Heathrow, where it was finally loaded onto Flight 103.

On 21 January 2001, Abdelbaset Ali Mohmed al-Megrahi was convicted of the bombing and sentenced to life in prison in Scotland, after a trial that was riddled with inconsistencies and dubious evidence. His co-accused, Lamin Fhimah, was acquitted. The judges talked of uncertainties and qualifications in the case against al-Megrahi, but, despite their misgivings, were able to conclude that the evidence fitted into 'a real and convincing pattern'. 'There was, however, nothing remotely real or convincing (let alone any kind of pattern) in the case against Megrahi', wrote Paul in another *Private Eye* special: *Lockerbie: The Flight from Justice*.[14]

'There was no evidence that the bomb went on in Malta, still less any evidence that Megrahi put it there.' All the other evidence against him was plagued by those 'uncertainties and qualifications' identified by the judges. 'Their verdict was a triumph for the CIA, but it did nothing at all to satisfy the demand of the families of those who died at Lockerbie.'

As so often before, Paul persuaded someone who knew the story inside out to help him with the special. Pam Dix's brother Bill died at Lockerbie, and she had followed every twist and turn of events from the day of the bombing. She became Paul's researcher for the special.

Paul also got to know several people who had lost children on the flight, including Jim Swire, whose daughter Florence had died; John Mosey, who had lost his son; and Martin Cadman, whose son Bill had also been killed. In February 1990, just over a year after the bombing, Cadman had been at the American embassy in London to meet members of the American president's Commission on Aviation Security and Terrorism. He described to Paul how, as they left, one of the senators had said to him: 'Your government and our government know exactly what happened at Lockerbie. But they are not going to tell you.'

All the stories that Paul covered in the mid 1990s – Lockerbie, Bryn Estyn, Stephen Lawrence, Scott – pitted ordinary people against the government, the police, judges, civil servants, and, in the case of the arms industry, those with an economic interest in maintaining secrecy.

Asked in an interview about the Scott Inquiry, Paul raised the issue that was for him at the heart of the matter: it was the arms industry itself that shaped the decision-making process inside government, aided by ministers and civil servants, in an entirely secretive form of government. 'People fought for the vote', he said.

> They argued that everyone had to have a vote, otherwise you couldn't have a fair or legitimate government, and they won it. So, people thought, you've elected the government and that's it. My argument is that the country is run by a group of people who are there because of their economic interests. Those people are not there because they've been chosen by the electorate.[15]

That, Paul felt, was at the very heart of the history of the twentieth century, and it would be the subject of his final book, *The Vote*.

In one way or another, Paul had been thinking about the vote all his life, beginning in a rather unformed way in 1945, at the tender age of seven, when he sensed that something rather important had happened in the Labour landslide after the war. The issue became more focused during the general election of 1959, when he was a Liberal and still contemplating the possibility that his own future career might include being an MP, and was invited to speak in support of the Liberal candidate in Westminster. Don't sound too pompous, his aunt Dorothy had warned him – and, to be sure he understood, she took him to hear the local Tory MP. 'You see what I mean by pompous?' she whispered as they emerged.[16]

He initially discussed his ideas for the book with Adam Sisman, his editor at Macmillan, who had taken so much care in ensuring that the Colin Wallace book saw the light of day. That was in the summer of 1989. Adam had left Macmillan by the time Paul's proposal was written and the book had been commissioned, the working title of which was to be *The Power and the Vote*. The plan – hopelessly optimistic – was that it would take about two years to write.

Returning to *Private Eye* helped, as he was back to the week-on, week-off routine, which allowed more time for writing. By December 1993 he was making progress, though there was a new pressure on the way, because he was about to become a father again, at the age of fifty-six, to Kate, his first and only daughter. She was born in January 1994, after Clare, desperate at her refusal to appear, jogged around Springfield Park.

Eventually, in an abject letter to his publisher, Paul committed himself to getting the first chapter done by August 1995. He thought it better to explain than to apologise. The reasons were money, or the lack of it; journalism, which kept him rather busy as story after story came back into the news; and confidence, which was an odd explanation, coming from Paul. 'I wish I had the arrogance of my youth', he wrote,

> when I would set out to write books on subjects I knew nothing about without a care in the world. I think funnily enough I do know a little about this one but am constantly intimidated by the sheer enormity of the task. These Levellers have absorbed me completely for so long now that I'm sure that once I'm free from them, the book will move much faster.[17]

'These Levellers' were the contemporaries of Oliver Cromwell, whose history Paul had grown up with. His grandfather's house was full of busts and portraits of Cromwell, and Isaac was a founder member of the Cromwell Association. Milton, Cromwell's secretary, was another favourite of his grandfather, and Isaac kept all his Milton quotes in one of his notebooks, which in time Paul would inherit. And it was with Cromwell, the English Revolution and the defeat of the king in 1646 that Paul began his story.

The year 1647 was one of uproar and agitation. Levellers were everywhere in the city, and agitators spread throughout the army. For the first time, the idea that all people – that is, all men – should have a vote was circulating throughout the country. As the elected representatives of the New Model Army debated its future in Putney, Colonel Thomas Rainsborough got to the point. 'Every man that is to live under a government', he said, 'ought first by his own consent to put himself under that government . . . The poorest he that is in England hath a life to live, as the greatest he.'[18]

Cromwell and his generals, like Henry Ireton, would have none of it. Wealthy people like themselves could not contemplate giving the vote to everyone. Only those with a 'permanent fixed interest in the kingdom' could possibly vote. Why? Because the majority had no property, and if they elected the government they would vote to take away the property of the rich. Ireton believed power should lie with 'the persons in whom all land lies, and those in corporations in whom all trading lies'.

Paul argued through his ideas on these momentous events at a series of Marxism meetings in the mid 1990s, where he spoke along-side Brian Manning, an historian of the English Civil War, and John Rees, his comrade in the SWP, and later the author of his own book on the Levellers.[19] In July 1997 they were joined by Caryl Churchill, whose play *Light Shining in Buckinghamshire* had so brilliantly shone its own light on the Putney Debates and the part played by Rainsborough. Another year they were joined by the veteran Marxist historian Christopher Hill, who Paul held in high regard. As Hill made clear in his book *Milton and the English Revolution*, Milton got his ideas from talking to his contemporaries and, Paul wrote, made it clear that *Paradise Lost* and Milton's other long poems 'had more to do with the "loony left" – mid-seventeenth century Levellers, Diggers, Ranters, Muggletonians etc. – than with any classical text or Latin scholarship'.[20]

Once he was free of the Levellers, the next chapters followed much faster: first the Reform Act of 1832, then the ups and downs of the Chartist movement between 1838 and 1848, whose radical demands were ultimately met with failure. The pressure for the Chartists' reforms, Paul made clear, came from people who would gain nothing from the agitation. 'Why, then', he asked, 'were so many prepared to strike and march and protest for so few?' There were, he thought, two reasons. First, reform seemed to most people to be some sort of progress – a response based on hope. But there was something more than hope, something that Paul identified with: a movement from below that might change society.

> There was the unusual and as yet underdeveloped feeling of the people's own power: a sense that, by agitation, by striking, by defying the law about what they should read and when and where they should meet, by secretly storing arms and talking about them, they, the lowest of the low, had appropriated a fragment of the political power which had been held exclusively by the rich and powerful.[21]

In the late 1830s and '40s, the Chartist movement dragged people out of the gloom. Everywhere, ordinary people suddenly became members of committees and spread the agitation, overcoming the more common discriminations and prejudices. They were people like Robert Lowery, a tailor by trade, who was so physically disabled that he could not walk; William Cuffay, the son of a black Caribbean slave; and the Irish Chartist leaders, like Feargus O'Connor and Bronterre O'Brien. There were women, too. The story of Mrs King was the sort of story Paul liked to retell, and it was one he learned from the historian Dorothy Thompson. Mrs King, of Manchester, wanted to name her child James Feargus O'Connor King, after the Irish Chartist leader. The registrar asked her if her husband was a Chartist. 'I don't know', was her reply, 'but his wife is.'[22]

Paul's notebooks listed the books he read – page numbers noted, the first line of quotes written out in his always illegible handwriting. And then the books became presents, as more than one copy made its way into his hands: 'The best book about the Chartists and George Julian Harney', he wrote to his son Matt at Christmas 1994, inside a copy of Albert Schoyen's *The Chartist Challenge*. 'It took me ten years to find mine – and now I've found another one – for you.'

The struggle for the vote continued through the rest of the nineteenth century, and Paul continued to track the story through to the Suffragettes, and on into the history of the vote in the twentieth century. No doubt Paul would have made faster progress if there had not been the pressure of politics, and his irrepressible desire to argue all the time, at any meeting, anywhere. The pressing need for income was another hindrance. *Private Eye* paid extremely well – but a new column in the *Guardian*, which began soon after he left the *Mirror*, would top it up.

At the *Guardian*, there was little restraint on what he could write, albeit with the usual caveats about using his column as a platform for the SWP. All he had to do was produce 800 words, on time, once a fortnight – and he was able to write to that precise length with amazing ease. His son Tom remembers how they would be settling down to watch *Match of the Day* on a Saturday evening when Paul would disappear upstairs, and come down half an hour later with the column done and dusted. He would begin with serious matters of the moment and follow with short pieces, triggered by one event or another, reflecting the rich mosaic of his own life: lunch with Churchill, when Paul was a teenager and his father was governor of Jamaica. 'We don't want to become a magpie nation, do we?' was how Churchill had expressed his anxiety about immigration from Jamaica. 'Magpie nation?' Foot senior muttered to himself all the way home, until he exploded: 'Magpie nation, that's nothing but bloody racialism.'[23]

In another column he came to the defence of his uncle Michael, when he was smeared by the *Sunday Times* as a Soviet agent, code name Agent Boot. Paul was quick to point out that he certainly had not been a security risk back in the 1970s, when he was appointed as secretary of state for employment by Harold Wilson.[24] That story followed hard on the heels of revelations in the *Times* that Richard Gott, a *Guardian* journalist, had taken trips to the Soviet Union paid for by the KGB. The *Times* tried to further smear the *Guardian* by revealing that Arthur Ransome, the *Manchester Guardian*'s correspondent in Russia in the years after the 1917 revolution, later famous for his *Swallows and Amazons* children's books, was 'the most important secret source of intelligence on British foreign policy' to the Russians.[25] Paul knew all about Ransome's past: he had just written a long introductory essay to a reprint of Ransome's three short books – *The Truth about Russia*, *Six Weeks in Russia 1919* and *The Crisis in Russia 1920* – for Redwords, and there was little secret about his time in Russia throughout most of the war. He spoke Russian and knew all the Russian leaders.[26] The books were written after meetings with the security services of both sides.

There was also a surprising amount of poetry in Paul's *Guardian* columns. Shelley, of course – and Byron, berating Robert Southey for being such a wimp as Poet Laureate.[27] Keats also featured, and the question he posed, which Paul thought should be emblazoned over the Stock Exchange and all similar institutions:

> Why were they proud? Again we ask aloud,
> Why in the name of Glory were they proud?[28]

Walt Whitman also appeared, with his description of revolutionary Europe in 1848:

> God, 'twas delicious!
> That brief, tight, glorious grip
> Upon the throat of kings.[29]

So did Louis MacNeice's *Autumn Journal*, written as war loomed in 1938, yearning for a new world:

> Where skill will no longer languish nor energy be trammelled
> To competition and graft,
> Exploited in subservience but not allegiance
> To an utterly lost and daft
> System that gives a few at fancy prices
> Their fancy lives.[30]

Alongside Shakespeare, Voltaire, George Eliot and Oscar Wilde, there was a song Paul remembered from his Glasgow days, sung to the tune of 'The Red Flag'. It came to him in the run-up to the Labour Party conference in 1994:

> The cloth cap and the working class
> As images are dated.
> But we are Labour's *avant garde*
> And we are educated.
> And we are sure if we persist,
> To make the New Year's Honours List.

So just to show we're quite sincere
We sing the Red Flag once a year.[31]

Leon Rosselson, who wrote the song, points out that Paul had delivered a slightly mangled combination of two verses of the original. They were written in the Hugh Gaitskell days of the early '60s, and, he says, came back, as if newly minted, in the New Labour years.

Paul could never refuse a meeting about Shelley. But in the 1990s he also came to appreciate Byron, and agreed to speak on Byron's epic poem *Don Juan*. Clare remembers how they read it to each other in bed at night, and on the last night had to keep going until the early hours so that Paul would at least know how the poem ended.

Nor could Paul refuse an invitation to talk to miners. To talk to miners about Shelley was a double pleasure. In March 1999, he combined the two at the annual event held in memory of David Jones and Joe Green, the two miners killed on the picket line during the 1984 strike.

Rose Hunter attended every year. The ceremony began early, with a wreath-laying outside the Barnsley headquarters of the NUM, followed by a piper playing the Gresford (the miners' mourning hymn). Then they moved into the beautiful and ornate council chamber, draped with NUM banners and decorated with the portraits of former miners' leaders. It was here that miners debated the general strike in 1926, and where they began their strike in 1984. Now they were listening to Paul talking about poetry.

'When he started to speak about Shelley, I thought – this is going to be well boring', remembers Rose. 'But what a fantastic lecture it was. He brought Shelley to life. We all stood and clapped and a feeling of wow! He was so inspiring. We were used to powerful speakers, but I was absolutely blown away.'

It would be Paul's last meeting for quite some time.

25

Head and Heart

In the early hours of Easter Saturday, 1999, Clare telephoned Matt. 'It's Paul', she told him. 'He's had a heart attack.' Paul was in an ambulance on his way to hospital, and she was scared. They agreed she would stay at home with Kate, and Matt would go to Homerton Hospital. When he arrived, he was greeted by Paul telling him, rather dismissively, 'You shouldn't have bothered.' But, as Matt sat and watched his father, it was clear that something was desperately wrong. Paul was in pain and getting weaker by the minute. He seemed to be dying in front of Matt's eyes.

By the time Matt and Clare switched roles, the doctors knew it was not a heart attack. Paul's aorta was leaking. If it burst, he would die. To make a bad situation worse, the hospital had given him blood thinners, the standard treatment for a heart attack, but the worst possible option for a leaking aorta.

Two miles down the road, at the London Chest Hospital, an emergency team of surgeons was being assembled. Paul was to be transferred; if he survived the journey, they would operate. Clare followed the ambulance in her car: 'I thought I was following a dead man.' He survived the journey, but the operation lasted so long that Paul's sister Sarah and her husband Tim had time to drive up from Cornwall. His brother Oliver flew in from some distant corner of the world; his son John had hopped on a plane in Milan; and Tom and Matt had reassembled at the hospital.

Then the surgeons told the waiting family that the worst had happened: Paul's aorta had ruptured on the operating table. The good news was that somehow, amazingly, they had managed to patch him up. The bad news was that the danger of it bursting again would be a constant. If it did, that would be it. All there was to do now was to wait for the bleeding to stop. But it didn't – it went on for hours, and there was no return to consciousness. The prognosis was not good.

In the days that followed, crisis followed crisis. Paul's kidneys failed. His liver failed. He contracted pneumonia. After two weeks, with little sign of life remaining, the consultant in the intensive care unit sat them down and told them that it was most likely that Paul's brain had not survived. If he emerged from the coma at all, he would be in a persistent vegetative state. What did the family want to do? Would Paul want to be like this? They had a night to think about it. They were at their lowest ebb.

Clare had been reluctant to take Kate to the hospital to see her dad. She was only five, much too young to comprehend what was happening or cope with the tubes and wires, machines and dials. But now Clare knew she had to take her. When she saw her father, Kate immediately climbed up on the bed and kissed him on the cheek. And then Paul smiled. There was even the faintest movement in his left hand. There was life; he was not brain-dead.

Gradually, the physical crises slowed and stopped. But the coma continued for five weeks. No one could tell them what was going on in his brain – although they would soon find out.

As the crisis ebbed, Paul was moved out of intensive care, and then out of the Chest Hospital and back to the Homerton. There, he drifted in and out of the present, rambling on to his visitors about things that had happened but never happened, places he had been but never been, a combination of paranoia and fantasy, somewhere between coma and consciousness. He was in Australia – or was he lying on a sandbank in New Guinea? The reality was even grimmer. He shouted at the nurses and, much to Clare's embarrassment, at a young Asian man in the bed opposite, whom Paul kept calling a fascist and a threat.

Slowly, he started taking sips of water and spoons of jelly. Very slowly he became saner, the moments of lucidity grew longer, the paranoia abated. There were even, incredibly, moments that made the family laugh. One psychologist asked Paul to draw something on a pad. He produced a terrible squiggle, and Clare was told, in all seriousness, that there had clearly been damage to that part of the brain. What she knew was that that squiggle was about as good as it got when they all played *Pictionary* together.

Paul's memory was tested, and, worryingly, he could not remember anything about himself, where he was born, or even where he was. But when he was asked if he could remember a phone number, he began to reel off screeds of them. And a question about a remembered line of poetry produced the entire prologue to *Henry V*, before Paul started on *The Mask of Anarchy*. There was, it seemed, going to be nothing wrong with his brain. What about his body? The scans appeared to show that Paul would be paralysed, perhaps from the chest down, perhaps from the waist down. In either case, a rather pompous consultant told Clare, he would not walk again. Then, another miracle: Clare noticed that Paul was, almost imperceptibly, by a millimetre or two, wiggling one of his toes – and their hopes soared.

There was, John felt, a bit of a soap opera atmosphere at the hospital, as people arrived and waited for news, or expressed their opinions about what should happen next. The old friends were all there: Richard Ingrams, of course, Ian Hislop from the *Eye*, and Tariq Ali too. What Paul really needed was a place in the Homerton's rehab unit. He was in the queue, but there were few places, and nothing was assured. Tariq took the initiative, rang the consultant, and pleaded that Paul be prioritised. Once she found out, Clare was mortified, and knew that Paul would be too. Ian Hislop also tried to help, with offers of private insurance and BUPA. Richard took a more priestly route, telling Paul he was praying for him, just to wind him up. They all meant well, and Clare explained to the consultant that Paul would not want to be treated differently to anyone else.

However it happened, Paul was moved into the rehab unit in July. He was conscious; he was eating; he was even watching television. There were therapists galore, and an urgent request to Clare from Paul's medical team to re-establish some sort of family routine, to help Paul get back to something like a normal life. All of this made for tough days for Clare. She would arrive with Kate in the early morning, so they would all eat breakfast together. Then she would drive Kate to school and make her own way to work, returning for lunch with Paul, and then back to school to collect Kate.

The evenings were for visitors. Clare would ring them up and book them in – an amazing array of friends and neighbours, MPs and campaigners, even the odd Lord.

To begin with, Paul hated rehab. He shared his ward with two other patients, one in such physical difficulty he had a mattress on the floor. But as the weeks went by and Paul's fitness improved, his visitors would help him into a wheelchair and push him out of the back door of the hospital, and down the road to a very welcoming Vietnamese restaurant. After six months, he was finally allowed home. His spine was damaged, but he was not paralysed or confined to a wheelchair. The tiny movement in his toe had grown to the point where he could sort of walk, stagger really, with the aid of crutches. It was not easy, and he could not go far. The staff in the rehab unit were rightly proud of their success, and his physio continued until the crutches were eventually replaced by two walking sticks.

Clare's house was tall and narrow, with steep staircases. Moving might have been a good plan, but Paul would not consider it. Jim Nichol had been doing all he could to help Clare with Paul's perilous finances, and now rang around his friends and raised enough money to install a lift between the sitting room and the bedroom above. There was money too for a good-quality upright armchair that Paul could get in and out of. But he liked nothing better than lounging on the sofa. The problem was that, once he had sat down on it, he could not get up again, and Clare would find herself running down the road, knocking on doors, looking for a neighbour to help hoist him out. He didn't much like the lift, either, and the minute he learned to haul himself up the stairs using the handrails, it became redundant.

Paul had not been out of hospital for long before he wrote a diary piece for the *London Review of Books*: 'I had managed only one speech against the war in Kosovo when I was carted off to hospital in the middle of the night', he wrote. The war was still raging, and enraging Paul, when he came back out.

Then he wrote to Alan Rusbridger, the *Guardian*'s editor, confirming that he would be able to resume his column in November, and a short explanation duly appeared at the end:

I was expertly patched up and looked after, but widely written off. I spent about six weeks unconscious or off my rocker, but gradually my brain came back, followed slowly by my sense of outrage at the way the allegedly sane world is run.

He thanked his *Guardian* readers for all the letters and get-well cards that had arrived.[1]

His regular return to the *Eye* would take a little longer. While he was in hospital, he had started writing bits and pieces for the investigative pages, renamed 'In the Back' after the demise of 'Footnotes'. And then, in late December, he produced a long piece about Jeffrey Archer, who had finally met his political end, and was forced to stand down as the Conservative candidate for the prestigious new post of London Mayor. Now he could be frank about him: fiddler, forger, bully, liar, shoplifter, fantasist, plagiarist, perjurer, lucky husband, insider-dealer – the stories that went back to the 1960s and his early days at the *Eye*.[2] A note at the end announced his return, starting with the first issue in the new year.

Getting to the *Eye* offices, and up the stairs once he was there – it was another tall, narrow building with steep stairs – was going to be tricky. A solution was soon found when his son Tom took over driving duties. Paul had a terrible old car, a Nissan Micra, which he gave Tom on condition that Tom drive him to and from the *Eye*. 'I would drive over at 7.30 in the morning', he remembers, 'and then drive him in, three or four days a week, every two weeks. I loved doing it. It was nice to spend that time with him, and everyone at *Private Eye* was very welcoming.'

As Paul's walking improved, he and Clare returned to Springfield Park, source of so many memories. She told Paul about the decision they had been asked to make that dark night in the hospital. Would he have wanted them to switch off his life support? If there was no sign of life, would he have wanted to exist like that? He would not have wanted the machines turned off, he told her, never mind the expected prognosis. She understood: 'Such was his love of life, he said he would have found something to enjoy.'

26

Skinning the Tiger

When Paul was carted off to hospital with the life ebbing out of his heart, four chapters of his book were with his publisher, and he was on to the familiar territory of votes for women. His mind was so focused on the chapter that, even after that near-death experience, he was working on it again before he left hospital.

For Paul, the militant suffrage campaign spearheaded by the Pankhursts represented one of the spectacular moments in political history. Its meetings filled the Albert Hall again and again, and it brought a quarter of a million women to a demonstration in Hyde Park in 1908. But it was met by a wall of obstruction in parliament. Although MPs voted in growing numbers in favour of change, neither Tory nor Liberal governments would countenance it. And the emerging Labour Party was not much better.

Women were demanding votes 'on the same terms as men', or 'Ostam'. And Ostam, argued some of the most left-wing delegates at the Labour Party conferences in those critical years, was a retrograde step. It would enfranchise middle-class women. It would tip the class balance in favour of the ruling class, not the working class. The demand should be for adult suffrage, universal suffrage. In each of the conferences between 1906 and 1908, the delegates voted, in growing numbers, in support of adult suffrage and against women's votes on the same terms as men.[1]

Paul was with the minority. To vote against the women's campaign was to duck the issue and vote to do nothing. The argument for adult suffrage was a diversion, because there was no campaign for adult suffrage. The Labour Party was certainly not running it. In truth, the argument against the women's vote was a thin cover for the misogyny that pervaded some sections of the left and the trade unions. Ernest Belfort Bax, the former leader of the Social Democratic Federation, was a good example. In his book, *Essays in Socialism, New and Old*, written while this debate raged, he described how women had smaller brains than men: 'Not merely is the female brain absolutely smaller but relatively smaller.'[2]

In the end, the First World War changed everything. In August 1914 Emmeline and Christabel Pankhurst tossed aside their single-minded campaign for the women's vote in support of the war effort, and the women's movement split. Yet the demand for the vote became more pronounced, not less – and from the most politically conservative quarters. As one Conservative MP said, men fighting in the trenches should have the vote, and not many would argue with that. But what about women, fighting in the trenches at home, making the bombs and the rest of the ordnance? Shouldn't they also get the vote?

Within two years, parliament was debating an extension of the franchise to all men and women, or at least women over thirty. The debate ran through the winter of 1916 and into 1917, when a bill to extend the franchise was introduced. Finally, in February 1918, the bill received royal assent, and all women over thirty became able to vote in the first post-war election.

Paul asked: Could we look back and say that it would have happened anyway? He was adamant in his reply: we could not, for the very simple reason that the ruling class does not easily give up its power: 'If no one disturbed the rule of the class in power, then that class would continue to rule without concession.'[3] The years of argument, the terrible sacrifices of the militant suffragettes, the anguish and the passion – these had driven the change.

Not long after he came out of hospital, the chapter was finished – and in the summer of 2000 he spoke again at the SWP's Marxism event. It was no longer the pleasure it had once been, he wrote in a letter to Tom:

Marxism looms. I'm much less confident than I used to be. I remember some Marxisms where I didn't even prepare my talks, but this time I have been slogging away at two complete drafts, and I'm still not satisfied. The problem with growing old is you grow less confident, not more, which seems unfair.

That year, one of those talks was on socialism and democracy, the other on votes for women.

He anticipated some controversy, as there had been about his articles in *Socialist Worker* back in 1978. Then he had been told he had 'the wrong line' on the suffragettes – wrong for supporting Ostam, and wrong too about what the suffragettes had achieved. Twenty years later, he asked bluntly what the SWP would have done if it had been around all those years ago. Would it have supported Ostam? Or sided with the adult suffragists? Or, to put it another way: 'When you look at the agitation at the time, are you in favour of votes for women, putting an end to fifty years of blatant discrimination and moving things forward, or are you not?'

There was no controversy. Twenty years earlier, Paul's main antagonist had been his old friend and comrade Tony Cliff; but Cliff had died earlier in the year, and the arguments that had preoccupied them both in the 1970s and '80s had slowly died away, too. Mark Steel, then a young comedian establishing himself on the radio with a series of lectures about famous people, remembers Paul ruminating on his arguments with Cliff. 'I was preparing a lecture on Sylvia Pankhurst, and Paul told me with such delight that he and Tony Cliff had had great arguments about her. He'd said to Cliff, "In your book on women you are completely dismissive of the role of the suffragettes." Cliff denied it. Paul got out the book, turned to the page and put it in front of him.' There it was, in black and white: 'Was the Act of 1918 the outcome of the activities of the suffragettes? Not at all.'[4]

Tony Cliff was not the only person to challenge Paul's arguments about votes for women. There was also his aunt, Jill Craigie – although she came at the question from a very different point of view. Paul loved Jill deeply, and she had been the person who had first fired his interest in the suffragette movement. Her knowledge, as well as her collection of books and suffragette memorabilia, was vast, and Paul had delighted in his conversations with her. 'Again and again, I would ring her up or even drive all the way to Pilgrims Lane to try to untie some of the knots in my brain about the struggle for women's suffrage.'[5] They disagreed about the Pankhursts, and when she gave Paul a copy of Christabel's autobiography, she wrote on the flyleaf: 'For the only member of the Foot family, Paul, to get better with this subject.'

Jill had died soon after Paul came out of hospital, and he always regretted that she had not lived to see what he wrote on her subject. In Jill's memory, Michael gave Paul a copy of *The Young Rebecca*, which included all Rebecca West's writings on the suffragettes. 'For the belated education of Paul Foot in the passion and wisdom of Jill, January 2000', he wrote. Inside the book, Paul kept his notes for his Marxism talk on the suffragettes.

That autumn Paul's uncle John also died, and a few weeks after Paul left hospital, Matt drove him and uncle Michael to Devon for John's funeral. Michael had used a stick since a car accident many years before, and his walking was impaired. 'By long tradition we stopped off at a second-hand bookshop at Ashburton', Matt wrote of that journey. 'The trip from the car to the bookshop took an inordinate time as the two men competed in a Monty Python ministry of funny walks contest. I think it resulted in a draw.'[6]

A few months later, Paul's aunt Dorothy also died. He had loved her deeply, too – loved her inexhaustible hospitality in her flat by the Albert Hall. He remembered her with great fondness at her funeral.

> My friend Richard Ingrams called her The Duchess, not because she was in any way royal but because, whatever the anxieties and torments underneath, she glided through life as if it were a glorious sunny day in Venice in her native Italy: *La Serenissima*.[7]

Paul had been saddened by all these deaths, and had been particularly shocked by Cliff's. In his obituary for the *Guardian*, he described how that first meeting with Cliff in Glasgow 'had lifted a veil about the nature of the society we live in. That veil has never come down again.'[8] He respected Cliff's immense intellectual power and his ability to explain his libertarian Marxism in simple language, and had loved his wit and his ridiculous jokes – though none of that respect stopped them arguing when it mattered. They had shared platforms all over the country, at meetings large and small. Most of the time, Paul would speak first, so that Cliff could subtly correct him if he deviated in some way. 'Paul, you are soft', was Cliff's constant jibe, which Paul would answer with a laugh and a nod. But Paul also respected Cliff's strong sense that what mattered was what you did, as much as what you thought. 'Of all the awful crimes of the Left, none infuriated Cliff like passivity. For people who knew the world was rotten, to sit back and do nothing about it was for him the ultimate aberration.'[9]

Passivity was not an option for Paul, either. He had been out of hospital for a little over four months, and was still under the care of physiotherapists and doctors, when he agreed to stand as a candidate for the Socialist Alliance – the loose confederation of most, but not all, of the groups to the political left of the Labour Party – in the election to the new Greater London Assembly in 2000. Perhaps, with a book to finish and having committed himself to start writing again for both *Private Eye* and the *Guardian*, and his seat on the editorial board of *Socialist Review*, and articles to write for both the *Review* and *Socialist Worker*, it might have been a good idea to say no. But Paul could not. All the writing would be of no significance if he turned down the opportunity to take part in such a campaign.

Although Paul rather grumpily described their house in Stamford Hill as the military HQ for the Socialist Alliance campaigns, it was not too onerous for him – he was just one candidate on a list of many. But Paul's name gave the Alliance campaign a terrific boost, as he had just been crowned Campaigning Journalist of the Decade in the *What the Papers Say* awards. At the ceremony for the award – precisely the sort of event Paul hated and would only have attended under some pressure – the judges highlighted his work on the Hanratty and Bridgewater cases, and the story of Lynn Siddons. 'At the end of the 1990s', said the compere, Clive Anderson, 'we look back and see how many times Paul Foot's campaigns have made a difference. His persistence is a lesson to all journalists who want to do likewise.'[10]

Bridgewater and Siddons had both come to a satisfactory conclusion, but the Hanratty story was not yet over. In 2002, the case was to be heard at the Court of Appeal, where Henry Blaxland, an old friend of Paul's, was part of the team representing the Hanratty family. The issues to be decided were whether procedural flaws in the original trial, and in the judge's direction to the jury, made the conviction unsafe. But before the appeal could get under way, the ground shifted significantly. There was new DNA evidence. Henry's heart sank when he heard what had been discovered. 'I knew there could only be one outcome when I heard about the DNA evidence. We had to exhume the body and there was a full DNA match. It nailed the case.'

Paul could not accept the outcome. He hung on to the Rhyl alibi: if Hanratty was 200 miles away in Rhyl, there must be something seriously wrong with the DNA evidence. But the converse was also true. If the DNA evidence was right, there was something seriously wrong with the Rhyl alibi – an argument Paul would not have accepted; he was loyal to the Hanratty family to the end.

There would be no dramatic result to the GLA election campaign. The combined left-of-Labour vote, which was just enough to win a seat, had splintered between those who had joined in the Socialist Alliance and those who had not. Paul's old enemy, sectarianism, still thrived.

But there was more campaigning for Paul. He contributed a short pamphlet for the Socialist Alliance during the general election in 2001, and stood as the Alliance candidate for mayor of Hackney the following year. This was on home territory; he had been living in Hackney for thirteen years, his daughter was at a local school, and he had played golf and tennis in the local parks. He had had to give up tennis, but even with his sticks he still insisted on playing golf, his ball flying all over the place – sometimes, embarrassingly, into groups of other golfers. This campaign would also be a lot more work. The issues were mostly local, but the campaign was fought against the background of the looming war in Iraq, and of Paul's own indebtedness to Homerton Hospital. 'Thanks to the NHS and all those nurses and physiotherapists and ancillary workers at the hospital, I still have my brain, my indignation and my voice, which I am itching to use on behalf of the people of Hackney', he was quoted as saying in the campaign's election free sheet.[11]

Paul spoke as often as he could. 'I can still struggle to my feet for short bursts', he wrote to an old acquaintance, 'which at least stops me being long-winded.'[12] Michael Rosen, the children's author, who also lived locally, joined Paul on the platform at a rally at the Hackney Empire, together with Mark Steel and Mark Serwotka, general secretary of the civil service union PCS – quite a line-up for the local media. In fact, the campaign caught something of the zeitgeist, causing Paul to become a little concerned that he might actually win. For him it was all about the campaign, the meetings, the talking. He need not have worried: he was up against an effective Labour Party machine. But he received nearly 13 per cent of the vote – just 300 votes behind the Conservative candidate, and two votes ahead of the Lib Dem.

There was another election for the London Assembly two years later, in 2004. This time Paul was on the list of candidates for Respect. After the war in Iraq, the SWP had teamed up with George Galloway, the Stop the War Coalition and the Muslim Association of Britain to form a new coalition of the political left, including the peace movement, the anti-war cause and the Muslim community. It had thereby simply abandoned its previous commitment to the Socialist Alliance. Clare was furious, because she and Paul had done so much to build the Alliance, and Paul had no great enthusiasm for anything involving George Galloway. But in the end he was loyal, and went along with the SWP's decision. He was low down the list for the election, and not expected to do a great deal in the way of campaigning. His main contribution was to pen a very short pamphlet setting out Respect's policies.

Through all this campaigning, Paul kept working on his book. The chapter on women had concluded the first part, on how the vote was won. Next, Paul turned his attention to what really intrigued and bothered him: how the long struggle for the vote had ended up in a parliamentary cul-de-sac of impotence. 'Why were elected politicians committed to socialist ideas so palpably incapable of putting them into practice?' he asked in the introduction. Why had elected socialists been so pathetic in office?[13]

The general election of 1918 was the first to include any women. The Labour vote increased considerably, and fifty-seven Labour MPs took their seats. A disappointing result, thought Paul, considering the radical times, so soon after the revolution in Russia and the end of the

First World War. Ramsay MacDonald was not particularly concerned. He was a thinker and writer with numerous books about socialism to his name: about the collectivism of the socialist idea, about municipalisation and nationalisation. In 1919, he added another, a short and timely pamphlet, *Parliament and Revolution*, in which he set out his view that universal suffrage changed everything:

> A Parliamentary election will give us all the power that Lenin had to get by a revolution, and such a majority can proceed to effect the transition from capitalism to socialism with the co-operation of the people, and not merely by edict.[14]

As Labour Party leader, he was about to find out just how that transition might work.

MacDonald led two minority Labour governments, neither of which was a success. The first was in 1924, and short-lived. The second, in 1929, was brought to power by the first election under universal suffrage, and was the first time Labour had won more seats than any other party – on a commitment to end the scourge of unemployment. Then, on 23 October 1929, five months into the new government, the US stock market crashed, and unemployment rocketed. All the traditional Labour areas were laid waste: mines and shipyards closed; engineers and electricians lost their jobs.

Just when something dramatic was called for, a Labour government proved unable to deliver it. There was no nationalisation, no support for jobs. MacDonald lamented that there was nothing the government could do. In his last speech to a Labour Party conference, in 1930, it was clear he had no practical or tangible solution to unemployment. The speech 'teetered on the edge of sanity', Paul wrote; and then, when MacDonald got on to the subject of unemployment, 'he careered right over it'.[15] He suggested that people go and work on the land, where their health and strength would grow along with their food, and a meal might appear on the table. Paul was dismayed to read that this clear proof that their leader was losing his faculties was met with a great roar of applause.

With no answers to hand, MacDonald was propelled into a national government composed almost entirely of Tories and Liberals.

At the general election in October 1931, Labour was reduced to just fifty-two MPs, while many of the party's leaders lost their seats. The few who survived were mainly on the left, and George Lansbury became the new party leader.

Paul had a lot of time for Lansbury, and often spoke at SWP meetings about events in Poplar in 1919, when Lansbury was the local mayor. At the time, Poplar's councillors were faced with a terrible dilemma. Poplar was a deprived area, and the only way for the council to pay poor relief to those in the most extreme poverty was to raise the money from their other already poor residents. The councillors felt this was unfair on the people of Poplar, and argued that rates in London should be shared between the boroughs, so that the better-off areas supported the poorer ones. By 1921, the situation in Poplar was desperate, and Lansbury led his council in revolt against levying higher rates. He and all the Poplar Labour councillors, men and women, went to prison for not putting the financial squeeze on their very poor population.

What happened in Poplar was contentious. Some Labour historians and constitutionalists argued that it cost the Labour Party dear. So Paul took a close look at the results of the elections that followed. While it was true that, in the next round of borough elections in early November 1922, three Labour councillors in Poplar lost their seats, it was also the case that next door, in Hackney – where Herbert Morrison had refused to support the Poplar councillors – they lost all of them. On the plus side, the immediate consequence of the developments in Poplar was that the rates were equalised across London, as they remained until Margaret Thatcher abolished the Greater London Council in 1986.

The lesson to be learned from the display of defiance, according to George Lansbury himself, was simple: 'The workers must be given tangible proof that Labour administration means something different from capitalist administration and, in a nutshell, this means diverting wealth from wealthy ratepayers to the poor.' When the system stopped him doing that, he made it clear that he preferred contempt of court to contempt for the poor.[16]

In his post-mortem on Labour's tragedy of 1931, the economic historian R. H. Tawney argued that the problem at its core was the conflict between working people's legitimate demand to live a decent life and a capitalist class which was not going to surrender its privileges. Paul had read a lot of Tawney – a life-long supporter of the Labour Party who had warned throughout 'that capitalism and democracy were in permanent conflict. Either democracy, through Labour, would tame capitalism, or capitalism would overwhelm democracy.'[17] For Tawney, the 1931 Labour government had been bent on proving that, far from being different from other governments, it could rival the most respectable of them in its cautious conventionality. He wanted to see something quite different.

A Labour government should use political democracy to forge an economic democracy, he argued, that would end the distress and misery of the workers and the poor. 'Who is to be master?' Tawney had asked – socialism or capitalism? In the coming battle to replace the latter with the former, he used a graphic metaphor: 'Onions can be eaten leaf by leaf, but you cannot skin a tiger paw by paw: vivisection is its trade, and it does the skinning first.' Unless a Labour government confronted capitalism as something that needed to be tamed, its ministers would disappear down the throat of the tiger.[18]

Years later, as Paul discovered for himself, Tawney was eulogised by right-wing leaders of the Labour Party. But as they struggled to skin the tiger paw by paw, few of them bothered to read the professor's

> furious attacks on the compromisers, vacillators and honours-grubbers of the second Labour Government, nor his consistent warning, which he went on delivering until he died in 1962, that political democracy without economic democracy was an 'unstable compound' and would devour more powerfully based Labour governments than either of Ramsay MacDonald's.[19]

In 1936, just as General Franco was launching his war against the elected Republican government in Spain, the publisher Victor Gollancz was launching the Left Book Club in Britain. Gollancz was close to the Communist Party but was not a member. Together with Harold Laski, a prominent academic and member of the Labour Party, and John Strachey, who had been a Labour MP, they chose the Club's titles. Many of their choices were books generally influenced by the CP, which was where the energy for the Club was coming from. Consequently, in Paul's opinion, many were quite unreadable Stalinist trash. But there were gems, too: the first edition of George Orwell's *The Road to Wigan Pier* and Arthur Koestler's *Scum of the Earth*. Paul particularly liked *Hammer or Anvil*, Evelyn Anderson's account of Germany from 1918 to the seizure of power by the fascists, and *Our Street*, a novel of anti-Nazi resistance, written by Jan Petersen and smuggled out of Germany. Christopher Hill thought A. L. Morton's *A People's History of England* was a classic.

Gollancz had aspired to build up a list of five or six thousand members. What he ended up with was closer to 57,000. Millions of books were distributed, and he created perhaps the most astonishing publishing venture in British history. And then, when the pact was sealed between Stalin and Hitler, it faltered. All three of the Left Book Club's selectors distanced themselves from the Communist Party, as did a host of other left-wing intellectuals and writers. Several of them, including George Orwell, contributed to Gollancz's effort to set the record straight in *The Betrayal of the Left*, published by the Club in 1941 – a book that would split the Club apart.

Paul had started collecting all the Club's monthly choices in the 1970s, and this title was one of the hardest to find, not least because Club members in the CP would not touch it, and relatively few copies entered circulation. Another rarity was *The Adventures of the Little Pig* – the only children's book published by the Club. Paul mentioned his search for the book during a BBC radio programme he made about the Club in 1990, and a listener immediately offered up the missing gem.[20] By contrast, the bulk of the Stalinist 'trash' was easy to find, as Paul's sons remember. After rummaging around in secondhand bookshops, they would proudly present Paul with a familiar orange jacket, only to discover that Paul already had more than one copy himself.

Paul had interviewed Barbara Castle for his radio programme. By then she was a former cabinet minister, and an old hand in British Labour politics. But she remembered clearly what the menace of fascism had felt like when she was a young woman and a councillor for St Pancras: 'We were terrified. There was a sense of helplessness as we saw the governing class of Britain appeasing like mad.' The Club revitalised the left. Even if you didn't read all the titles, she felt that it 'gave one the feeling that there was a climate of authority behind our ideas, which was vital after the timidity and squirming of the Labour cabinet of 1929–31'.[21]

The exception to this revitalisation on the left was the Labour Party itself. Labour was simply not plugged into this enormous interest in ideas about socialism, and kept its distance from the Club and anything organised by the Communist Party – including its campaign for a popular front against fascist forces in Spain, or anywhere else.

The Second World War transformed Labour's fortunes. In July 1945, people voted to dispense with the old political order: Labour won 393 seats, and had an overall majority of 146. The Conservatives secured 210, and the Liberals just 12. This was a massive majority for a Labour government voted in on a socialist programme.

As a young man, Paul had assumed he might become an MP and join in the parliamentary life. He became a Labour Party member in 1962 in Glasgow, and he left in the spring of 1967 after a grim evening canvassing for Labour in the Greater London Council elections. The previous year there had been much enthusiasm, and his Hampstead constituency had turned Labour for the first time ever. Pounding the same streets in Kilburn a year later, people were sour, even hostile. 'Vote Labour. Why should we? Can you give us a single good reason to do so?' He could not, so he left.[22]

What had happened? A financial crisis and a run on the pound in the summer of 1966 had forced Labour prime minister Harold Wilson to reverse election pledges he had made just four months earlier. He slashed public spending – a move that devastated the Labour vote. Labour lost control of the Greater London Council and hundreds of council seats. By-elections were also lost, even in seats that had been Labour for decades.

That was the push factor. The pull factor for Paul was a far more exciting political life outside the Labour Party. 'At the time', he wrote,

> it seemed to those of us who were taking part in the agitations that there was an increasingly unbridgeable gulf between Labour politics at Westminster, where the Government was constantly compromising

with the American war in Vietnam and the colonels in Greece, and the revolutionary spirit that was emerging among the youth.[23]

The two seemingly unbridgeable worlds – the dull world of compromise in parliament and the revolutionary spirit beyond it – collided in a by-election in April 1969. Bernadette Devlin was elected as MP for Mid-Ulster, on a poll turnout of 91 per cent. She was, Paul thought, a miracle, bringing to Westminster 'a flavour of the revolt that was taking place not just in Northern Ireland but in many other places too'.[24] On May Day in 1969, she marched with the unions against the anti-union proposals in Labour's *In Place of Strife*. When rampaging police killed a Catholic worker in Derry, she formed a one-woman, all-night picket outside 10 Downing Street. She was a brilliant public speaker and, wherever she went, she drew huge crowds, sometimes accompanied by Paul on the same platform.

Paul was writing from his own experience when he described in *The Vote* the 'unparalleled blossoming of democracy' in 1972, the year he joined *Socialist Worker*. 'Political discussion and debate, for so long confined to parliamentary chambers, suddenly became part of the daily lives of many thousands of workers.'[25] The fight by the miners, the railway workers and then the engineers in Manchester, the dockers in London, and the councillors at Clay Cross, were all stories Paul had covered for *Socialist Worker*.

This eruption of industrial muscle and democratic ideas also transformed the Labour Party. At its conference in 1973, shadow chancellor Denis Healey promised there would be 'howls of anguish from the rich' at his proposals for redistribution of income in Britain. There would be nationalisation, the government taking substantial stakes in a wide range of industries. *Labour's Programme*, published for the conference, was far to the left, in Paul's opinion, of anything from 1945. 'We are a democratic socialist party and proud of it', was its opening line.

It continued with the age-old question: 'Who wields economic power in Britain?' An elected government? Or the financial wizards and speculators? It committed the Labour Party to a pledge that echoed the pledges from Labour's earliest years: 'a fundamental and irreversible shift in the balance of power and wealth in favour of working people and their families'. But it never happened. Another financial crisis tipped sterling into a slide on the international money markets, and once again, as Wilson knew, it was the 'bailiffs' of the money markets forcing the pace, not the elected government.

In the cabinet, Barbara Castle calculated that health and social services were going to take a hit, and passed a note to a cabinet colleague: 'I see no reason for a Labour Government. We have adopted the Tory mores. The only difference is that we carry out Tory polices more efficiently than they do.'[26] Michael Foot, at Employment, got the job of defending the government, and employed familiar weather analogies to absolve the government of responsibility: it had been blown off course by an 'economic typhoon'. In his memoirs, Denis Healey, the man at the centre of this particular typhoon, made clear how little control he had over anything. The government turned to the International Monetary Fund, and, in return for loans, the IMF demanded cuts in every area of public spending, all of which the government agreed to.

When Paul joined *Socialist Worker*, he had believed the capitalist world was on the verge of a revolution, and that the organised workers of Britain would be in the forefront of that revolution. How quickly things changed. By 1977, when he wrote *Why You Should Be a Socialist* and stood for election in Stechford, he watched as a rock-solid Labour seat in the Midlands was lost to the Tories. Next door, Walsall went the same way. The vote in traditional Labour seats was already crumbling.

Those losses were an early warning sign. Margaret Thatcher's victory two years later heralded a different sort of politics. First, she hobbled the unions; then she took the nationalised industries back into private hands. Her Employment Acts removed the right of workers to strike in solidarity, protected the rights of non-union members, tied union officials up in bureaucratic string, and made sure any union that stepped out of line would be fined or have its funds taken away by the courts. She then defeated one union after another – at British Leyland, in the steel industry, on the railways – before she took on the miners in 1984. They stood up to her in what Paul described as 'the greatest act of sustained defiance in the history of British labour'.[27] And they went down to a terrible defeat.

Re-establishing the undemocratic nature of industry, Thatcher privatised gas, the bus industry, British Airways and the British Airports Authority and British Steel, as well as the water and electricity companies. By the time Thatcher left office, almost all the industries so carefully brought into public ownership by the post-war Labour government were back in the hands of shareholders, bankers and speculators.

Thatcher also abolished the Greater London Council – and then the Inner London Education Authority, and the old elected metropolitan boroughs that controlled the big urban areas. The Conservatives could not abide any of them, because they were democratic, and generally controlled by Labour.

The final privatisation was to be the railways. The Labour Party was against it, and so was the country – only 11 per cent of those polled were in favour. At the Labour Party conference in 1993, John Prescott promised the railways would be renationalised. Frank Dobson said the same in 1994, as did Michael Meacher in 1995. Then the pledges stopped. There was a new leadership in the Labour Party. At first, Tony Blair appeared to commit a future Labour government to a publicly owned and publicly accountable railway, but there was no mention of it in the Labour manifesto for the 1997 general election. Nor were there proposals to reconstitute the GLC, the ILEA or the metropolitan councils. There was no attack on the anti-union laws or the privatisations. Clause IV, committing the party to public ownership, was rewritten – replaced, as Paul wrote, with 'a series of semi-literate clichés that no one remembers'.[28] What had happened? The Labour Party had, for the first time in its history, abandoned its historic mission to democratise British society.

Having succeeded John Smith, Tony Blair had at once, and with tremendous energy, set about establishing New Labour – a party based on the mass Labour vote and the politics of the old Labour right. 'The net result of a hundred years of compromising with capitalism has ended with New Labour, an allegedly social democratic organisation which has surrendered both socialism and democracy.'[29]

There was one last chapter to write before *The Vote* was finished.

27

Perfidious Financial Idiocy

By the time Paul was labouring with the final chapter of *The Vote*, he was writing about contemporary events, and he shared his ideas, as he so often did, with his audience at Marxism. 'New Labour is the rejection of social democratic politics', he told them. 'State pensions, gone, council housing, gone, comprehensive education, gone, public transport, gone, and even the diamond in the social democratic crown, the NHS, being pinched and lessened.'

He titled the talk 'Some mysteries of New Labour', although for Paul there was no great mystery at all as he tracked Tony Blair's break with all that Labour had once stood for. It wasn't just about personnel and policies, but the historical heart of the Labour Party. The talk, and the chapter, were a culmination of years of work on one particular topic: the Private Finance Initiative.

When Paul left the *Mirror* in 1993, there had been no shortage of offers to make television programmes. There were various pilots, even the BBC floated the idea of running his *Mirror* column on television, but the problem was he didn't feel as comfortable on screen as on paper. 'It's not me to be the objective interviewer when the person is talking absolute bollocks.'[1]

He was a regular on *What the Papers Say,* with a format that played to his strengths. It was topical, political and, as the presenter, he read his own carefully crafted script to camera, and actors voiced the newspaper extracts he had chosen. He was also supremely confident being interviewed about his books, his political scalps, developments in the stories he was following. He was even prepared to make long-form documentaries, when he really needed to, about Shelley or the Bridgewater Four, even if he complained about all the standing around that the making of television seemed to require. An exception to this general rule was *Streetlegal*, a series he made for Channel Four in 1993, which he co-presented with Patricia Hewitt. They'd known each other since their days at the National Council for Civil Liberties, back in the 1970s, when she was its general secretary and Paul was elected to its executive, and he continued to track her career as a Labour MP and minister.

One programme he was pleased to have made, as part of the fiftieth anniversary celebrations of the NHS, was *Private Wealth v National Health*. Christopher Hird produced, and alongside Paul were Jeremy Hardy and Linda Smith, better known for their comedy but equally at home with serious documentary making. The programme was packed with stories about the state of the national health service and the competition from the private sector. And the familiar revolving door – this time of high paid executives – the charitable status and associated tax advantages of private hospitals, and the proliferation of profitable consultancies, like Andersen Consulting and Ernst & Young.[2]

Two things had happened while they were working on the programme that confirmed for Paul that they were asking the right questions. First, when their researcher rang a Labour MP and asked a few questions about the health service, they got a call back from a special adviser and 'a torrent of abuse'. It was Paul's first direct experience of what he described as the overweening arrogance of New Labour.

Then he travelled to Scotland and had to do the interview with those very people he deemed to be talking bollocks. The Royal Infirmary of Edinburgh, an old city centre hospital, was to be closed and a new, state of the art hospital, would be built in the suburbs. It was a Private Finance Initiative, PFI, project. When Paul questioned the plans, he was met with disdain. 'Everything was lovely, the outcome would be great, there wouldn't be fewer beds.'[3] 'Jeremy had some good stuff about PFI hospitals', Paul said of the programme. 'We were miles ahead on PFI, but we didn't quite have the formula for doing it.'[4] So, it remained a one-off project, and Paul reverted to writing about PFI in his *Guardian* column, and in enormous detail in the pages of *Private Eye*.

Once again, there was a back story. In his very last published column for the *Daily Mirror*, in March 1993, Paul had written about the Wessex Regional Health Authority and the scandal of the millions of pounds it spent and lost on a new, failed, computer system.

The contract had been won by Arthur Andersen and IBM. The House of Commons Public Accounts Committee was appalled. Arthur Andersen Consulting had both advised the Health Authority and tendered for the contract, which it won. You can't do that, was their blunt appraisal. Paul was interested because it so happened that two brothers called Ray and Brian Currie, husband and brother-in-law of Edwina Currie, a junior minister in the Department of Health, worked for Arthur Andersen at the time. A spokesman for the company was at pains to point out that neither of the brothers had anything to do with the computer contract; they worked for the audit section, Arthur Andersen. The contract for the computers in Wessex was won by Arthur Andersen Consulting, a separate enterprise. Although both were, it seems, ultimately bound together in a worldwide partnership. And here the long quote from the spokesman for the company, which Paul published in full for the edification of his *Daily Mirror* readers, slipped into ancient history with a reference to the laws of the Medes and Persians.[5]

By the mid 1990s the Tory government was in considerable disarray. Things were so bad within the Conservative Party that Prime Minister John Major stood down as party leader and then won the contest to be the new leader. His party was losing seats, through defections and by-elections. The Labour Party, under Tony Blair, was in the ascendancy and looked like it might win the next general election. This was the context in which Andersen Consulting began looking into the political future, wooing Labour. It provided its services free to Labour's Commission on Social Justice, and in 1994 it employed Patricia Hewitt, the deputy chair of that Commission, as its own director of research. And in the summer of 1996, it laid on a vast event at Templeton College, Oxford for the entire team of prospective Labour ministers – more than a hundred Labour MPs – to discuss their future as government ministers. Paul wondered what on earth they thought they were going to learn from a bunch of consultants.

The following year, Labour won the election and Paul began tracking Hewitt's rise. She was now Labour MP for Leicester West, and within a year she would became Economic Secretary to the Treasury, within two years a Minister, and by 2001 was in the cabinet as Secretary of State for Trade and Industry. Paul had always thought she was on the left but noted in his *Guardian* column that Bill Morris, the general secretary of the transport union, described Trade and Industry under her leadership as 'the provisional wing of the CBI'.[6]

In 1993, the same year that Paul was laying out the story of the Wessex Regional Health Authority in the *Mirror*, David Willets, the Conservative MP for Havant, published a pamphlet called *The Opportunities for Private Funding in the NHS*. In it, Willetts argued for private enterprise to fund and build hospitals for the NHS, and then, at the end of the process, to inherit them too. Initially at least, both the TUC and the Labour Party were against the idea. Sam Galbraith, a member of Labour's shadow frontbench and an internationally respected neurosurgeon, said PFI was 'a financial sleight of hand, a massaging of figures as a result of which the increase in the public sector borrowing requirements is not shown and is thus a matter of deceit'.[7]

By 1997 such caution and criticism had been ditched, and the newly elected Labour government was ready and willing to go down the PFI route. The mastermind behind the change in Labour's thinking was Geoffrey Robertson, MP for Coventry. Within six weeks of Labour's accession he had a report on PFI ready, and legislation in the pipeline that would remove any hurdles to the signing of new contracts. The second reading of the National Health Service (Private Finance) Bill was introduced by Alan Milburn, who Paul remembered meeting in the Days of Hope bookshop in Newcastle, back when Milburn had been considered left-wing (and the bookshop was known locally as the Haze of Dope). The people who had been helping Geoffrey Robertson were at Andersen Consulting. They had worked on ways of making the rules on PFI contracts less onerous to the private sector, and by the end of 1997 PFI had soared into orbit. No one in government or the Labour Party seemed to care that the flow of new investment carried with it a heavy burden of new debt. By the time Paul was writing this story into *The Vote*, Arthur Andersen had gone bust over its involvement in the Enron scandal. All that advice had come from an utterly corrupt enterprise.

The person who had helped Paul with the Royal Edinburgh Infirmary story for the television programme was Allyson Pollock, a doctor and professor in public health policy. Her research achieved some fame when the *British Medical Journal* published an editorial entitled 'PFI – Perfidious Financial Idiocy'. It concerned a series of articles the *BMJ* was publishing, based on research by Allyson and her team at University College London, that showed, contrary to the reassurances Paul had been given, that the number of beds across Lothian, which includes Edinburgh, had declined by almost a quarter.[8]

The *BMJ* was loudly denounced by Labour MPs, but Paul cautioned them: remember what happened in Wyre Forest, a parliamentary constituency in Worcestershire where the Wessex Health Authority's plans for a shiny new PFI hospital ran into difficulty. To finance the new hospital, the health authority planned to downgrade a smaller, local hospital in Kidderminster. Initially supportive of local campaigners against the cuts in their services, the Labour MP for Wyre Forest, David Lock, soon changed sides, as he climbed the political ladder in the New Labour government. At the next general election, Wyre Forest elected retired hospital consultant and campaign leader Richard Taylor as its MP. David Lock was out – providing a cautionary tale for his fellow Labour MPs.

Despite the campaigns and objections, the number of new hospitals being built under PFI contracts continued to grow. Building costs were spiralling, bed numbers were shrinking, and running costs growing. What was the difference, asked Frank Dobson, New Labour's health secretary, as he opened the new PFI hospital at South Tees? Hospitals were previously being built by the same profit-making companies who were now involved in building PFI hospitals. Nothing had changed. As *Private Eye* explained, everything had changed:

> Dobson cannot see the difference between hiring a plumber to put in your new bathroom and letting the plumber take over your whole house on condition he rents it back to you for the next 30 years – and paying him extra to do your cooking and cleaning.[9]

The hospital stories continued to roll into the *Eye*. At the 2003 Labour Party conference, the schools minister, David Miliband, announced that all future school building would be under PFI, too – even though an Audit Commission report had shown that the first seventeen contracts for schools were neither cheaper nor quicker.

Then there were the computer and IT projects for pension records, benefit payments at post offices, court records, immigration and asylum claims, and passports. All ran into difficulty, costing the government millions of squandered pounds. Some were complete duds. Paul pulled all the stories together for another *Eye* special: *P. F. Eye*.

True to form, he persuaded Allyson Pollock to help with the project, sending sections back and forth for her comments. He invited her to a *Private Eye* lunch at the Coach and Horses, and in return she invited him to speak to a meeting of the NHS Consultants Association: 'Paul arrived at the meeting with a copy of Aneurin Bevan's leaflet setting up the NHS', with its announcement that the service would provide everyone with all their medical care, paid for by taxpayers.

What intrigued Paul about the whole PFI story, besides the mounting public debt and the enrichment of some building companies, was the critical transfer in power from public to private. Why was New Labour so in love with business and projects like PFI? He had a theory. When the Social Democratic Party was formed in 1981 through the defection from Labour of four right-wing MPs, the new party was intent on ditching everything associated with traditional Labour. As far as Paul was concerned, they were, in truth, Liberals. For evidence, Paul produced his uncle Dingle. Dingle Foot had been a Liberal during the war, and had been defeated as a Liberal in three successive post-war elections. In 1957 he joined the Labour Party. How else was he to sustain a political career? He was instantly selected to fight a by-election in Ipswich, which he won – and then held the seat until 1970.

> I can vouch for the fact that my uncle's politics never deviated an inch from his Liberal origins, even when he became a member of the Labour Government. Many Liberals like him, in Parliament and outside it, went the same way. They did not especially like trade unions and were deeply suspicious of public ownership, but they tolerated their differences quite comfortably in exchange for office.[10]

The SDP was extremely successful for quite a long time, even though it would eventually vanish into oblivion, and its leaders into the Liberal Party, renamed the Liberal Democrats. But the young, aspiring Tony Blair never joined. Why not, Paul asked. His politics had proved to be far more in tune with theirs than the Labour Party's traditional politics of socialism and trade unionism. Paul speculated that Blair must have decided it would be better to stay and change Labour from within. In his early days he sported a CND badge; but as soon as he became leader, and then prime minister, he built around himself a powerful group of people who would reject the socialist tradition of the Labour Party.

Just days before the contest for the leadership was over, Blair had made clear the intended direction of travel: 'The trade unions will have no special and privileged place in the next Labour government. They will have the same access to it as the other side of industry.' It was as if, Paul reflected, the two sides of industry were like two football teams, and the government an even-handed referee. These were echoes of the past, he thought, as Blair and his team prepared the ground for 'an assault on Labour voters more outrageous and contemptible than even Ramsay MacDonald ever imagined'.[11]

The plan was set out in *The Blair Revolution*, an 'execrable' book, according to Paul, badly written and badly argued, the point of which was to reject everything collective, comprehensive or universal, and anything to do with trade unions. It was written by Peter Mandelson, grandson of Herbert Morrison and Labour MP for Hartlepool, and Roger Liddle, a founder member of the SDP, but by 1996 a member of the Labour Party. The book is littered with familiar names: Attlee, Bevan, even R. H. Tawney; but little of their politics survived. The authors' position was quite clear: New Labour was 'literally a new party'.[12]

The government of that new party also became littered with famous names from the SDP and the Liberals. Paul named them all in a little chart in *Private Eye*, showing how they related to each other, sometimes by marriage, but more significantly by the company they kept, particularly their public relations companies. The SDP names included Lord Rogers, Lord Jenkins, Lord Newby, Matthew Oakeshott, Sir Ian Wrigglesworth, Lord Taverne, Derek Scott and, of course, Roger Liddle. The Liberals added Lord Thomson of Monteith, Lord Holme, and

Andrew Adonis to the tally. None of them had been voted in, and most were not even members of the party that had been voted in.[13]

'Labour came into existence to represent trade unionists and socialists in Parliament', Paul wrote in the introduction to *Labour Party PLC*, David Osler's book on the Labour Party's growing connections with business.

> In the various periods before 1997 when they have achieved office with a parliamentary majority, the influence of those socialists and trade unionists, though waning, has at least been detectable enough to worry big business and their media. Systematically and with tremendous application and dedication, New Labour has striven to tear up the roots left by Old Labour and to turn itself into a business party every bit as credible and friendly to big business as the Tories had been.

The cost of tearing up the roots would be high:

> Where there is no difference between two big political machines paid for by big business, ordinary peoples' interests in and involvement in politics collapses. Less people vote and less people care. All politics becomes contemptible, and the way is open for the racialist and the dictator.[14]

28

The White Radiance of Eternity

In the summer of 2003, Michael Foot reached the grand age of ninety, and there were to be parties for family members and political allies. Paul took responsibility for organising the family birthday present: a book, naturally, and an exceptional one at that – a copy of Jonathan Swift's *Polite Conversation*, published in 1738, and a welcome addition to Michael's vast Swift collection. 'From his devoted nephews, nieces, great-nephews and great-nieces, in law and out of law', read the inscription, lightly written in pencil.

There was a dinner for family members at the Gay Hussar in Soho, and a celebration at Downing Street, hosted by Tony and Cherie Blair, for this longstanding and much venerated member of the Labour Party. All were invited, but Paul and Clare declined to go. The problem was Ariel Sharon, the Israeli prime minister who was then on a visit. In response, a Palestinian protest had been organised against the man widely held responsible for the massacre at the Sabra and Shatila refugee camps in 1982, in which hundreds, and possibly thousands of people had died. Paul and Clare would not cross such a picket line, and Matt joined their boycott. John did go in, however, as did his younger brother Tom. 'We filed in, in our suits, feeling very lame', remembers Tom. 'And then downstairs and on into the garden, to shake hands with Tony Blair and Michael. Paul would have died there. Michael was so loyal to the Labour Party he would never say anything publicly about Blair. Not at that time.'

Besides the problem of Ariel Sharon, another possible reason why Paul did not want to go and stand around at a garden party was the state of his health. For months, he had been in agony, caused by the pressure of his disability on his back. Sitting was almost impossible, and much of each day was spent lying down. He had to have help with everything. Clare remembers how sad and depressed he became.

He needed an operation on his back to relieve the pressure, but the risks from another general anaesthetic were life-threatening. The doctors had explained all this, and the operation was put off for as long as possible. But by the summer of 2003 he had got to the point where he couldn't go on, whatever the risks. The night before the operation, Paul was tearful, propped up in his bed in the Royal London Hospital. Clare gave him a copy of Robert Harris's *Pompeii* to distract him. Unable to put it down, he read it through the night, and was then ready for whatever lay ahead.

He survived, recovered, and walked again, though still with two sticks. He could sit once again at his desk and drive his adapted car. Life was suddenly much better. Now, finally, he could finish *The Vote*.

Paul had, as usual, been optimistic that he would be able to do so before the operation. But it was October before the manuscript was with the publisher and selected readers had been asked for comments. After so many years, so many books read, so much thought, it was finally complete in June 2004. All that remained were the footnotes.

As he reached the end of his story, Paul reflected in its last pages on his own life and politics, and his doubts about the revolutionary path he had taken. Privately, he had always had doubts. It was a way of judging himself. He remembered how, one night in 1975, as the great industrial upheaval of the previous years began to dissipate, he had shared those thoughts with Geoff Ellen, as they waited for the page proofs of *Socialist Worker*. The change they had hoped and worked for had not come, and was not going to come from Harold Wilson or Denis Healey.

> In the decline of the movement, the issue seemed to have changed. Was the revolution going to come at all? And if not, what was to become of us if our grand aim in life was to be frustrated and even ridiculed? To my enormous relief, Geoff cheered me up with his speciality: a huge all-enveloping grin. 'If the revolution doesn't come'

he said, 'there is nothing much we can do about that. Whether it comes or not, there is nothing for us to do but what we are doing now, fighting for it, fighting for the workers and the poor.' Some years later Geoff Ellen, still a young man, went to bed one night with a headache, and died from a brain haemorrhage. All his adult life he stuck firmly by his advice to me that dark winter evening in 1975, and so, I hope, have I.[1]

Paul had been thinking about his book on the vote for a large part of his adult life – certainly since 1975, when he mentioned in an interview in *Isis* that it was one of the books he was contemplating writing.[2] When finished, it became a manifesto of his political ideas, the culmination of a lifetime of political thought, political activity and reading.

At last, he, Clare and daughter Kate could plan a holiday. There were just one or two commitments and deadlines to meet first. In May he was speaking on Shelley at University College Oxford, where his interest had first been piqued, and in June he was making a special appeal in his *Guardian* column for funds to assist the ninth Baron Abinger, a distant descendant of the poet Shelley. Rather an unusual request for Paul, but the circumstances demanded it. The Baron had sold a collection of Shelley papers to the Bodleian Library at Oxford. But the Library was short, by £300,000, of the necessary funds. Paul was excited by the prospect of the papers becoming available. They included original manuscript pages of Mary Shelley's *Frankenstein*, with Shelley's notes, and hitherto unpublished material by Mary's father, William Godwin, as well as her mother, Mary Wollstonecraft. It was not his readers he was appealing to, but those at the top end.

There is so much money sloshing around the rich nowadays that surely there are a hundred people with £3,000 to spare for such a national treasure. In return they can get a facsimile of the pill box with which Shelley illustrated his pamphlet *Proposal for Putting Reform to the Vote*, which he wrote in Marlow in 1817, not to mention a place reserved forever in what he called the 'white radiance of eternity'.[3]

Then he was off to Marxism, and a meeting on the Chartists, reviving the arguments of one of the finest chapters in *The Vote*. And his talk on the mysteries of New Labour. There was one more column for *Private Eye*, and another for the *Guardian*, before they could fly off to Dublin. Richard Ingrams would also be in Ireland, and they had promised to meet up.

The piece for the *Guardian* was to mark the tenth anniversary of the bombing of the Israeli embassy in London, for which two young Palestinians had been sent to prison for twenty years. Paul believed, with good reason, that the convictions of Samar Alami and Jawad Botmeh were miscarriages of justice. They had been set up by a mysterious Palestinian called Moghrabi, who had since disappeared; and, whereas they were a couple of amateurs, the bombing was clearly a professional job. They had cast-iron alibis for the bombing itself, but were convicted on charges of conspiracy.

Adding to the evidence in their defence was the fact that MI5 had received advance warning of the bombing, about which they did nothing. It was from a credible source, which suggested it was a professional operation, and had nothing to do with either Alami or Botmeh. In a familiar pattern, MI5 had not disclosed this to the defence at the trial, and the government had denied for years that the warning existed. Paul needed to speak to Gareth Peirce, their solicitor, before he wrote his piece, so he packed his notebook into his bag and left a long message on her phone. He would catch up with her later from Dublin.

On Sunday 18 July, the family made it as far as Stansted airport, where Paul Foot's heart finally gave out.

His notebook remained in his bag. No one ever wrote the article. 'He brought us hope', Jawad said, years later. He never met Paul, but 'his belief in justice reached us in our darkest moments'.[4]

Acknowledgements

My thanks go to all the members of the Foot and Fermont families, who gave their time in interviews, and shared their photos, books and other materials, without which this portrait of Paul's life would not be complete. I'm particularly grateful to Clare Fermont, Paul's sons, John, Matt and Tom Foot; Paul's cousins, Kate Illingworth, Win Foot, Christina Thistlethwayte, Lily Angus and Charlie Burbury; and Monica Foot. And also to Rose Foot for her rather wonderful book *With Love from Paul*, her photo collection of Paul's books, given and received.

Special thanks to Bryan Rostron, who shared an office with me at the *Daily Mirror* and persuaded me I could write this book. To Jo-Anne Richards and Richard Beynon, whom I met while working in Johannesburg, South Africa, and who mentored me and many other aspiring writers in their All About Writing school. And all those friends who read all or part of the manuscript.

I'm indebted to Tony Harcup, who shared the full text of his wide-ranging interview with Paul, from which he quoted in his books *The Ethical Journalist* and *Journalism: Principles and Practice*; Nuala Rowland, who kindly sent me a chapter of her late husband Robert's unpublished memoir, covering his trip with Paul to the United States in 1960 to debate the death penalty; and to Lee Huebner, Airlie Professor of Media and Public Affairs, George Washington University, who retrieved a recording of the debate for me. To Joe Diviney for his research into the cabinet papers for 1984, and to all the miners and their families I met in Barnsley.

I'm also indebted to John Houston for his skill with the book's photographs, and to John Rudge, who has worked for years to assemble a complete record of the pamphlets published by the International Socialists and the Socialist Workers' Party, and whose efforts saw the publication, after thirty-six years, of Paul's talk on *Orwell & 1984*.

I would like to extend my thanks to all those I interviewed:

Tariq Ali, Lily Angus, Anthony Arblaster, Richard Barber, Colin Barker, Mary Beckinsale, Nancy Berwick, Jane Birdsell, Geoffrey Bindman, Ian Birchall, Norman Birnbaum, Henry Blaxland, Christopher Booker, Piers Brendon, Richard Brooks, Geoff Brown, Alasdair Buchan, Margaret Callaghan, Gordon Carr, Dave Cash, John Charlton, Judith Chernaik, Janet Cunliffe-Jones, Peter Clark, Patrick Cockburn, Gill Coleridge, Jeremy Corbyn, Michael Crick, Tam Dalyell, Nicholas Deakin, Marion Dee, Michael Denny, Jane Deighton.

Kelvin Everest, Liz Elliott, Laurie Flynn, Lesley Foster, Nigel Fountain, John Foster, Maria Fyfe, Lindsay German, Bob Gillespie, Alan Gibbons, Tim Gopsill, Grey Gowrie, Roy Greenslade, Jean Gray, Chris Hall, Peter Hain, Joe Haines, Maureen and Michael Hanratty, Jeremy Hardy, Tirril and Nigel Harris, Vincent Hickey, Christopher Hird, Ian Hislop, Sandy Hobbs, Paul Holborow, Clive Hollick, Goretti Horgan, John Houston, Roger Huddle, Rose Hunter.

Richard Ingrams, Peter Jay, Avtar Jouhl, Bill Keach, Richard Kirkwood, Anne Koch, Richard Kuper, Tim Laxton, Laurence Le Quesne, David Leigh, John Lewthwaite, Fred Lindop, Ken Loach, Neil Lyndon, Mary McAuly, Jimmy McCallum, Gus Macdonald, Jean McCrindle, Sheila McGregor, Eamonn McCann, Ken McPherson, Gordon McCulloch, Mike Molloy, Janet Montefiore, Fergus Nicol, Jim Nichol, Joe O'Brien, Paul O'Brien, John Palmer, John Pilger, Allyson Pollock, Eddie Prevost, Christine Protz, Roger Protz.

Balwinder Rana, John Rees, Jeremy Roberts, Jack Robertson, John Rose, Michael Rosen, Leon Rosselson, Bryan Rostron, Michael Rustin, Sally Sampson, Red Saunders, Juliet Schubart, Stephen Sedley, Mark Serwotka, Mike Simmons, A. Sivanandan, Geoffrey Spencer, Adam Sisman, Hugh Stephenson, Mark Steel, Norman Strike, Adrian Sugar, Alison Taylor, Christina Thistlethwayte, Martin Tomkinson, George Tomlinson, Ricky Tomlinson, Bill Thompson, Phil Turner, Peter

Usborne, Colin Wallace, Sam Webb, Francis Wheen, Mary-Kay Wilmers, Pat Williamson, Susan Wooldridge.

Thanks also to the many librarians and archivists who have assisted me: Shrewsbury School and University College; The Gleaner, Kingston, Jamaica; London School of Economics; University of London Senate House Library; the Modern Records Centre, University of Warwick; and, in particular, the librarians at the British Library, where most of this book was written.

Readers may wonder why I haven't mentioned many of the meetings Paul spoke at, articles he wrote, strikes he reported and campaigns he supported. I was cautioned very early on by Francis Wheen, who worked with Paul at *Private Eye* and is himself the author of two very fine biographies – of Karl Marx and Tom Driberg – not to squeeze in every fact I discovered and, above all, to tell stories. I have tried. All the omissions, and any mistakes, are mine.

I'm deeply grateful to everyone at Verso, in particular Tariq Ali, who thought my book worth publishing, and to John Merrick for being a patient editor.

Finally, I'd like to dedicate this book to Jim Nichol, who has lived with this book for so long. And to the two young people for whom I wrote it: Kate Fermont, who was ten when her father died, and my son Nick Renn Nichol, who was eighteen.

The following kindly gave permission to reproduce copyright material: David Higham Associates for permission to quote Louis MacNeice; the Macmillan Archive, Macmillan Publishers International Ltd; Penguin Books Limited and The Random House Group Limited for material from the Penguin and Jonathan Cape archives; the RCW literary agency; the Shrewsbury School Archives; the Master and Fellows of University College, Oxford.

Photo credits: Second Lieutenant Foot and the Jamaica regiment: Wally Allen, Kingston, Jamaica; Paul Foot speaking at an anti-apartheid rally, 1970: Chris Davies, Report; Paul Foot with Ricky Tomlinson: John Sturrock; Paul and the National Union of Journalists banner: John Sturrock; Paul Foot speaking to striking miners in 1984: Rik Walton; Paul Foot with Arthur Scargill, 1990: Steve McTaggart/Socialist Worker archive; Paul Foot speaking in defence of the Bridgewater Four: Clare Clifford; Paul Foot and partner Clare: Eamonn McCabe.

Bibliography of Paul Foot Works

BOOKS

Articles of Resistance, Bookmarks, London, 2000

The Helen Smith Story: Paul Foot in Cooperation with Ron Smith, Fontana, Glasgow, 1983

Immigration and Race in British Politics, Penguin, Harmondsworth, 1965

Ireland: Why Britain Must Get Out, Counterblasts No. 2, Chatto & Windus, 1989

Murder at the Farm: Who Killed Carl Bridgewater?, Sidgwick & Jackson, London, 1986

The Politics of Harold Wilson, Penguin, Harmondsworth, 1968

Red Shelley, Sidgwick and Jackson, London, 1981

The Rise of Enoch Powell, Penguin, Harmondsworth, 1969

The Vote: How It was Won and How It was Undermined, Viking, London, 2005

Who Framed Colin Wallace?, Macmillan, London, 1989

Who Killed Hanratty?, Jonathan Cape, London, 1971

Words as Weapons: Selected Writing, 1980–1990, Verso, London, 1990

PAMPHLETS

(Published by the International Socialists, Vietnam Solidarity Campaign, Socialist Workers Party, Socialist Alliance and Respect)

'An Agitator of the Worst Kind': A Portrait of Miners' Leader A.J. Cook*, Socialist Workers Party, 1986

The Anti-Cameron Report, a Rank and File pamphlet, 1967

The Case for Socialism, What the Socialist Workers Party Stands For, Socialist Workers Party, 1990

Down with the War, Respect, 2004

How to Fight the Tories, Socialist Worker, 1970

The Postal Workers and the Tory Offensive, International Socialists, 1971

Stop the Cuts, Rank and File, 1976

'*This Bright Day of Summer*': *The Peasants' Revolt of 1381*, Socialist Workers Party, 1981

Three Letters to a Bennite from Paul Foot, Socialist Workers Party, 1982

Unemployment: The Socialist Answer, Labour Worker Glasgow, 1963

Vietnam and Trade Unionists, Paul Foot, Martin Bernal, Sabby Sagall and Ian Birchall, date unknown, Vietnam Solidarity Campaign

While Tories Shriek . . . Socialism Has an Answer, Socialist Workers Party, 1979

Why You Should Be a Socialist, Socialist Workers Party, 1977

Why You Should Vote Socialist, Socialist Alliance, 2001

Workers against Racism, International Socialists, 1973

PUBLISHED POSTHUMOUSLY

Orwell & 1984, a Talk by Paul Foot, Redwords, 2020

Toussaint Louverture and the Haitian Revolution, Two Talks by Paul Foot, Redwords, 2021

BOOKS AND PAMPHLETS WITH INTRODUCTIONS BY PAUL FOOT

Chris Cowley, *Guns, Lies and Spies*, Hamish Hamilton, London, 1992

Hugo Dewar, *Arsy-versy World, Poems by Hugo Dewar*, Bookmarks Publications, London, 1981

Michael Gillard, *A Little Pot of Money: The Story of Reginald Maudling and the Real Estate Fund of America*, Private Eye Books, London, 1974

Roger Huddle et al. (eds), *Blood, Sweat and Tears: Photographs from the Great Miners' Strike, 1984–1985*, Artworker Books, London, 1985

David Osler, *Labour Party PLC: New Labour as a Party of Business*, Mainstream Publishing, Edinburgh and London, 2002

Arthur Ransome, *Arthur Ransome in Revolutionary Russia* (incorporating *Six Weeks in Russia, 1919* and *The Crisis in Russia, 1920*), Redwords, London, 1992

Olive Schreiner, *From Man to Man*, Virago, London, 1982

Percy Shelley, *Shelley's Revolutionary Year: Shelley's Political Poems and the Essay A Philosophical View of Reform*, Redwords, London, 1990

Steel Workers' Power, Joe Herbertson and Nick Howard, *Socialists Unlimited for the SWP*, 1980

The Walrus, *Brilliant! Out He Goes! Which Way Forward for Amicus?*, Socialist Workers Party, 2002

Tony Cliff, *A World to Win: Life of a Revolutionary*, Bookmarks, London, 2000

PRIVATE EYE SPECIALS

Hearts and Grafts – An Examination of the Heart Transplant Craze, 1968

Lockerbie – The Flight from Justice, 2001

Not the Scott Report – Arms to Iraq Special, 1994, with Tim Laxton

P. F. Eye – An Idiot's Guide to the Private Finance Initiative, 2004

Ripping Yarns – Sonia Sutcliffe – The Press and the Law, 1991

Rock Bottom – The Gibraltar Killings – Government and Press Cover-Up, 1989

Tax Dodge Report – the Artful Dodger – Inland Revenue/Mapeley Deal, 2003, with Richard Brookes

Notes

1. MANGOES IN THE BATH

1 Hugh Foot, *A Start in Freedom* (London, 1965), pp. 27, 33.
2 Ibid., p. 13.
3 Ibid., p. 48.
4 Paul Foot, *The Vote: How It Was Won and How It Was Undermined* (London, 2005), p. 319.
5 Paul Foot, 'London Diary', *New Statesman*, 29 June 1979.
6 Richard Barber, *The Story of Ludgrove* (Oxford, 2004), p. 157. Paul gave the interview not long before he died on condition that Barber include his view that all schools should be part of the state education system.
7 Ibid., p. 173.
8 Ibid., p. 247.
9 Personal interview. From hereon, I won't cite material that came from personal interviews.
10 Michael Foot, *Debts of Honour* (London, 1980), p. 18.
11 Sarah Foot, *My Grandfather Isaac Foot* (Bodmin, 1980), p. 73.
12 Foot, *A Start in Freedom*, p. 27.

2. AN INKY LITTLE BOY

1 Paul Foot, 'Diary': 'The Buttocks Problem', *London Review of Books*, 5 September 1996.
2 Mark Peel, *The Land of Lost Content: The Biography of Anthony Chevenix-Trench* (Edinburgh, 1996), p. 1.
3 Paul Foot, 'Jolly Beating Weather', *Private Eye*, 11 April 1969.
4 Paul Foot, 'Diary', *London Review of Books*, 5 September 1996.
5 Shrewsbury School Archives.

6 Ibid.

7 Frank McEachran, *Spells* (Oxford, 1954), p. 4.

8 Ibid., p. 198.

9 Richard Ingrams, *My Friend Footy* (London, 2005), p. 19.

10 Shrewsbury School Archives.

11 Harry Thompson, *Richard Ingrams, Lord of the Gnomes* (London, 1994), p. 44.

12 Paul Foot, 'London Diary', *New Statesman*, 13 October 1978.

13 Paul Foot Reporting, 'Tarzan tans the old school toffs', *Daily Mirror*, 16 November 1990.

14 Anthony Holden, Atticus, *Sunday Times*, 30 January 1977.

15 'Diary', *London Review of Books*, 5 September 1996.

16 Michael Lindsay Charlesworth, *Behind the Headlines: An Autobiography* (Wells, 1994), p. 187.

17 Shrewsbury School Archives.

18 Ibid.

3. PARADISE ON EARTH

1 Paul Foot, 'SW signs TV star', *Socialist Worker*, 31 March 1979.

2 *Called Up*, BBC One, 22 November 1983.

3 Paul Foot, 'Come Here, Botham', *London Review of Books*, 9 October 1986. Gary Sobers's record lasted for thirty-six years, until it was beaten by Brian Lara, another West Indian cricketer. The term 'Chinaman', for a left-arm wrist spin, has now been banned by *Wisden*.

4 'I have always felt the need to come to Coke', *Daily Gleaner*, Jamaica, 18 November 1957.

5 University College, 1959, UC:CO3/A4/789, Paul Foot student file, University College, Oxford.

6 Ibid.

7 Richard Ingrams, *My Friend Footy* (London, 2005), p. 21.

8 Ibid., p. 28.

9 Harry Thompson, *Richard Ingrams, Lord of the Gnomes* (London, 1994), p. 83.

10 Ibid. p. 84.

11 Union Report, *Isis*, 19 November 1958.

12 Paul Foot, 'Eternal Summer', *Oxford Opinion*, 31 January 1959.

13 Recording of the debate courtesy Lee Huebner, Airlie Professor of Media and Public Affairs, George Washington University.

14 Robert Rowland, unpublished memoir, private collection.

15 Hugh Stephenson, *Isis*, 9 November 1960.

16 Paul Foot, 'Things are looking up', *Guardian*, 22 January 2003.

17 Thompson, *Richard Ingrams*, p. 103.

18 Ingrams, *My Friend Footy*, p. 27.

19 Thompson, *Richard Ingrams*, p. 103.

20 Paul Foot, *Words as Weapons: Selected Writings 1980–1990* (London, 1990), p. x.

21 Paul Foot reviews Robert Skidelsky's book on Oswald Mosley, *Searchlight*, May

1975; Robert Skidelsky, *Oswald Mosley* (London, 1974), p. 381. In a later edition of his book, Skidelsky changed the sentence 'must take a large share of the blame' to read 'some of the blame'.

22 Iconoclast, *Isis*, 26 April 1961.

23 Paul Foot, 'Liberty or Selfishness', *Isis*, 14 June 1961.

24 Hugh Foot, *A Start in Freedom* (London, 1965), p. 33.

25 Paul Foot, private papers.

4. NO MEAN CITY

1 Christopher Huhne, 'Left and Still Moving', *Isis*, 20 February 1975.

2 Tony Harcup, 'Interview with Paul Foot', (November 2001), private collection.

3 Tony Harcup, 'Interview'.

4 Tony Cliff, *A World to Win: Life of a Revolutionary*, Introduction by Paul Foot (London, 2000), p. xii.

5 Paul Foot, 'By George, they've got it', *Guardian*, 1 June 2003; Cliff, *A World to Win*, p. xii.

6 Ibid., p. xiv.

7 Paul Foot, 'All his life a fighter', *Socialist Worker*, 23 April 1988.

8 'State Capitalism: back to square one?', *Tribune*, 21 August 1964; Paul Foot, 'Café, table, tactics', *Socialist Worker*, 4 July 1987.

9 Paul Foot, 'Never mind the City, give us sex', *Guardian*, 6 June 1994.

10 Paul Foot, 'Marx: From the Chartists to the Paris Commune', Marxism 1998, audio, private collection.

11 Ibid.; Marx, 'The Civil War in France', (International Working Men's Association, 1941), p. 45.

12 'Angry Gaitskell hits back', *Daily Record*, 7 May 1962.

13 Paul Foot, 'London Diary', *New Statesman*, 8 December 1978.

14 'Sir Hugh's son in Labour row', *Evening Standard*, 20 November 1962.

15 Colin Barker Correspondence, undated, MSS.152/1/3/1, Papers of Colin Barker (1939–2019): International Socialists, 1938–c1976, Modern Records Centre, University of Warwick.

16 Ibid.

17 Harry McShane, 'Lessons of the March', *Labour Worker*, October 1963.

18 Paul Foot, 'Unemployment, the Socialist Answer' (pamphlet), *Labour Worker*, 1963.

19 'Sir Hugh's son weds', *Sunday Express*, 24 June 1962.

20 Paul Foot, private papers.

21 Paul Foot, private papers.

22 Richard Ingrams, *My Friend Footy* (London, 2005), p. 34.

23 Richard Ingrams, ed., *The Life and Times of Private Eye, 1961–1971* (London, 1971), p. 15.

24 Paul Foot, 'Big Bill Breezes In', *Daily Record*, 30 October 1963.

25 Paul Foot, *Words as Weapons: Selected Writings 1980–1990* (London, 1990), p. x.

5. THE LEPER

1 Paul Foot, 'The people who want your vote', *Sun*, 16 September 1964.
2 Probe, *Sun*, 8 October 1964, where the quote appeared without the asterisks.
3 Foot, Sir Hugh, Confidential correspondence between the UK Mission to the UN and the Foreign Office, 1962, FO371/166844, National Archives.
4 Nicholas Deakin, *Colour and the British Electorate, 1964: Six Case Studies* (London, 1964).
5 Paul Foot, 'Immigration and Race in British Politics', August 1965, Editorial files 052/S, Penguin Specials series, DM1107/S245, University of Bristol, Special Collections.
6 Ibid.
7 Paul Foot, *Immigration and Race in British Politics* (Harmondsworth, 1965), p. 125.
8 Ibid., p. 126.
9 Harold Wilson, *Hansard*, 3 November 1964.
10 Foot, *Immigration and Race*, p. 160.
11 Ibid., p. 75.
12 Ibid., p. 53.
13 Foot, *Immigration and Race*, p. 62.
14 Ibid., p. 106.
15 Foot, 'Immigration and Race', Penguin Specials series.
16 Norman St John-Stevas, 'Immigration – humbug dispelled, brickbats all round', *Sunday Times*, 29 August 1965.
17 Roy Hattersley, 'Open Door Policy', *Observer*, 29 August 1965.
18 Foot, 'Immigration and Race', Penguin Specials collections.
19 Paul Foot, 'Is Britain Going to be Next?', *Sunday Telegraph*, 22 August 1965.
20 Paul Foot, 'Churchill: Hero or Thug', *Labour Worker*, February 1965.
21 Paul Foot, 'The Politics of Harold Wilson', September 1968, Editorial files 052/S, Penguin Specials series, DM1107/S265, University of Bristol, Special Collections.
22 'Grandma objects as Lord Caradon's grandsons "march"', *Sunday Express*, 2 June 1968.

6. A BEE TO THE HONEYPOT

1 From a 1962 interview in the *Sunday Pictorial*, quoted in Paul Foot, 'Half, Bird, Half Fish, Half Unicorn', *London Review of Books*, 16 October 1997.
2 Stephen Glover, *Secrets of the Press: Journalists on Journalism* (London, 1999), p. 81.
3 Paul Foot, *Who Killed Hanratty?* (London, 1971), p. 353.
4 Paul Foot, 'Hanratty, the Case for an Enquiry', *Queen*, 14 September 1966.
5 Richard Ingrams, *My Friend Footy* (London, 2005), p. 49.
6 Paul Foot, *Words as Weapons: Selected Writings, 1980–1990* (London, 1990), p. xii.
7 Footnotes, 'The Humphry and Jeffrey Laugh In', *Private Eye*, 5 December 1969.

8 Footnotes, 'The Man with the Golden Hands', *Private Eye*, 19 January 1968. Emphasis in original.

9 Paul Foot, 'Hearts and Grafts – an Examination by Private Eye of the Heart Transplant Craze', *Private Eye*, December 1968.

10 Footnotes, 'Decline and Fall of Ronan Point', *Private Eye*, 30 August 1968.

11 Footnotes, 'Ronan Scandal', *Private Eye*, 8 November 1968.

12 Ray Fitzwalter, 'The Master Builder', *Telegraph and Argus*, 9 April 1970.

13 'Reggiecide: Mister Maudling's Pension Scheme', *Private Eye*, 1 August 1969.

14 Footnotes, 'The Slicker of Wakefield', *Private Eye*, 24 April 1970.

15 Footnotes, 'The Slicker of Wakefield, Chapter Two', *Private Eye*, 30 June 1972.

16 *Any Questions?*, BBC Radio 4, Nottingham, 21 July 1972.

17 Paul Foot, 'The Fall & Fall of Reginald Maudling', Editorial files 052/S, Penguin Specials series, DM 1952/557, University of Bristol, Special Collections.

18 Michael Gillard, *A Little Pot of Money: The Story of Reginald Maudling and the Real Estate Fund of America* (London, 1974).

19 'Maudling lawyers scrutinize new book', *The Times*, 11 May 1974.

20 Auberon Waugh, *Will This Do? The First Fifty Years of Auberon Waugh* (London, 1991), p. 109.

7. TIGHTNITS

1 *Not Wanted on Voyage: The Seamen's Reply to the First Report of the Court of Inquiry into Certain Matters Concerning the Shipping Industry* (pamphlet) (Hull, 1966). Paul used the quote at much greater length in a *Guardian* column many years later. By then one of the signatories, an idealistic young seafarer called John Prescott standing up for his class, had become 'a portentous deputy prime minister', siding with the employers against the firefighters. Paul Foot, 'Strange Loss of Memory', *Guardian*, 11 December 2002.

2 Illustrated London News, *Private Eye*, 8 July 1966.

3 Paul Foot, 'Frank Cousins – Where will he lead the Left?', *Labour Worker*, 5 August 1966.

4 Robin Blackburn and Alexander Cockburn, *The Incompatibles: Trade Union Militancy and the Consensus* (Harmondsworth, 1967).

5 Ibid., p. 208.

6 Paul Foot, 'The Politics of Harold Wilson', September 1968, Editorial files 052/S, Penguin Specials series, DM1107/S265, University of Bristol, Special Collections.

7 Paul Foot, *The Politics of Harold Wilson* (Harmondsworth, 1968), p. 94.

8 Ibid., p. 89.

9 Ibid., p. 91.

10 Ibid., p. 98.

11 Paul Foot, 'Pipe Dreams' Obituary of Harold Wilson, *Socialist Review*, June 1995.

12 Andrew Marr, *A History of Modern Britain* (London, 2007), p. 241.

13 Foot, *Politics of Harold Wilson*, p. 21.

14 Philip Oakes, Atticus, 'Left Foot Forward', *Sunday Times*, 11 August 1968.

15 'Michael Foot, on Paul Foot, on Harold Wilson', *Tribune*, 27 September 1968.

16 Paul Johnson, 'Israel: the Militant Peacemaker', *New Statesman*, 18 July 1969.

17 'Death of a Marriage' by a mother of two, *Forum*, January 1972.

18 Richard Burton, *The Richard Burton Diaries*, ed. Chris Williams (New Haven, 2012), p. 221.

19 Paul Foot, *The Rise of Enoch Powell* (Harmondsworth, 1969), p. 113.

20 Ibid., p. 7.

21 Londoners' Diary, 'Foot's feat', *Evening Standard*, 18 February 1969.

22 Kenneth O. Morgan, *Michael Foot: A Life* (London, 2007), p. 249.

23 Foot, *Rise of Enoch Powell*, p. 104.

24 Ibid., p. 119.

25 Ibid., p. 139.

26 Paul Foot, 'The Rise of Enoch Powell', November 1969, Editorial files 052/S, Penguin Specials series, DM1107/S279, University of Bristol, Special Collections.

27 Paul Foot, 'Beyond the Powell', *Socialist Review*, March 1998.

8. WHO KILLED HANRATTY?

1 Barry Miles, *The Beatles Diary* (London, 2001), p. 362.

2 'Did Britain Murder Hanratty?', private collection; youtube.com.

3 Jonathan Cape/Penguin Random House archive.

4 Lord Russell of Liverpool, *Deadman's Hill: Was Hanratty Guilty?* (London, 1965).

5 Paul Foot, 'City Boffins Wrong Again', Guardian, 17 November 1998.

6 Jonathan Cape/Penguin Random House archive

7 Paul Foot, 'The Archer: An everyday story of fiddling folk', *Private Eye*, 14 September 1971.

8 'Hanratty – The Mystery of Deadman's Hill', produced by Bob Woffinden and Ros Franey, Yorkshire/Channel 4, 1992.

9. ONE GLORIOUS SUMMER

1 Christopher Hitchens, *Hitch 22: A Memoir* (London, 2010), p. 149.

2 Paul Foot, 'Has "T. Dan Wilson" Ratted on the Working Class?', *Socialist Worker*, 2 May 1970.

3 Paul Foot, *How to Fight the Tories* (pamphlet), *Socialist Worker*, 1970.

4 Ibid.

5 Ralph Darlington and Dave Lyddon, *Glorious Summer: Class Struggle in Britain* (London, 1972), p. 25.

6 Paul Foot, *The Postal Workers and the Tory Offensive* (pamphlet) (London, 1971).

7 Ibid.

8 Paul Foot, *Workers against Racism* (pamphlet) (London, 1973).

9 Lewis Baston, *Reggie: The Life of Reginald Maudling* (Stroud, 2004), p. 411.

10 Senate House Library Special Collections, Rich.MS 117/ SH 209/file 6.

11 Paul Foot, 'Orwell', 1984, MSS.348/2/6; Bookmarks Publications, drafts, correspondence; Modern Records Centre, University of Warwick.

12 Socialist Worker flyer, *Private Eye*, 25 February 1972.

13 Paul Foot, 'I'm a high paid miner who's better off on sick pay', *Socialist Worker*, 15 December 1973.

14 Senate House Library Special Collections, Rich.MS 117/Box 209/file 6; Box 211/ file 1; Box 221/file 1.

15 Paul Foot, 'Socialist Worker: Don't just read it...write for it!', *Socialist Worker*, 20 April 1974.

10. Y, OH LORD, OH WHY

1   Tony Harcup, 'Interview'.

2   Paul Foot, 'Clay Cross: We will not pay', *Socialist Worker*, 27 January 1973.

3   Paul Foot, 'Gone to seed', *Socialist Worker*, 3 February 1973.

4   Paul Foot, 'Think what we could do if union was run by the rank and file ...'; 'Sadie's motto: You get nothing out of society unless you fight for it – so fight', *Socialist Worker*, 21 February 1976.

5   Paul Foot, 'Another victory for socialism', *Socialist Worker*, 8 February 1975.

6   Michael Foot, *Hansard*, House of Commons, 13 February 1973 – quoted in *Socialist Worker*, 15 February 1975.

7   *Paul Foot, 'Gas men must win!'*, Socialist Worker, 17 February 1973.

8   Paul Foot, 'TUC abandons the unemployed', *Socialist Worker*, 6 September 1975.

9   'I won't let them forget Des', *Socialist Worker*, 13 September 1975.

10 Laurie Flynn, *Defend the North Wales 24 – Pickets on Trial*, IS Industrial Pamphlet, 1973; Laurie Flynn, 'Workers Against the Law: The Truth about the Shrewsbury Trials' (pamphlet), London 1977.

11 Paul Foot, 'Free the Six! 140 Years of Law and Order', *Socialist Worker*, 4 May 1974; George Loveless, *Victims of Whiggery* (London, 1837), p. 32.

12 Paul Foot, 'I didn't let the bastards grind me down', *Socialist Worker*, 2 August 1975.

13 Paul Foot, 'The takeover bid for Africa ...', *Socialist Worker*, 26 May 1973.

14 Paul Foot, *Workers against Racism* (pamphlet) (London, 1973), p. 6.

15 Ibid.

16 Paul Foot, 'The Strike at Courtaulds, Preston', Institute of Race Relations (London, 1965).

17 Foot, *Workers against Racism*, p. 17.

18 'Put Politics in Command', *Race Today*, editorial, Vol 5, No. 8, August 1973.

19 'Government moves against Socialist Worker', *Socialist Worker*, 22 June 1974.

20 Paul Foot, 'Y, oh Lord, oh Why', *Socialist Worker*, 13 April 1974.

21 Donald Young, 'Naming Mr Y is "contempt" says Janie case judge', *Daily Mail*, 18 April 1974.

22 Paul Foot, Contempt of Court, 1974–5, 2/5405, National Archives.

23 Ibid.

24 *The Times*, Law Report, 18 October 1974.

25 'Spain? Fly me, I'm Clive', *Socialist Worker*, 15 February 1975.

26 Paul Foot, 'We owe him a huge debt', *Socialist Worker*, 28 September 2002.

27 David Widgery, 'Under the Influence', 1981, MSS.348/2/1; Bookmarks Publications, drafts, correspondence; Modern Records Centre, University of Warwick.

28 Paul Foot, 'David Widgery', *New Left Review* I/196 (November–December 1992).

29 Ibid.

30 Ibid.

11. VOTE FOR FOOT

1 'Alison is 8 – and dying. Thanks to you, her life's hardly worth living', *Socialist Worker*, 10 January 1976.

2 Paul Foot, *Stop the Cuts* (pamphlet), Rank and File, 1976; *The Labour Party Manifesto* 1974, p. 15.

3 *Economist*, 10 April 1976 – quoted in Foot, *Stop the Cuts*.

4 Paul Foot, 'Shelley: The Trumpet of a Prophecy', *International Socialism Journal*, First Series, June 1975; Richard Holmes, *Shelley: The Pursuit* (London, 1974).

5 Tony Cliff, 'Why we need a socialist worker's party', *Socialist Worker*, 9 January 1977.

6 Steve Jefferys, 1966–1969, MSS.244/2/1/1; International Socialists/Socialist Workers Party, internal papers 1966–1969, Modern Records Centre, University of Warwick.

7 Paul Foot, *Why You Should Be a Socialist* (pamphlet) (London, 1977).

8 Paul Foot, 'Strachey, from Marxism to peanuts', *Socialist Worker*, 14 July 1973.

9 Foot, *Why You Should Be a Socialist*, p. 35.

10 Ibid., p. 38.

11 Ibid., p. 41.

12 Ibid., p. 88.

13 Ibid., p. 93.

14 Anthony Holden, Atticus, *Sunday Times*, 30 January 1977.

15 'Stechford: Why We Are Standing', *Socialist Worker*, 12 March 1977.

16 'Corruption in City is Rife', *Birmingham Evening Mail*, 17 March 1977.

17 Ian McBride, 'Chris Bryant Charged', *Birmingham Evening Mail*, 23 March 1977.

12. HONEY ON THE ELBOW

1 Roger Huddle and Red Saunders, *Reminiscences of RAR: Rocking Against Racism 1976–1982* (London, 2016), p. 195.

2 David Widgery, 'The Tories, the NF, the Queen and me', *Socialist Worker*, 25 June 1977.

3 *Books and Bookmen*, July 1977, Paul Foot, review, Martin Walker, *The National Front* (London, 1977).

4 Paul Foot, 'BBC gives free rein to the racists', *Socialist Worker*, 25 December 1976.

5 *Books and Bookmen*, July 1977.

6 Paul Foot, 'Police on racist rampage', *Socialist Worker*, 11 June 1977.

7 'Foot – the face in the crowd', *Police*, July 1977.

8 Paul Foot, 'The SWP doesn't incite, provoke, intimidate', *Police*, November 1977. Emphasis in original.

9 Jack Dromey and Graham Taylor, *Grunwick: The Workers' Story* (London, 1978).

10 Paul Foot, 'Grunwicks – A grim reckoning', *Socialist Worker*, 12 November 1977.

11 Paul Foot, 'The headless union', *Socialist Worker*, 21 January 1978.

12 'If you like the old SW you'll love the new one ...', *Socialist Worker*, 11 February 1978.

13 Workers at Lucas Fazakerly, 'And there was a gnashing of teeth and a tearing of boilersuits', *Socialist Worker*, 6 May 1978.

14 'Magic!', *Socialist Worker*, 6 May 1978.

15 Anna Paczuska, 'Then one day we burned down the railway station', *Socialist Worker*, 10 June 1978.

16 Prisoners (Temporary Discharge for Ill-Health) Act.

17 Paul Foot, 'Unshackled! But Not Yet Free', *Socialist Worker*, 10 June 1978.

18 Tony Cliff, miscellaneous drafts (1990s), MSS.459/2/20; Draft books, articles and speeches by Tony Cliff (1917–2000), Modern Records Centre, University of Warwick.

13. THE DITTO MAN

1 Richard Ingrams, *My Friend Footy* (London, 2005), p. 76.

2 Auberon Waugh, *The Last Word: An Eyewitness Account of the Trial of Jeremy Thorpe* (London, 1980), p. 23.

3 Paul Foot, 'The Ditto Man', *Private Eye*, 21 July 1978.

4 Auberon Waugh, *Will This Do? The First Fifty Years of Auberon Waugh* (London, 1991), p. 231.

5 Waugh, *Last Word*, p. 239.

6 Paul Foot, 'Report from Portugal', *New Statesman*, 19 December 1975.

7 Paul Foot, 'Hammer and Anvil – the Warning of the Past', Socialist Worker, 20 September, 1975; translated into Portuguese and reprinted in *Republica*, 29 October 1975.

8 Paul Foot, 'London Diary', *New Statesman*, 13 October 1978.

9 Paul Foot, 'Black Jacobin', *New Statesman*, 2 February 1979.

10 Paul Foot Reporting, 'The things they say', *Daily Mirror*, 24 November 1983.

11 Paul Foot, 'London Diary', *New Statesman*, 15 June 1979.

12 Paul Foot, 'Super PiGs', *Socialist Worker*, 19 May 1979.

13 Paul Foot, 'Blair: Our brother and our friend', *Socialist Worker*, 16 June 1979.

14 Paul Foot, 'London Diary', *New Statesman*, 24 August 1979.

14. POETRY AND REVOLUTION

1 Paul Foot, *Red Shelley* (London, 1981), p. 10.

2 Paul Foot, 'Shelley: The trumpet of a prophecy', *International Socialism*, June 1975.

3 Foot, *Red Shelley*, p. 206.

4 Paul Foot, 'Socialists and books', *Socialist Worker*, 30 July 1983.

5 Geoffrey Matthews, 'A Volcano's Voice in Shelley', *Journal of English Literary History* 24 (1957).

6 Judith Chernaik, *The Lyrics of Shelley* (London, 1972).

7 Paul Foot, 'Shelley, the Restless Revolutionary', *New Statesman*, 6 October 1978.

8 Paul Foot, 'London Diary', *New Statesman*, 13 October 1978.

9 G. M. Matthews, 'Othello and the Dignity of Man', in David Craig, *Marxists on Literature: An Anthology* (Harmondsworth, 1975), pp. 110, 113.

10 Paul Foot, 'Shelley: Religion Beyond Rhyme or Reason', *Guardian*, 18 April 1981.

11 Brian Sedgemore, 'The visionary poet who loathes authority', *Tribune*, 15 May 1981.

12 Marilyn Butler, 'Death in Greece', *London Review of Books*, 17 September 1981.

13 Richard Holmes, 'Unbeautiful effectual angel', *The Times*, 14 May 1981.

14 *Poetry and Revolution*, BBC Radio 3, 20 September 1991.

15 Paul Foot, 'Diary', *London Review of Books*, 4 July 1985.

16 Channel 4, *The Trumpet of a Prophecy*, 1 November 1987.

17 *Shelley's Revolutionary Year: The Peterloo Writings of the Poet Shelley*, Introduction by Paul Foot, first edition, (London, 1990), p. 15.

18 Ibid., p. 14.

19 Foot, *Red Shelley*, p. 105.

20 Ibid., p. 108 – on *Epipsychidion*.

21 Ibid., p. 15.

22 Paul Foot, 'Shelley and Revolution', SWP Recordings, 1977.

23 Paul Foot, 'A sad day for Shelley freaks', *Socialist Worker*, 9 February 1984.

24 Foot, *Red Shelley*, pp. 194–202.

25 Paul Foot, 'Shelley and Revolution'.

26 Foot, *Red Shelley*, p. 201.

27 Paul Foot Reporting, 'Do you really want another 5 years of this?', *Daily Mirror*, 3 April 1992.

28 Timothy Clark and Jerrold E. Hogle, eds, *Evaluating Shelley* (Edinburgh, 1996), p. 76.

15. LOOK IN THE MIRROR

1 Paul Foot, *Words as Weapons: Selected Writings 1980–1990* (London, 1990), p. xiii.

2 Stephen Glover, *Secrets of the Press: Journalists on Journalism* (London, 1999), p. 83.

3 'Paul Foot Reporting, Britain's top investigative reporter is in the Mirror TODAY', *Daily Mirror*, 10 October, 1979.

4 'Lord Harris Replies to Britain's Top Investigative Reporter', *Daily Mirror*, 13 October 1979.

5 Paul Foot Reporting, 'Why Foot Got the Boot', *Daily Mirror*, 7 November 1979.

6 Paul Foot, 'Hit the Families', *Daily Mirror*, 13 December 1979.

7 Paul Foot, 'Why did Lynn's killer stay free for 18 years', *Independent*, 3 August 1996.

8 Paul Foot, 'Killer on the Loose', *Unsolved* 3: 30 (1984).

9 Paul Foot Reporting, 'Moscow's alright for some', *Daily Mirror*, 18 June 1980.

10 Tony Benn et al., *The Crisis and the Future of the Left: Debate of the Decade* (London, 1980); British Library Audio Archive.

11 Paul Foot, 'The Labour Left's Brightest Star', *Socialist Review*, March–April 1980 – reprinted from *Books and Bookmen*, March 1980; Tony Benn, *Arguments for Socialism*, ed. Chris Mullin (Harmondsworth, 1979).

12 Joe Herbertson and Nick Howard, *Steel Workers' Power: The Steel Strike and How We Could Have Won It* (pamphlet) (London, 1980).

13 Paul Foot, 'The Rotherham lads are here!', *Socialist Worker*, 2 February 1980.

14 Tariq Ali, 'Bringing the Labour Party back to socialism', *Guardian*, 20 November 1981.

15 Paul Foot, 'Why even Benn doesn't have the answer', *Socialist Worker*, 26 September 1981.

16 Paul Foot, 'Unity swamps the left', *Socialist Worker*, 25 September 1982.

17 Paul Foot, 'Up against the politics of pessimism', *Socialist Worker*, 5 December 1981.

18 Paul Foot, *Three Letters to a Bennite* – SWP pamphlet (London, 1982).

19 Ibid.

20 Ibid.

21 Paul Foot Reporting, 'Sunk! Peace that went down with the Belgrano', *Daily Mirror*, 5 May 1983.

22 Tam Dalyell, *Misrule: How Mrs Thatcher has misled Parliament from the sinking of the Belgrano to the Wright Affair* (Sevenoaks, 1987), p. 43.

23 Paul Foot Reporting, 'Belgrano: How much DID Thatcher know?', *Daily Mirror*, 12 May 1983.

24 Paul Foot Reporting, 'Belgrano: The long silence of Mr Pym', *Daily Mirror*, 19 May 1983.

25 'The Sinking of the Belgrano, Francis Pym Replies', *Daily Mirror*, 20 May 1983.

26 Paul Foot, 'How the Peace was Torpedoed', *New Statesman*, 13 May 1983.

27 Slideshare, 'Margaret Thatcher: Poll Rating Trends', 9 April 2013, at slideshare. net.

28 Tam Dalyell, 'Obituaries: Paul Foot' *Independent*, 20 July 2004.

29 Letter from Jeddah, *Private Eye*, 22 June 1979.

30 Paul Foot, 'They've got something to hide', *Socialist Worker*, 28 August 1982.

31 Paul Foot Reporting, 'Men, Parties and Nurse Helen', *Daily Mirror*, 16 September 1980.

32 Paul Foot with Ron Smith, *The Helen Smith Story* (Glasgow, 1983), p. 285.

33 Ibid., p. 277.

34 Ibid., p. 279.

35 Paul Foot Reporting, 'Seven vital questions', *Daily Mirror*, 10 December 1982.

16. THE ENEMY WITHIN

1 Roger Huddle, Angela Phillips, Mike Simons and John Sturrock, eds, *Blood, Sweat and Tears: Photographs from the Great Miners' Strike 1984–1985*, with an introduction by Paul Foot (London, 1985).
2 'Economy: Report of Nationalised Industries Policy Group (leaked Ridley report)', Margaret Thatcher Foundation, 30 June 1977, at margaretthatcher.org.
3 Paul Foot Reporting, 'Fouled up by police', *Daily Mirror*, 26 April 1984.
4 Paul Foot Reporting, 'Your freedom is at stake!', *Daily Mirror*, 12 July 1984.
5 Paul Foot Reporting, 'Mine hosts?', *Daily Mirror*, 21 June 1984.
6 Paul Foot, 'Miners' Strike No 10 Sensation', *Daily Mirror*, 6 June 1984.
7 Cabinet Minute: TNA: CAB: 128/78, Cabinet: CC(84)21st Conclusions, Minute 4, 7 June 1984, pp. 1–2.
8 Michael Foot, *Hansard*, 7 June 1984.
9 Paul Foot, 'Miners' Strike No 10 Sensation', *Daily Mirror*, 6 June 1984.
10 Paul Foot, 'The price of being decent', *Socialist Worker*, 31 March 1984.
11 Tony Harcup, 'Interview'.
12 Paul Foot, *The Vote: How It Was Won and How It Was Undermined* (London, 2005), p. 405.
13 Paul Foot, 'What the miners do not need', *Socialist Worker*, 21 April 1984.
14 Paul Foot Reporting, 'So much for sabotage', *Daily Mirror*, 24 May 1984.
15 *Sun*, 15 May 1984.
16 'The Truth that Scargill Dare Not Tell', *Daily Express*, 9 May 1984.
17 Paul Foot, 'Then there was one', *Socialist Worker*, 19 May 1984.
18 Paul Foot, 'A general who supports pit strikes?', *Socialist Worker*, 2 June 1984.
19 Paul Foot Reporting, 'We saw a policeman hit Scargill', *Daily Mirror*, 5 July 1984.
20 Foot, *The Vote*, p. 375; Margaret Thatcher, *The Path to Power* (London, 1995).
21 Paul Foot, 'A mining village mourns', *Daily Mirror*, 18 September 1984.
22 Huddle et al., *Blood, Sweat and Tears*, p. 7.
23 Paul Foot, *Words as Weapons: Selected Writings, 1980–1990* (London, 1990), p. xv.
24 Paul Foot papers, private collection. Emphasis in original.
25 Tim Sanders, cartoon, *Socialist Worker*, 21 July 1984.
26 Paul Foot, 'Hey-Day Depression', *Socialist Worker*, 11 May 1985.
27 Paul Foot Reporting, 'The Miner birds', *Daily Mirror*, 20 December 1984.
28 Martin Adeney and John Lloyd, *The Miners' Strike, 1984–85: Loss without Limit* (London, 1986), p. 168.
29 Paul Foot Reporting, 'Ballot blocks', *Daily Mirror*, 9 August 1984.
30 Paul Foot Reporting, 'The Birch won't be standing', *Daily Mirror*, 13 September 1984.
31 Huddle et al., *Blood, Sweat and Tears*, p. 8.
32 Paul Foot Reporting, 'Why McGregor must go', *Daily Mirror*, 20 September 1984.
33 Paul Foot, '"Posh" papers fight their class war', *New Statesman*, 5 October 1984.
34 'The Poisonous Embrace', *Daily Mirror*, 30 October 1984.
35 Paul Foot Reporting, *Daily Mirror*, 1 November 1984.
36 Paul Foot, 'Hey-Day Depression', *Socialist Worker*, 11 May 1985.

37 Huddle et al., *Blood, Sweat and Tears*, p. 9.
38 Ibid.
39 Paul Foot, 'A Class war Wonder Woman?', *Socialist Worker*, 16 February 1985.

17. PAMPHLETEER

1   Paul Foot, 'What a way to spend Easter', *Socialist Worker*, 13 April 1985.
2   Paul Foot, 'By George, they've got it', *Guardian*, 1 June 2003.
3   Paul Foot, 'George Orwell', 1984, University of Warwick – audio available at mrc-catalogue.warwick.ac.uk.
4   George Orwell, *Homage to Catalonia* (Harmondsworth, 1966), p. 102.
5   Paul Foot, 'George Orwell', 1984, University of Warwick.
6   Paul Foot, *'This Bright Day of Summer': The Peasants' Revolt of 1381* (pamphlet) (London, 1981).
7   Ibid.
8   It was eventually published by Redwords as Paul Foot, *Orwell & 1984: A Talk by Paul Foot* (London, 2020).
9   Foot, 'George Orwell'.
10 Paul Foot, *'An Agitator of the Worst Kind': A Portrait of Miners' Leader A. J. Cook* (pamphlet) (London, 1986).
11 Ibid., p. 5; Beatrice Webb, *Diaries* (London, 1924–1932), p. 116.
12 Paul Foot, 'United in battle for the class', *Socialist Worker*, 26 May 1984.
13 Paul is referring to the Department of Health and Social Security, which later became the Department of Social Security and finally the Department for Work and Pensions.
14 Foot, *'An Agitator of the Worst Kind'*, p. 30.
15 Paul Foot, A. J. Cook, 1985, MSS.348/2/16; Bookmarks Publications, drafts, correspondence; Modern Records Centre, University of Warwick.
16 Tony Cliff, 'The tragedy of A. J. Cook', *International Socialism Journal* 2:31, Spring 1986.
17 George Orwell, *The Collected Essays, Journalism and Letters of George Orwell, Volume 2* (London, 1970), p. 324.
18 Paul Foot, *Ireland: Why Britain Must Get Out* (London, 1989), p. 1.
19 Ibid., p. 65.

18. BALDRIC'S CUNNING PLAN

1   Paul Foot, 'Shattered at the Mirror', *Socialist Worker*, 21 July 1984.
2   Paul Foot, 'The worst Friday 13th', *Guardian*, 3 April 2001.
3   Kenneth O. Morgan, *Michael Foot: A Life* (London, 2007), p. 237.
4   Stephen Glover, *Secrets of the Press: Journalists on Journalism* (London, 1999), p. 87.
5   Terry Pattinson, 'Scargill to Ballot Miners on Final Offer', *Daily Mirror*, 10 September 1984.

6　Tom Bower, *Maxwell: The Outsider* (London, 1988), p. 296.

7　Letter to the author, July 1985.

8　Ibid.

9　Ibid

10　Tony Harcup, 'Interview'.

11　Richard Stott, 'A Sad Farewell', Association of Mirror Pensioners, mirrorpensioners.co.uk.

12　Richard Stott, *Dogs and Lampposts* (London, 2002), p. 256.

13　Paul Foot Reporting, 'Archer: The Making of a Tory Chief', *Daily Mirror*, 30 October 1986.

14　Paul Foot, 'Those Suits', *London Review of Books*, 7 September 1995.

15　Paul Foot Reporting 'Useful swing on the golf course',, *Daily Mirror*, 5 March 1987; Kevin Barron, *Hansard*, 26 February 1987.

16　Paul Foot Reporting, 'Wrathful Mr Ridley "it's not everyday I get a writ from a cabinet minister"', *Daily Mirror*, 19 March 1987.

17　Paul Foot Reporting, 'Who cares about state schools?', *Daily Mirror*, 10 December 1987.

18　Paul Foot Reporting, 'Left to rot', *Daily Mirror*, 18 December 1986.

19　Ibid.

20　Paul Foot, 'The Card-Players', *London Review of Books*, 18 December 1986.

19. WHO KILLED CARL BRIDGEWATER?

1　'Guilty! The Cruel Killers of Carl the Newsboy', *Daily Mirror*, 10 November 1979.

2　Paul Foot Reporting, 'Points that link killer with Carl', *Daily Mirror*, 12 November 1980.

3　Paul Foot, 'I Lied About Carl's Killer', *Daily Mirror*, 3 September 1986.

4　Paul Foot, *Murder at the Farm: Who Killed Carl Bridgewater?*, 5th edn (London, 1998), p. 273.

5　Ibid., p. 290.

6　Ibid., p. 291.

7　Ibid., p. 296.

8　Ibid.

9　Paul Foot Reporting, 'Men of straw', *Daily Mirror*, 23 March 1989.

10　Foot, *Murder at the Farm*, p. 297; 'Beyond belief', *Daily Mirror*, 19 April 1990.

11　Foot, *Murder at the Farm*, p. 298; 'The language of innocence', *Daily Mirror*, 4 May 1990.

12　Foot, *Murder at the Farm*, p. 302.

13　Ibid., p. 318.

14　Paul Foot, 'For a change – one cheer for Michael Howard', *Guardian*, 29 July 1996.

15　'Framed', *Daily Mirror*, 21 February 1997.

16　Foot, *Murder at the Farm*, p. 333.

17　Ibid., p. 334.

20. A RATTLING GOOD YARN

1 Paul Foot Reporting, 'How they put the squeeze on Clockwork Orange man', *Daily Mirror*, 9 April 1987.
2 Ibid.
3 Ibid.
4 Paul Foot, 'Who Framed Colin Wallace?', Editorial file T0122, The Macmillan Archive, Macmillan Publishers International.
5 Paul Foot, *Who Framed Colin Wallace?* 1st edn (London, 1989), p. 53.
6 Ibid., p. 70.
7 Ibid., p. 46.
8 Ibid., p. 116.
9 Paul Foot Reporting, 'Truth about Kincora forgery', *Daily Mirror*, 20 April 1989.
10 Foot, *Who Framed Colin Wallace?* 1st edn, p. 236.
11 David McKittrick, 'Doubts over Ulster murder claims', *Independent*, 2 September 1987.
12 Foot, *Who Framed Colin Wallace?* 1st edn, p. 258.
13 Ibid., p. 248.
14 Ibid., p. 268.
15 John Stalker, *Stalker: Ireland, Shoot to Kill and the Affair* (Harmondsworth, 1988), p. 46.
16 Paul Foot Reporting, 'The hounding of Stalker', *Daily Mirror*, 3 July 1986.
17 Paul Foot Reporting, 'The crook behind the Stalker smear', *Daily Mirror*, 11 September 1986.
18 *What the Papers Say*, 14 March 1988, script, private collection.
19 Paul Foot, 'Rock Bottom: The Gibraltar Killings, Government and Press Cover-Up', *Private Eye*, February 1989, p. 4.
20 Ibid., p. 8.
21 Ibid., p. 2.
22 Paul Foot Reporting, 'What a plug!', *Daily Mirror*, 22 December 1988; *The Other Side of Freedom*, BBC Radio 4, 27 December 1988.
23 Foot, 'Who Framed Colin Wallace?' Correspondence files T122.
24 R. W. Johnson, 'R. W. Johnson Writes about a National Disgrace', *London Review of Books*, 6 July 1989.
25 Richard Ingrams, *Observer*, 14 May 1989.
26 *Private Eye*, 26 May 1989.
27 Godfrey Hodgson, 'Wallace: the Spy Left Out in the Cold?', *Independent*, 10 June 1989.
28 Anthony Cavendish, 'Failures of Intelligence', *Sunday Times*, 28 May 1989.
29 Archie Hamilton, *Hansard*, 30 January 1990 – quoted in full in Paul Foot, *Who Framed Colin Wallace?* 2nd edn (London, 1990), p. 415.
30 'Press Council backs Wallace complaint', *Guardian*, 9 March 1990.
31 Foot, *Who Framed Colin Wallace?* 2nd edn, pp. 421–2.
32 'Wallace to get compensation', *Sunday Times*, 5 August 1990.
33 David Calcutt QC report, 10 August 1990, private collection.

34 Paul Foot Reporting, 'Nobblers go free', *Daily Mirror*, 21 September 1990.
35 Historical Institutional Abuse Inquiry, NI, document KIN 103353, 4 August 1987.
36 *Private Eye*, 18 October 1996.
37 Foot, *Who Framed Colin Wallace?*, 1st edn. p. vii.

21. TO DIVIDE IS NOT TO TAKE AWAY

1 Paul Foot, *Red Shelley* (London, 1981), p. 108.
2 Paul O'Brien, *Shelley and Revolutionary Ireland* (London/Dublin, 2002).
3 Marianne Elliott, *Partners in Revolution: The United Irishmen and France* (New Haven/London, 1982).

22. THE HIRED BRAVOS

1 'Scargill and the Libyan Money, The Facts', *Daily Mirror*, 5 March 1990.
2 Paul Foot Reporting, 'Heads you lose . . .', *Daily Mirror*, 6 July 1990.
3 'Defend Scargill – Defend the NUM', *Socialist Worker*, 21 July 1990.
4 Seumas Milne, *The Enemy Within*, 2nd edn (London, 1995), p. 111.
5 Ibid., p. 409.
6 Ibid., p. 138.
7 Paul Foot, 'In memory – Simon Guttman', *Socialist Worker*, 27 January 1990.
8 Paul Foot, 'The question lingers on', *Socialist Worker*, 1 July 1989.
9 Paul Foot, 'All His Life, a Fighter', *Socialist Worker*, 23 April 1988.
10 Paul Foot, *The Case for Socialism, What the Socialist Workers Party Stands For* (pamphlet) (London, 1990).
11 'It All Ends in Tears', *Daily Mirror*, 23 November 1990.
12 Paul Foot, 'Bye Bye Baghdad', *London Review of Books*, 7 February 1991.
13 Paul Foot Reporting, *Daily Mirror*, 1 February 1991.
14 Paul Foot, 'It's Aimed at Our Troops', *Daily Mirror*, 25 January 1991.
15 Paul Foot Reporting, 'Law against the war', *Daily Mirror*, 1 March 1991.
16 Foot, 'Bye Bye Baghdad'.
17 Paul Foot Reporting, 'Like to borrow £330m, Saddam old pal?', *Daily Mirror*, 8 February 1991.
18 Percy Byshe Shelley, *Queen Mab*, IV, 178–9.

23. THE GREAT CROOK

1 'The man who saved the Daily Mirror', *Daily Mirror*, 6 November 1991.
2 Richard Stott, *Dogs and Lampposts* (London, 2002), p. 306.
3 Paul Foot Reporting, 'Coal sellers!', *Daily Mirror*, 6 April 1989.
4 Paul Foot Reporting, 'This is your captain cheating', *Daily Mirror*, 21 February 1992.
5 Tony Harcup, 'Interview'.

6 Paul Foot Reporting, 'Profs and Toffs', *Daily Mirror*, 27 March 1992.

7 Paul Foot Reporting, 'The coal scuttlers', *Daily Mirror*, 16 October 1992.

8 Paul Foot Reporting, 'The power and the gravy', *Daily Mirror*, 23 October 1992.

9 Paul Foot Reporting, *Daily Mirror*, 30 October 1992.

10 *Hansard* EDM 1587, 'Events at the Daily Mirror', 11 March 1993.

11 Paul Foot Reporting, reprint, *Socialist Worker*, 3 April 1993.

12 Will Bennet, Andrew Gliniecki, 'Foot offered sick leave after ban on column', *Independent*, 27 March 1993.

13 Paul Foot, 'Time to go', *Socialist Worker*, 3 April 1993.

14 Stott, *Dogs and Lampposts*, p. 327.

24. BACK TO THE HONEYPOT

1 *Hansard*: House of Commons Employment Committee, The Management of Redundancies, evidence, 1 February 1994.

2 'Monty's Finest Hour', *Private Eye*, 6 November 1992.

3 Paul Foot, 'The off-scot freemason', *Private Eye*, 29 January 1993.

4 Paul Foot, 'The Story You Don't Want To Read', Night&Day, *Mail on Sunday*, 10 May 1998.

5 In 2016 Gordon Anglesea was sent to prison for sexually abusing a boy at Bryn Estyn. He died in prison the following year.

6 Paul Foot, 'Tiptoeing by the truth', *Guardian*, 19 May 1998.

7 Paul Foot, 'Macpherson's Fundamental Failure', *Private Eye*, 5 March 1999.

8 Chris Cowley, *Guns, Lies and Spies*, Introduction by Paul Foot (London, 1992), pp. xvi–xvii.

9 Paul Foot and Tim Laxton, *Not the Scott Report*, *Private Eye* special, November 1994.

10 Ibid., p. 3.

11 'Scottcha!', *Private Eye*, 23 February 1996.

12 *Scott of the Arms Antics*, Channel 4, 10 February 1996, available at BFI Mediatheque.

13 Richard Ingrams, 'Paul Foot and The Eye', *Private Eye*, 1 October 2004.

14 Paul Foot, *Lockerbie: The Flight from Justice*, *Private Eye* special, May 2001, p. 27.

15 James Bowen, Claire Donnelly, 'Spotlight: One Foot in the Press', *Impact*, University of Nottingham, 13 March 1996.

16 Paul Foot papers,'Dorothy Herridge: Obituary', private collection.

17 Letter from Paul Foot to Kate Jones, 4 April 1995 (reproduced by permission, RCW Literary Agency).

18 Paul Foot, *The Vote: How It Was Won and How It Was Undermined* (London, 2005), pp. 28–9.

19 John Rees, *The Leveller Revolution: Radical Political Organisation in England, 1640–1650* (London, 2016).

20 Paul Foot, 'How history comes alive', *Socialist Worker*, 11 September 1993.

21 Foot, *The Vote*, p. 87.

22 Ibid., p. 116; Dorothy Thompson, *The Chartists* (Hounslow, 1984), p. 146.

23 Paul Foot, 'Ask the sick or the jobless if it's the best budget ever', *Guardian*, 6 December 1993.

24 Paul Foot, 'An astonishing comeback by the crazy gang', *Guardian*, 27 February 1995.

25 Paul Foot, 'Cold war gold undermines our independence', *Guardian*, 2 January 1995.

26 Arthur Ransome, *Revolutionary Russia*, Introduction by Paul Foot (London, 1992).

27 Byron, *Don Juan*, quoted in Paul Foot, 'City Boffins Wrong Again', *Guardian*, 17 November 1998.

28 Keats, *Isabella*, quoted in Paul Foot, 'Two clouts for the poor on my doorstep', *Guardian*, 6 November 1995.

29 Walt Whitman, *Resurgemus*, quoted in Paul Foot, 'Leaping like lightening in France', *Guardian*, 18 December 1995.

30 Louis MacNeice, *Autumn Journal*, section iii, quoted in Paul Foot, 'Time to defy those quangoes we don't trust', *Guardian*, 27 February 1995.

31 Leon Rosselson, *Battle Hymn of the New Socialist Party*, (mis)quoted in Paul Foot, 'Time to defy those quangoes we don't trust', *Guardian*, 15 August 1994.

25. HEAD AND HEART

1 Paul Foot, 'That's not fair, Gordon', *Guardian*, 16 November 1999.

2 Paul Foot, 'The Ten Faces of Jeffrey Archer', *Private Eye*, 24 December 1999.

26. SKINNING THE TIGER

1 Paul Foot, *The Vote: How It Was Won and How It Was Undermined* (London, 2005), p. 203.

2 Ibid., p. 188; Ernest Belfort Bax, *Essays in Socialism* (London, 1906).

3 Foot, *The Vote*, p. 236.

4 Tony Cliff, *Class Struggle and Women's Liberation* (London, 1984), p. 132.

5 Paul Foot papers, 'Obituary: Jill Craigie', private collection.

6 Matt Foot, 'Are You Awake? It's Paul. He's had a heart attack . . .', *Guardian*, 13 April 2000.

7 Paul Foot papers, 'Obituary: Dorothy Herridge', private collection.

8 Obituaries, Tony Cliff, *Guardian*, 11 April 2000.

9 Tony Cliff, *A World to Win: Life of a Revolutionary*, Introduction by Paul Foot (London, 2000), p. xv.

10 Paul Foot papers, What the Papers Say Awards, 25 February 2000.

11 Socialist Alliance Election Special, private collection.

12 Paul Foot papers, letter to Tony Topham, private collection.

13 Foot, *The Vote*, p. ix.

14 Ramsay MacDonald, *Parliament and Revolution* (Manchester, 1919), p. 92.

15 Foot, *The Vote*, p. 286.

16 Ibid., p. 259.
17 Paul Foot, 'The fright they deserve', *Guardian*, 29 October 2003.
18 Foot, *The Vote*, p. 296; R. H. Tawney, 'The Choice Before the Labour Party', *Political Quarterly*, Vol. III, July–September 1932, p. 336.
19 Foot, *The Vote*, p. 296.
20 *The Left Book Club*, BBC Radio 3, 26 March 1994.
21 Ibid.
22 Foot, *The Vote*, p. 362.
23 Ibid., p. 362.
24 Ibid., p. 364.
25 Ibid., p. 371.
26 Ibid., p. 388.
27 Ibid., p. 403.
28 Ibid., p. 412.
29 Ibid., p. x.

27. PERFIDIOUS FINANCIAL IDIOCY

1 Tony Harcup, 'Interview'.
2 *Private Wealth v National Health*, Channel 4, 24 June 1998, available at BFI Mediatheque.
3 Paul Foot, 'The price of arrogance', *Guardian*, 30 April 2003.
4 Tony Harcup, 'Interview'.
5 Paul Foot Reporting, 'What a Currie on', *Daily Mirror*, 19 March 1993.
6 Paul Foot, 'Listen to Prophet', *Guardian*, 22 January 2002.
7 Quoted in Paul Foot, *P. F. Eye*, *Private Eye* special, March 2004; *Hansard*, Sam Galbraith, 1 May 1996,
8 'PFI – Perfidious Financial Idiocy', editorial, *British Medical Journal*, 3 July 1999.
9 Foot, *P. F. Eye*, p. 4.
10 Paul Foot, *The Vote: How It Was Won and How It Was Undermined* (London, 2005), p. 401.
11 Paul Foot, 'Tony Blurs the past', *Socialist Worker*, 30 July 1994.
12 Peter Mandelson and Roger Liddle, *The Blair Revolution* (London, 1996), p. 21.
13 Paul Foot, 'Return of the Whigs', *Private Eye*, 22 January 1999.
14 David Osler, *Labour Party PLC: New Labour as a Party of Business*, Foreword by Paul Foot (Edinburgh, 2002), p. 10.

28. THE WHITE RADIANCE OF ETERNITY

1 Paul Foot, *The Vote: How It Was Won and How It Was Undermined* (London, 2005), p. 451.
2 Christopher Huhne, 'Left and Still Moving', *Isis*, 20 February 1975.
3 Paul Foot, 'Divided We Must Stand', *Guardian*, 23 June 2004.
4 'Remembering Paul Foot, 1937–2004', Marxism 2014, SWP TV, youtube.com.

Index